Knowledge Management

An Introduction

Kevin C. Desouza
and Scott Paquette

Neal-Schuman Publishers, Inc.

New York   London

Published by Neal-Schuman Publishers, Inc.
100 William St., Suite 2004
New York, NY 10038

Printed and bound in the United States of America.

The paper used in this publication meets the minimum requirements of American National Standard for Information Sciences—Permanence of Paper for Printed Library Materials, ANSI Z39.48-1992.

Library of Congress Cataloging-in-Publication Data

Desouza, Kevin C., 1979-
    Knowledge management : an introduction / Kevin C. Desouza, Scott Paquette.
        p. cm.
    Includes bibliographical references and index.
    ISBN 978-1-55570-720-0 (alk. paper)
    1. Knowledge management. I. Paquette, Scott. II. Title.

HD30.2D469 2011
658.4'038—dc23

2011017262

Contents

Chapter 3. The Concept of Management 73
Jongmin T. Moon with Kevin C. Desouza

PART II: PROCESSES OF KNOWLEDGE MANAGEMENT

Chapter 4. Knowledge Creation 99
Scott Paquette and Kevin C. Desouza

Chapter 5. Knowledge Organization 139
Scott Paquette

Chapter 6. Knowledge Transfer 179
Scott Paquette and Kevin C. Desouza

Chapter 7. Knowledge Application 213
Chen Ye with Kevin C. Desouza and Scott Paquette

PART III: BUILDING KNOWLEDGE MANAGEMENT PROGRAMS

Chapter 8. Building Global Knowledge Management Systems 247
Kevin C. Desouza and Chris Rivinus

Chapter 9. Building the Business Case for Knowledge Management . . 281
Kevin C. Desouza

Chapter 10. Managing Knowledge for Organizational Value 311
Scott Paquette and Kevin C. Desouza

List of Illustrations

FIGURES

TABLES

Preface

Knowledge management is getting the right information in front of the right people at the right time.
— Gordon Petrash

The discipline of knowledge management has matured over the past decade. Much of the interest in the field results from the simple reality that organizations compete on their *knowledge-based* assets. Even noncompetitive organizations (e.g., nonprofits and governmental departments) thrive or wither based on their ability to leverage their knowledge-based assets. Consider the case of nation-states, where indicators such as standard of living, economic prosperity, and even safety can be traced to the ability of the nation to leverage its knowledge assets in innovative ways. Similarly, nonprofits of all kinds compete for grants and funding based on their ability to show stakeholders that they are best equipped to use their knowledge toward social good. Even individuals, from students to budding entrepreneurs or information professionals, are assessed and rewarded on how they put their knowledge, expertise, and skills toward productive purposes. Simply put, all organizations strive to acquire the most advanced technology assets (within their budgetary constraints), hire the smartest people, and build robust, and innovative, business processes. In each of these efforts, successful organizations will be able to leverage knowledge in, and around, their midsts; connect disparate pieces of knowledge; and leverage it toward attaining organizational objectives.

The fundamentals presented in *Knowledge Management: An Introduction* hold equally applicable to all types of organizations: from hospitals to government agencies to *Fortune* 500 companies. The only factor that does change is the nature of *knowledge* one must manage. In this book, we take a discipline-agnostic view of knowledge management. Our goal is to help you appreciate the art and science of knowledge management through multiple lenses. We will share examples from corporations, libraries, nonprofits, government agencies, and even from lone rangers (such as individual entrepreneurs). We will share practices for enabling knowledge creation and transfer that can be applied in large or small organizations, government or nonprofit, albeit with some minor tweaking. To truly appreciate knowledge management, one must take a broad view of the concept and learn how to adapt practices and techniques found in a multitude of environments. After all, at the end of the day, we are concerned with the management of *knowledge*, which is a deeply human experience, and much can be learned from studying how diverse professionals, organizations, and even individuals engage in the acts of discovering, creating, transferring, and applying knowledge.

In the pages that follow, we aim to present actionable and foundational knowledge for the next generation of knowledge managers and workers. This book will draw heavily on both our research and practice experiences. Since 2000, we have been involved in knowledge management projects. These projects have run the gamut of knowledge management efforts: from the technical domain of knowledge discovery from databases, to the behavioral challenges associated with crafting incentives for knowledge transfer and consumption and the strategic realm which has looked at, among other issues, the crafting of organizational innovations. These experiences have profoundly impacted our views of what knowledge management is and how to do it right. We will attempt to share as much of our experiences as possible in the pages that follow. This effort will bring together practice-driven knowledge which is synthesized with knowledge arrived at from rigorous scientific inquiry.

The primary audience for the book is upper-level undergraduate and graduate students who are interested in the concept of knowledge management. Knowledge management courses are found in a wide assortment of academic disciplines from information and library science, to public policy and administration, management, and even engineering (e.g., industrial engineering). The only prerequisite for reading and comprehending this text is an open and inquisitive mind. We do not assume the reader to have any specific background or experience. Knowledge management courses are interdisciplinary in their orientation. As noted, due to the multifaceted nature of managing knowledge and the parallels one can draw from examining practices across a range of disciplines, it is not possible to teach a course on knowledge management that is specific to a given discipline. Therefore, we have written a book that students across a wide range of disciplines and lines of inquiries can appreciate and gain from.

The book is written in a conversational tone, which we hope will be engaging for the reader. When discussing concepts, we share some personal stories and experiences to help the reader digest the intricacies of critical issues. Illustrations come from our consulting and research experience. In each chapter, sidebars illustrate a multitude of examples of how knowledge management concepts play out in practice. In addition, a concluding sidebar highlights the top ten critical issues that knowledge management professionals need to pay attention to. Questions for discussions appear at the end of each chapter and can be used as springboards for constructive dialogue. Finally, each chapter's reference list may be consulted for deeper coverage on critical issues or used by instructors to assign additional reading.

ROAD MAP OF THE BOOK

The book is divided into three main sections. Part I, which consists of three chapters, covers the foundational concepts and introduces the reader to the key elements of knowledge management. Chapter 1 frames the concept of knowledge management within the larger agendas of information management and organizational innovation.

The focus of this chapter is that an organization must gain value from its efforts in knowledge management. This may occur when an organization realizes value from knowledge management in terms of operational and tactical efficiencies (e.g., optimized business processes) or even strategic gains (e.g., competitive advantages). The concept of knowledge management draws on, and contributes to, the information management and innovation agendas of organization.

Chapter 2 explores the concept of *knowledge*. It answers key questions including: What do we mean by knowledge? How do we differentiate knowledge from information or data? Is knowledge the same as intelligence (or wisdom)? Are there different types of knowledge? Who owns or controls knowledge (individuals, groups, organizations, interorganizational networks, or society)? The goal of this chapter is to help the reader understand the multifaceted nature of knowledge and how the lens through which it is viewed impacts the management of knowledge.

Chapter 3 concentrates on the concept of *management*. This chapter is not intended to serve as a replacement for a management textbook or course. Rather, the focus of this chapter will be on exploring how the management of an intangible asset, such as knowledge, differs from the management of a tangible asset (e.g., capital, land, machinery). The goal of this chapter is help students who do not have a background in management to gain an initial understanding of its various elements—planning, control, organizing, and directing. The chapter concludes with a set of guidelines for the management of knowledge (and information) assets.

Part II consists of four chapters that explore critical activities of knowledge management. Chapter 4 focuses on *knowledge creation*, the mechanics by which knowledge is drawn from information. The manner in which knowledge is discovered in organizations will depend on different circumstances. For example, when an organization encounters a problem, knowledge discovery might occur when a solution is crafted by exploiting its reservoir of knowledge. This effort has distinct mechanics when compared to the case where an organization needs to engage in blue-sky, broad-range thinking to chart its future course. Here an exploratory approach might be better suited. The process by which knowledge might be discovered here will be of a different nature. Both the discovery of knowledge from explicit information sources (e.g., databases and information records) through automated mechanisms (e.g., machine learning or statistical analyses), and the generation of tacit knowledge are covered here.

Chapter 5 focuses on *knowledge organization*. How do we organize knowledge? This chapter takes as it starting point the various dimensions of knowledge (covered in Chapter 2) and then explores the organization problem. In addition to traditional organization methods (e.g., by type of knowledge, source, or form), this chapter will explore nontraditional classification schemes (such as by value proposition or risk). Top-down and bottom-up (emergent) methods of organizing knowledge will be covered. For example, the chapter will discuss the concept of tagging, an emergent organization mechanism. Tagging, in its many variants, is a popular concept today, and raises many questions: How should organizations manage tagging of knowledge objects? Who should tag knowledge objects (producers or consumers, experts or novices)? How is tagging of information objects different than tagging of knowledge objects? While the majority of the chapter focuses on the organization of *explicit* knowledge artifacts, due attention is given to the organizational challenges surrounding knowledge of a *tacit* nature.

Chapter 6 explores the design and management of *knowledge transfer and sharing*. This chapter centers on the knowledge transfer problem and the issues that arise when trying to transfer knowledge across contexts (e.g., human to human, human to machine, or vice versa). It addresses design considerations for knowledge service, such as the design of push and pull mechanisms. The chapter also covers newer technologies such as web services and social media.

The purpose of Chapter 7 is to explore the manner in which knowledge is *applied* to meet organizational goals. An organization certainly gains value from knowledge management efforts if it can systematically use, and reuse, knowledge to further its goals and objectives. Today, we must manage both how humans use knowledge and how to build technologies that automate the application of knowledge. For example, think about customer service and other self-service technologies: these artifacts are coded with knowledge and act as interfaces for us to get work accomplished. The questions of how these technologies should be designed and managed (e.g., knowledge be updated, systems maintained) are non-trivial issues that require due consideration.

The third and final part of the book contains three chapters. These chapters take a strategic view of knowledge management in organizations. Chapter 8 covers salient issues surrounding the design of *global knowledge management systems*. Today organizations spread across continents, spanning multiple cultures, countries, and time zones. Organizations must be flexible enough to tap into knowledge resources anywhere on the globe and then to leverage them. This chapter will provide an overview of some of the pragmatic issues involved in building global knowledge management programs. For example, today it is commonplace for an intranet (i.e., an internal information space) to be constructed in the English language. Yet, when taking into consideration that there are many more Chinese students learning English than there are American or British students learning Mandarin, what language should be used?

Chapter 9 looks at the process a manager uses in *building a business case* for a knowledge management effort. When organizations do not devote the necessary resources to knowledge management efforts, it is often not due to a lack of resources, but rather because mangers have not made an appealing business case. You will be provided with guidelines of how to tie knowledge management efforts to an organization's goals, objectives, and key indicators (e.g., profit, revenue, and customer retention). In our experience, knowledge managers and information professionals are some of the least adept at making a business case for their efforts. One of the reasons is their failure to capture the true value of the effort in terms that matter to the organization stakeholders. This chapter provides actionable guidelines on how to craft a solid, valuable, and defensible, business case.

Chapter 10 provides a summary of the key issues explored in the book. In addition, it proposes guidelines for professionals who are about to embark into knowledge management jobs. It concludes with a look at how the future of organizations will undergo radical changes in the next few years, and why the criticality of managing knowledge will be as important as ever.

CONCLUDING THOUGHTS

As you begin to read this book, here are five critical things to bear in mind:

1. Knowledge management is a critical capability for organizations to master if they are to compete, and even simply survive, in their environments.
2. Managing knowledge begins, and ends with, empowering humans within and across the organization.
3. Technology plays an essential, albeit supporting, role in enabling organizations to manage knowledge effectively and efficiently.
4. Today, organizations have to build knowledge management programs that are relevant in a global context.
5. Knowledge management is an art and a science. The art comes from the fact that knowledge management practices need to be innovative in order for them to deliver differential value to the organization. The science stems from the fact that organizations of all kinds must engage in certain general principles and practices and do so in a systematic manner if they are to manage knowledge.

We welcome comments, feedback, and suggestions. Please do not hesitate to contact either of us. We do our best to respond to the e-mails that we receive and we will gladly incorporate feedback into future editions of the book. Happy reading!

Acknowledgments

Writing a book is never a solitary endeavor. There are too many individuals who have contributed to this project to name each one personally. So, let me apologize in advance if I do not single you out below. I do appreciate all your time and effort in this project. First, I would like to acknowledge the immense contribution of my coauthor, Scott Paquette. I have known Scott for little over six years now and have come to appreciate his kind nature and innovative ideas. It has been a true pleasure to collaborate with Scott on this project. Second, I would like to thank the executives and students who contributed to the book. Jongmin Moon, Peter Baloh, Chen Ye, and Chris Rivinus coauthored chapters in the book and brought critical ideas to the project. Trupti Deo did significant background research for the chapter on knowledge discovery. Subramaniam Ramasubramanian, my former graduate assistant, helped out with collecting case studies and reference materials for the project. Special thanks for Stan Garfield and Neal Myrick, who volunteered to be interviewed for chapters in the book. Third, Marissa Lavelle, my current graduate assistant, did a marvelous job reading through all chapters, editing them, and getting them formatted for final submission. Marissa also helped assemble a number of the cases and sidebars for the book. Fourth, Sandy Wood and Charles Harmon of Neal-Schuman deserve a lot of credit for the project. Sandy played a vital role in seeing the book through the production process. Charles Harmon recognized the value for the book, and has been extremely kind in his handling of the project. Finally, I would like to thank my wife, Sally Desouza. Sally has been a vital source of calm, energy, and love during the project.

Kevin C. Desouza
Seattle, Washington

The most rewarding part of writing a book is reflecting on those numerous friends and colleagues who contributed towards our efforts. First, I would like to thank Kevin Desouza for presenting me the opportunity to work with him to develop a new and refreshing look at knowledge management. I have admired Kevin's work in expanding the field of KM and educating those who practice KM in corporations, and it was a pleasure to finally collaborate with him. My previous work in this field with individuals such as Chun Wei Choo, Brian Detlor, Lynne Howarth, Herman van den Berg, and Colin Furness helped shaped my ideas surrounding knowledge management. My more recent projects with Bo Xie, Dave Yates, Paul Jaeger, Jen Golbeck, Molly Brown and Sarah Trainor has given me the opportunity to explore new areas of KM and innovative ways it is used in organizations and society. The people at Neal-Schuman Publishers who guided us through the process were immensely helpful in refining our work. Finally, thanks to my parents, my wife Andrea, and my son Ben for all of their support and encouragement.

Scott Paquette
College Park, Maryland

Part I

The Basics

1

An Introduction
to Knowledge Management

Kevin C. Desouza

OBJECTIVES

- Introduce knowledge management and its components.
- Define knowledge management as it is used in organizations.
- Provide introductory examples of how knowledge management is and is not used in organizations.
- Argue why knowledge management is an important activity for an organization's success.
- Describe the structure and content of the book.

INTRODUCTION

Knowledge management has been present as a discipline of inquiry and practice for decades. One might argue that as a field of inquiry, it has been active for centuries dating back to the early philosophers who put forth theories regarding the nature of knowledge. In practice, knowledge management gained traction in the 1990s. Several high-profile case studies on knowledge management programs at British Petroleum, Chevron, Xerox Corporation, Toyota, and Dow Chemical Company, among others, drew the attention of managers and consultants (Brown, 1998; Dyer and Nobeoka, 2000; Petrash, 1996). Soon, many significant management consulting firms developed practice areas in knowledge management. Several prominent books intensified interest in knowledge management, including *The Knowledge Creating Company* by Ikujiro Nonaka and Hirotaka Takeuchi (1995), *Working Knowledge* by Thomas H. Davenport and Laurence Prusak (1998), and *Intellectual Capital* and *The Wealth of Knowledge* by Thomas A. Stewart (Stewart, 1997, 2001). This was immediately followed by an explosion of research papers about knowledge management in a wide-array of academic disciplines from economics to strategic management, and information and library science to public administration, and even in law and engineering journals (Alavi and Leidner, 2001; Argote, McEvily, and Reagans, 2003; McInerney and Day, 2002).

Unfortunately, like most novel ideas, the promise of knowledge management was inflated and hyped. With the surge of interest in knowledge management, organizations invested in knowledge management programs not because they knew what they were doing, but because they wanted to keep up with the competition. Knowledge management became a trendy buzzword, and soon every executive wanted to sponsor a knowledge management project to show that they understood the concept and its implications on their corporate strategy. After the fad of knowledge management receded in the early 2000s, the field went through a period of deep introspection, evaluation, and renewal (Hislop, 2010). Old ideas were refined or discarded and rigorous research into the concepts of knowledge management took place. These efforts revived the interest in knowledge management from both a practice and a scholarship perspective.

Today, it is fair to say that the field is alive and thriving. Knowledge management programs are important for the strategy and competitiveness of all organizations. Knowledge management impacts organizations of all types, from the for-profit to the government and nonprofit sectors. Government agencies such as the US Navy, US Army, Federal Aviation Administration, and National Aeronautics and Space Administration have all built knowledge management programs. Successful organizations understand why they must manage knowledge, develop plans as to how to accomplish this objective, and devote time and energy to these efforts. Organizations are holding senior executives and administrators accountable for knowledge management, while they continue to employ corporate librarians, taxonomists, system builders, consultants, designers, and intellectual property personnel on their staff to support their knowledge management efforts. To prepare students for these opportunities, universities and colleges now offer courses on a wide assortment of topics related to knowledge management, including some degrees that have knowledge management specializations. Professional organizations such as the Special Libraries Association have dedicated divisions that bring together knowledge management practitioners (Special Libraries Association, 2011).

This introductory chapter will cover some of the background of knowledge management. To begin with, how is knowledge management defined? What does (and does not) constitute knowledge management? It explores the four central components of knowledge management: knowledge, people, process, and technology. Knowledge management is an interdisciplinary space that draws from and contributes to a multitude of scholarly and professional disciplines. This book will explore a few of the most critical disciplines that have made fundamental contributions to our understanding of knowledge management. It also presents discussions of knowledge that exists at the individual, group, organizational, and societal levels.

DEFINING KNOWLEDGE MANAGEMENT

Definitions of knowledge management are as varied and myriad as the backgrounds of the authors who propose them. Knowledge management is a highly interdisciplinary field that attracts scholars and practitioners from such varied areas as economics, management, philosophy, innovation, public policy, information science, information systems, engineering, and sociology, among others. With many disciplines contributing to knowledge management, a search engine might produce several hundred definitions of what is (and is not) knowledge management. While it is not possible to consider all definitions here, the two most pragmatic and classical definitions of knowledge management are as follows:

> KM is to understand, focus on, and manage systematic, explicit, and deliberate knowledge building, renewal, and application—that is, manage effective knowledge processes. (Wiig, 1997: 2)

> Knowledge management is getting the right information in front of the right people at the right time. (Petrash, 1996: 370)

As noted by both Wiig and Petrash, knowledge management is about increasing an organization's effectiveness through application of its knowledge assets. It is important to note that knowledge management is not exclusive to any particular type of organization. Organizations of all types must manage their knowledge if they are to adequately perform in their environments. No matter their missions, all organizations have knowledge assets that need to be leveraged. This raises the question, what are knowledge assets of an organization? The next chapter explores the concept of knowledge assets further, but for now the definition provided by Thomas H. Davenport and Laurence Prusak (1998: 5) is adequate:

> Knowledge is a fluid mix of framed experience, values, contextual information, and expert insight that provides a framework for evaluating and incorporating new experiences and information. It originates and is applied in the minds of knowers. In organizations, it often becomes embedded not only in documents or repositories but also in organizational routines, processes, practices, and norms.

Knowledge assets are the physical and logical manifestations of knowledge. And, simply put, knowledge management is about helping an organization utilize its knowledge assets in the attainment of objectives and goals. There must be a clearly identified organizational goal and motivation for undertaking knowledge management. Put another way, the organization must feel confident that it will reap returns for its knowledge management investments.

Not everyone agrees that knowledge can be managed or that knowledge management is sensible. For example, T. D. Wilson, editor of *Information Research*, in his 2002 paper, "The Nonsense of 'Knowledge Management,'" writes: "The inescapable conclusion of this analysis of the 'knowledge management' idea is that it is, in large part, a management fad, promulgated mainly by certain consultancy companies, and the probability is that it will fade away like previous fads" (Wilson, 2002: under "Conclusion"). Wilson goes on to point out:

> according to the rhetoric of "knowledge management," "mind" becomes "manageable," the content of mind can be captured or down-loaded and the accountant's dream of people-free production, distribution and sales is realized—"knowledge" is now in the database, recoverable at any time. That may be Utopia for some, but not for many. Fortunately, like most Utopias, it cannot be realized. (Wilson, 2002: under "Conclusion")

Since we are still talking about knowledge management, and organizations of all sizes and forms are concerned about how best to manage knowledge, the *fad* has not faded. While Wilson was quick to prejudge and dismiss knowledge management, his article does point out one critical issue—not all *knowledge* may be *manageable*. Consider for example, the case of a painter. Trying to capture the intricacies of how an artist paints is not easy. Even if the painter sat down and explained his mode of thinking and approach to painting, it would be difficult, if not nearly impossible, to document this in a manner that allowed someone else to read it, duplicate it, and perform at the same level. In this case, trying to manage the artist's knowledge might prove to be difficult. Here, we might want to explore a different approach. For instance, we might want to have someone work with the artist in an apprenticeship mode. Through the process of interacting, dialoguing, observing, and visualizing the artist at work, the novice might learn the necessary skills to become a good painter. In this case, we are not focused on managing *knowledge* as much as trying to manage (or direct others to) the *source of knowledge* which is usually the individual who possesses the knowledge. We explore this issue at greater length in Chapters 2 and 3.

Collison and Parcell describe knowledge management as "herding cats":

> Stop for a minute and imagine yourself in a field full of cats, trying to herd them towards one corner. Not going well, is it? So if you can't herd cats, how could you get them to do what you want? You might suggest providing scratching-posts, saucers of milk, warm fires and balls of wool—components that go to make up the right environment . . . and this is exactly the view when thinking about knowledge management. You can't manage knowledge—nobody can. What you can do is manage the environment in which knowledge can be created, discovered, captured, shared, distilled, validated, transferred, adopted, adapted and applied. (Collison and Parcell, 2003: 24)

Knowledge management is more than managing *knowledge* or *sources of knowledge*; it involves managing the environment where knowledge is exchanged. As we will explore in later chapters the sharing of knowledge, a salient capability within knowledge management, is dependent on having an organizational culture where members of the organization are motivated to, and rewarded for, sharing their knowledge. Otherwise, members will view their knowledge as a source of power and hoard it from others. In addition to managing *knowledge*, an organization trying to apply the principles of knowledge management must also ensure that its *environment* facilitates the creation, capturing, sharing, and utilization of knowledge. While no universal definition of knowledge management currently exists, we can begin to develop one by acknowledging several key facts:

1. It involves leveraging knowledge towards attainment of organizational goals and objectives.
2. It must encompass managing knowledge artifacts, the human sources of knowledge, and the process of how knowledge is generated and applied.
3. It must ensure that the organizational culture that springs from it fosters the knowledge of discovery, sharing, and learning.

Three additional points are important to consider when defining knowledge management. First, a knowledge management program can be implemented by either individuals or groups. While there are some differences between how individuals manage their knowledge when compared to managing knowledge in a collective setting, the underlying processes are similar. Just as an individual must create knowledge, so does a team or an organization. Similarly, at all levels of analysis we must uncover mechanisms for knowledge transfer.

Second, knowledge management should not be distinct from the other activities conducted by an organization. Managing knowledge must be ingrained into the activities and processes conducted by an entity. Ideally, an organization should not have to think about knowledge management but instead practice it unconsciously as it becomes embedded in work routines and practices. For example, if employees are required to stop their work to add an entry to a knowledge repository, then something needs to be improved. Ideally, as employees conduct their work, relevant knowledge is being captured and being made available to the organization.

Third, in order to make knowledge management function properly, one must have a clear understanding of the goals of the entity. What does the entity (organization) want to achieve, why does it want to achieve its goals, how does it plan to achieve its goals, and what are the factors that might impact its goals? The knowledge management programs and strategy must contribute to and be aligned with the organizational agenda. Failure to do so will lead to the creation of a knowledge management program that does not contribute to the organization.

This book examines knowledge management as it is used in organizations. One perspective of managing knowledge views it as a process, where many activities are formed to carry out key elements of an organization's KM strategy and operations. In Figure 1.1, this process is depicted where an organization must first identify and capture knowledge, and then organize it in order to bring knowledge within the organizational boundaries. Next, knowledge is transferred and shared throughout the organization using both human and technological means. Through this transfer, the members of the organization can apply the new knowledge to their work activities, which can include the use of knowledge management systems or developing the business case for an organization's knowledge management projects. Underlying these activities are the fundamental elements of knowledge and management. Figure 1.1 also denotes which chapters examine each part of this process.

CASES OF KNOWLEDGE MANAGEMENT USE (OR NONUSE)

In order to appreciate the critical importance of knowledge management, we will look at three incidents where *knowledge* was *not managed*.

The Case of Napster

In 1999, Shawn Fanning created Napster, a program that allowed users to swap music files via the Internet. Its immediate success demonstrated the music industry's inability

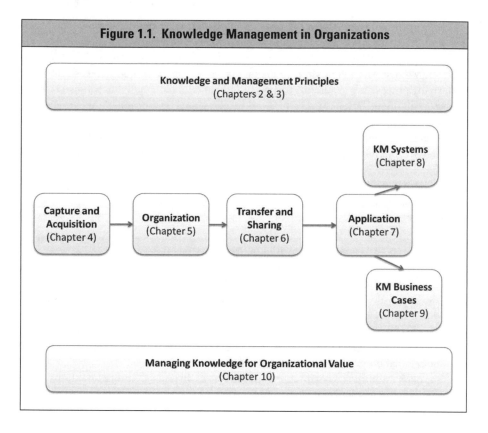

Figure 1.1. Knowledge Management in Organizations

to recognize and adapt to the rapid technological changes occurring in their own market. The Record Industry Association of America's (RIAA) only available response was to file suit against the 19-year-old Fanning. This weak and unimaginative response served as little more than a stopgap measure while the RIAA members struggled with ways to "legitimize" a Napster clone that would provide revenues (McManus, 2003). Today, various Napster clones exist, and iTunes has revolutionized the way music is purchased.

What does this incident demonstrate? In the first case concerning the RIAA, knowledge regarding the changing nature of customer purchase preferences was ignored. Had the RIAA understood the latent implications of Napster, it may have been able to respond differently to the situation by more effectively changing its distribution model and conforming to the preferences of its customers. Sony, the company that gave us the Walkman, also missed out on this trend. Sony was the first company to create a portable device that allowed people to play music on the go. Yet the company, like the RIAA, missed out on being the first to market with a device to take advantage of digital music. Apple, with iTunes and the iPod, filled this void by adequately identifying and acquiring knowledge from its business environment and utilizing its internal knowledge, experience, and know-how to build a product that consumers embraced.

The Case of the US Invasion of Iraq

During the build-up to the Iraq War in 2003, the US government misrepresented knowledge regarding Iraq's weapons of mass destruction (WMD) capabilities. Critical and accurate knowledge was misused or not shared, while inaccurate knowledge was used as the basis of the Bush administration's claim that Iraq possessed WMDs. In one incident, the Central Intelligence Agency (CIA) relied heavily on one source, an Iraqi defector named Rafid Alwan who provided inaccurate and misleading information regarding Iraq's biological weapons program. It is interesting to note that Alwan's primary handler was Germany's Federal Intelligence Service (BND). The BND had warned its American counterpart, the CIA, about doubts it had regarding the authenticity of Alwan's claims yet the CIA went ahead and placed a lot of credence on the information he provided. In another incident, substantial amounts of material provided by the CIA in Colin Powell's speech to the United Nations, whose purpose was to rally international support for the war, was found to be faulty. For example, the US Department of Energy and Air Force have disputed the claim that the aluminum tubes depicted in Powell's presentation could be used to transport uranium (Desouza, 2003).

This second case illuminates the dire consequences that might occur when knowledge is not adequately created and shared. The US intelligence community, which is made up of agencies whose sole agenda is to generate actionable knowledge to help elected leaders plan for a wide assortment of threats to America's national and global interests, provided poor information that lacked credible sources. Knowledge was not shared between the various intelligence agencies. Moreover, in cases where knowledge was shared, it was not duly appreciated and accounted for by the receiving agency. Furthermore, inaccurate assessments were made as information was manipulated by the Bush administration to meet a predetermined outcome.

The Case of Hurricane Katrina

In August 2005 Hurricane Katrina, one of the five deadliest hurricanes in US history, struck the Gulf coast of the United States. Sadly, many of the efforts to provide relief to those affected by Katrina were laden with mismanagement and failures. Communication failures occurred between first responders (disaster management, law enforcement, and relief personnel) and to the public that resulted in poor resource utilization. For example, the city of New Orleans made accommodations to evacuate residents using school and municipal buses. However, residents were not told the locations where they could board the buses and the transit authority failed to plan adequately for drivers, routes, and traffic. As a result, many residents of New Orleans were not able to evacuate. Knowledge of past natural disasters, especially those that were near the scale of Katrina, was not used effectively for planning purposes (U.S. House of Representatives, 2006).

This again points to the devastating outcomes that ensue when knowledge is not managed in a timely manner. During the minutes, hours, and days after Katrina made landfall, various agencies, including the Department of Homeland Security, Federal Emergency Management Agency (FEMA), and the Office of the Governor of Louisiana, did not receive—and hence could not act on—timely information and knowledge about how the situation on the ground was developing. Although much of the infrastructure was damaged, some response units with capable communication technology were present, but they were not being utilized for knowledge sharing. This case also points out how organizations can fail to learn even when there is a vast reservoir of knowledge and experience.

In all three of these cases, knowledge management was poorly executed. The results speak for themselves: lives were lost, organizations were destroyed, people were injured, businesses suffered, and opportunities were not leveraged for public benefit. Managing knowledge is not a luxury for an organization. It is a necessity, both for survival and for thriving in turbulent environments. While knowledge management is not going to protect an organization from all possible problems that may arise, it will help the organization better sense oncoming concerns and plan for them. Organizations that are successful in managing knowledge may secure competitive advantages. Knowledge management, when done properly, produces results and benefits that are not directly attributable to knowledge management initiatives. However, if the knowledge management is not done, or done poorly, the organization will witness devastating consequences that can be directly attributed to knowledge management.

Knowledge Management in the Life of a Curious Student

To better appreciate the intricacies of knowledge management, the case of a graduate student who wants to try conducting research provides an excellent example.

> Take a few minutes to think about the process and write down the major steps. Think through the various steps and outline: (1) what kind of knowledge do you need, (2) how do you get it, (3) what do you do with it, (4) how do you progress through various milestones, and (5) how do you know when you have achieved your goal, and what do you do next?

Table 1.1 contains a summary of the knowledge management steps carried out by "the curious student."

Suppose that your goal is to become a world-class researcher. Establishing this goal is a first and important step that will help you guide your next steps in this process. One way to think about this is that reaching your goal will represent your desired state. Where you are today is your current state. Through knowledge management, you must find the best way—the most effective and efficient way—to get from your current state to your desired state. In order to do so, you must be able to take inventory of what you know by identifying your current knowledge, skills, and experiences. Did you take a class in statistics or qualitative research? Do you have the necessary knowledge of how scientific inquiry is conducted? If not, then these will represent gaps that must be filled in if you are going to achieve your goal.

Once you identify your gaps, the second step will be to begin to fill them. In order to learn the craft of scientific inquiry, one might take graduate classes in the philosophy of science, research methodologies, and explore theories of interest. Through these experiences, you will gain knowledge about *how* to conduct research. This knowledge will come from both reading of explicit knowledge artifacts (e.g., books, journal articles)

Table 1.1. Knowledge Management Steps: The Curious Student	
Step	**Description**
Perform gap analysis	• Take a knowledge inventory in order to identify gaps between existing knowledge ("current state") and desired knowledge ("desired state").
Fill the gaps	• Acquire the needed knowledge through a combination of explicit artifacts (such as books or journals) and tacit sources (such as interactions with professors and peers).
Utilize knowledge	• Use new knowledge to formulate a solution.
Collect evidence	• Collect evidence such as qualitative or quantitative data to support the conclusions (which can stand up to review and scrutiny).
Analyze data	• Analyze the data collected in order to identify patterns and carry out interpretations (construct new knowledge).
Transfer knowledge	• Communicate the findings (new knowledge) to stakeholders in the accepted formats.

and from interactions with knowledge sources (e.g., professors, fellow classmates) in order to acquire *tacit* knowledge. Tacit knowledge cannot be shared in an explicit form, as it is difficult to separate from the knowledge source. Through the course work, one gains knowledge that we might consider as fundamental to one's objective. Without this knowledge it might be difficult to undertake rigorous scientific inquiry, but simply getting it does not transform one into a world-class researcher.

The next step (which might occur in tandem with the previous one) is to begin to utilize the recently acquired knowledge to undertake scientific research. You will need to begin by formulating a research problem. This can be considered akin to working on problems like those encountered at work. Regardless of the nature of problem, one must use one's knowledge to formulate a solution. While many times the problems we work on might not be unique, the manner in which each of us goes about solving problems tend to be more idiosyncratic. The budding researcher must construct research questions, develop a hypothesis, and arrive at a research methodology. These stages are laden with the aspects of innovation. Here is where the creativity and uniqueness of the researcher's individual perspective begins to bear fruit.

Once knowledge has been applied to arrive at tentative ideas or hypotheses for a solution, the next step is to go about collecting data and empirically (either quantitatively or qualitatively) testing these notions. At this stage, the researcher will be best served by using established knowledge in the discipline to execute various research methodologies in a rigorous manner. Innovation is not as paramount because the researcher must be able to show evidence for his or her conclusions that can stand up to peer review and other scrutiny. How data is collected, processed, and analyzed is the major component of research scrutiny, so research methodologies must be adhered to. For example, if the researcher did not build a scientifically reliable survey instrument (e.g., if the questions are poorly worded or are leading), then the results based on analysis of the data will be of little to no value. Similar issues arise if issues of scientific reliability and validity are not adhered to.

Once the data is analyzed, it is transformed into information. The next vital step is to begin to analyze the information. Here, you will examine if the information supports or refutes the hypotheses, signals latent trends and patterns, or contains outliers that must be investigated further. Through the process of interpretation, you are beginning to *construct new knowledge*, also known as interpretations. These interpretations will then lead to recommendations. In the information and social sciences, recommendations can take the form of interventions for phenomenon (e.g., methods to increase attention to information), guidelines for the design of new systems (e.g., design considerations for learning systems to be used by autistic children), or even policy recommendations (e.g., policies to improve knowledge retention).

Just coming up with the new knowledge is not sufficient (it is good, but not enough!). You must spend the necessary time and effort to communicate—that is, *transfer* this knowledge to various stakeholders. In the case of scientific research, this is normally scientific and professional organizations. Here, the knowledge being transferred will be received (through submission of the paper to a journal or scientific meeting), evaluated (through peer review), and then either deemed to be credible and useful or not. In the case that it is deemed credible and useful, the knowledge will be made available to others so that they can use, build upon, and extend the work. In the case that it does not make the cut, you will be given feedback on how to improve the work to bring it to a place where the quality merits further consideration.

Upon the completion of one successful research cycle (from problem formulation to generation of ideas, empirically validating the ideas and generating new knowledge, and transferring the knowledge to stakeholders) you will learn a lot about the intricacies of scientific inquiry. You will learn how to define problems, execute various stages of the research methodology, interpret results, and even become skilled in the art of writing a scholarly paper and presenting findings to stakeholders. The first time any researcher completes a research project, the learning curve will be quite steep and intense, but soon his or her knowledge base will begin to develop and deepen. These experiences will not only be the outcome of the research undertaken by the individual but through the process of socialization in scientific communities. By networking with peers and experienced researchers, the researcher will learn and get acquainted with not only knowledge that is found in books, but gained from the experiences of others. For example, most scientific communities organize colloquiums for doctoral students and new scholars so that they can connect with experts outside their immediate circles and learn from the best and brightest in the field. These experiences are invaluable when it comes to developing as a scholar. Over time, through disciplined effort, practice, and innovations, you will achieve your goal as a world-class researcher. As you attain this status, not only will your knowledge about how to conduct research deepen and increase in value, you will become well attuned to know-how in your field of expertise and attain the status of an expert in your scholarly field. You will help increase the knowledge base of other researchers while helping your field advance through the discoveries you make and through others building off your discoveries. You will become intertwined in a never-ending cycle of knowledge.

These stages represent the process of knowledge management in an academic setting. Knowledge management in organizations takes a similar trajectory. Individuals circle through these stages through the conduct of their work. The goal of knowledge management is to increase the effectiveness and efficiency through which individuals and organizations cycle through these various stages. Each individual works like a researcher by examining data of interest, calculating information, drawing interpretations, and conducting necessary actions to benefit the organization. Alongside this, each organization as a whole must work *collectively* to engage in knowledge management. This is akin to collaborative research undertakings. Groups of researchers, each of whom may bring complementary knowledge and experiences, must work collaboratively to solve a complex problem. One reason for collaboration is that no single researcher may be able to solve the problem alone, or it is too costly for them to solve it in isolation. Collaborations call for researchers to share knowledge, appreciate diverse perspectives, and jointly construct artifacts. An organization can be visualized as a series of collaborative research projects that all aim to address a common goal or objective. Each project undertaken is related to others and influences other efforts. Knowledge management must occur *within* and *across* such efforts, to further the overall objectives of the organization. The role of the organization is to determine what knowledge it possesses, what it might be able to access (for example, through strategic alliances), and then decide where (the areas of interest) and how (the process) best to apply this knowledge to develop innovative products and services that are valued by customers.

Given this quick illustration into what knowledge management is, you should see that knowledge management is something that you are engaged with on a daily basis. We are all in some ways knowledge workers and managers. Some of us are better than others at managing knowledge, and normally we can begin to trace the success that peers have to how capable they are at managing their knowledge. The same thinking applies at the team/group and organizational level. Groups that are better at taking advantage of diverse perspectives through effective and efficient communication and collaboration will fare better, in most cases, than groups that cannot synthesize diverse perspectives and communicate effectively. Organizations, and even interorganizational networks, operate in much the same way.

KP²T: KNOWLEDGE, PEOPLE, PROCESSES, AND TECHNOLOGY

In order to manage knowledge, we must pay attention to four components: knowledge, people, processes, and technology. Throughout the book, we will come back to each of these four concepts as we discuss the various intricacies of knowledge management.

Knowledge

Without *knowledge* to manage, there would be no *knowledge management*. What kinds of knowledge are there in organizations? A basic condition of knowledge management is to manage knowledge that one deems valuable. Differences in how knowledge is *valued* will lead to differentials in resources assigned to manage them. For instance, consider security programs that protect valuable knowledge. All nations take great care securing valuable knowledge in the context of national security operations and missions. Access to these knowledge artifacts, programs, and processes are limited to (1) people who possess necessary security credentials which determine access levels, and (2) those who need to know. Similar dynamics occur within private organizations, as they use a wide assortment of legal protective measures to secure their intellectual property and assign value to their knowledge.

Knowledge can be found in multiple forms and reside in multiple sources. The ideal knowledge management program will appreciate the diversity of forms and sources and find the right method to manage them. At the highest level, we can think of two broad categories of knowledge: (1) knowledge that is *fundamentally tied* to the source and (2) knowledge that can be detached from the source. Here, the source can be a person, team, organization, or any other instantiation of human artifacts. For now, consider an individual as the source. In daily work routines and tasks, it is common to encounter highly skilled individuals who are unbelievably creative, imaginative, and skillful in their trades. These might be the chef at a restaurant, the musician at the local pub, or even the professor who is so bright that he knows more than he can communicate through formal lectures. As in the earlier example of the painter, even if these people are able to articulate their work processes, the chances of anyone duplicating the results with the same amount of grace and clarity are almost nil. Here, the best management approach will be to build an environment where knowledge seekers can connect with the source of knowledge and interact with it in order to get their aid and help as problems arise. For example, through modes of apprenticeship and socialization, rookies can learn from experts. They can observe experts at their work, try to imitate them, seek counsel as problems arise and then through time build up their reservoir of their own knowledge and add elements of their own creativity and talent to it. Today, through a wide assortment of social networking technologies and websites such as LinkedIn and Facebook, individuals are finding newer ways to connect with each other and share knowledge, information, collaborate on projects, or just keep everyone up-to-date on their daily lives. Organizations are also using these new services and technologies to promote knowledge sharing in their workplaces, which will be discussed further in Chapter 6.

In cases where knowledge can be detached from the source, the focus of knowledge management becomes how best to get sources to articulate their knowledge, what is the right mode of capture, and how best to manage the artifacts in which such knowledge is captured. The classical example of this can be found in scholarly publications. Books and other scientific publications can be looked upon as knowledge artifacts. These knowledge artifacts encapsulate experiences, know-how, and ideas. They are prepared by creative and skilled individuals in their domains and normally involve some level of credibility and validation checks. For example, a journal article goes through various peer review assessments where the material is put through scrutiny. Through these checks, the basic tenets of the knowledge are questioned and evaluated, and assessments are made. Once knowledge passes the tests, it is deemed acceptable, and goes through the lengthy and expensive publication process. Today, with online journals and books, the time and cost to publish material is decreasing, but it is still not cost-free. This knowledge goes through the process of organization (e.g., the development of structured abstracts and keywords) and is then stored in repositories. The goal of these repositories is to facilitate easy access to and retrieval of the knowledge. Knowledge, once retrieved, can be utilized without direct connection to its source. Over time, people build on each other's work and the repositories grow in volume, variety, and quality. Similar to the process followed through for scholarly publication, various private and government organizations have built knowledge management systems, also known as document repositories or intranets, to promote the sharing of knowledge that can be captured as explicit knowledge artifacts. Newer technologies such as blogs and wikis are increasing the efficacy of these forms of knowledge management systems.

To summarize, a fundamental understanding of the type of knowledge that is being managed is very critical to the success of any knowledge management effort. There must be some value, or expected return, to expend the resources for knowledge management. The greater the return, the greater the resources one might spend to manage the knowledge. An appreciation for the diversity of knowledge sources and forms is essential as well. These ideas will be explored further in Chapter 2.

People

The second component of knowledge management, the people, is equally salient when compared to the knowledge component. People are the sources of knowledge, either directly or indirectly. Our ability to think creatively and uniquely, coupled with our experiences and talents, make us valuable sources of knowledge. In a direct sense, people are the creators and consumers of knowledge. On a daily basis, individuals consume knowledge from multiple sources in addition to taking in huge influxes of information (e.g., from various news outlets). We also create knowledge as part of our daily lives. Knowledge management begins, revolves around, and ends, with people.

The late Peter F. Drucker originally coined the term *knowledge workers* in the 1950s. In *Management Challenges of the 21st Century* (Drucker, 1999: 142), he noted six determinants of knowledge worker productivity:

1. Their ability to question the nature of their tasks and/or work assignments and understand them in a deep manner
2. Being responsible for their own productivity and managing themselves
3. Being responsible for continuous innovation as part of their work assignments
4. Being responsible for continuous learning, and, equally important, teaching, as part of their work
5. Being evaluated by the quality of their output, and not solely on the quantity as was common in the days of the industrial/mechanical society
6. Being treated as assets and not merely as costs, as reflected in knowledge workers' desire to contribute to their organization

These six are vitally important considerations for all organizations to heed.

In deploying knowledge management processes, systems, and programs, organizations should keep these six considerations at the forefront of their attention. After all, any processes or systems should enhance, and not curtail, the productivity of the knowledge workers of the organization. Drucker emphasizes this by stating, "The knowledge worker cannot be supervised closely or in detail. He can only be helped. But he must direct himself, and he must direct himself towards performance and contribution, that is, towards effectiveness" (Drucker, 1999: 7). Managing knowledge workers is not about directing, instructing, or even controlling them. The ideal organization, and to that end, the knowledge management program, will *enable* the knowledge worker. One reason why knowledge workers need to be enabled is that, as Drucker notes, "In fact, that they know more about their job than anybody else in the organization is part of the definition of knowledge workers" (Drucker, 1999: 18). Knowledge workers do not have "supervisors" in the technical sense; they have advisors, associates, and sources of counsel. Since the people they report to may not know the intricacies of their work to the extent that they do, they cannot really be supervised or controlled in how they do the very specific details of their work. The people they report to, however, may know more about how the organization operates, and can offer knowledge and advice, changing the role of manager from *supervising* to *enabling*.

One aspect of enabling is to provide knowledge workers with resources that they can take advantage of as part of their daily work assignments. A critical resource is access to knowledge and other knowledge workers. As part of their daily assignments, knowledge workers face emergent knowledge needs (needs that cannot be predicted). When these needs arise, the knowledge worker needs to be supported through tools, processes, and protocols to seek, integrate, and apply relevant knowledge. As Drucker pointed out, knowledge workers need to be able to seek out knowledge, experiment with it, learn from it, and even teach others as they innovate so as to promote new knowledge creation. Knowledge workers must be enabled in the sense that they feel empowered to use, and contribute to, knowledge repositories, and are able to explore the various networks, both formal and informal, to discover knowledge that may not be found in repositories. Having a knowledge management program that enables this sense of the importance of knowledge is very important. In Chapter 3,

---

The BBC

One of the oldest broadcasters in the world is the British Broadcasting Corporation (BBC). It has taken a different path with its implementation of a KM strategy by not purchasing large, expensive systems, but instead focusing on the needs of the people by using small tools that helped social interactivity throughout the organization, such as blogs, forums, and social networking tools. The objective is to connect people and encourage the creation of new knowledge.

Soon after the initial KM endeavors, the organization's needs grew; the more people began using these technologies, the more information they wanted to share. The BBC then started implementing wikis, which are editable web pages that many can use and create. Researchers used these pages to combine their knowledge, documents were created and edited by multiple people in many departments, and projects were run with the help of such tools. The BBC found that keeping the technology simple, encouraging shared ownership of the work, and focusing on the people and what knowledge they require to perform their jobs was the key to its KM strategy (Semple, 2006).

we will discuss at greater length the intricacies *of how this enabling* fosters productivity among knowledge workers.

Processes

Processes are mechanical (an assembly plant) or logical (submitting expenses for reimbursement) artifacts that guide how work is conducted in organizations. Processes are critical to the functioning of organization. Organizations construct, manage, upgrade, and even dismantle processes on a regular basis. Processes range from those that are local to a given department, to those that are global in the sense that they span, or impact, the entire organization. Organizations often utilize interorganizational processes, which govern exchanges among two or more organizations. One example that can be used to illustrate interorganizational processes is the interlibrary book loan program. Libraries have arrangements for their patrons to borrow books that they do not carry from their partner institutions. The manner in which information is transmitted, shared, and recorded to make the borrowing and returning of the books possible is an example of an interorganizational process.

Processes govern work in organizations. Knowledge workers are expected to take advantage of, and work within, processes and at times even circumvent and innovate around them. As such, it is important for a knowledge management program to recognize their saliency. Processes might be made of, and executed by, humans, machines, or a combination of the two. Processes range from the highly structured and programmable to the very unstructured and emergent. Highly structured processes may be candidates for automation where one can inject and "code" knowledge directly into the process. As an example, consider the case of online FAQs (frequently asked questions) and product diagnosis tools. Today, especially for products such as computers, vendors provide sophisticated online diagnostic tools. These tools, as we will explore at greater length in later chapters, codify knowledge into a series of rules that allow the user to walk through the process without any human intervention. The reason why these processes can be programmed is that they are easily discernable, specifiable, and hence can be programmed.

On the other hand, organizations may have highly unstructured processes. Consider the case of an artist or a writer working on a project. It would be difficult, if not impossible, to predict all their knowledge needs. It would also be difficult for anyone from the outside to think of various systems to deploy to help the individual beforehand. Similar issues arise as innovators work on their projects. As they work, needs and problems arise and solutions are crafted. As projects like these are continuously changing, it is not feasible to think of building a system such as an online FAQ. Instead, as needs arise along this dynamic process, there must be a way for the individuals to understand and tap into various options to support their knowledge needs. Here, the critical determinant of a good knowledge management system will be to minimize the cost or disruption to the work being done in the provision of knowledge. Knowledge management systems provide a combination of push and pull mechanisms to guide how the needed knowledge is provided, which will be demonstrated in Chapter 8.

A critical requirement for knowledge management is to be able to understand work processes and how to map them. By mapping them, you will be able to describe the inputs, outputs, personnel, resources, and work being conducted in a given process. Mapping of processes will help to depict what is really going on in the organization and how work is being accomplished. The next step will be to articulate knowledge needs found along the process and deploy the requisite technology or human interventions to meet these needs, with the goal of increasing effectiveness and efficiency.

Italian F1 Motorsports

F1 motor racing is one of the most popular events in the world, and is viewed by millions on a weekly basis. Italy-F1 includes the involvement of many big name automotive manufacturers and smaller suppliers. The challenge for this producer of racing engines was to link its suppliers together in order to not only share knowledge, but cocreate new products and innovations. Italy-F1 approached this from a process-based perspective, and looked at how people work and use knowledge.

The first step was to connect people in different supplier organizations and have them know the work of other related suppliers. Once relationships were established, knowledge began to flow and collaborative ideas emerged. How daily activities were performed began to change as they naturally involved more outside sources when making a decision, tackling a problem, or searching for new information. Formal and informal meetings played a large role in this collaborative culture, especially through gathering engineers with a diverse set of backgrounds and industry experience together to share their personal knowledge on a problem. Eventually, Italy-F1 and many suppliers offered joint training programs for their engineers to foster new relationships and learning that could combine their valuable industry experience (Mariotti, 2007).

Technology

The last component of knowledge management is technology. Spending on knowledge management technologies continues to grow at an astounding rate. A 2007–2008 spending study by AMR Research, which surveyed 350 technology executives, estimated spending on knowledge management *software* at $73 billion (AMR Research, 2007). The study estimated that spending would grow 16 percent in 2008 (AMR Research, 2007). Unfortunately, with the advances in information technologies and computing over the past few years, many think that knowledge management can be attained through technological solutions. While technology is important, and can significantly enable knowledge management, it is not a solution in and of itself. No matter how sophisticated a given technology is, unless the underlying concerns are addressed, the problem will not go away and the opportunities for improvement will not be realized.

Consider the example of a major technology firm. Facing intense competition and in an attempt to bolster its offerings, the firm began to consider knowledge management as a possible line of business. The firm had deep expertise in the construction of information technologies, but did not understand among other things some of the critical drivers behind how people shared knowledge or the complexities associated with articulation of knowledge. It continued to invest in research and development in search and database technologies, impressing clients with the technological sophistication of its offerings. Yet, as it implemented solutions such as a knowledge repository that was powered by a sophisticated organization schema they encountered a problem: no knowledge was submitted to the system. The firm failed to devise incentives for people to contribute to the repository or keep the existing knowledge assets up-to-date. As a result, its clients never realized any value from their investment. Unfortunately, cases such as these are not rare. Organizations continue to look at technology as a silver bullet. Technology will not make your organization share knowledge, but if people want to share it, technology can increase the reach and scope of such exchanges.

Technology is a critical enabler for knowledge management; this is a common theme that is present throughout the book, beginning with Chapter 3. Technology-enabled techniques of data mining allow people to parse through large collections of data to discover latent patterns. Even technologies as basic as video cameras help us in the discovery of knowledge by recording experiences. Similarly, when discussing knowledge services, we will cover issues of how self-service technologies are becoming knowledge-laden, automated providers of knowledge-based services. Self-service technologies are becoming common in a variety of areas such as airlines and their self-service check-in desks.

In the deployment of technology-enabled solutions, several considerations are important to bear in mind. First is the KISS principle—Keep it Simple, Stupid! Too often, technology designers get caught up loading a solution with overzealous features, websites that are too busy and complex to navigate, and solutions that are not user-friendly. These are some of the most common reasons why technology-enabled knowledge management solutions are abandoned. Second, as noted in the previous section, knowledge management solutions should neither constrain nor restrict but instead empower individuals. In most cases, individuals use technologies in ways that the original designers did not consider. Knowledge workers are not passive users of technology. They innovate by customizing these tools to meet their work contexts. Designers of technology must find a way to tap into these "super-users" to get ideas for new versions/releases of the technology. Third, technologies need to be flexible and ingrained into the work practices of individuals. The more pervasive and ubiquitous technology is, the greater the chance it will be used. The more

---

The United States Navy

In order to help their people manage their careers and be involved in training and development, the US Navy has created a portal that provides customized web pages based on a sailor's interests and career path. The Navy Knowledge Online (NKO) website creates a common gateway to the important knowledge needed to advance through this branch of the service. Communities of practice have been established to connect members across functional areas that may not be reachable through their "Knowledge Home Port" (Walter, 2002).

Knowledge in this system is useful not only for day-to-day operations, but for lifelong learning and development that is crucial to assist individuals in preparing for changes in this vast organization. Rear Admiral Harry Ulrich states, "We wanted to provide every sailor with a personalized gateway to the Navy's knowledge base of information on professional and personal development" (Government Technology, 2002). The goal for the Navy is to make NKO the centerpiece of its KM and learning strategies, through focusing on the current and future needs of its people.

immersed an individual is in the technology, and the more technology immersed is into the work of the individual, the greater is the chance that it will be used, on a regular, and sustained basis. As an example, consider those who use Facebook. Most users find Facebook *sticky*; that is they check it regularly, update it, and use it for all kinds of purposes not considered by the original designers. Employees need to find that the knowledge management system at work is a similar sticky gateway to their organization.

KNOWLEDGE MANAGEMENT: AN INTERDISCIPLINARY PURSUIT

Knowledge management is a highly interdisciplinary scholarly discipline that draws its roots from a number of other traditional academic disciplines. These disciplines inform what we know about how organizations, groups, and societies manage their knowledge. As knowledge management continues to emerge as a distinct discipline in its own right, it is making contributions to its root disciplines. Today, papers on knowledge management are appearing in the major journals of disciplines such as public administration, innovation and technology management, law, psychology, sociology, health care, and strategic management among others.

The discipline of philosophy can be considered as the main root of knowledge management. Since the days of Aristotle and Plato, philosophers have been interested in the concepts of knowledge and the act of knowing. Much of the current understanding on what is knowledge can be traced to epistemological discourses and debates dating back through the centuries. One of the most commonly cited philosophers by knowledge managers is Michael Polanyi (1891–1976). Polanyi is well known for his contribution to the development of the concept of tacit knowing (Polanyi, 1966). Philosophy, especially the branch of epistemology, has influenced thinking on how knowledge is produced, how knowledge claims are evaluated, and how knowledge is communicated among various parties. Other influential philosophers who have shaped significant aspects of knowledge management include Rene Descartes, John Locke, Immanuel Kant, and John Dewey. In addition to philosophy, three other major disciplines have played an influential role in the formation of knowledge management (Descartes, 1986; Locke, 1959; Kant, 1949; Dewey, 1958).

Economics

The field of economics has played a vital role in the development of the knowledge management discipline. For centuries, economists have examined a wide range of problems that make up critical tenets of knowledge management. Consider the work of Friedrich August von Hayek (1899–1992), an Austrian-born economist who received the Nobel Prize in 1974. While the major work for which he received the Nobel Prize centers on issues on the theory of money and economic (market) movements, his 1945 paper, "The Use of Knowledge in Society" is considered a seminal work in knowledge management. In this paper, Hayek notes:

The peculiar character of the problem of a rational economic order is determined precisely by the fact that the knowledge of the circumstances of which we must make use never exists in concentrated or integrated form but solely as the dispersed bits of incomplete and frequently contradictory knowledge which all the separate individuals possess. The economic problem of society is thus not merely a problem of how to allocate "given" resources – if "given" is taken to mean given to a single mind which deliberately solves the problem set by these "data." It is rather a problem of how to secure the best use of resources known to any of the members of society, for ends whose relative importance only these individuals know. Or, to put it briefly, it is a problem of the utilization of knowledge which is not given to anyone in its totality. (Hayek, 1945: 519)

These words are salient, as they make for a critical argument for knowledge management. As Hayek notes, knowledge is unequally distributed across members of society, thereby making it difficult for individuals to be able to take full advantage of their knowledge without coordination with their peers. Herein lies the fundamental issue of knowledge management: how can you leverage knowledge that is distributed across people, synthesize it, and transform it in order to achieve the goals of collective entities?

Another seminal economist whose contributions are important to the field of knowledge management is Kenneth Joseph Arrow. Arrow, who won the Nobel Prize in Economics in 1972 at the age of 51, still remains the youngest person ever to win the prestigious award. Arrow is recognized as one of the founders of neoclassical economic theory, with his major contributions being in social choice theory and laid the foundation of what has become the field of information economics. He studied how information asymmetry, cases where one party has more information than another, creates incentives for cheating (i.e., acting with guile). Through provisions such as warranties, third-party authentication, and other protocols, markets address information asymmetries (Arrow, 1963). This work has played a vital role in the development of electronic markets, and continues to influence the thinking behind knowledge markets, a topic discussed in Chapter 8. Arrow's work has also made significant contribution to theorizing about the role played by information in risk management and decision making.

To find other contributions from economists to the field of knowledge management, one must examine the domain of information economics (or economics of information). A subdiscipline of microeconomics, it is focused on inquiries that examine how information effects decisions at the individual, and organizational levels. Information economics studies questions such as how is information priced, how one signals the value of information, how information goods are bundled, and how information is used to reduce the uncertainty associated with decision making. Information economists' findings have directly and significantly impacted our understanding of knowledge goods. Some of the seminal information economists are George Akerlof, Hal R. Varian, A. Michael Spence, and Joseph E. Stiglitz (Akerlof, 1970; Spence, 1973; Stiglitz, 1975). Other economic disciplines such as political economics, which examines the role of knowledge assets and human capital in economic development, have also influenced the knowledge management field. The work of 1992 Nobel Laureate Gary Stanley Becker is credited with developing the concept of human capital. He argued for investment in human capital and his work showed how investments in human capital lead to differential payoffs (Becker, 1964).

Management Science

The broad discipline of management science has also shaped what we know about how to manage knowledge in organizations. Management science, if one takes a simplistic and pragmatic view, is about helping organizations increase their effectiveness and efficiency in order to attain goals and objectives. Subdisciplines such as strategic management, innovation management, organizational behavior, information systems, project management, and accounting and finance inform aspects of knowledge management.

Among the various subdisciplines of management science, the area of strategic management has been one of the most critical contributors to knowledge management in recent times. Even a cursory review of the major journal of the discipline, *Strategic Management Journal*, will uncover the popular interest in knowledge management problems and issues. The major focus of researchers and practitioners in this domain is learning about how knowledge is leveraged within the organization in order to strategically position and competitively differentiate it in the marketplace. Robert M. Grant, one of the most cited management science researchers in the field, developed the "knowledge based theory of the firm." Grant's theory, which builds on the resource-based view of the firm proposed by economist Penrose (1959), asserts that knowledge is the most important resource of the firm. More important, it goes on to note that knowledge application, and not knowledge creation, is the primary responsibility of the firm. Grant argues that knowledge resides in individuals, and hence the role of the firm is to foster the effective and efficient application of knowledge in collected settings. Grant's knowledge-based theory of the firm has fostered research into how organizations develop strategies and processes, foster knowledge sharing and transfers, enable the application of knowledge in distributed settings (e.g., within multiple departments in a firm or in firms that belong to inter-organizational networks), and even optimize organizational design (e.g., how to design formal structures so as to enable optimal decision making).

The work of David Teece is also notable in the strategic management discipline. Teece and his colleagues developed the concept of **dynamic capabilities** and their prominence in firm performance. Teece, Pisano, and Shuen noted that it was not merely the differences in resources possessed by firms that led to performance, but it was in fact the firm's ability to leverage resources through their dynamic capabilities that was more salient. They define dynamic capabilities as "the ability to integrate, build, and reconfigure internal and external competencies to address rapidly-changing environments" (Teece, Pisano, and Shuen, 1997: 516). The notion of dynamic capabilities has been advanced in recent years by various scholars in the strategic management domain and remains a cornerstone of understanding regarding how firms leverage their resources for strategic advantages. The concept of capabilities is critical as we begin to understand the processes associated with knowledge management. Knowledge management can be viewed as the collection of capabilities that are required to integrate, build, and reconfigure knowledge-based competencies. Moreover, the ability of a firm to manage its dynamic capabilities lies in how well knowledge is managed in and around the firm.

In addition to Grant and Teece, it is fruitful to review the writings of other well-known and influential strategic management scholars such as Richard R. Nelson, Sidney G. Winter, Kathleen Eisenhardt, Alfred D. Chandler, and Edith Tilton Penrose. Each of these scholars has made significant contributions to what we know about knowledge management.

Another pivotal contributor to knowledge management has been the broad subdiscipline of technology management, which examines various facets of how organizations employ technology towards organizational objectives. Areas of investigation under this discipline include topics of innovation, management of information systems, project management, technology development and commercialization, and research and development programs. Much of what we know about how to deploy technological systems to foster knowledge management stems from work conducted within this domain. Each of the strategic management scholars previously mentioned has contributed to the literature on technology management as well.

Library and Information Science

The library and information science discipline has contributed many foundational elements to the field of knowledge management. Libraries have been the major repositories of societal knowledge for thousands of years. At one point in time libraries were the only places where care was taken to preserve local experiences, know-how, and inventions. The first library dates back to around 1200 BC and existed in Ugarit in Syria. Excavations in Ugarit led to the discovery of a palace library, two private libraries, and one temple library. The most famous ancient library is the Library of Alexandria, which dates back to 200 BC. The library contained close to 500,000 artifacts in its collection, many of which were handwritten works and hand-drawn reproductions. Thomas Jefferson's collection of books was known as the Monticello library and also played a prominent role in American history. During the War of 1812, the Congressional Library was destroyed. After the war, Jefferson donated his books to Congressional Library collection, which led to the creation of what we presently know as the Library of Congress (Library of Congress, 2006.). Beyond tracing the LIS tradition to the creation of libraries and library administration, one can look at the vast history of the academic discipline of information science (IS). Information science has a rich and vast tradition but has only recently been organized into a discipline. Some attribute the formation of the field to the publishing of Vannevar Bush's article "As We May Think" that appeared in 1945. Others attribute it to one of the first major conferences on the topic, the Royal Society Scientific Information Conference that took place in 1948. Some point to the founding of formal organizations such as the International Institute of Bibliography, which was formed in 1895 as the International Office of Bibliography, in Brussels, Belgium, by Paul Otlet (Otlet, 1990).

Classical works from leading LIS figures such as Melvil Dewey (1851–1931), Henry Bliss (1870–1955), and Sir Francis Bacon (1561–1626) continue to influence how we think about knowledge organization. The ideas and solutions that have been developed from their original works impact the work of librarians, the functioning of libraries, and the organization of knowledge artifacts in corporate settings.

Too often, the principles of library and information science are not well known to those working in the field of knowledge management. As Marcia Bates notes:

> Recently, digital information and new forms of information technology have become the focus of tremendous amounts of attention and energy in our society. Money is pouring into the development of all manner of technologies and information systems. The excitement penetrates not only the business world and the general society, but also academia, where computer scientists, cognitive scientists, and social scientists are thinking about information and the social impacts of information technology in new ways. This new context poses a challenge to information science. Currently, the wheel is being reinvented every day on the information superhighway. Our expertise is ignored while newcomers to information questions stumble through tens of millions of dollars of research and startup money to rediscover what information science knew in 1960. We in the field need to make our research and theory better known and more understandable to the newcomers flooding in—or be washed away in the flood. (Bates, 1999: 1043)

As Bates observes, the knowledge and skills developed in the LIS academy need to be applied to the current information and technological challenges facing organizations and society. As Bates (1999: 1048) frames it, information science explores three big questions: "(1) the physical question: What are the features and laws of the recorded-information universe? (2) The social question: How do people relate to, seek, and use information? (3) The design question: How can access to recorded information be made most rapid and effective?" These questions are not so different from the challenges explored by knowledge management practitioners and scholars. As we will explore in the next chapter, knowledge, like information artifacts, has certain features that must be appreciated and managed. How do we design social protocols for engaging individuals into the collective act of knowledge management so as to promote the rapid, effective, and efficient creation and consumption of knowledge?

To make knowledge management work, we need professionals who are skilled in the various aspects of LIS: from curators to archivists, cataloguers to reference specialists, and architects to researchers. As noted by Saracevic:

> I suggest that information science has three such powerful ideas, so far. These ideas deal with processing of information in a radically different way than was done previously or elsewhere. The first and the original idea, emerging in 1950s, is information retrieval, providing for processing of information based on formal logic. The second, emerging shortly thereafter, is relevance, directly orienting and associating the process with human information needs and assessments. The third, derived from elsewhere some two decades later, is interaction, enabling direct exchanges and feedback between systems and people engaged in IR [information retrieval] processes. (Saracevic, 1999: 1052)

The three tenets of information science—retrieval, relevance, and interaction—are critical foundations that knowledge management researchers draw upon in their daily work. This book will illustrate how specialized knowledge and experience held by LIS professionals can be brought to bear on various knowledge management problems. For example, individuals who are skilled at providing services at the reference desk are sorely needed in the knowledge services sphere—they can be ideal brokers between knowledge seekers and knowledge producers. In many organizations, knowledge management programs are run by individuals who have a background in LIS, especially those who are interested in working in special libraries. While these individuals understand how to manage information and knowledge artifacts, they often do not have sufficient training and knowledge in the management aspects of running organizations. Issues such as how to successfully plan, finance, and market their knowledge management programs seem to become significant challenges to these professionals. This book intends to offer some guidance on how a background in both of these areas might prove to be useful.

Library 2.0

In the 1990s most websites were just pages of information that were presented to the viewer. Websites were very unilateral with little to no interaction between the viewer and the website, which was primarily due to the limitations of the technology at the time. As technology advanced the websites evolved and became much more interactive, provided a richer user experience, and involved the users more in order to harness their collective intelligence. This increase in interaction and collaboration is what we now refer to as **Web 2.0** (O'Reilly, 2005). Other industries have begun to adopt similar principles by fostering collaboration and having users and/or customers more involved in initiatives and projects undertaken by organizations, which has led industries to adopt the *2.0* label in order to indicate that they have begun to evolve as well (e.g., Business 2.0). Libraries are no different. Library 2.0 brings in patrons as contributors to tailor library services to fulfill their own needs as well as the needs of others by offering services such as personalized library pages, user comments, tags, and ratings to feed user-generated content back into the library pages (Casey and Savistinuk, 2006). Just as Web 2.0 is harnessing the collective intelligence of web users, Library 2.0 seeks to harness the collective intelligence of patrons to provide better service and identify areas of improvement. Libraries are also increasingly becoming a space used by groups of people for collaboration—resulting in the demand for librarians to understand the technologies used by people to support collaboration.

Helene Blowers, IT director at North Carolina's Charlotte and Mecklenburg County public library, developed a program called Learning 2.0 that helped train library staff in the latest web technologies, which Christine MacKensie, director of the Yarra Plenty Regional Library in Melbourne, Australia, used to make sure that staff would be able to help patrons with questions regarding things like Flickr or Second Life (Hanly, 2007). Librarians are increasingly required to help patrons manage and interact with the knowledge found through these technologies. While being well versed in the latest technologies and their uses is critical for libraries (as well as other organizations), it is easy to overlook the increasing need of more "traditional" technologies, such as power outlets. It is common to see a group of people sitting around a table with each person using at least one portable device like laptops and smartphones, if not many. All of these devices require power outlets—a traditional technology that Tracy Lauder, assistant dean for Library Administration at the University of New Hampshire, says is a "fairly big issue for [the library]" (Kelley, 2010: under "Universities Struggle to Keep Up").

CRITICAL REASONS DRIVING THE NEED FOR KNOWLEDGE MANAGEMENT

When asked for the top reasons why they must manage knowledge, executives who are responsible for knowledge management programs usually offer three fairly consistent points including organizational survival, competitive differentiation, and the effects of globalization. These points are discussed in detail in the following sections. Another commonly cited reason is an aging workforce. Most organizations are facing a graying of their workforce and soon, much knowledge is going to leave their organization. This intellectual capital needs to be captured so that future generations in these work environments do not have to repeat mistakes and reinvent knowledge. While some organizations realize that they are going to lose knowledge as the baby boomers retire and are actively preparing for it, others are not too concerned. They seem to think that the old knowledge is of limited value today and do not want to hold on to it. This idea seems a bit strange until you think about the fact that some of the latest technological innovations such as Google and Facebook were not developed by experienced professionals but were developed instead by college students. These students questioned the status quo and went on to build truly innovative solutions. In certain environments, the purging of old knowledge may be beneficial for renewal and changing perspectives. But at a company such as Boeing, there is a need to be able to sustain knowledge regarding the design and maintenance of their airplanes (which are in service for decades). Table 1.2 summarizes the factors that are driving the need for knowledge management.

Survival and Operational Excellence

The single most important factor that is driving the need for knowledge management is the realization that an organization *must* manage its knowledge if it is to survive in today's dynamic and competitive marketplace. Survival concerns are not limited to private or for-profit firms as nonprofits, public agencies, and even nation-states have all realized the value of knowledge management. Without adequate care in how knowledge is managed, organizations will not be operating optimally. This will result in the ineffective and inefficient creation and delivery of products and services leading to unsatisfied customers, which is what ultimately leads to the demise of the organization. One of the most famous cases of an organization that used knowledge management to boost is operational excellence is the Xerox Corporation (Mottl, 2001). In the mid-1990s, Xerox allowed a grassroots knowledge management effort called Eureka to blossom. Eureka enabled the sharing of knowledge amongst its 25,000 technicians who attended to over 1 million service calls in regard to Xerox's products—printers, copiers, and

Table 1.2. Critical Reasons for Knowledge Management	
Reason	**Description**
Organizational survival	• Effective knowledge management allows organizations to adapt and survive in a dynamic and competitive marketplace.
Competitive differentiation	• Knowledge management is a critical driver of competitive advantages because it enhances the capacity of organizations to innovate.
Globalization	• Globalization creates an urgent need for organizations to be able to manage knowledge across countries and continents.
Aging workforce	• Managers are anticipating baby boomers' retirement in large numbers and are actively preparing for knowledge transfer to younger workers.

network infrastructure. During service calls, technicians encountered problems for which they did not have a readily available solution. Either the problem was novel, or the solution as described in the manual did not fix the problem. These problem encounters were costly as technicians spent hours trying to debug the problems and find solutions through trial and error. Customers experienced downtime of equipment, not to mention the increased cost for service calls. The need to increase operational excellence was embraced by the technicians and built on a simple premise—as they encountered novel problems and created solutions, they documented this knowledge and shared it with other technicians. The technicians realized that while they might not gain from the knowledge they contributed, they would gain from the knowledge submitted by their peers. The exchange of knowledge is only one benefit of such a system.

Another significant benefit is that Eureka became the artifact around which technicians got to know one another and learn about one another's expertise. Before Eureka, technicians were limited to phone calls and e-mails with the eight or so individuals who worked with them in a given geographical region. Now Eureka can be accessed by technicians through their laptops and contains the knowledge from and contact information of technicians across the globe. Within Eureka, different products have different databases to capture the technicians' tips. In order to ensure quality and trust in tips provided by technicians, a group of gatekeepers known as Tigers are involved. Tigers ensure the authenticity and quality of tips entered by technicians and are usually product experts in the field. Validation by Tigers is about having a conversation with the technician about the tip versus simply accepting or rejecting a tip. The knowledge schema to capture the tips from technicians is straightforward; it includes symptom(s), cause(s), test(s), and action(s). Moreover, knowledge transfer and exchanges are not limited to localities or geographic clusters, but can take place globally. Through the implementation of Eureka, Xerox significantly increased the operational excellence associated with its service calls. The cost savings from handling calls, the increase in customer satisfaction, and the overall increase in employee (the technicians) morale were just a few of the benefits. The results from the Eureka effort prompted several other knowledge management projects and programs at the Xerox Corporation and other multinational organizations.

Competitive Differentiation

Once survival and operational excellence is attended to, the next most common reason for conducting knowledge management is to help in competitive differentiation. It is easy to think of the term *competitive differentiation* as being restricted to for-profit firms. However, it is important to remember that all organizations compete within a sector. For example, a public library may have to compete with other libraries and information providers to secure a government grant to expand its services. One of the most often cited reasons why the United States developed a competitive edge in the technological and economic arena was its ability to attract the best minds from across the globe through its immigration program. Skilled individuals migrated to the United States, leaving their home countries to suffer brain drain while the United States benefited. Similarly, nonprofits compete for grants, recognition, and volunteer time and energy. The nonprofit that is able to leverage its know-how and present its unique capabilities in a superior manner will be better off than one that does not know how to manage its knowledge.

Promoting knowledge management is a critical driver of competitive advantages as it enhances the capacity of the organization to innovate, thereby differentiating itself from its competitors. In order to innovate, an organization must be able to generate ideas and construct inventions, and then take these inventions and turn them into products and services to sell in the marketplace. Organizations that are unable to innovate at a sustainable pace will lack the ability to continuously attract new customers, which in turn will lead to their demise. Organizations that are able to innovate will be able to secure, and even retain, their competitive positions in the marketplace.

Consider the case of Siemens AG. Siemens AG is Europe's largest engineering conglomerate. Siemens' international headquarters are located in Berlin and Munich, Germany. Siemens AG is a global powerhouse with 15 divisions and three main business sectors: Industry, Energy, and Healthcare. Multinational corporations (MNCs) like Siemens build up their competitive advantage through their subsidiaries' ability to create knowledge within their local networks and to share it with sister units located in different countries. If knowledge sharing between units is the main reason for the existence of the MNC, as well as the source of its competitive advantage, then the velocity and scope with which knowledge is circulating is a key determinant of such advantage. ShareNet is an example of a global knowledge-sharing tool used by Siemens. It was developed in 1999 and has been recognized as a unique example of knowledge sharing because of its sophisticated software applications and substantial number of users. It provided employees of the many subsidiaries of Siemens worldwide an opportunity to access all kinds of knowledge and information. The ShareNet website contains a structured section with "communities" and "knowledge libraries" where information is categorized by topic, and another less structured section with "discussion groups," "urgent requests," etc., aimed at promoting a more direct form of communication. It is structured to allow users to perform the four basic functions: inserting knowledge, browsing knowledge, networking, and user support. ShareNet is grounded on the idea that its users should participate in knowledge sharing for their mutual good, and therefore the system contribution to knowledge sharing is dependent on the users' activities within the system. This is sustained by specific incentive and reward systems and is based on users' reciprocal evaluation of each other's contributions achieved through feedback and content evaluation activities on the bases of the quality and reusability of the knowledge inserted. Thus, at the same time, users can be contributors, receivers, knowledge reusers, and quality editors. Siemens attributes a significant amount of its competitive success to the ability to solve the world's most complex problems through the construction of commercially viable and sustainable products and services. Unsurprisingly, this is possible because it can manage its knowledge in a far superior manner than its competitors (Nielsen and Ciabuschi, 2003).

Globalization

The world is getting "flatter," more connected and interdependent (Friedman, 2005). Evidence of these trends can be found by examining the financial crisis that began in late 2007 or early 2008. No country has been immune from the effects of the crisis. Some have felt the effects of crisis more severely than others, but all of the world's economies are trying to battle their way out of it. The crisis, largely due to the mortgage and housing collapse in the United States, impacted banks in Europe, affected the economies of countries (such as Iceland and Lithuania), and even made life difficult for people living various countries in Asia due to cuts in corporate spending and global expansion plans. The trend of globalization and increased interconnectivity and dependency is not going away, and will only intensify in the future. This poses an urgent need for organizations to be able to manage knowledge across countries and continents.

Consider one outcome of globalization—outsourcing. Today, not only do organizations outsource the manufacturing of physical goods (e.g., cars or clothing) but knowledge work such as software development is also being outsourced. Organizations are taking advantage of the availability of skilled knowledge professionals in foreign countries where there are cost advantages when compared to workers in their own localities. In addition, by outsourcing work, the organization can operate all through the day or night by taking advantage of time zone differences. If one were to trace the evolution of outsourcing, organizations moved from the sourcing of simple, structured, manufacturing assignments, to the outsourcing of knowledge work which was of a structured nature such as call centers, to the present time, where high-end knowledge work involves a high degree of knowledge exchanges and even the codevelopment of new knowledge.

Organizations face a daunting challenge in managing the risks associated with the outsourcing of innovation; most of these risks can be traced to the ability of an organization to sustain a viable knowledge management program within itself and also collaborate on knowledge management with its business partners. Many organizations have realized that they cannot reach business goals by conducting all activities internally. Cooperating with business partners and leveraging the know-how found in an organization's midst is a salient determinant of competitive successes. Organizations often struggle to increase the intensity and success of partnerships. When organizations outsourced only manufacturing, business partners simply assembled raw materials, and life was easy. Business partnerships then moved to simple knowledge work, as was the case when the outsourcing of software development and IS maintenance efforts became popular in the mid-1980s. Today, leading organizations rely on their business partners for innovation and process goals. The outsourcing of innovation involves engaging with business partners in ways that are significantly binding and have strategic implications.

For example, Boeing actively solicited business partners in the innovation process for its new 787 jetliner (Baloh, Jha, and Awazu, 2008). A team of 15 worldwide companies was created just to make the structural sections of the plane. For example, Mitsubishi Heavy Industries (Japan) is responsible for the wing box, while Vougut and Alexia (Italy) are building the horizontal stabilizer and the center and aft fuselage. Suppliers thus become interested and involved in the success of the new jetliner. In doing so, a partnership based on shared interest in the end product develops and is sustained throughout each interaction. Toyota is another excellent example of a firm innovating with business partners. Despite the amount of research conducted on the Toyota Production System and the fact that Toyota provides tours of its operations to other companies' representatives, competitors have not been able to achieve the outstanding level of productivity present at Toyota. One important reason for this is that knowledge resides and is owned at the network level. Participating suppliers benefit from knowledge sharing as they themselves gain from others' knowledge. Eli Lilly formed the subsidiary InnoCentive to create a business model of external knowledge acquisition (Arndt, 2003). The process is similar to bounty hunting in the Old West: "Wanted" posters describe a scientific problem and offer a reward online. Scientists then compete in an online project room to answer first and best. Over 95,000 scientists from around the world now participate.

Several common themes emerge in these cases:

- In innovation-based outsourcing programs, both parties are engaged in developing novel products and services.
- The chances of the two parties successfully meeting their objectives is very low as the project space is undefined and new, with a greater chance of failure.
- These alliances are premised on the fact that both parties will benefit and, if they gain, will share the rewards.
- The knowledge sharing and intellectual property issues within (and around) these alliances is emerging and sometimes indeterminate.

The saliency of good knowledge management programs cannot be understated here. As globalization intensifies, organizations will need to come to grasp with how to integrate knowledge found across cultures, manage in multiple languages, design systems that promote knowledge sharing in online and virtual settings, and identify processes to optimally leverage the collective knowledge found in disparate pockets.

THE STRUCTURE OF THE BOOK

This book aims to present an introduction to the field of knowledge management through the structure presented in Figure 1.1 (p. 8). Chapters 2 and 3 discuss the fundamentals of both the concept of knowledge and the practice of management. These two chapters provide a foundation for the discussions in the remaining chapters. Chapter 4 examines how both individuals and organizations create knowledge. As this is the first step in knowledge management, we begin with examinations of what causes knowledge creation, and of knowledge creation's impact to the organization. Once knowledge is in possession of the organization it must be organized for easy retrieval and use, which is the subject of Chapter 5. Included in this chapter are conversations about different methods for organizing knowledge and the effect of the Internet on this process.

Chapter 6 examines the means available for organizations to ensure their knowledge is transferred to the right people and groups within the organization. Also presented is the idea of transferring knowledge across organizational boundaries to partners, supply chain members, and customers. How organizations apply their knowledge to both strategic and operational processes is the topic covered in Chapter 7, including the positive effects knowledge can have on an organization's success. Chapter 8 introduces the application of knowledge management systems within an organization, but expands on many traditional ideas and concepts to understand the effects of globalization on these systems and their users. Chapter 9 presents an in-depth examination of how an organization creates a business case for knowledge management, including the justification for resources for KM projects. Finally, in Chapter 10 we review many of the fundamental concepts of knowledge, and look at how organizations can derive value from knowledge within and outside their organization. Leadership is an important component of this discussion.

As discussed earlier in this chapter, organizations and the world in which they operate have undergone changes of enormous magnitude since knowledge management became a popular topic during the 1990s. As many of the early concepts of knowledge management have been refined, two significant factors have emerged, impacting how both organizations and society in general manage knowledge. The first, as introduced in this chapter, is the globalization of business markets. Secondly, the advent of social media services and technologies has permeated our personal lives and is now creating change within the corporate world. Both of these factors have impacts on the organization that are not yet fully understood The intent of this book is to have each of these phenomenon as underlying themes throughout our discussion of knowledge management and its concepts.

We also place an emphasis on innovation work within organizations, as this is not only a source of new knowledge, but also a key driver in the use of both internal and

---

Recap: The Major Points for Knowledge Managers to Consider Regarding Knowledge

1. Although knowledge management is relatively a new field, coming into maturity during the mid-1990s, it has grown into an important aspect of managing and organizational strategy.
2. Many useful case studies and examples exist on how companies have been successful implementing and executing knowledge management activities.
3. Although many definitions of knowledge management exist, they all center on knowledge being an important strategic asset that is essential for an organization's competitive success.
4. Knowledge management can occur at the individual, group, organizational, or societal levels, and at all of these levels it should be closely integrated with other business activities.
5. The four key components of knowledge management are knowledge, people, processes, and technology.
6. Although technology is not required to manage knowledge, it can become a critical enabler and foundational element of a holistic knowledge management plan.
7. One reason for the effectiveness of knowledge management in a wide array of situations is its interdisciplinary roots. KM has its origins in business, economics, library science, sociology, and psychology.
8. The advent of globalization has driven the need for knowledge management, as organizations search to find effective tools and methods for acquiring and sharing knowledge over many structural and cultural barriers.
9. Creative and innovative firms have not only used knowledge management to improve learning and business practices, but have developed competitive advantages over their competition and used KM to drive their sustainability in a marketplace.
10. Knowledge management is a fundamentally important skill for anyone working in any type of organization and has many important aspects that contribute to form a strong knowledge management strategy. This book will serve as a guide for understanding the entire picture of knowledge management.

external knowledge. As organizations must be innovative in their products, services, work processes, and use of technology in order to compete in today's marketplace, it is vital that managers understand the role of knowledge management in innovation. It is therefore important for knowledge managers to recognize not only these business changes and their potential effects on organizations, but also how they can enable or hinder an organization's knowledge management activities.

DISCUSSION QUESTIONS

1. Do you believe that an organization can "manage" its knowledge? What are the challenges faced in creating a program or strategy that involves knowledge management?
2. What components of the organization must managers be aware of when managing knowledge? How does each component contribute to knowledge management?
3. The contribution of many fields toward the study of knowledge management has made it a truly interdisciplinary field. What were the major contributions of other fields to our understanding of knowledge and knowledge management?
4. What advantages can be had by organizations that embrace the concept of managing knowledge and integrate KM within their organizational strategies?
5. How can nonprofit organizations benefit from knowledge management?

REFERENCES

Akerlof, G. A. 1970. "The Market for 'Lemons': Quality Uncertainty and the Market Mechanism." *Quarterly Journal of Economics* 84, no. 3: 488–500.

Alavi, M., and D. Leidner. 2001. "Knowledge Management and Knowledge Management Systems: Conceptual Foundations and Research Issues." *MIS Quarterly* 25, no. 1: 107–136.

AMR Research. 2007. "Knowledge Management Software Spending to Hit $73 Billion in 2007." Tekrati, September 27. http://software.tekrati.com/research/9391/.

Argote, L., B. McEvily, and R. Reagans. 2003. "Introduction to the Special Issue on Managing Knowledge in Organizations: Creating, Retaining, and Transferring Knowledge." *Management Science* 49, no. 4: v–viii.

Arndt, M. 2003. "Finding Bounty Hunters for Science." *BusinessWeek*, November 21. http://www.businessweek.com/technology/content/nov2003/tc20031121_1327_tc024.htm.

Arrow, K. J. 1963. "Uncertainty and the Welfare Economics of Medical Care." *American Economic Review* 53, no. 5: 941–973.

Baloh, P., S. Jha, and Y. Awazu. 2008. "Building Strategic Partnerships for Managing Innovation Outsourcing." *Strategic Outsourcing: An International Journal* 1, no. 2: 100–121.

Bates, M. J. 1999. "The Invisible Substrate of Information Science." *Journal of the American Society for Information Science* 50, no. 12: 1043–1050.

Becker, G. S. 1964. *Human Capital: A Theoretical and Empirical Analysis, with Special Reference to Education.* Chicago, IL: University of Chicago Press.

Brown, J. S. 1998. "Internet Technology in Support of the Concept of 'Communities of Practice': The Case of Xerox." *Accounting Management and Information Technologies* 8, 227–236.

Casey, M., and L. Savastinuk. 2006. "Library 2.0." *Library Journal*. September 1. http://www
.libraryjournal.com/article/CA6365200.html.

Collison, C., and G. Parcell. 2003. *Learning to Fly: Practical Lessons from one of the World's Leading Knowledge Companies*. Milford, CT: Capstone Publishers.

Davenport, T., and L. Prusak. 1998. *Working Knowledge: How Organizations Manage What They Know*. 2nd ed. Boston: Harvard Business School Press.

Descartes, R. 1986. *Meditations on First Philosophy: With Selections from the Objections and Replies*. Edited by John Cottingham. Cambridge: Cambridge University Press.

Desouza, K. C. 2003. "Dissipation of Intelligence." *Competitive Intelligence Magazine* 6, no. 5: 42–44.

Dewey, J. 1958. *Experience and Nature*. New York: Dover.

Drucker, P. F. 1999. *Management Challenges for the 21st Century*. New York: HarperBusiness.

Dyer, J. H., and K. Nobeoka. 2000. "Creating and Managing a High-Performance Knowledge-Sharing Network: The Toyota Case." *Strategic Management Journal* 21: 345–367.

Friedman, T. L. 2005. *The World Is Flat: A Brief History of the Twenty-First Century*. 1st ed. New York: Farrar, Straus, and Giroux.

Government Technology. 2002. "U.S. Navy to Build Knowledge Management Portal." *Government Technology*. October 9. http://www.govtech.com/e-government/US-Navy-to-Build-Knowledge-Management.html.

Hanly, B. 2007. "Public Library Geeks Take Web 2.0 to the Stacks." *Wired*, March 29. http://www.wired.com/culture/education/news/2007/03/learning2_0.

Hayek, F. A. 1945. "The Use of Knowledge in Society." *American Economic Review* 35, no. 4: 519–530.

Hislop, D. 2010. "Knowledge Management as an Ephemeral Management Fashion?" *Journal of Knowledge Management* 14, no. 4: 779–790.

Kant, I. 1949. *Fundamental Principles of the Metaphysic of Morals*. Translated by Thomas Kingsmill Abbott. New York: Liberal Arts Press.

Kelley, Michael. 2010. "A Digital Generation Scours the Library for a Plug." *Library Journal*, December 30. http://www.libraryjournal.com/lj/home/888602-264/a_digital_generation_scours_the.html.csp.

Library of Congress. 2006. "Jefferson's Legacy: A Brief History of the Library of Congress." Library of Congress. Last modified January 11. http://www.loc.gov/loc/legacy/.

Locke, J. 1959. *An Essay Concerning Human Understanding*. New York: Dover.

Mariotti, F. 2007. "Learning to Shape Knowledge in the Italian Motorsport Industry." *Knowledge and Process Management* 14, no. 2: 81–94.

McInerney, C., and R. Day. 2002. "Introduction to the JASIST Special Section on Knowledge Management." *Journal of the American Society for Information Science and Technology* 53, no. 12: 1008.

McManus, S. 2003. "A Short History of File Sharing." Sean McManus. August. http://www.sean
.co.uk/a/musicjournalism/var/historyoffilesharing.shtm.

Mottl, J. N. 2001. "How Xerox Got Its Engineers to Use a Knowledge Management System." *TechRepublic*, September 24.

Nielsen, B. B., and F. Ciabuschi. 2003. "Siemens ShareNet: Knowledge Management in Practice." *Business Strategy Review* 14, no. 3 (June): 33–40.

Nonaka, I., and H. Takeuchi. 1995. *The Knowledge Creating Company*. New York: Oxford University Press.

O'Reilly, Tim. 2005. "Design Patters and Business Models for the Next Generation of Software." Oreillynet. September 30. http://www.oreillynet.com/oreilly/tim/news/2005/09/30/what-is-web-20.html.

Otlet, P. 1990. *International Organisation and Dissemination of Knowledge: Selected Essays of Paul Otlet.* Translated and edited with an introduction by W. B. Rayward. Amsterdam: Elsevier Science, B.V.

Penrose. E. T. 1959. *The Theory of the Growth of the Firm.* New York: John Wiley.

Petrash, G. 1996. "Dow's Journey to a Knowledge Value Management Culture." *European Management Journal* 14, no. 4: 365–373.

Polanyi, M. 1966. *The Tacit Dimension.* Terry lectures, Yale University. Garden City, NY: Doubleday.

Saracevic, T. 1999. "Information Science." *Journal of the American Society for Information Science* 50, no. 12: 1051–1063.

Semple, E. 2006. "Rise of the Wiki." *Inside Knowledge* 9: 1–3.

Special Libraries Association. 2011. "SLA KM's Home Page! Knowledge Management Division—SLA's Wiki Spaces." Accessed March 12. http://wiki.sla.org/display/SLAKM.

Spence, M. 1973. "Job Market Signaling." *Quarterly Journal of Economics* 87, no. 3: 355–374.

Stewart, T. A. 1997. *Intellectual Capital: The New Wealth of Organizations.* 2nd ed. Volume 1. New York, NY: Doubleday.

Stewart, T. A. 2001. *The Wealth of Knowledge: Intellectual Capital and the 21st Century Organization.* New York, NY: Doubleday.

Stiglitz, J. E. 1975. "The Theory of Screening, Education and the Distribution of Income." *American Economic Review* 65, no. 3: 286–300.

Teece, D., G. Pisano, and A. Shuen. 1997. "Dynamic Capabilities and Strategic Management." *Strategic Management Journal* 18, no. 7: 509–533.

U.S. House of Representatives. 2006. "A Failure of Initiative: Final Report of the Select Bipartisan Committee to Investigate the Preparation for and Response to Hurricane Katrina." GPO Access, February 15.

Walter, J. D. 2002. "Navy Building Knowledge Management Portal." Navy.mil. Released September 26. http://www.navy.mil/search/display.asp?story_id=3709.

Wiig, K. M. 1997. "Knowledge Management: Where Did It Come From and Where Will It Go?" *Expert Systems with Applications,* 13, no. 1: 1–14.

Wilson, T. D. 2002. "The Nonsense of 'Knowledge Management.'" *Information Research* 8, no. 1 (October). http://informationr.net/ir/8-1/paper144.html.

2

The Concept of Knowledge

Peter Baloh with Kevin C. Desouza and Scott Paquette

OBJECTIVES

- Review the classical and current perspectives on what constitutes knowledge.
- Describe the different dimensions of knowledge, including taxonomies such as tacit and explicit knowledge and hierarchical levels such as individual, group, organizational, interorganizational, and societal knowledge.
- Understand the multifaceted nature of knowledge and how the lens through which it is viewed impacts the management of knowledge.

INTRODUCTION

Human resources, and therefore people, are the heart of today's organizations. They are the ones who, in the process of their work, locate, package, create, apply, or reuse knowledge. In 2007, these **knowledge workers** were the majority of all workers in the United States (Marks and Baldry, 2009). According to US Bureau of Labor statistics from 2010, knowledge workers received increasing salary premiums and many of these professions were also listed as jobs where employers will have to actively compete for excellent workers (US Bureau of Labor Statistics, 2011). To accomplish their work successfully, knowledge workers need to access the knowledge residing in organizations to create new products, business processes, or satisfy customers. Individuals interact with multiple forms of knowledge located within or outside the organization such as facts stored in documents, in databases, in memos, and within people. How successful they are in their jobs is directly linked to their capability to seek the relevant knowledge out, understand it, generate new knowledge, and apply it in performing their tasks. The goal of managing knowledge is to aid individuals in the performance of their duties when they solve problems individually or in groups (Grant, 1996a). In other words, improving how fast and how well knowledge (available inside organization and externally) is utilized and how new knowledge is created has a direct influence on organizational performance. For individuals' activities to be productive, they need to minimize "reinventing the wheel" and capitalize upon their own existing knowledge and organizational knowledge institutionalized in shared routines, operating procedures, and business processes. Knowledge workers must also generate new knowledge individually or through social interaction and avail organizational members of this new knowledge. One of the most challenging endeavors for organizations lies in understanding their knowledge-related needs and requirements. This can include identifying the types of knowledge required and instituting knowledge-related practices that will improve how available knowledge is managed by the organization.

In this chapter, we explore the fundamentals of the concept of knowledge. We begin by exploring the relation of knowledge to the concepts of data, information, intelligence, and wisdom. We then outline several philosophical perspectives that inform our understanding of what knowledge is and how should we go about managing it. Next, we conduct a quick overview of organizational learning and show how it is related to the knowledge possessed by an entity. Finally, we discuss the most commonly studied dimensions of knowledge and approaches to knowledge processing in organizations.

THE ARTIFACTS: DATA, INFORMATION, KNOWLEDGE, INTELLIGENCE, AND WISDOM

Businesses thrive when people make correct, timely, mission-critical decisions. In order to facilitate effective decision making, workers need to be able to access knowledge, solve problems systematically, and experiment with new approaches and alternatives. Employees must be given the ability and tools to support learning from their own experiences and from the experiences and best practices of others. In any organization, knowledge needs to be transferred quickly and efficiently between individuals, groups, and stakeholders.

In this context the differences between data, information, knowledge, intelligence, and wisdom emerge. These terms are unfortunately often used interchangeably or with no consideration of the distinct differences between the concepts. Without understanding what knowledge is and how it fits among this hierarchy, it would be difficult to understand how to identify, acquire, store, and use knowledge in typical organizational processes and activities.

Data and information can be linked with each other, but do not share a linear, hierarchical relationship with knowledge, intelligence, and wisdom. **Data,** which is raw facts and numbers, becomes **information** when it is useful or meaningful for the recipient in a particular context. The same facts can be considered either data or information, based on the person who receives them and the context in which they reside. For example, a retail chain may possess pieces of data that are part of the total daily transactions within one store, and may include items such as the amount and volume of sales of a particular product. This can also be considered information for managerial decision makers, as they can use this information to make relevant sales and procurement decisions. The CEO of the retail chain will consider this same string of numbers data, as his responsibility does not usually demand that he examine operational, day-to-day decisions.

Knowledge, on the other hand, is what people believe based on meaningful and organized accumulation of information; it can be combined with other information, interpreted, and acted upon. Continuing the example of the retail store, when a procurement decision for a particular product needs to be made, proper pieces of information are fed into the mental schema, models, concepts, and judgments of the decision maker. Knowledge allows an individual to interpret, analyze, and act upon this information. Therefore, knowledge becomes a collection of justified beliefs that increase an entity's capacity for action. Knowledge can be based on history and past experiences, as well as an individual's judgmental ability.

Intelligence is the act and state of knowing something, along with the ability to comprehend a piece of information for a particular purpose. In the context of our example, intelligence would be the ability to analyze and synthesize relevant information. **Wisdom**, finally, is accumulated knowledge and experience in a particular context, which leads the decision maker to choose the best ends and most rational means to reach them. The relationships between these concepts are depicted in Figure 2.1.

Putting the Concepts into Context: Libraries and Librarians

The concepts of data, information, and knowledge are easily illustrated through examining an important source of societal knowledge, the library. Within its bounds, a library maintains data on the books that are in the collection (via the card catalog or OPAC system), the patrons and what they have borrowed (via the checkout and inventory system), and other important aspects of the administration of the organization. However, librarians are vital to the operation of the library: they use this data to serve patrons who are looking for information. For example, during a reference interview a librarian may be asked to locate a specific book on a subject. She could easily search the online catalog and point the individual towards a book. However, she will more likely ask questions to determine the patron's actual information need, and by combining the data on the books available with the information she receives by talking with the patron, she can direct the patron towards the most helpful and relevant resources. Over time, she may encounter many similar requests from different patrons, and the librarian will build experiential or tacit knowledge that makes her a valuable resource for people using the library to search for information. This process of converting the data on the library's resources and the information provided by a patron into the knowledge a librarian develops over time is what makes librarians skilled knowledge workers who cannot be replaced by low-skilled workers or computers.

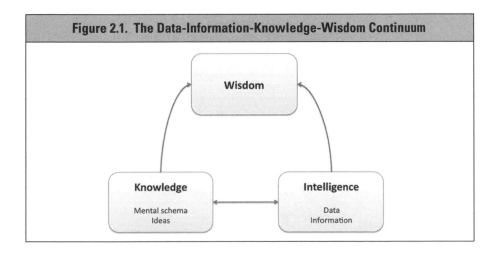

Figure 2.1. The Data-Information-Knowledge-Wisdom Continuum

Wisdom

Knowledge

Mental schema
Ideas

Intelligence

Data
Information

To understand the relationship between these concepts more clearly, consider an example of a university research project. One might start a research project by employing wisdom, where knowledge and experience of a particular research field(s) is combined with known opportunities for research. A researcher first attempts to define the problem to be solved. Then, the researcher moves on toward a stage where he attempts to solve the problem. The researcher employs his intelligence to gather and comprehend data and information for the purpose of progressing through the stages of solving the research problem. When the problem is solved, new knowledge has been created in the form of scientific and practical advancements (i.e., the solution enriches existing areas of research and adds to the ideas practitioners can use to improve their practices). The researcher has enriched his existing knowledge on how to perform the process of research. The activity of moving from wisdom to knowledge is called the **theory-driven approach to knowledge generation** and is depicted in Figure 2.2.

The direction of the conversion of knowledge can be reversed from the previous example. A research project may begin by first gathering data in the field, which would then be combined and interpreted through the employment of scientific research methods (i.e., grounded theory) to create new knowledge. By employing intelligence, this information would be synthesized into new findings related to possible explanations of the phenomena on which the data has been collected. The findings would become wisdom when they can be explained or utilized in a new or different setting, as the wisdom has gone beyond being context specific and can be applied in many situations. This process of moving from data toward wisdom is the **data-driven approach to knowledge creation**, and is shown in Figure 2.3.

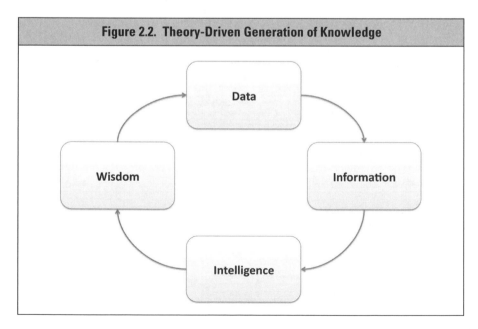

Figure 2.2. Theory-Driven Generation of Knowledge

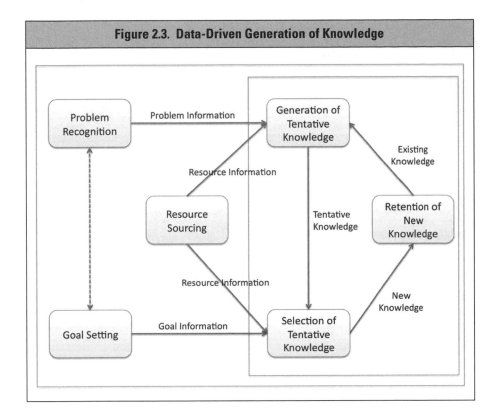

Figure 2.3. Data-Driven Generation of Knowledge

PHILOSOPHICAL VIEWS OF KNOWLEDGE

There is a significant divide between two fundamental perspectives on knowledge, which can lead to different approaches to managing knowledge within organizations at both the individual and corporate levels. The first perspective sees knowledge as an **object**, something that can be stored, manipulated, and exists separately from the human mind. Many who hold this view argue for knowledge management systems that enable as much storage and accumulation of knowledge in codified form as possible. The second perspective sees knowledge strictly as a complex result of human construction; thus, it cannot exist independently but only through personal interaction. This perspective assumes that the only way to improve knowledge management activities is by fostering an environment that facilitates social and human interaction (i.e., the creation of communities of practice).

These two diametrically opposed views have intrigued philosophers since the ancient Greek period (and even earlier). Thinkers in the field of epistemology are concerned with the questions on the nature of knowledge: what is knowledge, how is it acquired, what do people know, and how do we know?

Rationalism and empiricism are two great epistemological traditions, the first arguing that some a priori knowledge must exist which can be discovered by rational

---

Communities of Practice in Action

Creating a community of practice, or group of people who share similar interests or work-related tasks, is an effective way of connecting people in order for them to establish relationships that will support knowledge sharing. For example, the United Nation's Department of Peacekeeping, which is responsible for the management of all global peacekeeping operations, discovered that the typical peacekeeping mission could accumulate terabytes of information from operations and administrative work that needs to be managed during the time the troops are in the field. Typical information systems would not suffice in this case, as there are often issues with unreliable Internet connections and electricity, and the unique and varying needs of peacekeeping troops. In fact, many missions include people from over 114 countries, making the number of languages being used very difficult to manage.

In order to deal with these challenges, groups of similar workers were grouped together and different communities of practice were organized. They shared common goals and needs, so connecting these people allowed for the increased sharing of knowledge. Some support systems were developed to allow for a portal to access common information, but mainly they relied on troops communicating with each other to share their knowledge (Myint, 2007).

---

reasoning grounded in axioms, and the second claiming that the only source of knowledge is experience (a posteriori knowledge). In modern times, these opposing views are visible in important works of Rene Descartes and John Locke. Descartes, a Continental rationalist, devised rules for rational thinking and devised the "method of doubt," reflected in the question, "What can I hold as true beyond any doubt?" In contrast, Locke, a British empiricist, criticized the rationalist idea that the human mind is already equipped with true ideas that can be discovered through reasoning. He compared the human mind to a *tabula rasa* (blank slate) that has to be filled with sensations and reflections. Descartes was the first to identify the mind with the self-consciousness and self-awareness and to distinguish it from the brain, which was the seat of intelligence.

Immanuel Kant, in his *Critique of Pure Reason*, tried to synthesize rationalism and empiricism when he argued that knowledge arises only when both the logical thinking of rationalism and sensory experience of empiricism work together. In Kant's view, a priori intuitions and concepts provide us with some a priori knowledge, which also provides the framework for our a posteriori knowledge. Things as they are "in themselves" are unknowable. For something to become an object of knowledge, it must be experienced, and experience is pre-structured by the activity of our own minds. John Dewey, the American philosopher, also addressed the ontological gap between the mind and the body. He was one of the most influential pragmatists, arguing that all of human knowledge consists of actions and products of acts in which men and women participate with other human beings, with animals and plants, as well as objects of all types, in any environment. He emphasized the relationship between knowledge and action and tried to overcome the "spectator theory of knowledge" described in Cartesian dualism (Nonaka, 1994).

These two contrasting arguments remain today in philosophical foundations of **positivism** and **interpretivism**. Positivist theories conform to the Cartesian dualistic view on the body-mind split where knowledge is objective and exists separately and independently of humans. Interpretivist theories pose that it is impossible for humans to attain objective social knowledge existing separately from subjectivity. These are important to understand, as the viewpoint held by a person or organization will inform the design of knowledge-related activities in organizations. For example, the positivist view sees knowledge as a stock, an organizational asset that can be codified, stored, transferred, and measured (Edvinsson and Malone, 1997; Zack, 1999); and organizational interventions (processes and technologies) will focus on these activities (e.g., measuring intellectual capital or creating databases and document management systems). Those who are closer to humanistic and "learning" approaches see knowledge as complex, foundationless, constructed, practical, and pragmatic. They emphasize the human and social aspects of knowledge creation and argue that knowledge on its own does not exist and that it can only be constructed in social interaction between people; thus, organizational interventions will be about fostering collaborative get-togethers.

Nevertheless, there is a growing realization that a holistic approach in which both perspectives are appreciated is needed. An objective view on knowledge results in over-occupation with knowledge itself, while social constructivists are mostly trying to go beyond the knowledge and concentrate on a "knowledge happens only during conversation" concept. For some organizational contexts, knowledge can be explained and treated as something that can be codified in various formats that another person with appropriate mental models understands as knowledge, when it is read. For other settings and situations, knowing something requires a one-to-one social construction process, and knowledge can be treated as such. In successful business cases, both views are taken into account. Even though there is a seemingly significant epistemological gap between the two perspectives, we can see that when they are combined, they reflect both the concepts of an organization's knowledge and its learning and knowledge creation capability as the main sources of its competitive advantage.

ECONOMIC AND SOCIAL TRAITS OF KNOWLEDGE

It is a common belief that knowledge is a difficult asset to manage due to its intangible nature. Traditionally, organizations are adept at working with tangible assets, which are easily identified, valued, and recognized by an organization's many members. Finance and accounting professionals have developed sophisticated methods for valuing tangible assets and reflecting their value in financial statements. A manufacturing company can easily identify all of its production machinery and inventory of raw and finished goods, and place a value on these assets based on their age and condition. However, traditional accounting valuation procedures have limitations when applied to **intangible assets**, those that are not physical in nature. These include patents, trademarks, brands, goodwill, and knowledge. Organizations would like to recognize the value of the knowledge possessed by their employees, as ultimately this knowledge can become the bulk of an organization's value if it is a true knowledge-based organization such as a consulting firm, law firm, or a software development company. Unfortunately, despite many attempts by multiple organizations, standards to measure the value of knowledge have not been accepted by the business community. The process of valuing knowledge and knowledge management projects will be discussed further in Chapter 9 in the section on building a business case for knowledge management.

Measuring Knowledge

Many companies have tried to recognize the value of intellectual capital as being the difference between market capitalization and book the value of the company. Once such company was Skandia Insurance, a Swedish insurance company, which categorized its valuable knowledge as customer capital, human capital, and organizational capital. Using various metrics for valuing these three components of knowledge, the firm placed a value on its intellectual capital and stated their measures in an appendix to its annual report. Some of the measures that were used included the following:

- Competence development expenses per employee
- Employee satisfaction
- Training expenses per employee
- Information gathering expenses per existing customers
- Total number of patents held
- Employee attrition rate
- Dollar figure value of loss per employee who leaves
- Number of ideas implemented compared to those suggested
- Time spent on packaging knowledge created from a completed project (Dalkir, 2005)

Skandia posited that if you could measure each aspect of a company's intellectual capital, you could target it for investment and growth. Furthermore, by identifying knowledge in a way that managers could understand, you could also identify important sources of both tacit and explicit knowledge. For example, creating a better understanding of an organization's human capital would allow for not just hiring smart people, but also ensuring their intelligence and knowledge can be shared amongst their colleagues and across boundaries (Stewart, 1997).

The inability to measure knowledge has presented difficulties for managers responsible for organizations' knowledge, as they cannot easily determine the return on investment (ROI) for a knowledge project when presenting an initiative to other members of the organization. Both the value of the knowledge contained within the individuals of the organization, and its importance to the strategy, competiveness, and operations of the organization are difficult to empirically" demonstrate. The axiom "if you can measure it, you can't manage it" applies here, as managers will not recognize opportunities to apply knowledge in daily routines or unusual situations that present themselves during the course of business. Table 2.1 lists some special characteristics of knowledge that make it challenging to measure and manage.

Table 2.1. Special Characteristics of Knowledge	
Characteristic	**Description**
Non-rivalry	• When sharing knowledge with others, the source of the knowledge does not lose the ability to use the knowledge himself or herself.
Intangibility	• Knowledge can exist independent of space and in nonphysical forms.
Subjective valuation	• Knowledge's value is dependent on factors such as timeliness, accuracy, and relevance to the user. • Value is often derived from *subtracting* information, or from preventing knowledge overload by filtering out only the relevant, valuable knowledge that is needed in a given context.

Knowledge also possesses many characteristics that are not consistent with traditional economic thinking. Knowledge is a public good; therefore it can be used without being consumed. When sharing knowledge with others, the source of the knowledge does not lose the ability to use the knowledge themselves, so it is easily duplicated. Therefore, the costs of producing knowledge are the same no matter who will eventually possess or use it. Knowledge can exist independent of space, which means it can be in two places (or held by two individuals) at the same time. This causes a problem, as the buyer cannot judge the worth of a piece of knowledge until they have it, but once they have it they no longer need to purchase it. Similar to this problem, once you sell a piece of knowledge, you are not prevented from selling it to someone else; you still hold that knowledge. Consultants can design best practices for an organization that may see these practices as a source of a competitive advantage, but unless knowledge is controlled in a legal fashion (e.g., copyright, trademark, patent, restrictive contract) the competitive advantage lasts only until the consultants sell the best practices to the organization's competition.

Therefore, the intangible nature of knowledge prevents it from obeying the economic laws of supply and demand. Value of an economic good can be derived through scarcity. For example, gold is a scarce commodity and is therefore worth more than more abundant commodities, such as copper. The value of knowledge depreciates over time as it becomes outdated or obsolete, but not through use. Knowledge value is dependent on factors such as timeliness, accuracy, and relevance to the user. Many argue that knowledge is not scarce, as it is easy to produce. Every employee within an organization produces either explicit or tacit knowledge during the course of his or her job. Value is often derived from *subtracting* information, or from preventing knowledge overload by filtering out only the relevant, valuable knowledge that people need.

The economic qualities of knowledge require managers to change how they manage this intangible good. First, the cost structure of producing knowledge is different from tangible goods. When producing a product such as a piece of furniture, there are some up-front costs, but the majority of costs are spread out over the time that the goods are produced. For knowledge, the costs are almost all up-front. For example, producing the first book (which includes writing it) is substantially higher than producing any of the following copies (which are essentially copies of that first book). The more intangible or knowledge-based the product, the greater the discrepancy between marginal costs and the initial sunk costs. Second, the laws of diminishing returns do not apply to the production of intangible assets. For example, if it is determined that it will take ten people approximately four months to develop a software application, 40 people probably cannot complete the project in one month, as in many instances the production of knowledge can be done by only one person at a time (Brooks, 1995). In fact, the laws of increasing returns may apply here: the more people who use a knowledge-based project, the more valuable that product becomes. This is why companies such as Microsoft will spend millions of dollars to produce software that will sell for barely $100; the value is based on the wide use of the software. This idea can be successful due to the concept of networked externalities, where the larger the network utilizing the product, the higher the value the product has to that network.

Organizations must determine how to create processes and routines that are capable of handling knowledge that exists in multiple forms. By nature, knowledge is multifaceted, and in order to establish a comprehensive knowledge program, organizations must be able to recognize, create, store, and use knowledge in the form in which it is available. Furthermore, the complex nature of knowledge challenges organizations and their knowledge managers to be flexible in the use of processes and technologies in order to have the ability to adapt to an ever-changing business environment. For example, knowledge management systems that are designed to support processes surrounding customer and market knowledge must allow the user to collect information from formal sources (market research organizations), from informal sources (salespeople who inter-act with customers), in written form (sales and marketing analysis reports), in spoken form (conversations between various sales people), and electronic form (emails received from customers or potential customers). Organizations cannot predict which of these forms a certain piece of knowledge will take; therefore, they must be prepared to work with all forms in order to prevent knowledge loss. All of these forms of knowledge create value for the organization when they are combined and used to create an overall understanding of the organization's market and its customers. Using technology and systems for the management of knowledge will be explored in more depth in Chapter 7.

ORGANIZATIONAL LEARNING

Organizations must continually strive to create or acquire knowledge through two distinct activities that capitalize on the benefits of experience and knowledge (Roth, 2003): effectively translating ongoing experiences into distinct knowledge products, and transferring those products across boundaries within the organization. O'Dell and Grayson (1998) observed that while transferring knowledge across organizational boundaries, such as role and department boundaries, is difficult, the process can yield enormous benefits to an organization. The transfer of knowledge across an organization is said to be "one of the most important components of organizational learning and competitiveness" (Koch, 1999: 48). Successful knowledge transfer is in fact one of the major mechanisms through which *learning* can be achieved at the organizational level, which can in turn lead to improved overall performance. Table 2.2 outlines the steps whereby organizations learn and build organizational memory.

Organizational learning can be viewed as organizational activities that result in any of its units acquiring knowledge that it deems potentially useful and valuable to the organization. Every component of the organization does not need to learn the knowledge that is required, since learning occurs as long as the organization gains the knowledge and it becomes available to the other areas of the organization. However, the more areas of the organization that go through the learning process, the better it is able to establish a deep foundation of common knowledge throughout the organization. The learning process should result in the acquired knowledge being stored within the **organizational memory** that allows for future use.

Organizational learning can occur via a single-loop process, which is where the organization matches and acquires the knowledge it needs, yet no change occurs to the underlying governance, values, or culture. Double-loop learning occurs when the organization acquires new knowledge through learning processes, and a reevaluation

Table 2.2. Organizational Learning: The Steps in Building and Refreshing Organizational Memory	
Step	**Description**
Transfer of individual Learning	• Individuals in networks share their knowledge, beliefs, and assumptions to create new knowledge for the organization.
Validation of learning	• Collective thinking allows for the creation of workable solutions to address the organization's sustainability problems.
Institutionalization of learning	• New solutions are objectively recognized and identified as part of the corporate memory and can stand as evidence of organizational learning.
Adaptation	• Knowledge should be constantly refreshed in order for an organizational memory to contribute toward innovation and decision making.

or shift occurs in its policies, values, and culture. This form of learning is nonroutine and has a greater impact on the organization as a whole. Both forms of learning can occur intentionally, when the organization is actively trying to gain knowledge through learning via a knowledge management or search process, or unintentionally, when through the course of regular business routines and operations knowledge is gained and skills are learned through experience and activities (Huber, 1991).

Knowledge management processes affect organizational learning by transferring the knowledge of individual network members to the organizational level. Organizational learning is a cyclical process through which the learning that occurs on an individual and group level is embedded in the organizational level and the corporate memory. New knowledge, especially external knowledge, can be a strong stimulus for organizations to learn, change, and improve their operating systems and procedures.

Learning at the organizational level, however, is a process that can occur only once the learning and knowledge at the individual and group levels have been collectively recognized, accepted, and used as organizational knowledge. As Crossan et al. (1995: 347) explain, "there must be some shared understanding or transfer of knowledge from the individual to the broader community and eventually to the formal organization before it can be considered organizational learning." The results of the learning process should be retained independent of employees by embedding the results in the corporate memory and by institutionalizing them into systems, structures, routines, and prescribed practices.

An organization's memory is made up of all the tangible and intangible rules, processes, procedures and cultural instructions that dictate the ways in which the organization works. This suggests that organizations as a whole cannot truly benefit from learning until that learning has been embedded in the corporate memory. "This embedding, or institutionalizing of new ways of working, is complete when old tacit routines are removed and replaced with new taken-for-granted ways of working" (Tranfield and Smith, 1998: 126). Within a network environment, this implies that the knowledge and learning of the network members has been collectively validated as reliable and valuable for use in the organization. Organizational learning and the

---

Organizational Learning at JPL

Part of the National Aeronautics and Space Administration, the Jet Propulsion Laboratory (JPL) develops science and technology that help with the exploration of our own and neighboring planetary systems. JPL implemented a web-accessible database of general organizational knowledge in order to allow employees working on different projects to share their knowledge and build upon past successes. The system required an extensive development and implementation plan, which was focused on not only developing adequate technology, but also educating and encouraging users to contribute toward and use the system.

The implementation team at JPL used a variety of techniques to encourage knowledge sharing. They advertised the system and its features to the employees through e-mail, newsletters, display screens throughout the buildings, and other media. Each time a new awareness campaign was launched, they saw a spike in usage. They also measured individual learning through the system by surveying users and evaluating their knowledge via quizzes that determined gaps in organizational knowledge and the types of knowledge that were served well by the system. Overall, JPL recognized a substantial increase in the levels of individual learning, and eventually organizational learning, through the implementation and use of the system. They surrounded the system with other, nontechnical means for sharing knowledge that encouraged contact beyond an individual's immediate coworkers or project team. As the individuals began to learn more, the result could be seen throughout the organization (Cooper, Nash, Phan, and Bailey, 2005).

---

validation processes that occur in networks play a critical role in shaping organizations' governance, operations, and performance measurement.

Knowledge networks support the transfer of learning and knowledge from individual and group levels into the organization's corporate memory through the validation processes that occur in networked environments. Individuals in networks share their knowledge, beliefs, and assumptions to create new knowledge for the organization, allowing for the creation of workable solutions to the organization's sustainability problems. The process of collectively validating knowledge acts as the bridge between local and organizational learning. The validated knowledge and actionable solutions can then become institutionalized in the way the organization changes its structures, systems, procedures and culture. In validation and implementation, the new solutions are objectively recognized and identified as part of the corporate memory and can stand as evidence of organizational learning (Husysman and Dewit, 2004).

Once a base for an organization's memory is established, it can be difficult to alter the knowledge contained within the organization. Many companies that experience a strategic shift or an external shock find that adapting their knowledge to the new marketplace or environment is quite challenging. Furthermore, the knowledge within the organizational memory may become locked in, and either prevent the organization from accepting new knowledge it receives or impair its innovation or new learning. Such is the example of the United States intelligence community and their inability to learn from their failures that surrounded the 9/11 terrorist attacks. The knowledge contained by this community on threats and adversaries was highly segmented by organization. Each organization, such as the CIA, FBI, and NSA, had mature knowledge processes in place for the acquisition, use, and internal transfer of knowledge in order to build upon its organizational memory (Desouza and Vanapalli, 2005). However, barriers to sharing this knowledge across organizational boundaries prevented the accumulation of the knowledge regarding domestic threats and left all agencies unable to piece together the existing knowledge that suggested a major threat was imminent. After building the knowledge of how to conduct intelligence and a corpus of specific intelligence knowledge over decades, these organizations had great difficulty adapting to a changing a dynamic global environment. This problem of learning about new situations occurs in many organizations, as they rely on previous knowledge and try to apply it to new problems and situations. To be robust and adaptive when managing their organizational memory, organizations require a destructive capability, where they are comfortable in destroying their old knowledge and replacing it with new, untested or external knowledge. They must be willing to accept the cost of creating or acquiring this new knowledge, and the risk that it may not be entirely accurate or proven. Most knowledge that is deposited within an organizational memory will have a high rate of depreciation. Organizations must be aware that knowledge should be constantly refreshed in order for an organizational memory to contribute toward innovation and decision making (Desouza and Awazu, 2005).

The importance and value of fostering an organizational learning environment within a corporation's strategy is crucial to competiveness. Organizational learning is at the heart of an organization's ability to adapt and respond to a changing environment, as it allows an organization to identify new threats and opportunities, as well as possible response strategies. The ability to adapt and respond to a changing environment can ultimately lead to improved business performance (Husted and Michailova, 2002; Marquardt, 2002).

DIMENSIONS OF KNOWLEDGE

There are many distinctions or taxonomies of knowledge available when determining how to identify, acquire, and use knowledge in organizations. Different forms of knowledge require different management processes and levels of involvement. Therefore, it is the responsibility of knowledge managers to be able to recognize the differences between various types of knowledge they encounter.

Blackler's Five E's of Knowledge

Blackler (1995) defines knowledge taking five distinct forms: embodied, embedded, embrained, encultured, and encoded. *Embodied* is knowledge that has been gained through training the body to perform a task. For example, in order to hit a baseball, athletes practice hitting balls in a batting cage for many hours, perfecting their swings. They are learning how to hit the baseball and training their body to gain knowledge about motions and actions used in the sport. The knowledge on how to hit becomes absorbed by the body through repetitive training. *Embrained* knowledge is the knowledge that a person can possess, but has difficulty expressing in words or sharing with other. It is not knowledge that one can easily write down, talk about with others, or represent with pictures or other tools. It is gained through experience over time and may reflect one's values, morals, perceptions, and opinions. Animals possess embrained knowledge through their ability to remember migration patterns, hibernation schedules, and routes to food sources. *Encultured* knowledge is a set of knowledge that is shared among groups of people who share a similar environment. Through the process of socialization, people can gain knowledge about their environment, such as what is accepted, what actions and opinions are considered normal, and what behaviors are expected of people. Encultured knowledge can be shared by small groups, areas of an organization, an entire organization, or parts of society such as an entire nation. *Embedded* knowledge is knowledge that is found in routines and systems. Organizational routines, or the common ways people go about their jobs, can hold embedded knowledge as the routines facilitate learning amongst the employees that go beyond their job tasks. Finally, *encoded* knowledge is a form of knowledge that can be easily written down, expressed in words or diagrams, and is transferable through multiple channels and means. Process diagrams, procedure manuals, recipes, and instructions on how to assemble a product are all examples for encoded knowledge; it is encoded in a physical form that is understandable by multiple people.

Tacit and Explicit Knowledge

The most common dimensions of knowledge recognized today are tacit and explicit knowledge. The dimensions originated in the notion of *knowing* as popularized by Polanyi (1966), philosopher of science and social science. Central to Polanyi's thinking was the belief that creative acts (especially acts of discovery) are charged with strong personal feelings and commitments. Polanyi's argument was that the informed guesses, hunches, and imaginings that are part of exploratory acts are not necessarily in a form that can be stated in propositional or formal terms. He argued through deduction of psychological experiments that "we know more than we can tell" and that knowledge creation and problem-solving abilities are rooted in our hidden tacit particulars and connections. Human skills, biases, and passions play an important and necessary role in guiding discovery and validation, and they are acquired within a local context, not having universal validity. In other words, a separate, subconscious knowing exists, and it influences the process of articulation (explaining what we know). Also, this knowing gives meaning to words when we hear or read them—that is, meaning is not robotized explanation of words, but rather, comes from our experience, from our tacit knowing. For companies, it is important that they pay attention to how they nurture, foster, and tap into employees' knowledge dimensions.

More specifically, tacit and explicit knowledge were popularized as important distinct dimensions of knowledge by Nonaka and Takeuchi (1995), who identified how knowledge creation occurs as a process of alternating between the two knowledge dimensions. The **explicit** dimension of **knowledge** is formal and systematic. It can be articulated, expressed in words or numbers, and shared formally, as people are aware of it. Usually it is transmitted in the form of items such as documents, manuals, technical specifications, blueprints, scientific formulas, or organizational designs. As it can be processed, transmitted, and stored relatively easily, it is not difficult for organizations to capture this knowledge in repositories, systems, or operating technologies and share it throughout organization.

The opposite form of knowledge, **tacit knowledge**, has both cognitive and technical elements. The cognitive element consists of mental models such as paradigms, schemata, beliefs, perspectives, and intuitions. The technical elements are personal know-how, crafts, and skills that apply to a specific context, developed over the years. Tacit knowledge is highly personal, and it is difficult to articulate and transfer to others. It is deeply rooted in action, procedures, commitment, ideals, values, and it can only be indirectly accessed.

An example of both explicit and tacit knowledge is a cooking recipe. Explicit knowledge used in cooking includes a list (and measures) of ingredients and a short description of the cooking process. Tacit knowledge would consist of an understanding of what and how much of ingredients to include, and also the process of actually preparing the particular dish (processes such as adding particular ingredients in a certain order or in a certain way, or using a certain method are often difficult to explain).

Managing Tacit Knowledge at SAP

SAP is the leading enterprise resource management software provider in the world. Based in Germany, it provides large enterprise systems to the largest corporations in the world. As part of its KM strategy, it developed online communities to connect people with similar interests and problems. It also used this platform to offer interactive events and knowledge-sharing opportunities to employees and customers located around the globe. It incorporated many interactive, real-time communication features including chat and video conferencing with company experts and leaders.

It encouraged its communities to post their knowledge for others to access, including supporting senior executives in blogging about the company and its latest endeavors. Within its first year of operations, the online community attracted over 50,000 participants in over 173 countries. These users describe the system as "a knowledge-sharing platform that provides them with insights into the way in which industry leaders think and behave" (Fahey, Vasconcelos, and Ellis, 2007: 190). SAP began to see immediate benefits from participation in communities including stronger peer-peer and customer relationships, increased brand awareness of the many SAP solutions, quicker purchase decisions by customers, ease of knowledge availability on product capabilities, and improved collection of industry and competitive knowledge, all on a global basis using cost-effective methods. Overall, SAP was able to leverage its online communities to bring people together in order to foster organizational learning and relationships. This increased ability to share tacit knowledge contained within and outside the company enabled better knowledge of the company's products and services from an internal and customer perspective, ultimately leading to stronger relationships with the customers and more knowledgeable and helpful employees (Fahey, Vasconcelos, and Ellis, 2007).

Tacit knowledge influences how we articulate ideas and perceive newly acquired knowledge. For the purposes of dissemination of knowledge inside the organization, attention needs to be paid to the form (substance) and the medium (communication channel) through which it is distributed. To ensure successful diffusion and subsequent application of knowledge, the most appropriate way to make particular knowledge explicit and shared needs to be selected. Both form of capture (e.g., structure of documents and databases, level of data) and communication/distribution channel (e.g., electronic document, personal presentation) have to be evaluated with consideration of the recipients' underlying knowledge base. To continue with the cooking metaphor, a great chef can develop a recipe that, when followed by an amateur cook, produces a dish that is almost unrecognizable as the original great chef's dish. In developing the recipe, the chef has included all the information that he was able to articulate about how to cook the dish (the explicit knowledge), but the recipe lacks the tacit knowledge that is embedded within the chef.

Organizations need to focus on enabling, improving, and accelerating conversion from tacit to explicit knowledge that can then be further transferred and appropriated by others. In terms of strategy, both explicit and tacit knowledge are very important; however, it is a common belief that tacit knowledge is strategically more important as it is embedded in people and extremely difficult for competitors to replicate. In terms of knowledge creating a sustainable competitive advantage for an organization, the knowledge must be unique, not available to the competitors, or protected by law. Explicit knowledge may be unique, but it can be easily shared or transferred to other people or organizations. Tacit knowledge is unique but resides in individuals; in order for a competitor to acquire valuable tacit knowledge, the competitor must acquire the individual, or lure the individual away from his or her present job. People may have knowledge regarding customers or other individuals with knowledge, and this relationship-based knowledge is non-replicable if the person leaves the organization. A person's tacit knowledge also includes the knowledge of his or her networks and his or her ability to source and acquire knowledge from many other sources. Most organizations have come to realize the importance of not only people, but also how their knowledge can provide the organization a competitive advantage over other organizations.

Informational and Procedural Knowledge

Knowledge can also be viewed as either informational or procedural. This distinction separates knowledge from being just a *fact* (know-what), to knowledge as being something that represents *knowing how to do something* (know-how).

Informational knowledge is equivalent to knowing *what* one needs to know about a topic. It is the basis or foundation for tasks that require specific goals to be achieved. It focuses on beliefs about information and relationships that exist amongst variables. For example, knowing the average rainfall for the area you live in for the last 50 years is informational knowledge that can be used to inform the choice of material suitable for the roof of a house. **Procedural knowledge** is equivalent to knowing *how* to go about accomplishing a task. It is the foundation for tasks that focus on how a specific goal or objective will be achieved. This form of knowledge outlines the processes or means that should be used to perform the desired tasks. Procedural knowledge is the knowledge that process-oriented tasks rely upon and is associated mainly with tacit knowledge. Note that tacit knowledge is *knowing* something subconsciously, which may difficult to explain or transfer to others. As such, the meaning of procedural knowledge is somewhat broader, as it also consists of know-how that can be externalized in explicit, codified knowledge, and the know-how that is difficult to explicate, similar to tacit knowing. Learning about measurements of the volume of flow for a river derived from an environmental analysis or a scientific experiment would be one example of gaining procedural knowledge.

An important concept for knowledge managers is that "knowing what" or "knowing how" in themselves are not sufficient for actually performing a task. This is known as the *knowing-doing gap*. Pfeffer and Sutton (1999; 2000) warn against a common phenomenon in organizations where knowledge is not being put into action even though the organization is in possession of the knowledge. Causes of this gap include organizations focusing on structured, codified knowledge and the technology that stores and transfers knowledge. This stems from treating knowledge as a tangible object and ignoring its intangible properties, such as those that exist in tacit knowledge. By having people creating explicit knowledge who do not have experiential knowledge or a deep understanding of the work being performed, only knowledge on the specific practices is captured, ignoring the cultural and philosophical nature of the work.

Organizations can employ multiple strategies to ensure they do not replicate the knowing-doing gap. Firstly, organizations must alter how they view change and adaptation within the organization. Instead of focusing on how they perform work or their operational procedures, they must ask themselves why they are doing something and what specific purpose it serves. This allows the organization's culture, perceptions, and beliefs about knowledge and its work to emerge, and guides employees by giving them a sense of purpose and direction. This philosophy of work will emphasize experience and the performance of tasks, which are foundational to creating tacit knowledge. You learn best by doing something, rather than reading about the task or listening to someone else who has performed the task. Once experience is gained, it is important to have the employee teach others, as people reinforce their learning through teaching. Learning can occur through multiple mediums and channels, such as distance learning, and does not necessarily occur in person or in a classroom.

Although these strategies focus on creating an understanding of the philosophy of knowledge, this should not be misconstrued to assume that action is not an important element to knowledge management. Recognizing and understanding the importance of knowledge to an organization is essential, but so is putting these plans and beliefs into action. Not only will valuable knowledge be created through actions, but the strategic importance of knowledge use will be realized. Organizations must realize that many times innovative and untried practices will lead to mistakes and problems, but this is a necessary risk in doing business. Mistakes can be viewed as opportunities to learn from action and ensure future work does not lead to similar errors. If employees sense that the organizational culture is somewhat forgiving of mistakes, they will feel empowered to take more risks and think more innovatively, which can realize valuable knowledge. The concepts of knowledge creation and innovation will be explored further in Chapter 4.

Organizations that desire to use knowledge to be more competitive need to remove the internal barriers and politics and focus on their competition. Having an outward view to the importance of knowledge to strategic decisions is essential in order to thrive in a dynamic and competitive marketplace. This will take strong leadership within the organization, in order to direct, empower, provide resources, and lead employees towards a culture and belief system that values and emphasizes knowledge. Leadership is the foundation for any knowledge management strategy, initiative, or project; without strong and dedicated people moving knowledge into measurable, actionable activities, knowledge will remain only at the conceptual level and never realize any of its value (Pfeffer and Sutton, 1999).

Individual and Societal Knowledge

Knowledge can be defined by identifying the level or entity where knowledge resides within an organization. Knowledge creation is a dynamic process, beginning at the individual level and expanding as it moves through communities of interaction that transcend group, departmental, divisional, and organizational boundaries. Knowledge can be contained by an individual, a team/group, an organization (including departments), interorganizational networks, countries and economies, and society.

Knowledge first resides within individuals. Knowledge creation begins with people when they acquire and process tacit knowledge through interacting with their (macro) environment. These knowledge holders need to create action with their knowledge through decision making or the execution of tasks, and therefore participate in the knowledge processing cycle.

However, the individual level is not the only level where knowledge resides. As Nonaka and Takeuchi (1995) describe, the processes of converting and creating new knowledge allows for knowledge to become shared by a group of people or team as they develop a mutual understanding of their work, and why their approach is the best way to perform their tasks. Knowledge can be viewed at higher levels, such as the departmental or organizational level. Organizational knowledge is what the organization as a whole uses in its routines and processes. This form of knowledge, also referred to as intellectual capital, is defined as "the knowledge that doesn't go home at night" (Stewart, 1997: 108). The idea of valuing knowledge within the organization stems from the notion that the physical assets of an organization contribute less to the organization's success than the intangible assets, such as knowledge. Most organizations define their intellectual capital as knowledge that has been identified, captured, and utilized to produce a high value asset.

Intellectual capital has three components that describe where it can be found in organizations. Human capital is the portion of intellectual capital that is derived from the organization's individuals and employees. Human capital is leveraged to create value by encouraging the transfer and sharing of knowledge throughout an organization. Companies that are adept at managing human capital are able to recognize the difference between paying employees and investing in their people. Structural capital is the component of intellectual capital that is most recognized by organizations, as it is the most visible. Organizations recognize that knowledge is an evasive asset, and they must invest resources in order to ensure it remains within the organization. Strategies such as building knowledge centers, connecting people with technology, looking beyond corporate boundaries, and giving people the tools to locate other people and knowledge all help build an organization's structural capital. The third component of intellectual capital is customer capital, which reflects the value of the relationships between the internal and external members of the organization. In order to ensure knowledge is shared, relationships between the senders and receivers of knowledge must be established, and therefore the stronger the customer capital, the better the flow of knowledge that will occur (Stewart, 1997). Incorporating innovative and unique mixes of internal and external people (customers) can allow for the generation of new and valuable knowledge for the organization. These three components of intellectual capital are crucial to an organization's competitiveness and performance (Bontis, Crossan, and Hulland, 2002).

A number of business processes are specified and formalized in detail, and others are developed informally. In either case, these organizational routines are developed over time and become embedded with organizational knowledge (Grant, 1996b). Ideally, they reflect the best way of doing things (what needs to be done in order to create and add value to the organization). Beyond procedures and business processes, organizational knowledge can also include shared values, joint mental schemas, organizational norms, culture, and shared strategies.

As organizations engage with stakeholders such as partners, customers, suppliers, and communities, all previously mentioned forms of knowledge continue further up the organizational hierarchy to reach new levels. Knowledge of interorganizational networks is created through shared understandings of processes, routines and innovations that can permeate multiple organizations' boundaries. Through dynamic interaction, knowledge created by the organization can trigger the mobilization of knowledge held by outside constituents such as consumers, affiliated companies, universities, or distributors. For example, Toyota is renowned for the ability to closely connect its manufacturing partners into knowledge sharing consortiums in order to develop better business products and processes. Members of their consortiums have knowledge sharing requirements and must contribute to the joint knowledge being created, not just receive it. Not only does this build close relationships with its partners, it fosters an interorganizational culture of knowledge sharing which benefits all companies involved, not just Toyota (Dyer and Nobeoka, 2000; Kogut, 2000). A further example is the articulation of tacit knowledge possessed by customers that they themselves have not been able to articulate. To address these issues, an increasing number of organizations deploy user toolkits that enable partners to join in innovating new products and services. The emergence of social media as a means to connect to individual customers in order to consolidate their knowledge has assisted in this knowledge gathering process. Companies such as Southwest Airlines, Starbucks, and Sears have formalized processes where they use social resources such as Twitter and Facebook to listen to customers, measure trends and comments being posted about their respective companies, and occasionally craft a unique response customized for an individual customer. They are relying on the knowledge posted by customers in public forums in order to learn about the customers' perspectives on their products, organization, and marketplace.

Finally, knowledge plays an important role at the societal level. Countries, economies, and society develop mutual knowledge and an understanding of the phenomena that exist in their environment. Much of this knowledge is considered cultural knowledge, which can be a factor in defining morals, values, traditions, and norms. For example, countries consist of economies, political spaces, media, individuals, and other stakeholders, which jointly reach some sort of consensus on matters of national interest. This results in policies, regulations, public opinion, culture, and values that reflect the knowledge found within the country itself.

Encouraging Societal Knowledge

Encouraging a group of employees or an organization to create and manage knowledge is one challenge, but how do we manage knowledge on a larger scale? Societies require knowledge to improve economies, living conditions, and create the necessities for living. Many nations now view knowledge at a country level to determine their competitiveness in a globalized world. *New York Times* columnist Thomas Friedman has argued that countries like the United States need to encourage education and the creation of knowledge at the earliest stages of life. Many of his ideas require strong leadership at the highest levels of government, and he has become quite outspoken about the role of government in the creation and management of societal knowledge.

One of Friedman's more popular ideas was to issue a challenge to President Barack Obama to create new programs that would lead children to develop an interest in learning, and specifically in the fields of science and technology. He called for new scientific endeavors such as a new series of manned missions to the moon, scientific lab days, and inserting more science into classrooms. Friedman's hope is that capturing the imagination of children will lead them towards a series of life-long learning endeavors, which are ultimately necessary to compete for jobs in a globalized marketplace (Friedman, 2010). By creating a focus on innovation, creativity, and discovery for children, who naturally have abilities to ask questions and look for answers, the goal is to foster the recognition of the importance of knowledge in society, and begin working toward a new culture of knowledge seekers and users.

Private and Public Knowledge

A discussion on the dimensions of knowledge is not complete without examining the issue of private versus public knowledge. Knowledge is inherently individual and private. However, people, organizations, countries, and society create knowledge, share it, and use it to achieve their goals. There is a constant struggle to encourage individuals who hold knowledge to share it with a larger group within an organization or society. Stakeholders strike a balance between opening their knowledge to others and keeping it private. Organizations may choose to have their knowledge remain private, as it may contribute to the establishment of a competitive advantage for the organization. The knowledge-based view (Conner and Prahalad, 1996) of the firm explains this further by describing knowledge as a valuable, rare, difficult to imitate, and non-substitutable asset that can become the source for sustainable competitive advantage. Individual employees prefer to hold much of their knowledge private, as it may be perceived that their knowledge is a source of their unique identity or reputation within the organization. By sharing what they know, they no longer may be perceived as an expert or person who possesses unique and valuable information. In some consulting firms, this hoarding of knowledge occurs frequently as employees compete for the best job assignments and projects by using their knowledge as leverage for their preferred projects. If there is the possibility of downsizing or layoffs within the organization, employees may not share knowledge in order to distinguish themselves from others in the hopes of retaining their jobs. Numerous organizations rely on private and protected knowledge as the foundation for innovations and new product development in order to create products that will secure their position in the marketplace (Desouza and Vanapalli, 2005). Therefore, it is vital that this knowledge remain private in order for the products to be unique and original in the minds of consumers. Organizations can utilize many tools to ensure that their proprietary information remains internal and is not captured by competitors. Trademarks and patents are commonly used to give organizations a legal right to exclusively use knowledge that they have created, preventing competitors from copying their ideas. The pharmaceutical industry uses patents extensively in order to have an exclusive right to distribute a new drug before other firms can create a generic version. Although organizations focus many of their information and knowledge security practices around the physical technology and codified information in their organizations, they must also consider the other intangible assets that they possess and the consequences security breaches would cause to the organization (Paquette, Jaeger, and Wilson, 2010).

Competitive Intelligence and Knowledge Management

The process for gathering knowledge about the external business environment and turning it into useful knowledge that can be applied to tactical or strategic decisions is termed competitive intelligence (CI). CI is an important part of knowledge management processes because the knowledge received from the external environment may have very little usefulness or relevance to the organization unless knowledge management can convert it into useful knowledge. The goal of a CI program is to gain knowledge that supports the sustained competitiveness of the organization within its industry or marketplace. KM processes can aid the collection of knowledge by assisting in identifying new knowledge, determining the best ways to acquire such knowledge, and then transferring the knowledge throughout the organization so it reaches the most appropriate decision makers.

The one major difference between KM and CI is that CI has a much broader scope and is less clearly focused. In order to defend the organization from competitive threats, intelligence-gathering activities are employed to scan a wide area of the economy, including related industries, new and emerging marketplaces, and even other countries. This will allow an organization to anticipate the actions of current and possible future competitors, and react accordingly to the competitive threats within its marketplace. The earlier the warning can be presented to the organization via the knowledge collected, the sooner they can react and maintain their position. Tools and systems that can assist with the knowledge identification and acquisition stages include research databases from third parties, Internet scanning including information located on social media sites, and information made publicly available by the competition. It is important for a CI program to mirror how KM assesses, validates, and filters such information to ensure only accurate and relevant information is used by the organization. Therefore, an effective and efficient CI process requires mature knowledge management strategy and processes within the organization that can be leveraged to acquire and manage vital knowledge that supports the competitiveness of the organization (Parker and Nitse, 2006).

Knowledge that is public is accessible by all within the business environment. If, theoretically, organizations were able to share all their knowledge with the other firms in their marketplace, all organizations would prosper from these rich knowledge flows. For example, von Hippel (1988) identified how steelworking firms that were in direct competition with each other shared their knowledge on how to comply with new, difficult environmental regulations, helping everyone in the industry comply with the regulations, and saving resources in the process. Although in competition with each other, these firms recognized the value of making their knowledge public in order to benefit from other external knowledge as well as help an industry that was struggling economically. A more radical example occurred in Goldcorp, when the gold company did something unheard of in the mining industry. In order to be more effective at finding gold deposits, the company released its geological data online to "crowd source" the search for gold. In this extremely secretive industry, geological data is considered precious and guarded at all costs. But in this case, it was put online with the offer of $575,000 in prize money to those who could find gold. The results yielded 110 targets which had an 80 percent success rate of yielding significant gold deposits. Even more valuable learning occurred in the process, which yielded knowledge of new methods for analysis of geological data derived from computer scientists. By taking the risk of making sensitive strategic data public, Goldcorp was able to benefit greatly financially and capabilities-wise (Tapscott and Williams, 2008). Other organizations choose to share their knowledge, but with a select group of partners in order to create new products, enter new markets, or improve their innovation processes. A deeper exploration of the topic of sharing and transferring knowledge to both internal and external entities will be presented in Chapter 6.

The key question individuals and organizations must ask themselves is at what level can the value of knowledge be extracted? In the examination of knowledge strategy in organizations, two clear perspectives have emerged. The first identifies the locus of knowledge at the individual level, where knowledge cannot be separated from the person who holds it. The second identifies the locus of knowledge at the collective level, which assumes that knowledge is created through social interaction with others (von Krogh, 2009). Proponents of the collective notion of knowledge center their argument on knowledge being engrained in business processes within organizations. As knowledge is created through the conversion of tacit and explicit knowledge, they maintain that a social setting with knowledge being created through groups and communities is a requirement for knowledge management. Knowledge cannot be separated from its environment and context, any more than it can be separated from those who hold it and use it. The body of literature that focuses on the individualistic nature of knowledge relate to Simon's cognitivist tradition (Simon, 1976), which assumes knowledge is an individual representation of a problem, a situation, or the external environment. The **knowledge-based view of the firm** (Spender, 1996) builds on Simon's work to state that knowledge work centers on the individual, and organizations use this knowledge in the application of goods and services. In this way, organizational processes use individual knowledge and integrate this knowledge into how the organization operates. It is therefore wrong to assume individuals are homogeneous and the processes of an organization are where organizational knowledge is located. Instead, all individuals are unique, as is their knowledge. It is this difference in individuals that creates differences amongst organizations. Once an organization determines where it believes its organizational knowledge is located, it can design structures and processes surrounding this knowledge in an attempt to create a competitive advantage.

VOLUME AND VOLATILITY OF KNOWLEDGE

When defining the challenge that organizations, and particularly knowledge managers, face in dealing with an organization's knowledge, it is useful to understand the challenges both the volume and the volatility of the knowledge can produce. The volume of individual (and therefore organizational) knowledge has grown exponentially over the years. As technology has provided more channels for the identification and collection of knowledge, organizations have been inundated with new forms and sources of knowledge that originate from both inside and outside the organization. Many of these technologies, although designed to encourage knowledge acquisition, do not have advanced filtering, sorting, and retrieval mechanisms that assist individuals in dealing with the deluge of knowledge that can occur once these technologies are put into use. The challenge now presented to organizations is to collect as much information as required from an exploding volume of knowledge sources and types, yet remember the basic principles of keeping information organized, findable, and filtered to allow for only useful and valuable knowledge. We will explore these principles further in Chapter 5.

Of course, one issue compounding this challenge is that filters and retrieval systems are not perfect, and whenever a filter is applied to a knowledge process, whether human or technical in nature, errors can occur in either allowing non-wanted information to be acquired or not allowing desired knowledge to reach those who require it. People charged with the responsibility of scanning the business environment for information are always susceptible to their biases or lack of perfect knowledge when determining what knowledge to share within an organization and what knowledge to ignore. No human or technical solution is perfect, yet organizations must have some processes in place to evaluate the knowledge received to minimize the effects of information overload.

The individuals within the organization charged with the responsibility of filtering external knowledge fall into one of two categories, gatekeepers or liaisons (Tushman, 1977; Tushman and Scanlan, 1981). **Gatekeepers** primarily convey external knowledge to internal organizational networks, allowing for the external knowledge to cross the organizational boundary and be shared amongst different people within the organization. These individuals are normally the communication stars of an organization, and have many connections to outside sources. This role is very specialized; usually gatekeepers have a few areas or fields of information in which they are most knowledgeable, and it is from these fields that they are able to acquire and share knowledge. In some cases, gatekeepers act as filters or screens to regulate the flow of knowledge into the organization, and they become concerned with the volume and the quality of knowledge being transferred. **Liaisons** assist in the mediation of communication between inside and outside networks. For example, they may help facilitate the innovation of new products by creating an interaction between internal departments such as new product development or engineering and other professionals in similar roles who belong to different networks. Their main role is to create the connections or links from inside employees to outside individuals, and it is these links that encourage the transfer of knowledge.

As the volume of information increases exponentially for individuals and organizations, so do reports of workers experiencing information stress, or the problem of dealing with an overwhelming amount of information and knowledge originating from many channels (both technological and human). Organizations must help their employees filter out noise and non-valued knowledge in order for them to pay attention to the important, relevant knowledge they receive. By giving their attention to a specific piece of knowledge, individuals are creating a focused mental engagement with the knowledge item. The attention process consists of two primary activities. The first occurs in a narrowing phase, where individuals actively screen out most of the knowledge that is received (either consciously or subconsciously) and select the knowledge which they deem important enough to give their attention to. At that point they enter the decision phase, where the decisions on whether to act on the knowledge and what actions to take occur. This phase results in an action, change in behavior, or the realization that more knowledge is required in order to act. Many forms of stimulus can trigger this process, including being exposed to an aversive or attractive situation, a captive or voluntary receipt of knowledge, or through either back-of-mind or front-of-mind awareness (Davenport and Beck, 2001).

Many organizations have leveraged technologies to assist people in managing their knowledge attention. Two distinct ideologies have been used, either to remove technology or to embrace technology as an enabler of attention. Many agree that technology has been one source of our attention deficit problems, as it has provided numerous channels that can overwhelm people with multitudes of knowledge. Many organizations create policies to remove technologies from the workplace, mainly social media applications, in order to have individuals focus solely on their work. Others leverage such technologies and their full capabilities to assist people in managing the flow of information they receive. Most technologies have incorporated filters that allow them to remove unwanted information but direct important knowledge toward individuals. However, the debate over whether distraction is good for overall productivity is still ongoing. Many feel that allowing employees to briefly divert their attention from work actually increases their ability to perform work functions over longer periods of time. Other organizations do not want to put this decision-making power into the hands of individuals, and therefore block network access to many popular websites. Others point to the phenomenon of "flow," and question whether this is a productive occurrence for employees. **Flow** is defined as a mental state where a person becomes completely immersed in a task and does not pay attention to external stimulus. Because it involves extreme focus and concentration, flow causes a distorted sense of time, a feeling of complete control over the activity, and in many cases a sense of intrinsic reward. For example, some people who play video games for many hours at a time do not realize how long they have been playing. Other people describe reading a book that is so interesting they are unaware of what is going on around them, and many hours of reading can feel like a single hour. Flow is an extreme example of attention by an individual and can occur in situations that both benefit and cause problems for an organization (Novak, Hoffman, and Duhachek, 2003).

The health care field is an example of an industry that has been affected by the growing amount of knowledge relevant to its business. Not only have new procedures and technologies been a constant source of knowledge that must be understood and evaluated for possible adoption into practice, but companies such as pharmaceuticals and medical products manufacturers have found new ways to provide detailed information about their products to those professionals who they rely on for recommendations. These firms have had to adapt their business practices to accommodate the new forms and demands for knowledge. A doctor in a small practice must maintain knowledge of new illnesses and treatments, including the medications that could be offered to patients. Many of these doctors rely on an office nurse as the gatekeeper, since the nurse is in a position to receive any incoming knowledge from external sources, quickly evaluate whether it is relevant to the practice, and then recommend the new knowledge to the doctor. The nurse can filter out unimportant messages or sales calls and ensure the doctor spends the bulk of his or her time caring for patients. In other cases, the nurse may also act as a liaison in order to link the doctor with other medical professionals or specialists if the knowledge required to help a patient is not immediately available. As many doctors and nurses rely on their professional organizations as a means to identify new knowledge sources, they become an excellent conduit to encouraging knowledge sharing between various offices and doctors.

The Volatility of Medical Knowledge

As part of total quality management (TQM) initiatives, many hospitals have begun to focus on how they manage knowledge, and specifically the management of medical knowledge used in practice. Studies of medical knowledge required by health-care practitioners have determined that one of the major challenged in managing such knowledge is that it is very volatile, or susceptive to changes. Some studies estimate that the average half-life for medical knowledge is less than five years, and this number is rapidly decreasing as new innovations and discoveries emerge (Rodts, 2001). Even explicit knowledge, which is easy to codify and share, faces the challenge that it can quickly become out of date or nonrelevant, which can lead to critical medical errors or even death. Combined with the complex nature of medical knowledge, the volatility of knowledge has become a major issue that health-care organizations must address.

Many KM techniques have been used to ensure that the knowledge created and transferred in a medical setting is accurate. For instance, technology can provide real-time updates on patient conditions, supply and effectiveness of drugs, or changes to recommended procedures. However, even more effective are strategies that focus on people and how they manage their individual knowledge. Creating incentives for sharing knowledge, participating in continual education programs, and learning how to question and evaluate knowledge have all increased the use of relevant and accurate knowledge and improved the overall management of medical knowledge in a health care setting (Chang, Tsai, and Chen, 2009).

As the volume of knowledge that organizations must manage increases, so does the volatile nature of the knowledge. New knowledge is usually an indication of change, and can have a direct effect on knowledge that has been received previously. Knowledge can easily become outdated in industries that face new competition, new customers, changing products, new technologies, and varying government and legal regulations. Organizations must realize that although they may utilize a great deal of effort to acquire knowledge, it can become outdated or incorrect in a short period of time. Industries involved in the manufacturing of complex and technical products have found that new technologies are constantly coming to market and they need to exert a great deal of effort to keep up with these technologies and assess what they mean to their businesses (Appleyard, 1996).

For example, consider volatility as a characteristic of knowledge. Knowledge that proved to be valid and useful yesterday may or may not be valid or useful tomorrow. Both the nature and the speed of knowledge change are important in deciding the best methods and processes to utilize in an organization's knowledge management activities. For some areas of work, new knowledge must be continuously created and adaptive solutions need to be applied to solve problems. Examples include the following scenarios:

- Building a house where basic knowledge of how to build a house must be customized to local conditions such as building codes, soil, weather, environmental and government regulations, and existing construction technologies
- A new strategy for an organization needs to be crafted by a group of senior executives and strategy-consultants, requiring knowledge of the organization's past, on its current state, and for predicting an ever dynamic future

In each case, knowledge management activities and processes oriented toward fostering a collaborative environment and connecting the right people together in order to create innovative solutions assist in ensuring that knowledge, although volatile, is kept current.

Knowledge management processes within an organization must have the support to identify obsolete or expired knowledge and replace it with more current knowledge. For example, if an organization relies on a corporate intranet to maintain much of its knowledge regarding essential work procedures, rules, or regulations, it is critical that the information provided is up to date to ensure employees do not receive obsolete knowledge and perform their duties incorrectly or expose the organization to the risk of going against regulations or laws. This can become even more complex as an organization expands its operations globally and must now continually assess and update knowledge from many countries.

Organizations that implement **environmental scanning** and other procedures to learn about their business environments can utilize these knowledge-updating processes in order to constantly evaluate and update their knowledge. Furthermore, offering employees the proper training will ensure they are maintaining up-to-date skills and knowledge regarding their jobs. Assigning and encouraging employees to fulfill boundary roles such as gatekeepers and liaisons can support any innovation initiative. Extending the use of boundary roles to other areas of the organization (e.g., implementing a new information system) can also help create more efficient and effective business processes. The number of boundary roles in one area of the organization (whether formal or informal) should be tailored to the knowledge needs of that area. Furthermore, managers should match a boundary role with the individual's knowledge, skills, and knowledge networks. The volatility of knowledge can be a challenge for organizations that rely on their knowledge management activities to remain viable; however, by ensuring that new knowledge is being constantly created or acquired at both the individual and organizational levels, these organizations can remain competitive.

In situations where knowledge is tacit and contained in a distributed environment, knowledge management activities and processes should be oriented toward providing efficient access to codified expertise. They should focus on the compilation, organization, and replenishment of their knowledge base in the form of databases and documents in document management systems, which can be easily accessed by employees. Organizations must realize, however, that codified information requires a substantial amount of effort to keep current and relevant. If codified information is allowed to become out-of-date, the resource that stores the knowledge (e.g., a manual or intranet) will be perceived by employees as not useful or valuable.

For better exploitation and exploration of knowledge to occur, organizations need to be structured in a manner to support and enable knowledge-related processes inside everyday activities of knowledge workers. This is a fundamental goal of knowledge management: creating an environment where the previous experience of organizational members is reachable and can be integrated to support many forms of decisions, and where new, high-quality solutions to business problems are developed efficiently.

KNOWLEDGE PROCESSING IN ORGANIZATIONS

The viewpoints and perceptions an organizational culture fosters regarding the definition, forms, and applications of knowledge will directly impact how an organization processes and utilizes knowledge in is business operations. When analyzing and improving work practices, it is necessary to understand the details of how individuals create and use knowledge in their daily routines and processes. This can lead to the creation of a sustained knowledge-focused environment that can eventually be supported by a culture that appreciates and values knowledge and its role in how people work (Choo et al., 2006).

The *evolutionary information-processing theory of knowledge creation* (Li and Kettinger, 2006) views organizations through workflows that describe how knowledge is utilized and created during the course of decision making, and how organizations can preserve knowledge in order to capitalize upon its value in the future. This theory (shown in Figure 2.4) links the concepts of knowledge utilization and creation directly to the everyday activities of an information worker, and specifically to an individual's decision making. It views decision-making activities as a six-stage process, where individuals use information and knowledge to generate a solution to an existing problem. Decision making begins with the recognition of a new problem and ends at the creation of new knowledge that enables the organization to solve the problem.

The process is triggered by a *problem recognition response* (e.g., an outdated product, customer complaint, receipt of new market information) and coordinated by *setting organizational goals* that specify the purpose, scope, and time constraints of the knowledge creation activities that will lead to generating a solution to the identified problem. Information functions as an input to the process, providing knowledge about the problem, alternatives, and possible goals. A key responsibility of managers is to recognize that a problem is evident and that a decision is required. Often, a problem exists when there is a difference between the current and the expected state. Within this model, the two-sided arrow connecting problem recognition and goal setting illustrates that both the problem and the goal usually evolve over time, due to the bounded rationality (Simon and Newell, 1958) or cognitive constraints of humans.

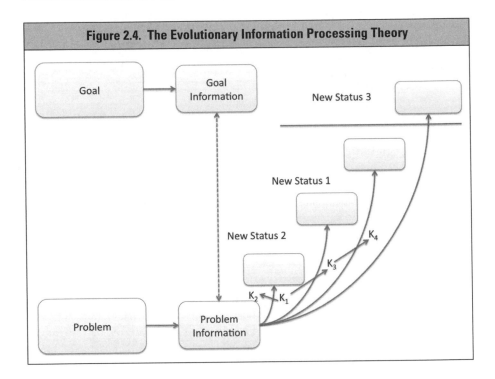

Figure 2.4. The Evolutionary Information Processing Theory

This concept reveals why it is hard to grasp the details of a problem at the beginning of the problem recognition step.

The process continues with an important issue related to knowledge creation, *resource sourcing*, which restricts the generation and selection of solutions that require certain organizational or external resources. Resources are treated as bottlenecks in the decision-making process: although they provide information, it takes time and resources to evaluate the information. However, due to the need for increased agility and constant adaptation, organizations should always be looking for opportunities to gain access to complementary or alternative resources in order to enrich their knowledge bases. Information about resources affects the many forms of knowledge that are generated, and informs the selection stage which determines whether the solution created is feasible.

The generation of tentative knowledge refers to the alternatives to existing knowledge located within and outside of an organization. Here, individuals *exploit and refine existing solutions* (which they retrieve from the organizational memory) or *explore and experiment with new ones* (March, 1991). The solution to the problem might not consist of the new tentative knowledge, as inferior knowledge for the solution could possibly be created if existing knowledge is applied, hence the need for new knowledge. This uncertainty is decreased with experience and previous successful problem solving, but preselection and heuristics might narrow the space in which new knowledge is searched. This uncertainty is necessary, leading to obligatory verification of tentative knowledge. Here, information functions as the indicator to the extent that the existing knowledge, received either from within or from outside of the organization, can solve the problem.

Tentative knowledge must be *verified and selected* before becoming an acceptable part of organizational knowledge. Selection is based on feedback information. First, it must be tested to what extent the tentative knowledge solves the problem by reducing the gap between the current state and the goal. This is done by applying tentative knowledge and analyzing feedback information on the status of the solution. Did the organization move toward the goal or not, and what is the remaining distance to reach the goal? Second, the problem is tested against resource information to determine if the solution is feasible with available resources.

Selected knowledge variation is then *retained* and becomes existing organizational knowledge, which can be used in further rounds of knowledge generation and selection or reused in the solving of other problems. Knowledge retention occurs in organizational memory in a form of individuals' memories, interpersonal relationships, documents, databases, work processes, products, and services (Stein and Zwass, 1995; Walsh and Ungson, 1991). As such, it becomes available for either the next round of solving the same problem or any other problem, as it enters the tentative knowledge generation as "existing" (verified and selected) knowledge. The key in this iterative knowledge generation-selection-retention phases is understanding of role of information: tentative knowledge is first only uncertainly generated and then selected based on feedback information (Li and Kettinger, 2006).

This sequence is illustrated in Figure 2.5. Knowledge variations are based on the gap between problem and goal (information). Feedback information shows that tentatively generated knowledge in the first iteration did not achieve the goal; however, as it moves towards the goal, it is retained in organizational memory and becomes new existing knowledge. The second variation of newly generated tentative knowledge is not retained in the organizational memory, as it is inferior to the existing knowledge. Thus, the third iteration starts from existing knowledge from the first iteration. The third knowledge variation fails to achieve the goal completely, yet it is much closer than the first one, and is therefore retained in organizational memory. The fourth variation is superior to the third, but it is limited by resource information, and thus the third variation is retained in the organizational memory (Li and Kettinger, 2006).

Knowledge Processing for Decision Making

Herbert Simon stated that problems are resolved through the decision-making activities of organizations. His model of decision making argues that decisions can be categorized along a continuum from repetitive and structured tasks (programmed decisions) to new and unstructured decisions (nonprogrammed). The four phases of decision making that occur in organizations—intelligence, design, choice, and implementation—factor into how decisions are made.

The intelligence phase is where the organization gathers knowledge to understand the problem, recognize the significance of the problem to the organization, identify the risks involved in the current situation, and determine the key factors that need to

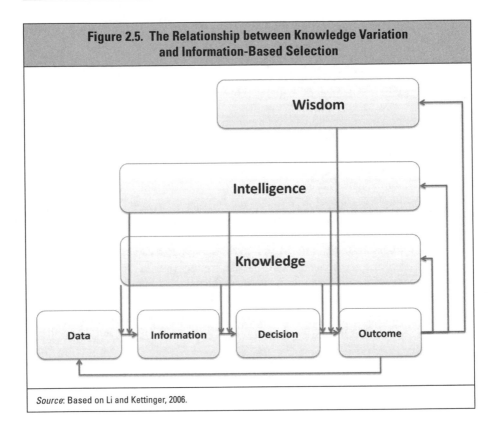

Figure 2.5. The Relationship between Knowledge Variation and Information-Based Selection

Source: Based on Li and Kettinger, 2006.

be considered during the decision process. In the second phase, the design phase, the organization gathers knowledge that is either existing or new to determine the available alternatives or different courses of action it may take. Much of this knowledge comes from tacit experience of the decision makers who have experienced either similar decisions or the organizational process during previous situations. The choice phase is the culmination of the decision-making process, and involves the selection of one alternative from a set of alternatives, based upon defined criteria. These alternatives also differ by the consequences that will be realized from them, and therefore decision makers must identify and weigh these consequences over the course of their decision. Therefore, choice is influenced by the expectation of what the alternative will bring to the organization. The act of choosing within a decision presents constraints in the form of cognitive limitations, incomplete or imperfect information, and time and cost restraints. Also influencing the decision are characteristics of the decision makers, including the amount of knowledge they possess relative to the decision, their ability in terms of intelligence and competence toward decision making, and the level of motivation they have to succeed (Harrison, 1995). The constraints can occur over a defined or an unknown time period, so the alternatives available in a decision maker's choice process may be limited to constraints of time. Therefore, when attempting to understand an organization's decision-making process, it is not wise to focus only on the act of making a choice. It is necessary to understand the recognition of the problem, how alternatives were derived, and what analysis was used leading up to choosing a solution. Finally, the implementation stage allows for feedback or learning by the organization to determine how successful or effective the chosen alternative was, and whether the knowledge used should be retained to be used in future decisions or not. These four processes are usually performed sequentially, but each one is an iterative process and can be repeated until satisfactory results are achieved (Simon, 1960).

Creating Knowledge in a Call Center

Consider the example of responding to a customer query in a call center. A call from a customer contains a description of a problem the customer has experienced, and triggers the need for the organization to find a solution in order to satisfy the customer. The customer service representative who handled the call initially searches for a plausible solution. If the problem/goal/resource combination has appeared before, a solution may be found in an existing knowledge base (e.g., the individual's own memory, existing documents and databases, or an experienced colleague who may know a satisfactory solution), or by reusing or applying the knowledge that had been previously stored in the organizational memory. Ideally, the customer replies to the employee that the problem is solved (positive feedback information), which means that there is no need for retention of "new" knowledge. However, if the customer uses a new version of a product that responds to the solution in a different manner than previous solutions created (feedback information is not positive), new tentative knowledge needs to be generated. This knowledge can be acquired by analyzing the architecture and design of the new version, consulting the engineers regarding the manufacturing process, or engaging employees furnished with the appropriate skills and capabilities that will finally integrate the new knowledge from the organizational memory and lead to a solution.

The evolutionary information processing theory addresses many of the challenges that are viewed as crucial for knowledge management to be successful, including systematic problem solving, experimentation with new approaches, learning from one's own experience and past history, learning from the experiences and best practices of others, and transferring knowledge quickly and efficiently through the organization (Garvin, 1993). The primary application of knowledge within an organization is decision making, which is addressed in the evolutionary information processing model that attempts to describe *how complex problems are systematically solved*, from decomposition of complex problems to the choice of the "best" solution. *Experimentation with new approaches happens* when information triggers tentative knowledge creation, which is based on existing internal or external knowledge, and how these new knowledge variations get selected based on feedback, goal, resource, and problem information. *Learning from one's own experience and past history*, and *learning from the experiences and best practices of others* is addressed with the process of knowledge retention, as selected variations are retained in organizational memory. The latter also acts as a mechanism for *quick and efficient transfer of knowledge through organization*. As such, this theory offers a comprehensive perspective on knowledge creation and utilization.

The evolutionary information processing theory illustrates two important implications for managers. First, it explains the information-knowledge relationship. For successful individual and organizational learning, the key to success is the exploitation of existing knowledge and exploration of new alternatives that replace established patterns of action. Information functions as a trigger for knowledge creation, where "tentative" knowledge variations are applied and then selected based on feedback, goal, and resource information. Two competing forces, exploration of new alternatives and exploitation of old certainties, push together for the creation of new knowledge. Existing knowledge from past activities resides in organizational memory and when accessed, supports current problem solving and decision making (Stein and Zwass, 1995).

Second, it defines problem solving as a structured knowledge process. Managers who design organizations and technology can now integrate their actions into the stages of decision making, which is an activity visible to many employees. The process-based approach utilized in the model fits a process-oriented perspective taken by the practitioners when designing organizations and information technology. This model can serve as an excellent starting point for structured analysis of knowledge

---

Knowledge Creation and Public Relations

Consider a public relations (PR) department that has to make a decision on whether to design and implement a new knowledge management solution. The first activity is to identify the business-critical work processes of the public relations department that need to be improved through the better utilization of knowledge. Secondly, the organization would identify what could be improved, or more specifically, which decisions made by knowledge workers require better knowledge resources. One such decision process would be the handling of a PR crisis, such as a sensitive business matter that requires experienced PR professionals to craft a specific message to the public, and the many decisions that are made by the PR employees during this type of critical event. The process of designing a suitable knowledge management solution can be aided by looking at the decision-making stages of this particular PR situation, and deciding upon the best knowledge-related activities and products required for each stage. For the problem recognition and goal setting stages, previous experience (with similar events) that is stored in documents and databases should be identified. Additionally, people who are considered experts in the field should collaboratively work on identifying the problem and the desired outcome of the decision process, forming a consensus about the facts and how best to proceed towards the solution. The problem needs to be accurately defined, including the goals that must be accomplished by the decision such as the mitigation of the risks regarding the decision, the communication strategy that will be employed, and the level of importance of the decision. These activities would be well supported with a knowledge management solution that contains provisions for research on previous cases and provides extensive background information, as well as giving the decision makers the ability to collaborate.

When the problem is recognized and goal is set, a tentative solution needs to be generated and, based on problem/goal/resource information, also selected for implementation. A good KM solution would foster a collaborative environment coupled with access to previous cases and experiences. Experts involved would have to study similar past events to understand what solutions were chosen and their rate of success. Knowledge retention will mostly happen in documents (lessons learned, abstracts of cases, maybe even videotapes of meetings with stakeholders) and inside people's heads (cumulative experience). A satisfactory solution would foster the codification of experience in documents, and also, documenting which of the employees have (or had gained) new experiential knowledge. This example illustrates that the complexity of designing a KM solution can be broken down with the help of discrete decision-making stages, as each one can visualize or design the most appropriate KM solution.

work in an organization; knowledge workers and managers can analyze the work of employees from a knowledge perspective and introduce changes to processes or technology with an understanding of the impact to organizational decision-making processes.

CONCLUSION

The transformation to a knowledge-based economy has required organizations to consider knowledge as a valuable asset that must be both understood and managed. Beginning with the individuals in the organization who identify, acquire, create, and use knowledge in their daily job routines and tasks, organizations must understand the knowledge that is important to their business and that can eventually become the foundation for the creation of a competitive advantage.

A major challenge for organizations is understanding the knowledge that is required by their employees in order to function. The many types of knowledge that are available to an organization must be evaluated though consideration of how such knowledge can be integrated into an organization. Looking beyond data and information, knowledge management techniques that support knowledge work performed by employees become valuable tools in managing the organization's knowledge, or creating the organizational memory. Different organizations harbor differing perspectives of what exactly constitutes knowledge, and these views shape the organizational practices, values, and knowledge culture that ultimately govern how knowledge is used.

Incorporating knowledge into the work routines of the organization has many challenges, stemming from the uniqueness of knowledge and its unconventional economic attributes. A new mindset is required to allow organizations to grasp the challenges and opportunities knowledge brings to an organization, and determine how this knowledge can benefit its strategy and decision-making processes. As knowledge can exist at many levels, organizations must determine the knowledge that is most accessible and of the best quality, given the resource limitations that may exist. Converting knowledge through the various levels (such as individual to organizational, or organizational to societal) allows not only for the sharing of knowledge and interaction among people, but also for the formation of new knowledge that can be mutually beneficial to both the sender and the receiver.

The goal for organizations is to create a solid understanding of their knowledge base and available knowledge to influence the behavior of employees, improving their efficiency and effectiveness. Integrating this understanding of knowledge into work practices is difficult but possible if the right resources, leadership, and strategies are in place. In any knowledge management project or initiative, knowledge use is the focal point for knowledge activities in order to extract the most value from the knowledge. The many forms of knowledge that can exist in the multiple levels of the organization and its business environment can be overwhelming and can possibly lead to overloading the organization with confusing, conflicting, and unnecessary knowledge. However, encouraging employees to gain an understanding of knowledge, its value, and how it can be used in their work can lead to success at all levels of the firm.

Recap: The Major Points for Knowledge Managers to Consider When Working with Knowledge

1. At the heart of any organization are its people, and any discussion on managing knowledge should focus on supporting and motivating employees.
2. The nature of work, and therefore the nature of managing, is constantly changing with the dynamics of the external environment. The knowledge economy is one example of such an external force.
3. Data, information, knowledge, and wisdom are four very different concepts and should be treated differently when being managed.
4. Examining data and information, and deriving knowledge from these sources, can create knowledge. Knowledge can also be created through creating a theory or hypothesis and testing the validity of that hypothesis.
5. As an organizational asset, knowledge does not follow many of the fundamental rules of economics. Therefore, through creative management, it can be used differently in varying situations.
6. Since knowledge is an intangible asset, it is very difficult to measure. This causes problems for knowledge managers, as they need to create ways of measuring knowledge and its value to an organization.
7. The overall gain of knowledge by an organization that creates value for the individuals and allows the knowledge to be retained is referred to as organizational learning.
8. It is important to understand the distinction between tacit (non-coded, very personal and difficult to articulate) knowledge and explicit (encoded, easy to share and transfer) knowledge. Although tacit knowledge is more difficult to manage, it creates the most value to an organization.
9. The flow of knowledge through an organization can be beneficial to people, as long as the distinction between private and public knowledge is clear. Employees must realize what knowledge should be encouraged to be disseminated publicly and which knowledge must remain private.
10. Knowledge presents challenges to an organization based on the ideas of volatility and volume. Knowledge is constantly changing and can become out of date very quickly. Knowledge can arrive at the firm in large volumes, and it is the responsibility of the knowledge manager to ensure employees and other management are not overwhelmed by knowledge.

DISCUSSION QUESTIONS

1. Are there methods that can be used to measure knowledge in organizations? What are the advantages to being able to measure knowledge? What are the risks an organization faces if it cannot measure its knowledge?
2. What is the benefit to an organization of having a strong organizational learning capability? Why is it essential to continually build an organizational memory?
3. Tacit and explicit knowledge are two very different types of knowledge that an individual may possess. What can a manager do to encourage the transfer and use of each type of knowledge?
4. Most knowledge is created and resides in an individual. How can this knowledge eventually be transferred into the group, organizational, and societal levels?
5. Although the goal of many organizations is to share their knowledge and allow access by as many internal people as possible, there are times when knowledge is most valuable when it is not shared. How can an organization protect knowledge and ensure it remains private, given the unusual nature of this asset?

6. Some argue that the problem with knowledge is it is no longer difficult to obtain, but often it is too easy to capture and people can feel overloaded with what they need to know. What steps can individual or organization take to avoid experiencing "knowledge overload"?

REFERENCES

Appleyard, M. M. 1996. "How Does Knowledge Flow? Interfirm Patterns in the Semiconductor Industry." *Strategic Management Journal* 17 (Winter Special Issue): 137–154.

Argyris, C., and S. Shon. 1978. *Organizational Learning: A Theory of Action Perspective*. London: Addison-Wesley.

Bartlett, C. A., and T. Mahmood. 1996. "Skandia AFS: Developing Intellectual Capital Globally." *Journal of Management Accounting Research* 12: 1–17.

Blackler, F. 1995. "Knowledge, Knowledge Work, and Organizations: An Overview and Interpretation." *Organization Studies* 16, no. 6: 1021–1046.

Bontis, N., M.M. Crossan, and J. Hulland. 2002. "Managing an Organizational Learning System by Aligning Stocks and Flows." *Journal of Management Studies* 39, no. 4.

Brooks, F. P. 1995. *The Mythical Man-Month*. Boston: Addison-Wesley.

Chang, H.-H., Tsai, Y.-C., and Y.-H. Chen. 2009. "Knowledge Characteristics, Implementation Measures, and Performance in Taiwan Hospital Organization." *International Journal of Business and Information* 4, no. 1: 23–44.

Choo, C. W., C. Furnes, S. Paquette, H. van den Berg, B. Detlor, P. Bergeron, et al. 2006. "Working with Information: Information Management and Culture in a Professional Services Organization." *Journal of Information Science* 32, no. 6: 491–510.

Conner, K. R., and C. K. Prahalad. 1996. "A Resource-based Theory of the Firm: Knowledge Versus Opportunism." *Organization Science* 7, no. 5: 477–501.

Cooper, L. P., R. Nash, T.-A. Phan, and T. Bailey. 2005. "Learning about the Organization via Knowledge Management: The Case of JPL 101." *International Journal of Knowledge Management* 1, no. 1: 47–66.

Crossan, M., H. Lane, R. E. White, and L. Djurfeldt. 1995. "Organizational Learning: Dimensions for a Theory." *The International Journal of Organizational Analysis* 3: 337–360.

Dalkir, K. 2005. *Knowledge Management in Theory and Practice*. Burlington, MA: Elsevier Butterworth-Heinemann.

Davenport, T. H., and J. C. Beck. 2001. *The Attention Economy*. Boston: Harvard Business School Press.

Desouza, K., and Y. Awazu. 2005. "Segment and Destroy: The Missing Capabilities of Knowledge Management." *Journal of Business Strategy* 26, no. 4: 46–52.

Desouza, K., and G. Vanapalli. 2005. "Securing Knowledge in Organizations: Lessons from the Defense and Intelligence Sectors." *International Journal of Information Management* 25: 85–98.

Dyer, J. H., and K. Nobeoka. 2000. "Creating and Managing a High-Performance Knowledge-Sharing Network: The Toyota Case." *Strategic Management Journal* 21: 345–367.

Edvinsson, L., and M.S. Malone. 1997. *Intellectual Capital: The Proven Way to Establish Your Company's Real Value by Measuring Its Hidden Brainpower*. London: Judy Piatkus.

Fahey, R., A. C. Vasconcelos, and D. Ellis. 2007. "The Impact of Rewards within Communities of Practice: A Study of the SAP Online Global Community." *Knowledge Management Research and Practice* 5: 186–198.

Friedman, T. 2010. "More (Steve) Jobs, Jobs, Jobs, Jobs." *New York Times*, January 24.

Garvin, D. A. 1993. "Building a Learning Organization." *Harvard Business Review* 71, no. 4: 78–91.

Grant, R. M. 1996a. "Prospering in Dynamically-Competitive Environments: Organizational Capability as Knowledge Integration." *Organization Science: A Journal of the Institute of Management Sciences* 7, no. 4: 375–387.

Grant, R. M. 1996b. "Toward a Knowledge-Based Theory of the Firm." *Strategic Management Journal* 17: 109–122.

Harrison, E. F. 1995. *The Managerial Decision-Making Process*. 4th ed. Boston: Houghton Mifflin.

Huber, G. P. 1991. "Organizational Learning: The Contributing Processes and the Literatures." *Organization Science* 2, no. 1: 88–115.

Husted, K., and S. Michailova. 2002. "Diagnosing and Fighting Knowledge Sharing Hostility." *Organizational Dynamics* 31, no. 1: 60–73.

Husysman, M. H., and D. Dewit. 2004. *Knowledge Sharing in Practice*. Dordrect, Germany: Kluwer Academics.

Koch, N. 1999. *Process Improvement and Organizational Learning: The Role of Collaboration Technologies*. Hershey, PA: Idea.

Kogut, B. 2000. "The Network as Knowledge." *Strategic Management Journal* 21: 405–425.

Li, Y., and W.J. Kettinger. 2006. "An Evolutionary Information-Processing Theory of Knowledge Creation." *Journal of the Association for Information Systems* 7, no. 9: 593–617.

March, J. G. 1991. "Exploration and Exploitation in Organizational Learning." *Organization Science* 2, no. 1: 71–87.

Marks, A., and C. Baldry. 2009. "Stuck in the Middle with Who? The Class Identity of Knowledge Workers." *Work, Employment and Society* 23, no. 1: 1–24.

Marquardt, M. J. 2002. *The Learning Organization: Mastering the 5 Elements for Corporate Learning*. Palo Alto: Davies-Black.

Myint, D. 2007. "Keeping the Peace: United Nations Department of Peacekeeping Operations." *Inside Knowledge* 10. http://www.ikmagazine.com/xq/asp/sid.0/articleid.365FD6DA-9D7B-4E58-8ABC-35CA6F12C8DE/eTitle.Case_study_United_Nations_Department_of_Peace keeping_Operations/qx/display.htm.

Nonaka, I. 1994. "A Dynamic Theory of Organizational Knowledge Creation." *Organization Science* 5, no. 1: 14–37.

Nonaka, I., and H. Takeuchi. 1995. *The Knowledge Creating Company*. New York: Oxford University Press.

Novak, T. P., D. L. Hoffman, and A. Duhachek. 2003. "The Influence of Goal-Directed and Experiential Activities on Online Flow Experiences." *The Journal of Consumer Psychology* 13: 3–16.

O'Dell, C., and J. Grayson. 1998. "If Only We Knew What We Know: Identification and Transfer of External Best Practices." *California Management Review* 40, no. 3: 154–174.

Paquette, S., P. T. Jaeger, and S. Wilson. 2010. "Identifying the Security Risks Associated with Governmental Use of Cloud Computing." *Government Information Quarterly* 27: 245–253.

Parker, K. R., and P. Nitse. 2006. "Competitive Intelligence Gathering." In *Encyclopedia of Knowledge Management*, edited by D. Schwartz. Hershey, PA: Idea.

Pfeffer, J., and R. I. Sutton. 1999. "Knowing 'What' to Do Is Not Enough: Turning Knowledge into Action." *California Management Review* 42, no. 1: 83–108.

Pfeffer, J., and R. I. Sutton. 2000. *The Knowing-Doing Gap*. Boston: Harvard Business School Press.

Polanyi, M. 1966. *The Tacit Dimension*. London: Routledge.

Rodts, M. 2001. "Few Things Are Carved in Stone." *Orthopaedic Nursing* 20, no. 4: 11.

Roth, J. 2003. "Enabling Knowledge Creation: Learning from an R and D Organization." *Journal of Knowledge Management* 7, no. 1: 32–48.

Simon, H. A. 1960. *The New Science of Management Decision*. New York: Harper and Brothers.

Simon, H. A. 1976. *Administrative Behavior: A Study of Decision-Making Processes in Administrative Organizations*. New York: Free Press.

Simon, H. A., and A. Newell. 1958. "Heuristic Problem Solving: The Next Advance in Operations Research." *Operations Research* 6, no. 1: 1–10.

Spender, J. C. 1996. "Making Knowledge the Basis of a Dynamic Theory of the Firm." *Strategic Management Journal* 17 (Special Winter Issue): 45–62.

Stein, E. W., and V. Zwass. 1995. "Actualizing Organizational Memory with Information Systems." *Information Systems Research* 6, no. 2: 85–117.

Stewart, T. A. 1997. *Intellectual Capital: The New Wealth of Organizations*. 2nd ed. Vol. 1. New York: Doubleday.

Tapscott, D., and A. D. Williams. 2008. *Wikinomics*. New York: Penguin.

Tranfield, D., and S. Smith. 1998. "The Strategic Regeneration of Manufacturing by Changing Routines." *International Journal of Operations and Production Management* 18, no. 2: 114–129.

Tushman, M. L. 1977. "Special Boundary Roles in the Innovation Process." *Administrative Science Quarterly* 22, no. 4: 587–605.

Tushman, M. L., and T. Scanlan. 1981. "Boundary Spanning Individuals: Their Role in Information Transfer and Their Antecedents." *Academy of Management Journal* 24, no. 2: 289–305.

US Bureau of Labor Statistics. 2011. *Précis, Monthly Labor Review Online*. Accessed April 12. http://www.bls.gov/opub/mlr/2002/01/precis.htm.

Von Hippel, E. 1988. *The Sources of Innovation*. New York: Oxford University Press.

Von Krogh, G. 2009. "Individualist and Collectivist Perspectives on Knowledge in Organizations: Implications for Information Systems Research." *Journal of Strategic Information Systems* 18: 119–129.

Walsh, J. P., and G. R. Ungson. 1991. "Organizational Memory." *The Academy of Management Review* 16, no. 1: 57–91.

Zack, M. H. 1999. "Managing Codified Knowledge." *Sloan Management Review* 40, no. 4: 45–58.

3

The Concept of Management

Jongmin T. Moon with Kevin C. Desouza

OBJECTIVES

- Provide a definition of management including its fundamental concepts.
- Link many accepted ideas in the field of management to related elements of knowledge management.
- Offer an overview of the activities of a typical manager, including examples and cases.
- Highlight recent trends and issues for managers of organizations in a global marketplace

INTRODUCTION

In every organization, managers play a critical role in shaping the future. The actions and decisions taken by managers on a daily basis can often result in the successful execution of operations for the organization. When a severe winter storm hit an unprepared Seattle in December 2008, the city came to a standstill. However, FedEx's managing director for the northwest region, Tom Campbell, was still able to deliver all packages with only a few being delayed, due to his knowledge gained from training in how to deal with severe weather problems (Girard, 2009). As with all good outcomes, the actions taken by managers can also lead to dire, if not fatal, consequences. The failure of managers on the Deepwater Horizon oil rig to notice key warnings signs of a mechanical failure led to the explosion on April 20, 2010, which resulted in the deaths of 11 men and created an environmental disaster that has cost BP tens of billions of dollars to date, with estimates continuing to rise as compensation is owed to many stakeholders (Associated Press, 2010). As senior managers such as the chief executive officer (CEO) deal with more strategic decisions and resources, their actions often have a greater impact upon the entire organization. The corporate image of Boeing was tarnished in 2003 due to a string of military procurement scandals that led to the resignation of then-CEO Philip M. Condit (Merle, 2005). Perhaps one of the most well-known examples of bad management and poor decision making was the collapse of Enron, whose senior management had created elaborate and illegal financial structures which they used to hide debt obligations and lie about company profits. After their actions were discovered in 2001, Enron filed for Chapter 11 bankruptcy later that year and has since become the image of corporate fraud and disastrous management (Eichenwald, 2005; McLean and Elkind, 2003).

The most important activity that a manager is engaged with on a daily basis is decision making. The effectiveness and efficiency of managers' decisions and decision-making processes ultimately determine the success, or failures, of their organizations through impacting competitive abilities (Mintzberg, Raisinghami, and Theoret, 1976). Critical to the success of decision making is the ability for individuals at the local level, and organizations at the global level, to leverage knowledge. The more accurate the knowledge that is available to managers, the better chance they have in making decisions that will result in positive and desired results. An underlying theme of this book is how organizations manage knowledge toward this end.

Management in the Library Context

High-caliber managers and leaders are necessary for all industries and ever more critical in times of crisis. Just as almost every entity is dealing with budget cuts as a result of the recession, libraries are facing critical budget cuts that may reduce their abilities to obtain library materials as well as change their operations as restructuring occurs to further reduce costs. The Montgomery County Public Libraries are operating with a materials budget that is half of what it was in 2008 (Fiscal 2008: $6.3 million; Fiscal 2011: $3 million), which has forced them to carefully select the materials for the library and led them to see significant cuts in niche material (Calamaio, 2010). Even the prestigious Harvard College Library is facing budget cuts that will require them to shuffle personnel and unavoidably face layoffs. Facing a crisis such as this requires managers and leaders to be more efficient and effective at decision making, especially in terms of advocating for resources, harness-ing knowledge, and conducting transformations to the classical institutions. A simple solution often does not exist and, instead, novel solutions and difficult decisions are carried out through increased levels of communication and collaboration. Administrators and senior managers at Harvard have encouraged cost-cutting measures such as the elimination of print subscriptions when the material is available online, and have even initiated a pilot program that shares research librarians between different libraries in an effort to address the $12 million budget reduction (Yi and Zhu, 2009).

In this chapter, the important high-level concepts of **management** are described. Understanding the discipline of management and its key concepts is crucial to anyone investigating the intricacies of management and use of knowledge in organi-zations. First, a definition of management is offered along with a discussion of the fundamental aspects of management: planning, organizing, controlling, and leading. Each of these components are defined and their relationships to the operations of a business are presented, including how these management components have changed in reaction to a dynamic business environment, and why they are critical to the suc-cess of the organization. Second, the tasks, routines, and processes that are normally performed by a manager are explored, along with the various levels of management and their different roles and responsibilities. This includes an examination of the traits of good (and bad) managers. Finally, current trends in management such as con-temporary issues, emerging approaches and ideas in organizational management, and the changes presented by knowledge workers are addressed. This chapter is not a complete and comprehensive exploration of management, but rather it is intended to address the key aspects of management that are important to managing knowledge in organizations.

TOWARD A DEFINITION OF MANAGEMENT

Management involves motivating resources, both human (e.g., employees) and artificial (e.g., technologies) to work in a coordinated fashion toward the achievement of organizational goals and strategies. It is possible to determine whether an entity has been managed adequately by examining the effectiveness and efficiency by which it achieved its goals and outcomes. At its core, management is concerned with the following critical activities: planning, organizing, controlling, and leading. Management and the practices that are employed by an organization can be altered whether the organization's products and services are tangible or intangible. Experienced and proficient managers are able to recognize what alterations of their routines are needed when dealing with intangible items, such as knowledge.

Classic works on the field of management present different perspectives on the role of managers. Peter Drucker, regarded by many as one of the greatest management thinkers of the last century, stated that a manager's job "is to direct the resources and the efforts of the business toward opportunities for economically significant results" (Drucker, 2006: 147). He believed that in order to achieve results, management and the organization need to recognize employees as assets rather than liabilities, and that the manager's job was also to prepare and free people to perform as knowledge workers (Drucker et al., 2008). Henry Mintzberg provides a different perspective. Mintzberg's approach posited that managers need to understand how to deal with three kinds of assets—action, people, and information (Mintzberg, 2009). Managers help organizations and units achieve their tasks, which is done by taking action. They also deal with the people taking action by motivating them, building teams, training them, among other activities, in order to help them to take more effective actions. Finally, managers must deal with information that guides people as they take action.

THE CLASSIC COMPONENTS OF MANAGEMENT

Although management scholars such as Drucker and Mintzberg provide different perspectives on the manager's job, the classical components of management are evident in all views: planning, organizing, controlling, and leading. Table 3.1 includes a summary of the components of management.

Planning

Among the most critical components of management is the ability to plan. Without the ability to prepare for the future, one will not be prepared to direct other management activities such as organizing, leading, and controlling. Many challenges are encountered

Table 3.1. Components of Management	
Component	**Description**
Planning	• A decision-making process whereby a course of action is created to move from a *current state* to a *desired state* • Includes phases such as gathering information, choosing the best course of action, and designing and developing the plan to implement the course of action • Not usually a fixed or rigid series of steps, but rather a framework that can be adapted based on changes in the internal and external environment
Organizing	• Involves securing resources, including human resources, financial resources, and physical resources, which are required to implement the plan • Requires good communication in order to justify needs and allocate scarce resources within an organization
Controlling	• The process of measuring and evaluating progress and outcomes, and taking corrective action as needed • Ownership, guidelines, and milestones must be established and clearly communicated to support effective measurement
Leading	• The ability to inspire shared vision and action among individuals or groups in order to achieve a common goal • Leadership traits include confidence and optimism, which leaders use to effectively inspire and motivate employees, especially during times of uncertainty

when leading a group or trying to organize and allocate resources without a predetermined plan that directs action. Planning is best conceptualized as a decision-making process whereby a course of action is created to move from a current state to a desired state. As a simple example, going from Boston (the current location) to San Francisco (the desired location) allows for a number of alternatives from driving a car, taking a flight, riding the train, or even using a combination of these transportation choices. In addition, you can choose whether to travel to the destination directly or via optional stopovers. A range of options based on price and features are also available. Based on your preferences and resource constraints, you are able to decide on a plan of action to reach the desired state.

Herbert Simon, who was best known for his work on decision making, identified its three major stages as intelligence, design, and choice (Simon, 1997). The intelligence phase is the stage where a manager recognizes that a new decision is needed. This situation arises due to changes in the external and/or internal environment. For example, new information may emerge in the business environment that necessitates a change in the organization's business processes, or a prior decision may have run its course and a new course of action is needed. Often, organizations do not enter this stage as they do not have the correct knowledge to inform them that a decision point has been reached. Design occurs when managers identify various alternatives that they believe will achieve the organization's objectives. Creativity and access to sufficient resources are critical in this stage to ensure that all the appropriate are identified and considered. The tradeoffs between the various options are also analyzed using tools such as a cost-benefit analysis. Finally, choice is the phase in which managers select the most viable option they believe will best meet the decision criteria considering their resources and other constraints. In considering the alternatives, it is not possible to select the most optimal solution; instead, managers engage in what Simon refers to as **satisficing** (Simon, 1991). As humans we are constrained by bounded rationality, as we seldom have access to all information or infinite amount of time or even all resources required to search exhaustively for all possible design options. People are also constrained by heuristics, which limit our cognitive ability to select the optimal alternative (Tversky and Kahneman, 1974). Hence managers must resort to finding a satisfactory, rather than optimal, solution given these constraints.

Nonprofits Facing Challenges

Nonprofit organizations (NPOs) are facing harsh challenges in the wake of the recession. Many NPOs are making quick and often drastic changes in order to respond to the challenges they face. Most NPOs rely heavily on state funding and charitable donations from foundations and individual donors to cover operation costs. With organizations facing budget cuts and a harsher economic environment, donations to charities and foundations are among the list of things that are quickly reduced, or eliminated. Sadly, NPOs are needed most during times of crisis as the people they serve, who are struggling to get through the recession, rely on them more and more for support. NPOs that are unable to cope with the financial challenges are faced with the decision to suspend operations, or worse—shut down. The Smokey House Center, a farm and forest center that works with kids at risk of dropping out of school in Vermont, temporarily suspended its educational programs after January 15, 2011 as it searches for a sustainable model in the post-recession economy (Keese, 2010). And other NPOs, unfortunately, are left with no other option than to close their doors. The Downtown Learning Center, a daycare center in Roanoke, was forced to shut down after realizing it had unpaid debts and only $3,000 for current expenses (Valencia, 2010). Other NPOs, however, have been able to rapidly adjust their plans to come up with innovative strategies to address their immediate funding needs. Kristopher Tucker of East Knoxville recorded and sold a CD of his Christmas music with all proceeds going to the Emerald Youth Foundation, an urban youth ministry where Tucker spent a part of his childhood sitting at the piano (Williams, 2009).

Once the decision has been made, the chosen alternative must be implemented and the plan must be put to action. Here, it is important to realize two things. First, decisions seldom are implemented as planned, given that a plan will need to be revised and updated as the implementation occurs and new knowledge is acquired. The US government has emergency and contingency plans in place in order to respond to natural disasters, but Hurricane Katrina demonstrated that sometimes what is planned is not enough to deal with an exceptional situation. Hurricane Katrina showed local, state, and federal governments that they were not prepared to deal with an overwhelming natural disaster, and they struggled to adapt their plans to deal with new and unforeseen issues. Instead of dealing with critical issues such as water, food, and shelter, officials in charge wasted valuable time and resources trying to establish a chain of command for decision making (Shane, 2010). Secondly, the execution of a plan relies on the people that will carry out the plan. A good plan, if given to incompetent people can lead to disastrous outcomes. In the wake of Hurricane Katrina, Rep. Charlie

Melancon contacted Michael Brown, then chief of FEMA, indicating that he had a medical specialist and a trailer of medical supplies that needed to be directed to a location where they were needed most, but it took Brown four days even to respond with an e-mail asking if the medical people were usable (CNN, 2005). Often, a bad plan given to competent people may not have such disastrous consequences, since competent managers implementing the plan will be adept at making changes and alterations to deal with the implementation as it unfolds.

Important components of the planning phase include creating a vision and mission statement, defining goals and objectives, and developing strategies. These are all aspects of planning activities, but different levels of management are more responsible for certain aspects than others. The executive-level managers are responsible for planning at the organizational level through the creation of a vision and mission statement. Middle management and those who deal with low-level operations are more focused on short-term planning. They are not concerned with the development of a vision and mission statement, but rather are focused on projects and tasks such as allocating resources and defining work schedules.

Plans can also be categorized into three different types: strategic, tactical, and operational. **Strategic planning** is at the highest level of the organization and is conducted by senior management as it used to define a direction or, in other words, the future state they wish to achieve. The vision and mission statement are important parts of a strategic plan; they provide guidance for determining what business strategies are most suitable for an organization. **Tactical planning** is establishing key initiatives that will help achieve the overall strategy. Goal and objective formulation is an important piece of tactical planning that can involve both senior and middle-level management. **Operational planning** is concerned with the details surrounding the processes and procedures necessary to achieve each goal and objective. Multiple projects are typically determined during the tactical planning process, and the managers assigned to each project are responsible for developing a specific project plan.

The nature of planning is constantly undergoing fundamental changes in organizations, given the dynamic nature of competitive external environments. Organizations recognize their planning windows are becoming smaller and acknowledge an increasing need to act quickly. Gone are the days were corporate strategic plans span multiple years; today, it is more likely that these plans will span a few months or one year at the most. The environments in which organizations operate in are characterized by dynamism and unpredictability, hence the longer the planning window, the greater the chance that the plans will not survive the future changes in the environment.

Traditionally, the planning process was done in a top-down manner by senior management and then passed down to lower level managers to execute. This was a common twentieth-century management practice; however, with rapid advances in transportation and communication, rapid globalization, accelerating innovation, and relentless competition, organizations have discovered that relying on top-down planning is risky. Organizations now understand that effective and efficient planning must be generated across the organizational hierarchies, involve as many stakeholder groups and voices as efficiently possible, and focus on aligning planning activities across functional, geographical, and hierarchical levels.

Top-Down versus Bottom-Up Approaches

As in other instances, the most effective approach often depends upon the context. A top-down approach is most appropriate for strategic and tactical planning such as setting the vision or goals. A bottom-up approach is more appropriate for brainstorming new ideas for products and services for the organization because they deal directly with customers and problems and often involve innovative ideas. While a top-down approach is better for strategic decisions like setting the overall vision, a bottom-up approach is often effective in determining goals and objectives because feedback from all levels of the organization can help in clearly defining the focus and measurements. It is important to remember that the most effective approach is not an either-or case, but instead a blend or hybrid of different methods. For example, crowdsourcing is viewed more as a bottom-up approach to finding solutions or ideas, but also involves a top-down approach because the overall goal or objective of the crowdsourcing effort is set by the organization. Once winning ideas or solutions are found, a manager needs to take responsibility and oversee the complete implementation and integration by the organization. Netflix established a $1 million prize in 2006 called the Netflix Prize, which gave teams three years to improve the company's recommendation algorithm for movies by at least 10 percent, and was awarded on September 21, 2009 (Netflix, 2006). Netflix's work does not end with the prize, as they still need to integrate the new algorithm into their own system and prepare for any situations that may occur when the solution is implemented.

Today, plans are seldom viewed as fixed or as a series of specifically defined rules or procedures. Rather, plans are used as frameworks to guide or steer the organization that can be altered when necessary. More emphasis is made on the process of planning as it is seen as a mechanism for creating consensus and focusing on broader strategies. While the exact path to reach the desired objectives may undergo revisions once the plan is implemented, the goals and objectives articulated by the plan will provide focus on the key success factors for the company. The Waterfall Model was a commonly used software development methodology involving a series of phases (requirements specification, design, and implementation) that required completion of one phase in order to move on to the next. This methodology was viewed as appropriate during a time when software development was maturing, and the business environment was not as dynamic as it is today. However, many organizations have come to realize that the Waterfall Model is insufficient for dealing with the rapid changes companies now experience. This new, volatile, and sometimes chaotic business environment has given rise to more "agile" methods designed to cope with the changing needs of projects and organizations. While the Waterfall Model emphasizes identifying all requirements and issues upfront, such as correcting errors in the early phases of a project, agile methods focus on coding quickly, identifying issues within the process, and fixing those issues before moving on. Agile methods understand that not everything can be accounted for and that unforeseen issues will arise during or after implementation. BT Group, a telecommunications company, began replacing its Unix-based phone-traffic monitoring system with a web-centric architecture in 2005 to allow traffic managers to make quicker changes to handle load more efficiently without overloading the system. Had they followed the Waterfall Model, the CIO of BT Group stated that it would have taken three to nine months for a third-party developer to gather specifications, 18 months for the development phase, and several more months afterward for software testing (Hoffman, 2008). Instead, the company was able to complete the entire project using its 90-day agile-development methodology. The decision to switch to such a project management ideology proved to be a key factor in the success of the project.

Organizing

Once the courses of action have been determined through the creating of strategic, tactical, and operational planning, the necessary resources must be secured in order to implement the actions outlined in the planning efforts. For instance, when cooking a meal, the recipe defines the necessary resources (ingredients) along with the steps necessary to create the final product. In this case, the recipe represents the plan. After deciding on which recipe to cook, it is necessary to identify what resources are currently available, and if any are missing, take the necessary steps to secure those resources. In this example, that would entail a trip to the grocery store. It is common that the organizations realize that the necessary resources such as technology or people are not available, in which case they must determine whether it is more efficient to continue with the plans through developing the resources in-house through research and development activities, or training new employees. Or, assuming they have the available capital, they may acquire the resources, such as buying or merging with another company that possesses the resources needed. For example, Hewlett Packard (HP) acquired ArcSight for $1.5 billion and stated that it "will enable the creation of a new type of security solution, one that serves the modern enterprise" (Rao, 2010), and also acquired 3PAR after a bidding war with Dell for $2.35 billion to "accelerate HP's Converged Infrastructure strategy and bolster [their] ability to provide customers with the industry's highest levels of performance, efficiency and reliability" (Hewlett-Packard, 2010). Organizations can also develop relationships with other organizations to share resources such as Apple's original contractual relationship with AT&T: AT&T

Crowdsourcing for Solutions

Solutions to complex problems are difficult to attain for many reasons such as budget constraints, insufficient knowledge, and incomplete information. Organizations can toil away trying to solve these problems and spend several million dollars, if not hundreds of millions, trying to find viable solutions or even new ideas. Crowdsourcing has proven to be an effective way of reaching beyond an organization's limitations by leveraging the knowledge and talent of others (e.g., customers, the public) to help fulfill an organization's need. Similar to the Netflix Prize, the X-Prize offers many competitions like the Progressive Automotive X-Prize: a $10 million competition for the best 100 MPG production-capable car. The X-Prize was created by the X-Prize Foundation, which uses prize philanthropy to organize resources and mobilize people to solve the grand challenges facing our world. Crowdsourcing differs from bottom-up communities, such as communities that build open-source software, because the work is managed by the organization to achieve a goal set by the organization. It is important to remember that leadership plays a critical role in the success of crowdsourcing efforts. In the case of Netflix, the chief product officer, Neil Hunt, was responsible for the Netflix Prize (Greenberg, 2009). RYZ, a small, high-end sneaker company in Portland, Oregon, has outside designers use RYZ's template to create new sneaker designs that are voted upon on RYZ's website with the winning design being produced, and the designer receiving $1,000 along with 1 percent royalties—an effort that founder and CEO Rob Langstaff says has allowed his company to move more quickly than more traditional methods at companies like Adidas (Kaufman, 2008).

agreed to sell Apple's iPhone on the AT&T network as long as they had an exclusive contract. This arrangement benefited both organizations with Apple revolutionizing the smartphone industry as it did the music industry with the iPod, and AT&T increasing its profit roughly 200 percent since it announced support for the iPhone in early 2007 (Siegler, 2010).

Mature communication processes are critical to promoting effective organization practices. Acquiring the right resources when they are needed, and getting them to where they are needed requires clear and consistent communication with those supplying and receiving, or reallocating, the resources. In the previously mentioned example of FedEx coping with severe winter weather, the regional manager was able to successfully deliver all packages during the Seattle snowstorm because of clear and consistent communication. His team was based in Portland, Oregon, and he and his eight-person staff implemented multiple daily conference calls with senior managers from each regional facility in order to share weather reports and details of truck arrival times (Girard, 2009). This allowed for better prioritization and organization of available resources, and translated into better service for the customers.

As organizations become globally distributed, there is a renewed focus on coordination. Managers need to communicate with and organize not only their local resources, but also resources in geographically diverse areas of the organization. The strategy behind the implementation of enterprise resource planning systems addressed this problem as companies required distributed systems to be integrated into one interoperating information system that would allow for effective coordination of their resources. Coordination also introduces the need to make changes to the span of control. Who is in charge of specific tasks and resources needs to be clearly communicated to everyone involved. However, it is important to avoid micromanaging as much as possible. While sometimes necessary, micromanaging can cause frustration and discontent among both the managers and the people being managed.

Organizational charts are the most common visual tools used to depict how employees are organized within the company structure. These charts also provide insight regarding the areas the organization considers important. A small or nonexistent R&D department can imply that the organization is not focused on the internal creation of knowledge and innovation. Similar to organizational charts, division of labor shows what capabilities people possess, and the division of responsibilities. Differing from organizational charts, division of labor schedules provide a more detailed view of the organizational structure, such as the different departments and the employees within this organization. They can also describe the goals and objectives of subgroups, including the employees who are assigned to perform tasks and responsible for achieving goals. Adam Smith argued that increasing the division of labor results in an increase in productivity (Smith, 2003). A single person working to accomplish a complex task may fail, but breaking the complex task into smaller, more manageable pieces allows for additional persons or groups to assist in accomplishing the task.

It is important to note that organizing should never be considered a one-time process, as internal and external changes will constantly affect the way an organization is structured. Uncontrollable events such as employees becoming ill or a natural disaster can require resources to be moved from one project to another or one location to a different one. Organizing must take place on an ongoing basis, and managers must continually optimize how the firm is organized. Organizations need to be able to demonstrate agility in how they move resources depending on changing conditions in their environments. This is a key requirement in being able to manage change and innovation. While the impact may vary, the act of reallocating resources causes many changes in the organization. Innovation requires the organization to be capable of distributing resources to new ventures, and to also have the foresight and plans in place to reorganize core aspects of the organization, including people and resources central to the organization's operations.

Controlling

Controlling, as part of managing within an organization, is not necessarily focused on directly controlling those being managed. Instead, it involves measuring, evaluating (benchmarking internally and externally), taking corrective action, and collecting feedback in order to better control operations and the outcomes they will produce. Clearly identifying authority, responsibility, and accountability is necessary for effective control. Authority is a manager's formal and legitimate right to make decisions, issue orders, and allocate resources to achieve desired outcomes for the organization. Responsibility refers to an employee's duty to perform assigned task or activities. Accountability allows those with authority and responsibility to report and justify task outcomes to those residing above them in the organizational hierarchy. While those being managed are responsible for the successful accomplishment of many of the tasks, the manager is the one who is ultimately held accountable for the overall success of the project. Measuring is set in place to ensure the right actions are occurring at differing levels of the organization. A traditional form of measurement would be tracking the hours of work completed. Milestones and requirements are also designed to place a level of control over projects and monitor the achievement of goals.

Evaluating is necessary to ensure that employees, teams, functional areas, and the organization as a whole are continuing to improve. It also illuminates the effectiveness and efficiency of current processes. For each process, a manager typically evaluates four aspects:

1. Effectiveness: Was the desired result produced?
2. Efficiency: Was it cost-effective?
3. Impact: What value was provided?
4. What best practices can be derived?

Management must constantly evaluate performance internally to determine if the performance observed is acceptable, and also to benchmark their progress against the competition. It is important that organizations evaluate themselves against their competition to identify strengths, weaknesses, opportunities, and threats (also known as a SWOT analysis).

When problems are identified, taking corrective action is necessary in order to make certain the desired outcome is achieved. These actions can be simple routines such as requesting an extension to the deadline due to unforeseen difficulties, or more difficult actions such as firing an employee for breach of contract. In any case, it is the manager's responsibility to identify the problem, recognize its cause, and take the necessary actions in solving it.

Collecting feedback involves gathering the perspectives of different stakeholders and creating new knowledge about the business environment. This knowledge can be compared to traditionally held opinions to identify any disconnects between different groups. Typically, the manager can derive the answers regarding the effectiveness, efficiency, impact, and best practices of a process by listening to people. The feedback from the other stakeholders involved is necessary in gaining a better understanding of the "big picture," and understanding how external people perceive the actions of an organization.

Guidelines, milestones, requirements, and schedules are tools in controlling business processes and projects. Much of these will be determined during the planning component and later implemented within specific projects and tasks. After-action reviews (AARs) are conducted following the end of the project to analyze exactly what occurred, why it happened, whether it was desirable, and what aspects of the project can be improved. These reviews are often used to build a culture of accountability. Performance reviews are also put in place to determine if employees are completing their work and operating at a satisfactory level. Incentives and rewards are used to promote desired behavior (Dixon, 2000).

There are two types of control associated with the management of organizations: output control and behavior control (Ouchi, 1978). Output control usually involves quantifiable measures set in place to control the outputs of behaviors. Sales quotas are an example of output control for sales teams. Behavior controls are more difficult because they are typically not quantifiable. Incentives and rewards are examples of tools used to control behavior. It should be noted that output control has an impact on behavior control. For better or worse, how sales quotas are set can affect the behavior of the sales team. If certain measures are not in place, people may do whatever it takes to meet their quotas, even at the expense of others.

Control can be exercised in a centralized or decentralized manner (Desouza and Awazu, 2006). Centralized control can be characterized by a tight structure, where the responsibility for decision making is normally restricted to a few individuals capable of top-down authority. Decentralized control is the reverse, where responsibility for managerial decision making is distributed amongst individuals across all levels of the organizational hierarchy. Which control mechanism an organization uses depends upon the context and the organization's individual characteristics. Within knowledge management, control mechanisms can be determined by three variables: the type of knowledge process, the type of knowledge workers, and type of knowledge being managed. Different control structures are appropriate for different types of knowledge processes. For example, the process of knowledge creation flourishes in a decentralized controlled environment, while the knowledge commercialization process is more efficient in a centralized controlled setting. Knowledge workers who apply knowledge in a standardized manner who excel under centrally controlled management, while those who use knowledge in a radical manner may demand responsibility and control to be distributed. Finally, public knowledge is effectively managed when knowledge is made available and accessible to all members of the organization. Bottom-up approaches to management assist in allowing the free flow of information within an organization. Private knowledge requires centralized controls as not all employees are allowed to access the knowledge, and its flow needs to be restricted within the organization due to security and privacy concerns.

Managing Digital Natives

Each new generation has grown up in a very different environment than the generation before them, which can influence many of the common values and behaviors that become viewed as characteristics of that generation. **Digital natives** (also called Generation Y or Millennials) refers to the next generation that has received much attention lately because they are the new workforce—which introduces change, and challenges, for management. For some, digital datives may be viewed as impatient, ungrateful, overly ambitious, and difficult to control when compared to other generations like Generation X or baby boomers. However, others have found that digital natives share common values and goals with baby boomers, such as making a positive contribution to society, achieving work-life balance through flexibility and remote working, and an increasing emphasis on intrinsic rewards over monetary rewards (Hewlett, Sherbin, and Sumberg, 2009). In managing digital natives, the focus is on conveying the value of the work being done as well as giving them the freedom in accomplish that work as opposed to telling them specifically how to work (i.e., micromanaging). Digital natives want their work to be engaging, or in other words, fun. To accomplish this, one manager holds occasional competitions with cash prizes, another comes to meetings dressed in different costumes, and one uses a marshmallow gun to shoot employees from time to time (Osteryoung, 2010). The managers enjoy themselves as well. The key point managers and leaders need to remember is that it is all about people. People are unique and diverse in their opinions and values, and this is true across all generations. Effective managers and leaders need to be able to work with people from diverse cultural and ethnic backgrounds—and digital natives are no different. As managers and leaders, it is important to remember not to be distracted by the label or surface value, but to dig deeper and understand the people with whom you are working.

Ensuring the correct incentives are in place is also important for managerial control. Bonuses are often used as rewards upon the successful completion of assigned objectives, but there are limitations to this form of incentive. Each individual is unique, and the incentives that work best for each person must be customized. For example, not everyone desires a monetary reward for a job well done. Some employees may covet a promotion, additional vacation time, or the opportunity to work on different projects. The manager must understand the motivations and needs of each individual and group. In terms of controlling, it is not about how you control people, but how you orchestrate the organization and its resources to the satisfaction of knowledge workers.

Leading

Management is doing things right; leadership is doing the right things.
—Peter Drucker

The most difficult component of management is leading people (Drucker, 2001). The ability to lead employees is not a trait commonly found in every individual, and is often a distinguishing factor for senior management. The difference between a leader and a manager is that a leader is one who inspires others to support the shared vision of the organization and take action. This is critical to what a leader does, including setting the overall vision and strategy, and hiring and retaining the very best talent for the company (Wilson, 2010). With leadership qualities such as the ability to motivate and inspire others, or getting them to believe and trust in an organization's strategy, a manager will be able to guide an organization to its desired state.

There are common traits found in good leaders. Upholding integrity and the values of the organization is vital. It is nearly impossible for executives who have lost the support of the organization to regain it. Mark Hurd, former CEO of HP, was forced to resign on August 6, 2010, after an investigation of sexual harassment charges revealed that he had tried to hide expense reports related to his relationship with a contractor (Carlson, 2010). Hurd achieved the lowest employee rating of any major technology CEO, with 34 percent, compared to Apple CEO Steve Jobs, who had an approval rating of 98 percent (Schonfeld, 2010). Other traits found in good leaders are optimism and confidence, which are critical especially during a crisis. Tim Westergren, who founded Pandora in 1999, was able to convince people to work on deferred salaries for over two years when the money ran out. He achieved this by displaying confidence in the potential success of Pandora's product, and in turn employees gained the same confidence (Wei, 2010). It is often the optimism and confidence exhibited by managers that draw talent to their startups. Managers need to command a certain amount of respect from people in order for employees to listen and follow a strategy or vision.

The organizational culture plays a profound role in shaping the organization, and the culture is almost always determined by the actions of senior management. The vision and mission statements developed by companies are often a reflection of the culture being set by the management team. Google also has a list of principles that guide the behavior of everyone in the organization, including the notorious "Don't be evil" principle. The policies set in place also reflect the existing culture and subcultures found in organizations.

The processes set in place to hire and retain the best talent are also a part of the organizational culture. Google is known for the "70/20/10 rule," which has employees spend 70 percent of their time on core tasks, 20 percent of their time on related tasks, and 10 percent of their time on anything they choose. Although it became well-known through Google, 3M was the company that pioneered this philosophy of giving employees freedom to pursue their ideas.

The manner in which organizations interact with stimulus outside their organization also reflects the values held by leaders. Product Red is a brand initiative that was started by Bono, lead singer of U2, and Bobby Shriver of DATA. Its goal is to raise money for the Global Fund to Fight Aids, Tuberculosis and Malaria. It has partnerships with several of the world's most iconic brands such as Starbucks and Apple, and each partner sells a product under the unique (RED) brand with 50 percent of the profits generated by the (RED) products going to the Global Fund. Warren Buffett and Bill Gates, two of the wealthiest people in the world, started the "Giving Pledge," which urged the richest people in the world to donate at least half of their fortunes to philanthropy (Blackburn, 2010).

As a leader, one must remember that although significant influence can be used over the organization, managing is more about leading, motivating, and encouraging employees residing at all levels to work effectively, efficiently, creatively, and successfully. The best leaders are the ones who lead by example, and serve those around them.

MANAGERS

Anyone who has responsibility over people and resources is a manager. Some managers are responsible for small groups, while others might be responsible for managing tens of thousands of people across multiple countries. Managers "manage" and are responsible for engaging in the acts of planning, organizing, leading, and controlling. Managers are given objectives and goals, and their ability to accomplish these measures is used to gauge their performance.

Management can reside at various levels due to different organizational structures, but typically they are on the front line, in middle management, or senior-management. Front-line managers are directly responsible for the production of goods and services, as well as supervision of clerical staff and floor employees. These managers deal with operations, and are more typically found in organizations with customer-facing operations such as stores. The managers found in Apple stores would be considered front-line managers. Middle management comprises managers who are in charge of specific departments or groups, or who serve as project managers. These managers are responsible for tactical operations, which involves implementing the strategy as presented by senior management. The senior-management is responsible for determining the strategy of various aspects of their organization. Vice presidents are considered part of senior management, and are usually in charge of entire divisions while reporting directly to the CEO and president. Managers at this level are focused more on strategy at the organizational level. As managers rise in the organization, they become less involved in daily operations and more involved in the art of strategizing, delegating, and responding to changes in the internal and external environments of the organization.

Most often managers are tested during times of uncertainty or difficulty, and these situations may determine a manager's reputation. Managers who are able to increase predictability, understanding, control, and compassion for their people will allow employees to accomplish the most in an emergency situation or crisis (Sutton, 2009). Predictability means providing people as much information as possible about what might happen in the future in order to reduce the shock of unexpected events. Understanding is when a manager explains why certain actions are being taken and requires communication, sometimes more than once. Control allows a manager to exercise authority over a situation and direct actions through their decisions. Being able to show compassion allows you to connect with the people, and will allow others to view you as someone they can trust and believe. Managers must also be able to empower their employees, not only by giving them new authority and responsibilities, but also by removing the barriers that prevent them from performing. These barriers are identified as the boss barrier, system barrier, and mind barrier (Kotter and Cohen, 2002). Managers create the boss barrier when actions and very words can prevent people from performing at their best. Subtle queues such as body language showing disinterest can cause employees to abandon their motivation and desire to work towards a solution to a problem. The system barrier refers to bureaucracy, which can tie the hands of employees who want to help. Performance evaluation and rewards can be the most difficult barriers as they tend to promote non-original approaches to thinking and knowledge creation, as opposed to innovative and creative ideas. The mind barrier needs to be removed to help people ignore their own predispositions by generating motivation and faith. Some people may feel intimidated by a task and could fail before they begin, despite being qualified and possessing the required knowledge, so the manager needs to be able to encourage and instill confidence in employees.

Knowledge Managers of the Organization

Kogut and Zander (1992) argue that the principal role of the organization is to integrate dispersed pockets of knowledge and to apply them toward organizational goal attainment. The people tasked with this very purpose are most prominently titled chief knowledge officers (CKOs), chief learning officers (CLOs), and chief privacy officers (CPOs) (Awazu and Desouza, 2004). Each of these officers has a different responsibility toward the knowledge assets of the organization.

CKOs are concerned with the transfer and flow of knowledge assets. To accomplish this, CKOs foster and develop social mechanisms that enable the exchange of information and knowledge. Organizations have come to recognize that interactions, both internal and external, play a critical role in generating innovation and new knowledge. Tools like intranets, videoconferencing, portable computing, Google Apps and salesforce chatter are fostering interactions and making collaboration among employees easier. Organizations also realize that external parties (such as customers) are capable of contributing to knowledge management, and they are taking a much more active role in managing knowledge for the benefit of the organization (Moon and Desouza, 2010).

CLOs are focused on helping the knowledge employees of the organization continue their learning through the acquisition of new skills and competencies. CLOs are responsible for assembling programs that foster the continued growth of their employees. Several companies like SnagAJob.com create "company universities" where in-house experts teach classes that employees take during the workday to continue their own learning (Buchanan, 2010). These types of programs not only improve the skills and competencies of the employees, which is an important advantage to organizations, but can also contribute to the employees' personal growth and help them achieve their own ambitions.

CPOs (or organizational security officers) are focused on protecting the organization's knowledge assets. They are responsible for implementing processes that prevent people without authorization from accessing sensitive or strategic information, and implementing rules and policies to prevent employees from abusing the data, information, and knowledge they possess. Google has run into serious privacy issues by providing confirmation that at least two engineers had breached internal privacy policies and accessed private accounts with one engineer using the account access to harass individuals (Kincaid, 2010). It is important to recognize that knowledge managers are not just employees who facilitate the exchange and creation of knowledge, but they also have a responsibility toward protecting knowledge (Desouza, 2007).

CURRENT TRENDS IN MANAGEMENT

Table 3.2 provides a summary of current trends in management.

Digital natives (also known as Millennials or Generation Y) are the new generation of corporate workers. A survey revealed that this generation shares a heightened sense of obligation to make a positive contribution to society and to the health of the planet, seek flexible working arrangements, value social connections, and prize other rewards of employment over monetary compensation (Hewlett, Sherbin and Sumberg, 2009). Unlike previous generations who have expressed loyalty to companies, digital natives have chosen to demand change or leave rather than "pay their dues." This has caused changes in management practices in order to cope with a new type of worker. Salesforce.com gives 1 percent of profits to its foundation, which pays for employees to volunteer 1 percent of their work time. Marc Benioff, CEO of Salesforce.com, states, "This program has dramatically increased our ability to recruit and retain high-quality employees" (Trunk, 2007). Other actions managers have taken include increasing communication since younger employees were raised receiving more feedback and

Table 3.2. Current Trends in Management	
Trend	**Description**
Digital natives	• Managers are adapting to changes in the workplace around the needs of younger workers (so-called Digital Natives or Millennials) who expect more frequent feedback and recognition, and more flexibility in the work environment, such as flexible work hours.
Retirement and knowledge retainment	• With retirement of the baby boom generation creating a significant demographic shift in the workplace, there are concerns around retaining their knowledge, especially tacit knowledge, which is integral to the organization.
Globalization	• With the globalization of the workplace, managers have an even greater need to listen to, learn from, and adapt to the needs of people with differing cultural backgrounds.
Project-based work	• With the rise in project-based work, project management offices (PMOs) will not only be critical in increasing the success of projects, but also in managing knowledge.
Design thinking	• Design thinking seeks to bring together intuitive thinking with analytical thinking in order to create innovation and value in organizations
Corporate social responsibility	• Corporations are increasingly seeking to show responsibility and accountability in their policies and actions around larger societal issues, such as protecting the environment.

recognition, changing policies such as the dress code to allow for more casual wear, and allowing options for more flexible working environments. The root of the challenge facing management, however, is not with digital natives, but with addressing the changing and various needs and desires of employees.

A major demographic impact beginning to affect corporations is the retirement of the baby boomers. However, the retirement of this older generation born after World War II presents a grave challenge for organizations—the knowledge lost when they leave the organization. For rapidly changing industries like information technology, knowledge related to specific technologies such as programming in COBOL will not have a significant impact on the organization unless the organization maintains legacy systems. However, the knowledge these workers have gained as they followed the trends in programming, learned how software is developed, and experienced the shift to new technologies can help to educate newer programmers and managers, and its loss will have a significant impact upon the organization's knowledge base.

Globalization continues to present challenges to managers as skills related to cross-cultural management become more important. As our world becomes more interconnected, organizations expand globally and distributed teams become more common, which results in more cultural diversity. Managers require capabilities to not only deal with people with differing cultural backgrounds, but also be able to adapt to being immersed in new cultures since their work can take them to multiple countries and varying cultural environments.

Evidence-based management is an approach to management that has drawn considerable attention from innovative organizations. "Evidence-based management entails managerial decisions and organizational practices informed by the best available scientific evidence.... Contemporary managers and management educators make limited use of the vast behavioral science evidence base relevant to effective management practice" (Rousseau and McCarthy, 2007: 84). The first principle behind evidence-based management is to view the organization and one's own knowledge as an unfinished prototype in order to take action and continue to learn more. The second principle is to focus on the facts, and remove biases, ego, opinions, or unproven notions from the decision-making equation. The third principle is encouraging managers to view themselves and their organizations the same way outsiders and external people do. The fourth principle is that evidence-based management should not be limited to the activities of senior executives. Everyone in an organization is involved in the success of the organization, thus everyone can contribute to improving quality and productivity, generating ideas, and designing experiments to test ideas. "[W]hen managers treat employees as if a big part of their job is to invent, find, test, and implement the best ideas, then managers make fewer mistakes, organizations learn more, and more innovation happens" (Pfeffer and Sutton, 2006: 35). The fifth principle is that leadership must take an active role in managing and encouraging all parts of the organization to accept this approach to management. The sixth principle is to slow the spread of unsuccessful practices if failure occurs on a regular basis. The seventh and final principle is to remember to ask the question "What happens when people fail?" Failure elicits fear in many people, yet without encouraging risk and helping people deal with failure, it is difficult for people to succeed and grow.

A rise in project-based work is occurring as the incoming generation of workers brings different expectations of what constitutes a corporate working environment. New entrants into the workplace are no longer viewing careers as long-term commitments to companies, but rather as a series of short-term projects that keep them interested and contribute to their own personal development (Melik, 2007). This presents an increased emphasis on the importance of managers and, in particular, project management offices (PMOs). IT projects are viewed as having a high failure rate, and much of its cause can be attributed to poor knowledge management that leads to mistakes being repeated. As the source of centralized integration and a repository of knowledge, a well-implemented PMO can resolve the most challenging project management issues by capturing and transferring knowledge, maximizing the power of cross-functional teams, regulating the demand of integrated technologies, and providing ownership and accountability for key efforts (Desouza and Evaristo, 2006). With the rise in project-based work, PMOs will be critical not only in increasing the success of projects, but also in managing knowledge.

Design thinking is receiving a lot of focus as a way of increasing an organization's ability to create value—or, in other words, be innovative. Roger Martin, dean of the Rotman School of Management at the University of Toronto, discusses two prevailing points of view on business: analytical thinking, which uses logic (deductive and inductive reasoning) to find answers through analysis (i.e. leveraging existing knowledge), and intuitive thinking, which relies on insight and creative thinking (i.e., exploration and invention) (Martin, 2009). These two points are seemingly at odds with each other, but Martin believes that both are necessary in order to truly create value because just one is insufficient—and this harmony is what he calls design thinking. Achieving a balance or harmony with extreme views (exploration and exploitation; reliability and validity) is a key aspect of design thinking. Martin offers five points in order to help develop as a design thinker (Martin, 2009: 168–177):

1. *Reframe extreme views as a creative challenge.* Most people are more inclined to one side of the spectrum—either reliability (consistency and predictability) or validity (producing a desired result). The design thinker needs to convey the value of each opposing view by finding ways to appeal to each point of view.

2. *Empathize with your colleagues on the extremes.* Just as a designer seeks to empathize with the user through user-centered design, the effective design thinker seeks to empathize with colleagues on different spectrums (analysis and intuition) to create a more productive, value-creating organizational context.

3. *Learn to speak the languages of both reliability and validity.* Similar to working in another country, it is necessary to learn the language in order to effectively communicate with each party. The best way to achieve this is by spending time with the people with whom you wish to work, in their environment.

4. *Put unfamiliar concepts in familiar terms.* Empathizing with the person you are addressing is critical to effectively conveying the value. If a person leans toward reliability, then repackage your argument in terms of reliability, and the same holds true with validity. Understanding the person you are dealing with is necessary to come up with an effective analogy.

5. *When it comes to proof, use size to your advantage.* Validity-type individuals like to explore and look to the future, which is something reliability-type individuals are uncomfortable with because the future is unknown. While validity-type individuals may want to jump ahead and address the future, it is necessary at times to scale back and create a small enough project that reliability-type individuals will be more inclined to while having a big enough project that allows for the innovation to still occur.

Tim Brown, CEO and president of IDEO, takes a different approach and conveys design thinking through its approach to achieving innovation. While most of the scientific management champions argue for a process made up of a sequence of steps, design thinking views innovation as an overlap of three spaces: "inspiration, the problem or opportunity that motivates the search for solutions; ideation, the process of generating, developing, and testing ideas; and implementation, the path that leads from the project room to the market. Projects may loop back through these spaces more than once as the team refines its ideas and explores new directions" (Brown, 2009: 16). Similar to Martin's view on design thinking, Brown also sees design thinkers as individuals who are able to bring a harmonious balance to various, sometimes opposing, factors.

Corporations are increasingly faced with the need to show how they are being socially responsible. A focus on corporate social responsibility has increased due to events such as the publicity brought on grand challenges facing our world like Al

---

Managing within Nonprofits and Government

Although concepts and ideas presented on management may sound like they apply only to corporations and for-profit organizations, this is not true. Any organization that wants to be effective in its mission (e.g., serving stakeholders, contributing towards progress in society, helping people) should practice sound management techniques in order to accomplish their goals.

Nonprofits and charities have very noble goals, yet limited resources to accomplish these goals. The more waste and inefficiencies they encounter, the fewer resources they have to serve their constituents or patrons. Any resources (time, money, etc.) saved by strong management can be reinvested or targeted towards providing new services or helping more people. Even though their ultimate goal is not to create a profit for owners, their ability to make a difference can be enhanced by the effective management of their strategy and operations.

Government and related government organizations are in a similar position to nonprofits and charities. They have limited resources that can be increased only through taxations or the expansion of government services, which are two options that are not favored by all citizens. Many voters judge government entities based on their accomplishments with respect to the resources they use. Therefore, a government will be regarded as responsible and effective by providing the most action with the least amount of resources, which ultimately come from the citizens of a country. Although policy leadership and strategic direction are often in the hands of elected officials, government managers who are tasked with realizing politicians' visions can work toward these visions through managing their departments in a manner that contributes to the overall goals of the government, and the expectations of the citizens and voters.

All organizations require leaders, strong management practices, sound decision-making processes, a clear and well-defined strategy, and the optimal allocation of resources in order to be successful. This holds true whether success is defined by profit, helping stakeholders, making a difference to society, or helping run and lead a country forward.

Gore's documentary *An Inconvenient Truth*, which focuses on global warming; the economic recession brought about largely by unsustainable financial practices; and environmental disasters like the Deepwater Horizon oil spill. These events have led to public outcry over corporations avoiding the responsibility they have to one of their most important shareholders—society. This has led many major corporations like Sony and Hasbro to create pages on their websites that specifically address how their corporations are being socially responsible (Goldner, 2010; Sony, 2010). Hasbro highlights three of its long-term commitments: (1) the environment: Hasbro has reduced the greenhouse gas emissions of its US operations by nearly half during the last seven years; (2) workplace conditions: it is one of the first toy companies to develop and implement a code of conduct for third party vendors; (3) community relations: the company has donated nearly $18 million to support children around the world. Sony highlights their "Road to Zero" program that aims to achieve a zero environmental footprint throughout the lifecycle of their products and business operations by the year 2050. Sony has embraced digital cinema as a step toward achieving its goal the technology helps reduce the CO_2 emissions generated from the packaging, distribution, projection, and disposal of conventional film.

CONCLUSION

Throughout the twentieth century, innovative organizations pioneered the principle that management should be treated like a discipline and a science. Common facets of management, such as planning, controlling, organizing, and leading, were accepted by the general population. Managers became important decision makers, strategic planners, leaders, human resource development officers, and motivators for organizations pursing a strategic vision. Now, in the twenty-first century, we see many shifts in management that are reflective of the changing economy and global business environment. New technologies and social networking applications have shifted the expectations of workers in terms of how they will communicate, relate to others in their organizations, and structure their work environment. A new generation of workers has emerged, with new priorities, values, and expectations that require new forms of management in order to create success within a people-centric organization. Although management techniques and frameworks will continue to change to keep pace with the rapidly changing environments and technologies that impact companies, the core constituents of management do not change—the people and employees within the organization and whom the organization serves.

DISCUSSION QUESTIONS

1. In your opinion, what makes a great manager? What criteria do you use to judge managers for whom you have worked?
2. What are the differences between a strategy, vision, mission statement, goals, and objectives? How are each used by various managers within an organization?

Recap: The Major Points for Knowledge Managers Regarding Management

1. No matter the type of organization (profit vs. nonprofit, government vs. corporate, small vs. large, regional vs. global), the fundamentals of management apply.
2. Much of management deals with the allocation of resources (financial, technological, or human), and the effective use of those resources.
3. Planning requires strong knowledge regarding the current state of the organization, and the ability to be forward thinking to define the future or desired state of the organization. A manager then develops a plan to bridge the gap between the two states.
4. Organizations can be managed from a top-down approach where executives and managers have great control over the direction of the organization, or from a bottom-up approach where responsibility and autonomy is granted to workers at all levels. The best approach for an organization fits with its structure, people, and culture.
5. Determining the metrics and procedures to evaluate the performance of an organization is an important part of how managers control the operations of a firm.
6. The ability to be flexible in management style is a great asset for any manager. Different approaches to managing vary in effectiveness with different types of people. Younger generations of workers respond differently to managers then older, more experienced workers.
7. Managers are not necessarily leaders, as leaders are those individuals (who may be situated at any level of the organization) who can define a direction, create consensus, and organize people to work towards a common goal.
8. Project-based management is very common for most organizations, as it is an approach to managing that takes on large problem or challenge and divides it into multiple smaller, more manageable pieces of work.
9. Design thinking is a management approach that combines analytical thinking and intuitive thinking to create value through new knowledge and innovation activities.
10. Although many traditional aspects of management that have become staples of business since the early twentieth century still apply today, it is important to reflect on the idea of management as new forces, dynamics, and technologies emerge.

---

3. Business has gone through many radical changes over the past decade. Identify some of these changes and what impact they have had on managers. How have managers adapted to meet the new demands of the organization and the business environment?
4. What is the difference between a manager and a leader, or are there any differences at all?
5. What types of people manage knowledge? Who is responsible for the overall management of knowledge within an organization, and how can they influence the entire organization's knowledge practices?
6. How can knowledge management be supportive of the activities performed by managers? When do managers require timely, relevant, and accurate knowledge? What are some of the sources of such knowledge?

REFERENCES

Associated Press. 2010. "Coast Guard Checks on Discolored Water Near LA." Yahoo! News, October 23. http://news.yahoo.com/s/ap/us_gulf_oil_spill.

Awazu, Y., and K. C. Desouza. 2004. "The Knowledge Chiefs: CKOs, CLOs, and CPOs." *European Management Journal* 22, no. 3: 339–344.

Blackburn, B. 2010. "The Giving Pledge: Billionaires Promise to Donate at Least Half Their Fortunes to Charity." ABC News, August 4. http://abcnews.go.com/WN/bill-gates-warren-buffett-organize-billionaire-giving-pledge/story?id=11325984.

Brown, T. 2009. *Change by Design*. New York: HarperCollins.

Buchanan, L. 2010. "Creating Your Own Company University." Inc.com, June 8. http://www.inc.com/top-workplaces/2010/creating-your-own-company-university.html.

Calamaio, C. 2010. "Selecting Montgomery County Library Books is a Balancing Act after Budget Cuts." Gazette.net, September 22. http://www.gazette.net/stories/09222010/bethnew 205421_32534.php.

Carlson, N. 2010. "HP CEO Mark Hurd Resigns After Sexual Harassment Accusations." Business Insider, August 6. http://www.businessinsider.com/hp-ceo-mark-hurd-resigns-over-sexual-harrassment-accusations-2010-8.

CNN. 2005. "'Can I Quit Now?' FEMA Chief Wrote as Katrina Raged." CNN.com, November 3. http://www.cnn.com/2005/US/11/03/brown.fema.emails/index.html.

Desouza, K. 2007. *Managing Knowledge Security: Strategies for Protecting Your Company's Intellectual Assets*. London: Kogan Page.

Desouza, K. C., and Y. Awazu. 2006. "Engaging Tensions of Knowledge Management Control." *Singapore Management Review* 28, no. 1: 1–13.

Desouza, K. C., and J. R. Evaristo. 2006. "Project Management Offices: A Case of Knowledge-Based Archetypes." *International Journal of Information Management* 26, no. 5: 414–423.

Dixon, N. M. 2000. *Common Knowledge: How Companies Thrive by Sharing What They Know*. Boston: Harvard Business School Press.

Drucker, P. F. 2001. *The Essential Drucker*. New York: HarperCollins Publishers.

Drucker, P. F. 2006. "What Executives Should Remember." *Harvard Business Review* 84, no. 2: 144–152.

Drucker, P. F., Jim Collins, Philip Kotler, Jim Kouzes, Judith Rodin, and V. Katsuri Rangan. 2008. *The Five Most Important Questions You Will Ever Ask About Your Organization*. San Francisco: Jossey-Bass.

Eichenwald, K. 2005. *Conspiracy of Fools*. New York: Broadway Books.

Girard, K. 2009. "What Went Right—and Wrong—in Three Real Cases of Uncertainty." BNET, May 4. http://www.bnet.com/article/what-went-right-and-wrong-in-three-real-cases-of-uncertainty/295107.

Goldner, B. 2010. "Corporate Social Responsibility." Hasbro. http://www.hasbro.com/corporate/corporate-social-responsibility/.

Greenberg, A. 2009. "The Netflix R&D Game." Forbes.com. September 21. http://www.forbes.com/2009/09/21/netflix-research-prize-technology-million-dollars.html.

Hewlett, S. A., L. Sherbin, and K. Sumberg. 2009. "How Gen Y & Boomers Will Reshape Your Agenda." *Harvard Business Review* 87: 71–76.

Hewlett-Packard. 2010. "HP to Acquire 3PAR." HP.com. September 2. http://www.hp.com/hpinfo/newsroom/press/2010/100902b.html.

Hoffman, T. 2008. "A Telco Giant Gets Agile: How BT Group Overcame Barriers to Agile Programming." *Computerworld* (April 28): 30–31.

Kaufman, W. 2008. "Crowd Sourcing Turns Business on Its Head." NPR, August 20. http://www.npr.org/templates/story/story.php?storyId=93495217.

Keese, S. 2010. "VPR News: Smokey House Center To Suspend Educational Programs." VPR (Vermont's NPR News Source). November 1. http://www.vpr.net/news_detail/89144/.

Kincaid, J. 2010. "Google Confirms That It Fired Engineer for Breaking Internal Privacy Policies." TechCrunch, September 14. http://techcrunch.com/2010/09/14/google-engineer-spying-fired/.

Kogut, B., and U. Zander. 1992. "Knowledge of the Firm: Combinative Capabilities and the Replication of Technology." *Organization Science* 3, no. 5: 383–397.

Kotter, J. P., and D. S. Cohen. 2002. *The Heart of Change: Real-Life Stories of How People Change Their Organizations.* Boston: Harvard Business School Press.

Martin, R. 2009. *The Design of Business.* Boston: Harvard Business Press.

McLean, B., and P. Elkind. 2003. *The Smartest Guys in the Room: The Amazing Rise and Scandalous Fall of Enron.* New York: Penguin.

Melik, R. 2007. "New Prescription: Adapt to Project-Based Work or Perish." *Machine Design*: 52.

Merle, R. 2005. "Boeing CEO Resigns Over Affair with Subordinate." *Washington Post*, March 8. http://www.washingtonpost.com/wp-dyn/articles/A13173-2005Mar7.html.

Mintzberg, H. 2009. "What Managers Really Do." *Wall Street Journal*, Business Insight Executive Briefing (interviewed by Martha E. Mangelsdorf), August 17. http://www.mintzberg.org/sites/default/files/mgrsreallydo.pdf.

Mintzberg, H., D. Raisinghami, and A. Theoret. 1976. "The Structure of 'Unstructured' Decision Process." *Administrative Science Quarterly* 21, no. 2: 246–275.

Moon, J. T., and K. C. Desouza. 2010. "Customer Managed Knowledge Factories." *Business Information Review* 27, no. 2: 94–100.

Netflix. 2006. "Netflix Prize: Home." Netflix. http://www.netflixprize.com//index.

Osteryoung, Jerry. 2010. "Managing Generation Y in IT." Inc.Tecnology.com. May. http://technology.inc.com/managing/articles/201005/osteryoung.html.

Ouchi, W G. 1978. "The Transmission of Control through Organizational Hierarchy." *Academy of Management Journal* 21, no. 2: 173–192.

Pfeffer, J., and R. I. Sutton. 2006. "Profiting from Evidence-Based Management." *Strategy & Leadership* 34, no. 2: 35–42.

Rao, L. 2010. "HP Continues Shopping Spree; Buys Security Software Company Arcsight For $1.5B In Cash." TechCrunchIT, September 13. http://www.techcrunchit.com/2010/09/13/hp-continues-shopping-spree-buys-security-software-company-arcsight-for-1-5-billion-in-cash/.

Rousseau, Denise M., and Sharon McCarthy. 2007. "Educating Managers from an Evidence-Based Perspective." *Academy of Management Learning & Education* 6, no. 1: 84–101.

Schonfeld, E. 2010. "Mark Hurd Had the Lowest Employee Approval Rating (34%) of Any Major Tech CEO." TechCrunch, August 10. http://techcrunch.com/2010/08/10/mark-hurd-lowest-approval/.

Shane, S. 2010. "After Failures, Government Officials Play Blame Game." *New York Times*, September 5. http://www.nytimes.com/2005/09/05/national/nationalspecial/05blame.html.

Siegler, M. G. 2010. "It's Hard to Feel Sorry for AT&T." TechCrunch, July 1. http://www.techcrunch.com/2010/07/19/att-iphone/.

Simon, H. A. 1991. "Bounded Rationality and Organizational Learning." *Organization Science* 2, no. 1: 125–134.

Simon, H. A. 1997. *Administrative Behaviour.* 4th ed. New York: The Free Press.

Smith, A. 2003. *The Wealth of Nations.* Bantam Classic ed. New York: Bantam Dell.

Sony. 2010. "Sony Global—Corporate Social Responsibility." Sony. http://www.sony.net/SonyInfo/csr/?j-short=csr.

Sutton, R. I. 2009. "How to Be a Good Boss in a Bad Economy." *Harvard Business Review* 87, no. 6: 42–50.

Trunk, P. 2007. "What Gen Y Really Wants." *Time Magazine*, July 5. http://www.time.com/time/magazine/article/0,9171,1640395,00.html.

Tversky, A., and D. Kahneman. 1974. "Judgement under Uncertainty: Heuristics and Biases." In *Judgement under Uncertainty: Heuristics and Biases*, edited by D. Kahneman, P. Slovic, and A. Tversky. Cambridge, UK: Cambridge University Press.

Valencia, J. 2010. "Roanoke Day Care Fixture Abruptly Closes Its Doors." *The Roanoke Times*, October 30. http://www.roanoke.com/news/roanoke/wb/265747.

Wei, W. 2010. "How Pandora Survived More Than 300 VC Rejections." *Business Insider*, July 14. http://www.businessinsider.com/pandora-vc-2010-7.

Williams, R. 2009. "Nonprofits Facing Money Woes Respond with Innovative Fundraising Strategies." Knoxnews.com, December 6. http://www.knoxnews.com/news/2009/dec/06/nonprofits-facing-money-woes/.

Wilson, F. 2010. "What A CEO Does." AVC.com, August 30. http://www.avc.com/a_vc/2010/08/what-a-ceo-does.html.

Yi, E., and P. Zhu. 2009. "Faced with Budget Cuts, Harvard College Library Consolidates." *The Harvard Crimson*, February 24. http://www.thecrimson.com/article/2009/2/24/faced-with-budget-cuts-harvard-college/.

Part II

Processes of Knowledge Management

4

Knowledge Creation

Scott Paquette and Kevin C. Desouza

OBJECTIVES

- Convey the criticality of knowledge creation to the competitiveness and viability of organizations.
- Describe how knowledge is created at the individual, group, and organizational levels.
- Examine important models of knowledge creation that describe the processes, technologies, and activities necessary to create knowledge.
- Discuss the role of technology in knowledge creation, including new and emerging technologies such as social media.
- Identify the barriers to knowledge creation, and discuss solutions for overcoming these individual, structural, and cultural challenges.

INTRODUCTION

Knowing is a social process. Individuals create knowledge through either their own personal activities or social interactions with others. **Knowledge creation** occurs throughout our daily activities, whether at work or in a more social, informal setting. Organizations thrive on our ability to learn new knowledge, be involved with new experiences, and collectively create new and innovative knowledge that can benefit both the organization and its customers.

The creation of knowledge occurs in many dynamic forms. Most often, it is through humanistic means, such as formal training, living through new experiences, or talking with people who share similar interests. Technical mechanisms also assist in the knowledge creation process, such as knowledge management systems, data warehousing, and data mining activities. Therefore, the significance of the employee and supporting knowledge technologies has grown substantially over recent decades. Organizations now live (and die) by their ability to create knowledge, innovate, and generate value with new knowledge. It can be knowledge that leads to new and innovative products, such as Apple leveraging its design and innovative knowledge to bring new and exciting products to market. It can be knowledge that improves internal processes and operations, such as Wal-Mart's position as a leader in logistics and supply chain information management, delivering products at lower costs than its competitors. Or it can be knowledge to improve the strategic decision-making capabilities and direction of the organization, such as General Electric determining what mix of businesses and markets to operate on a global scale, leading to a diverse conglomerate with operations range from manufacturing light bulbs to providing financial services. The ability to create knowledge and generate a competitive advantage is now essential for any organization that wishes to remain sustainable within its marketplace.

Libraries can serve as a locus of knowledge creation for individuals, organizations, and society. Libraries are currently facing the challenge of reduced usage of their services, including fewer print materials and a decrease in reference requests. Many point to the rise of readily available electronic materials as one factor contributing to this trend. However, libraries are not solely for the storage of books and other printed materials; they create a central communal space for a community and connect patrons with experts who can help them locate and acquire knowledge.

To highlight their role in the knowledge creation process, libraries are changing their strategies and physical layouts in order to serve the changing needs and demands of the public. They need to go beyond just providing a social setting for people, encouraging a sense of collaboration and productivity that fosters knowledge creation among individuals and groups. This is why many newly constructed libraries now focus on conference rooms, computer labs, seminar rooms, and even multimedia production centers. The innovative designs of libraries encourage people to act in a communal manner and create knowledge, which reflects a new role for the library in society (Gayton, 2008).

In a knowledge economy, it is essential that organizations continually create knowledge in order to improve their internal business processes, gain a better understanding of their environments, make effective decisions, create strategies that will move the organizations forward, and develop marketable products and services for their customers. To have value for the organization, any knowledge management initiative requires not only the identification of existing knowledge, but also the creation of new knowledge. Knowledge management tends to focus on knowledge creation because it is the key input to the process of managing knowledge.

This chapter will examine how individuals, groups, organizations, and communities create knowledge. A discussion of the differences in how knowledge is created through individual, collective, social, corporate, and technological activities will lead to a description of some important knowledge creation models. The role of technology in knowledge creation is discussed, including the emerging influence of social media technologies and data discovery techniques. The importance of knowledge creation for organizational activities, including innovation and new product development, is presented by examining recent research and ideas on the subject of creativity and its contribution towards knowledge creation. Finally, the barriers to knowledge creation are described, including possible solutions for both individuals and organizations.

INDIVIDUAL AND ORGANIZATIONAL KNOWLEDGE CREATION

Individual Knowledge Creation

People have always been considered central to knowledge creation, but this notion was popularized by Ikujiro Nonaka, who stated that "the prime movers in the process of organizational knowledge creation are the individual members of the organization" (Nonaka, 1994: 14). The act of creating knowledge can be both a conscious and an unconscious process. Much of the time we purposely create new knowledge when we write a paper, create a new method of doing work, or build a new piece of software. Many activities that occur at school or at work are purposely creating new knowledge for organizations and individuals. However, even when we are not intending to create new knowledge, we do so just by acting socially or interacting with our environment. For example, by participating in groups within a community, we are also learning about the culture, norms, and values that exist within the shared space that individuals within the community occupy. Therefore, what an individual learns in an organization is very much dependent on what is already known (or believed) by other members of the organization, and what kinds of information are present in the organizational environment (Nonaka and Takeuchi, 1995).

Unconscious Knowledge Creation

On many occasions we create knowledge without intention. Our minds are constantly taking in new information from the external environment and processing this information to create tacit knowledge for individuals. In other words, "we know more than we know," and this can lead to situations where we create new knowledge without trying.

For example, in 1864 the French chemist Louis Pasteur was working on developing a process that would prevent wine and beer from souring. Although an early solution to this problem was conceived in Japan in the mid-1500s, Pasteur stumbled on the modern version while conducting tests in his lab. However, in the process of reducing the souring of wine and beer, Pasteur realized he had also created a method to reduce microbial growth in food and liquids, especially milk. Utilizing this process, which was termed pasteurization after its founder, reduced the number of pathogens that could cause disease in milk and improved the lives of millions.

A similar situation when Dr. Spencer Silver, a chemist at the chemical giant 3M, developed a "low-tack," reusable adhesive when experimenting with new formulas for glue. Later, a colleague of his, Art Fry, used the formula to create adhesive bookmarks to mark pages in his hymnbook. Fry's application gained so much notice that in 1977 3M started marketing the product under the name Press 'N Peel, which we know today as Post-It Notes.

At an individual level, knowledge creation occurs through three key processes, depicted in Figure 4.1. These processes occur in repeated, iterative patterns, with each process capable of initiating the next (Mitchell and Nicholas, 2006). The first process is transmission, which develops a representation of what is known through the interpretation of received messages. This process relies on the receiver's tacit knowledge to help understand the environment. In cross-functional groups, this interpretation occurs when the meaning of words and phrases is investigated to create a meaningful message. An individual's ability to accurately interpret a colleague's message is dependent on the individual's ability to successfully apply his or her own experiential knowledge to the received content. For example, when introduced to a new working environment, an individual will spend a great deal of time initially determining the meaning of many local terms, learning how things work within the particular organization, and trying to gain an understanding of how his or her work fits into the bigger picture. The cognition process is the second step that involves both assimilating new knowledge and attempting to integrate it with other existing knowledge, and accommodation, where existing knowledge is altered or updated to integrate it with the new received knowledge. So continuing our example of new employees, they may have prior work experiences that they can bring to their new jobs, which will not only help them create a better understanding of the new environment, but enrich their knowledge by combining their old experiences with their new ones. Finally, task-focused positioning is where individual thought processes aimed at deciding strategies and tactics occur. As the understanding of issues related to their goal increases and individuals are able to integrate other perspectives with this knowledge, they use this new knowledge to prioritize activities, search for possible alliances and agreements, and locate opportunities for collaboration. Here is where new employees would take the new knowledge that they have created or combined with existing tacit knowledge and begin to create actions or new behaviors that leverage this new knowledge. The results of gaining the new knowledge are realized during this step.

Organizations can encourage knowledge creation at an individual level by ensuring three conditions exist. The first is encouraging intention, or generating a focus on knowledge creation. Intention deals with the conscious act of knowledge creation, where the result is a purposeful activity created after judging the value of the knowledge created. Second, knowledge workers thrive when they have some level of autonomy. Individuals have different intentions and different personalities, and this is very true with knowledge workers. Allowing for people to act autonomously will increase the possibility of creating not only intended knowledge, but also new and unexpected

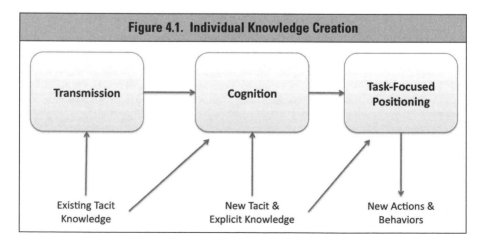

Figure 4.1. Individual Knowledge Creation

Transmission → Cognition → Task-Focused Positioning

Existing Tacit Knowledge   New Tacit & Explicit Knowledge   New Actions & Behaviors

knowledge. Autonomy allows for more flexibility in knowledge creation processes, but also for the development of motivation that gives individuals a sense of purpose when creating knowledge. Knowledge creation is an internal process, yet individuals must interact with their external environment in order for new knowledge to be developed. Third, fluctuations in the knowledge environment, including ambiguity, redundancy, and randomness, can stimulate a better understanding of the environment. This idea of creative chaos allows for breakdowns in generally accepted knowledge and encourages new perspectives, interpretations, and solutions (Smith and Paquette, 2010).

Individual Knowledge Creation: The Case of Radicals

An organization's ability to innovate and create new products is critical to its survival. This is especially true within the software development industry, where fierce competition with rapid innovation has encouraged software teams to be more collaborative and be aware of the knowledge that they are creating. They must identify, frame, and solve a problem through the development of new software in an efficient and timely manner. The problem-solving techniques now used within teams of developers are becoming more complex as the problems themselves become more complicated. New, radical engineering processes are used to allow individuals to break through traditional functional and organizational boundaries and use highly innovative processes to create the software. This may require more independence, extensive external contacts, the avoidance of internal politics, and a wider, more global scope than seen in previous management of software development. A less ordered and more chaotic regime will suit radical engineers and allow for them to create knowledge. Although traditional managers may find that these radical engineers are difficult to manage, they can be the driving force of knowledge creation within the software industry (Desouza, Awazu, and Kim, 2008).

Organizational Knowledge Creation

According to the knowledge-based view of the firm, an organization's ability to create knowledge is a key factor in maintaining its competitive advantage (Conner and Prahalad, 1996). **Organizational knowledge** comprises the sum total of knowledge residing in individuals or the social collective. Knowledge creation refers to the organizational processes that develop new knowledge or replace existing knowledge within an organization's knowledge repository; it encompasses activities such as new product development, business process design, skill development, and other innovative activities (Alavi and Tiwana, 2002). The knowledge materializes as product and services designs, business processes, working skills, and other organizational capabilities. Organizational knowledge creation occurs at both formal and informal levels.

At the organizational level, knowledge creation is enabled through the use of four knowledge processes (Brown and Duguid, 2001), depicted in Figure 4.2. Initially, the *accumulation* process involves all the combined individual inputs of knowledge that are theoretically available to everyone. The idea of accumulation is extended retrospectively to include the development of knowledge within the individual members' originating functional area or community of practice. Through extended in-depth interaction and shared practice, members of the same functional area or community have similar experiences and interpret those experiences similarly. These shared

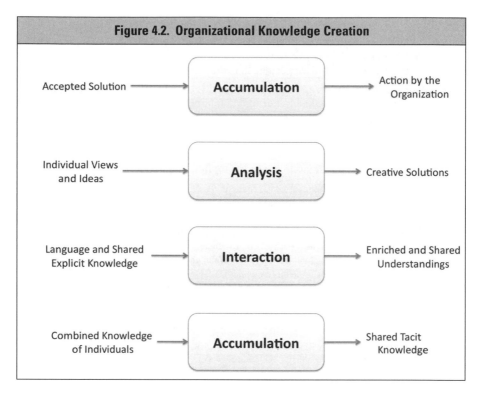

Figure 4.2. Organizational Knowledge Creation

experiences lead to the development of shared tacit knowledge. For example, in connecting individuals from various functional areas (in the form of cross-functional teams), new knowledge can be created that transcends the functional boundary. Many organizations employ brainstorming exercises to encourage the sharing of existing knowledge that is possessed by individuals. Secondly, within teams, *interaction* occurs when the use of language and other symbols are created to develop enriched and shared understanding. Interaction incorporates a desire to evolve deeper and shared understandings between members with different backgrounds operate from different perspectives underpinned by distinct cognitive structures due to their different work-related experience. Effective interaction relies on, and may be thwarted by, the ability to interact across the cognitive boundaries that underlie individual and group differences. Many groups working together not only establish a shared set of norms and routines, but also a shared syntax or list of terms that is understood by the group and used to represent their knowledge.

During the *analysis* process, group members debate points of view, assumptions, and the merits of possible solutions. The group's analytical discussion impacts individual analytical processes by highlighting certain pieces of knowledge, drawing attention to faulty logic, and presenting arguments in support of particular conclusions. Such reasoning facilitates creative solutions as it allows group members to link their inventory of past experiences to the current situation. By bringing together members from diverse backgrounds, group analytical reasoning has the potential to result in the application of a broader variety of experiences and knowledge than would be available to individuals operating alone. While the source of information regarding a previous problem or solution is the individual, the invocation, negotiation and manipulation of this information occurs through group interactions. Finally, *integration and creation* occurs when members create and accept the articulation of an agreed position or solution that integrates the best knowledge available. Here is where the activities of the group are finalized, made explicit so other members of the organization can understand them, and integrated with other organizational processes.

In summary, these four organizational knowledge creation processes attempt to accomplish two tasks when creating knowledge. They allow for individuals to convert their internal, tacit knowledge to explicit knowledge. Explicit knowledge can be more readily shared amongst individuals and can become more pervasive throughout the organization. They also attempt to move knowledge from an individual level to group, organizational, or interorganizational levels through facilitating collective knowledge creation activities that combine multiple individuals' knowledge into new knowledge.

Knowledge creation is essential for many organizational activities, including the gathering of competitive intelligence. In order to gain knowledge on the industry and an organization's direct competitors, it must continually acquire new knowledge that reflects a changing and dynamic business environment. Many sources of competitive knowledge are publicly available and easily accessible by any organization. However, it takes mature knowledge processes to identify, gather, and analyze such information in order to create valuable knowledge that can be used by decision makers to create strategies based on the activities and actions of competitors. Most organizations begin their competitive intelligence activities by mining information sources such as news releases, trade publications, news media, and social media sources that may contain information on competitors. Next, they sift through the information collected and search for information that can be combined with knowledge on the marketplace to predict the actions of other organizations. This action has become a large endeavor based on the volume of information that is available through the Web. Through the continual scanning and gathering of information on the external environment, an organization can become knowledgeable about its competitors and the industry in order to formulate strategies that will help it succeed in creating competitive advantages over other organizations. The value of external competitive information can be realized by establishing processes that acquire competitive information and transform it into knowledge of the business environment.

Organizations can participate in multiple activities that result in the creation of knowledge. They can acquire new knowledge by acquiring the source of the knowledge. The source can be either an individual capable of creating valuable knowledge, or an entire organization that possesses the desired knowledge. This acquisition comes with the challenge of integrating the new knowledge into the existing organizational knowledge so that it contributes toward new knowledge creation. Management, trust, structural, and cultural factors must be considered when deciding on acquiring others with knowledge. In some circumstances it may be a better solution to only rent the knowledge for a certain period of time and avoid any long-term commitments. Organizations do this by hiring consultants who bring with them new knowledge, or they can partner

---

Organizational Knowledge Creation

Singapore Airlines is one of the most successful airlines in Asia based on both financial performance and service delivery. Its business strategy focuses on innovation and new knowledge creation, which is reflected in its recognition as Asia's Most Admired Knowledge Enterprise. The development of mature knowledge management processes that drive innovation have led to the organization as a whole valuing innovation that can improve its business and service.

Singapore Airlines has developed methods to harvest knowledge from a diverse group of stakeholders, and has partnered with IBM to provide more in-flight services that lead to better knowledge of its customers. The airline tests many new service offerings that are both technology and nontechnology based to determine which ones can set it apart from its competitors. This strategy is based on the idea of collaborative knowledge creation, which identifies symbiotic knowledge creation opportunities and combines knowledge from a diverse group of industries, organizations, and people. Singapore Airlines has invested heavily in technology to create a networked community that can build relationships between people and facilitate knowledge sharing that leads to new knowledge. This organization has openly recognized that the center of its KM strategy is its people, who are the intelligent agents that drive the company's knowledge creation. Training, education, and retention of the best people contribute toward organizational learning and the use of knowledge to improve how they do business. Bottom-up knowledge processes, including employee initiatives, are the foundation of knowledge projects, and often new ideas which come from low levels of the organization are quickly accepted and supported by upper management. Singapore Airlines has integrated knowledge creation into its corporate strategy, and through a focus on networking and improving their people, they have energized their organization through creating new knowledge to improve their business and customer service (Goh, 2005).

---

with universities to fund research by knowledgeable scientists who will create and share new knowledge. The organization must address the important question of how it can retain the knowledge once the rented individuals leave the project. Knowledge absorption and retention processes will help capture and retain the new knowledge.

Organizations that place a very high value on the creation of new resources will have dedicated resources whose sole purpose is to create new knowledge and ideas. This solution has been used quite extensively for many years by companies such as Xerox (in the form of PARC), Microsoft (in the form of the company's research division), and even McDonald's (in the form of McDonald's University). Usually this option is reserved for larger organizations that have the ability to wait many years to realize the return on this financial intensive investment. Organizations that use dedicated resources must realize that this option does segregate many of the knowledge creation activities from the regular business, and an additional effort will be required to incorporate the generated new knowledge into the rest of the business.

In fact, it is very important for all organizations to merge, or fuse, knowledge creation activities with other knowledge and business processes. By bringing a diverse set of people together with unique knowledge and experiences, they have the ability to encourage the creation of innovative knowledge. Organizations such as Toyota are renowned for their rotation and mentorship programs that give the opportunity for many of their employees to work with and reside in departments outside their core knowledge area. New knowledge is formed from the synthesis of heterogeneous groups, creating value for the entire organization.

Adaptation is a strategy that is used by organizations for creating knowledge yet trying to keep up with a dynamic environment. Changes in the external business or market environment require new products and services, processes, and strategies. Organizations must resist the temptation to stay on a familiar and successful path, and instead be innovative in their decisions. This is often referred to the "if it's not broken, break it and fix it" strategy: organizations avoid complacency by making changes based on newly developed knowledge. The idea of adaptation requires the internal processes of an organization to be very flexible and easily changed based on what is learned from knowledge activities.

MODELS OF KNOWLEDGE CREATION

Nonaka's SECI Model

Nonaka's view of knowledge creation involves the transformation of knowledge between tacit and explicit knowledge (Nonaka and Takeuchi, 1995). He argues that in order to create new knowledge, individuals in organizations take existing knowledge and change it into a new form of knowledge. This model describes four types of knowledge transformations (see Figure 4.3): socialization, externalization, internalization, and combination.

Socialization is where tacit knowledge is converted into new tacit knowledge. This occurs mainly in social settings where experience is shared with individuals, and through these experiences new tacit knowledge is created. For example, when trade

Figure 4.3. The SECI Model

	Tacit Knowledge **TO**	Explicit Knowledge
Tacit Knowledge	**Socialization**	**Externalization**
FROM Explicit Knowledge	**Internalization**	**Combination**

professions such as electricians and plumbers train new employees, they use an apprenticeship model where the new employees shadow a more experienced one. Through their observation and eventual participation in the work, trainees receive tacit knowledge from the experienced worker and create their own tacit knowledge regarding the work and the profession. **Externalization** is where tacit knowledge is codified into an explicit knowledge form in order for it to be shared with others. Quite often when experienced employees are leaving their jobs, they are asked to document not only their procedures and role, but also other important facets of knowledge. This practice of externalization allows tacit knowledge to be transferred, allowing other employees to create their own knowledge. Externalization is a challenging procedure because most forms of tacit knowledge are difficult to convert and codify. **Internalization** occurs when an explicit knowledge transfer leads to the development of new tacit knowledge. For example, when reading messages posted to an online discussion forum, people not only receive the explicit knowledge codified within those messages, but also create their own tacit knowledge based on their impressions of the messages, who replies and how the replies are worded, what is commonly accepted by the members, and what hierarchy of leadership exists within the community. Finally, **combination** is where two objects of explicit knowledge are merged to create a new piece of knowledge. The reading of scholarly materials in order to write a new, original piece on the subject is an example of codification.

Nonaka has also developed two further concepts that along with the SECI model contribute towards an understanding of knowledge creation. The first is **ba**, which describes a shared physical, virtual, or mental space for individual relationships to converge in order to create knowledge. Ba serves as an area where the exchange and formation of new ideas is encouraged, and allows individuals to interact with other individuals and the environment. A second important factor in knowledge creation is the existence of knowledge leadership that provides the vision for all knowledge creation tasks. The job of knowledge leadership is to define and continually redefine the organization's knowledge assets in order to keep them aligned with the knowledge vision. They form, energize, and connect the various ba within the organization, and promote the activities surrounding the SECI model to enable knowledge creation processes. Like many corporate initiatives, leadership is a foundational element in knowledge creation activities (Nonaka and Konno, 1998).

The Herbert Simon Model of Problem Solving

This model of knowledge creation recognizes that problem solving often requires new knowledge in order to effectively and efficiently solve a problem. In this framework, knowledge creation occurs within three phases: problem recognition, idea generation, and solution selection (Simon, 1976). It begins from the recognition of a new or unique problem, where the complexity of the problem determines the organization and governance of activities involved in solving the problem (Nickerson and Zenger, 2004). Idea generation is the proposition of developing alternative solutions to the problem, which in some cases may be created from new knowledge. Finally, solution selection is the judgment and selection of the alternative that the organization perceives will best solve the problem. Each phase contains multiple activities through which new knowledge is created. This activity-based, goal-driven framework has been applied to various types of organizational knowledge creation, including new product development, process improvement, and systems development. Many of these activities are described in the sidebar example on Shell Oil, Inc.

Example: Shell Oil

Shell is an oil company of Dutch-British origin. The organization is divided among the three basic businesses of oil, chemicals, and exploration and production (E&P). The E&P division has 30,000 employees, of which about 70 percent are members of some kind of network. In 1998 Shell contained many small working groups comprised of 20 to 300 members. The groups were mostly informal in origin, with little structure or facilitation. In 1999, the small groups were combined into global networks called Communities of Practice. These new groups were quite large and had a formal position in the organizational structure. In E&P, the communities can be found on the issues of subsurface, surface, and wells. Each community has 1,500 to 2000 members. Smaller communities are dealing with issues of knowledge sharing, competitive intelligence, and HR aspects. The communities have "hub co-coordinators" for facilitation. They meet with other co-coordinators every three to four months. They are responsible for the coordination of all activities within the various communities.

The role of most communities is limited to daily problem solving. They serve mainly as a source of information for those members who have a problem in their work and seek the expertise of colleagues to solve this problem. Embryonic subgroups may form for a short time, discussing a specific issue. Members do not meet face to face, but send their questions and reactions via a simple discussion list facility. This means that the learning that takes place is single-loop learning, rather than double-loop, innovative learning. However, the department responsible for working standards regularly analyzes the emails to find elements that may be turned into standards. In this way shared knowledge is turned into organizational knowledge.

Problem solving generally relies on a selective search through large sets of possibilities, using rules of thumb (heuristics) to guide the search. As it would be impossible to capture a complete set of knowledge regarding the outcomes or impacts of the decision, decision makers rely on **satisficing**, or the search for alternatives until one is found that is "good enough." Therefore, knowledge is created until it is determined an acceptable solution has been created. Because realistic problem situations have a multitude of possible solutions, trial-and-error search would simply not work; the search must be highly selective.

Problem solving relies on large amounts of information that are stored in memory and that are retrieved whenever the individual recognizes cues signaling its relevance. For example, the expert knowledge of a doctor is evoked by the symptoms presented by the patient; this knowledge leads to the recollection of what additional information is needed to distinguish among alternative diseases and, finally, knowledge concerning the diagnosis is created.

One of the accomplishments of the contemporary theory of problem solving has been to provide an explanation for the phenomena of intuition and judgment frequently seen in experts' behavior. The store of expert knowledge, "indexed" by the recognition cues that make it accessible and combined with some basic inferential capabilities (perhaps in the form of means-ends analysis), accounts for the ability of experts to find satisfactory solutions for difficult problems, and sometimes to find them almost instantaneously. Being able to retrieve this tacit knowledge and combine it with either new tacit or explicit knowledge is an important factor in an individual's ability to form new knowledge.

The OODA Knowledge Creation Loop

The OODA loop (for observe, orient, decide, and act) is a concept originally applied to the combat operations process in military operations. Created by Colonel John Boyd, it arose as a concept in military strategy by analyzing the cognitive processes used by fighter pilots during air battles in order to understand what information they were using and gathering in order to defeat an opponent. However, Boyd later extended his ideas to larger aspects of military strategy, including historical battles fought by Napoleon and T. E. Lawrence. In this model, knowledge is created by the process of decision making within the mind of the individual, and therefore the organization. By accelerating the four stages of the loop, the organization can enable knowledge creation and gain competitive advantage.

The OODA loop's first phase is observation, where the learner simply observes the external variables that can include new information as a result of interactions with colleagues. These observations will feed into the cognitive activities in the next phase. Orientation occurs after taking note of the information in the environment. The individual analyzes the new information by including previous knowledge regarding norms, cultures, and traditions and tries to connect them to form a consistent foundation of knowledge. In the decision stage, the individual has developed a significant understanding regarding the new information and has to decide whether the newly created knowledge will be used or discarded. If the individual chooses to discard the new information, the process reverts back to the observation stage and the knowledge creation process starts again. Alternately, after deciding to accept the new information and create new knowledge, the individual quickly moves to put the new knowledge into action by creating and sharing the new source of knowledge with others in the organization (Brehmer, 2005).

Boyd determined that during battle, a soldier or pilot would continually loop through these stages in order to assess the situation and make decisions. For example, a pilot is constantly observing an enemy during a very dynamic and fast paced time period, while creating knowledge on the movement of the enemy, what it means, and how these actions fit into the overall battle. The decision to respond is created and then the appropriate action is taken. Sometimes, actions are used to confuse the opponent and eventually gain an advantage. During a typical air battle, a pilot goes through this cycle dozens of times in order to reassess the ever-changing nature of a battlefield.

The 7C Model for Organizational Knowledge Creation

The 7C model was developed as an extension of Nonaka's ideas of knowledge creation to emphasize the mostly tacit nature of knowledge, and the role that technology plays in the creation process. This model examines knowledge artifacts and how they become integrated in order for an individual to create new knowledge. In this model, it is important to note that knowledge creation is not viewed as a linear process, but rather a cycle that that flows through both the individual and organizational levels of the organization (Oinas-Kukkonen, 2005). In the model, the 7 Cs are composed of the following processes:

- *Comprehension*: Comprehension is the process of surveying and interacting with the external environment, and integrating the resulting intelligence with other existing project knowledge on an ongoing basis. The goal is to identify problems, needs, and opportunities through activities that create a learning experience.
- *Communication*: Communication is a process of sharing experiences between people and thereby creating tacit knowledge in the form of mental models and technical skills. This phase produces dialog records that emphasize the needs and opportunities, integrating the dialog along with resulting decisions with other project knowledge on an ongoing basis. At this stage, the learner gains new knowledge through communication with other people which results in the creation of the tacit knowledge that can now be transferred to others.
- *Conceptualization*: Conceptualization is a collective reflection process articulating tacit knowledge to form explicit concepts and systemizing the concepts into a knowledge system. in this stage, a project team produces knowledge products that form a comprehensive picture of the project and are iteratively and collaboratively developed. These knowledge artifacts may include proposals, specifications, descriptions, work breakdown structures, milestones, timelines, staffing, facility requirements, and budgets. Individuals now create their own knowledge artifacts, thereby converting their developed tacit knowledge into explicit knowledge. The learners can effectively express their tacit knowledge in a codified explicit form.
- *Collaboration*: With the newly created explicit knowledge, individuals are ready to work collaboratively in assembling the conceptualized knowledge using teamwork and demonstrating the value of new knowledge. The collective intelligence of the group is reflected in the newly created knowledge, which can be both visible and transferable to other individuals or groups. An example of this is illustrated in the example describing communities of practice at Unilever (see sidebar).

A summary of the knowledge creation frameworks discussed in this section appears in Table 4.1.

Table 4.1. Summary of Knowledge Creation Frameworks	
Knowledge Creation Framework	**Components**
Nonaka's SECI model	• Socialization • Externalization • Combination • Internalization
Simon's model of problem solving	• Recognition • Idea generation • Solution selection
OODA knowledge creation loop	• Observation • Orientation • Decision • Action
7C model for organizational knowledge creation	• Comprehension • Communication • Conceptualization • Collaboration

---

Example: Unilever

At Unilever, the Knowledge Mapping and Structuring Unit has begun initiatives such as "Knowledge Workshops" and "Communities of Practice" (CoPs) to enhance the efficiency of production and to improve innovative processes. In these initiatives, both knowledge exchange and knowledge creation processes play an important role. The first knowledge workshop was organized when the company faced problems in the processing of ketchup. Many experts concerning the production of ketchup were brought together. An unforeseen phenomenon occurred where the workshop gave birth to a community of experts, which was later called a "community of practice." Today, the communities of practice at Unilever concentrate mostly around certain production processes (e.g., of margarine and ketchup), but CoPs can also be found concerning principles of supply chain management and quality norms. Communities are set up through a formal process in which a "champion" is engaged and together with the champion, 10 to 20 employees are carefully selected and asked to join the community as representatives of their departments. Through this process, the CoPs become homogeneous groups of experts in a certain field. The experts are brought together for a weeklong workshop to exchange information, organize the group, and do team building. A facilitator coordinates the group activities, with the help of a handbook that is developed by the corporate Knowledge Structuring and Mapping Unit. The group is expected to communicate continually, but in actual practice the most intensive communication occurs during and around face-to-face meetings once or twice a year.

TECHNOLOGY-SUPPORTED KNOWLEDGE CREATION

Although technology is not a necessary ingredient for knowledge creation, most organizations have realized that strategically implementing knowledge management systems that support knowledge creation activities can have a positive effect on innovation and creativity (Paquette and Moffat, 2005). Human processes that support knowledge management within an organization can utilize the capabilities of knowledge management systems to help identify and connect people with similar knowledge interests, provide access to business data and information, and assist in creating new knowledge from this information.

The Impact of Social Networking

Digital social networks are gaining increasing importance for many people's work and leisure. This computer-mediated communication has become very popular with social sites like MySpace, Twitter, and Facebook, media sites like Flickr and YouTube, and wiki sites like Wikipedia. The term **Web 2.0** is also used to describe this type of interactive content. Although these systems are characterized by the large amounts of available content, their value to individuals is increased because they change the way the content and knowledge are created. With social media, users are not merely consumers of content but are transformed into content and knowledge creators.

A **wiki** is a website that can be edited by many people, often at the same time. Combining wikis and semantic web technologies is considered as a promising alternative for collaboratively creating and using knowledge. The user-friendliness of wikis for managing multisite content generation and the power of semantic technologies for organizing and retrieving knowledge may complement one another toward a new generation of web-based content management systems. Semantic wikis provide an original and operational infrastructure for efficiently combining semantic technologies and collaborative design activities. A semantic wiki can be seen as a wiki including an associated ontology, or an operational representation model of domain knowledge, that can be used for annotating the content of wiki pages and used for typing hyperlinks and testing consistency of contents.

A weblog, more commonly referred to as a **blog**, is a type of website that is usually maintained by an individual with regular entries of commentary, descriptions of events, or other multimedia material such as graphics or video. Blogs are perhaps the most significant recent movement in end-user knowledge creation on the web. Unlike earlier mechanisms for spreading information at the grassroots level, weblogs are open to frequent widespread observation, and thus offer an inexpensive opportunity to capture large volumes of knowledge creation at the individual level.

Technology-Facilitated Knowledge Creation

Communication and knowledge sharing within organizations can be relatively straightforward because there are few organizational and structural boundaries to cross. However, knowledge sharing within a large profession can be challenging, since knowledge must travel between many organizations and across great distances. Many librarians, who may work in only one library and have a limited number of colleagues, have taken to using blogs as a means for sharing knowledge of the practice.

Blogs allow for easy publication of thoughts, experiences, or opinions to a wide audience of readers. They are simple to set up and update, and allow for people of various technical abilities to share their ideas and knowledge with others. Librarians have embraced the use of blogs to communicate with others in order to grow their shared profession. These blogs are often filled with descriptions of experiences faced on the job, which allow for the librarian to transfer tacit knowledge gained through the course of working with others. New ideas and trends in libraries and services are described, including what can go right and wrong with implementing changes to the services patrons expect. Specific blog posts can include serving different groups of patrons, building the library as part of a community, and challenges faced when addressing a reference question. They span many types of libraries, including academic, public, government, and corporate libraries, which allows for the education of librarians on different environments and situations that may apply to their work. Often, a problem is presented, and the readers have the opportunity to comment and give advice on how the librarian could solve the problem. Blogs serve as a means for librarians to not only share their knowledge and ideas, but also to create a conversation that can enrich their experience in the profession (Kraft, 2006).

Microblogging, a relatively new phenomenon, lets users share brief text updates (usually fewer than 200 characters) via text messaging, instant messaging, e-mail, or the web. It is provided by several services including Twitter, Jaiku, and more recently Pownce. These tools provide a lightweight, easy form of communication that enables users to broadcast and share information about their activities, opinions, and status. Compared to regular blogging, microblogging fulfills a need for an even faster mode of communication. By encouraging shorter posts, it lowers users' requirements of time and thought investment for knowledge creation, one of its main differentiating factors from blogging in general. A second important difference is the frequency of updates. On average, a blogger may update a blog once every few days; a microblogger may post several updates in a single day. Twitter allows a user, A, to follow updates from other members who are added as friends. An individual who is not a friend of User A but follows her updates is known as a follower. Thus friendships can either be reciprocated or one-way. Several types of knowledge that can be created using Twitter:

- *Daily chatter*: Most posts on Twitter talk about daily routine and what activities people are engaged in. Friends or followers can reply to the author of the chatter, thus adding more information or knowledge through a conversation.
- *Sharing information*: Many posts on Twitter contain a URL that directs friends and followers to sources of information such as blogs or other websites of interest.
- *Reporting news*: Many users report latest news or comment about current events on Twitter. Some automated users or agents post updates like weather reports and new stories from RSS feeds.

Not long ago an individual web user was just a user, creating and collecting content accessible to others only if he or she was willing to create, host, and maintain webpages. Web 2.0 gives power to the users by providing services that allow them to create, collect, organize, connect, and share content without much effort or prior knowledge. Collaborative tagging is a process by which users of a web service add natural language keywords to commonly available information resources, thus organizing them and creating personalized collections of these resources specific to each user. Each user's personal collection created in this manner is made available to every other user of the service. The fact that more users have usually tagged the same resource allows for drawing connections between various users' collections and mutually tagged resources. It supports knowledge discovery, tag suggestion, and insight into resource popularity and interests and trends of users and communities.

The use of social media has been growing at an increasing pace. In July 2010, Twitter announced that it had published 20 billion posts, only two months after it had reached the 15 billion mark and five months after it surpassed 10 billion posts (Ostrow, 2010). Facebook, which launched in 2004, reached the milestone of 500 million users in July 2010; it had grown by 100 million users in the previous five months. One year earlier, its total user population was approximately 200 million (Axon, 2010). Much of this use can be attributed to organizations, which now use social media as a means to connecting with their customers and gaining their valuable knowledge (Paquette and Choo, 2008). Companies use Twitter in order to monitor online trends and discussions, find specific comments on their products and services, and respond to any problems that are mentioned online. Others use tools such as Facebook to build their online presence, communicate messages that are more difficult over traditional channels, and allow customers to talk to other customers as part of community building. Not only are the obvious marketing strategies being used, but organizations are also finding that social media is an effective tool to learn from customers and gain their knowledge about products and the marketplace.

Data Warehousing

Data warehousing is a collection of decision support technologies, aimed at enabling the knowledge worker (executive, manager, and analyst) to receive knowledge to improve decision making. A **data warehouse** is a "subject-oriented, integrated, time varying, non-volatile collection of data that is used primarily in organizational decision making" (Inmon, 1992: 1). Typically, the data warehouse is maintained separately from the organization's operational **databases**. The data warehouse supports online analytical processing (OLAP), the functional and performance requirements of which are quite different from those of the online transaction processing (OLTP) applications traditionally supported by the operational databases.

Online analytical processing is an approach to quickly answer multidimensional analytical queries. OLAP is part of the broader category of business intelligence, which also encompasses relational reporting and data mining. Databases configured for OLAP use a multidimensional data model, allowing for complex analytical and ad hoc queries with a rapid execution time. They borrow aspects of navigational databases and hierarchical databases that are faster than relational databases.

Data warehouses are targeted for decision support through creating knowledge based on vast amounts of stored data. Historical, summarized, and consolidated data is more important than detailed, individual records. Since data warehouses contain consolidated data, perhaps from several operational databases over potentially long periods of time, they tend to be orders of magnitude larger than operational databases. The workloads are query intensive with mostly ad hoc, complex queries that can access millions of records and perform a lot of scans, joins, and aggregates. Query throughput and response times are more important than transaction throughput.

In an example of how data warehousing can support knowledge creation, manufacturer Kimberly-Clark partnered with Food Lion supermarkets to ensure that the manufacturer's products remained in stock. A lack of stock is a common challenge for retailers, often resulting from a lack of information about inventory, the sales climate, and customer demand. Food Lion provided Kimberly-Clark with data about its sales, stock, and promotions. This knowledge allowed Kimberly-Clark and Food Lion to establish new quantities for store allocation, leading to lower out-of-stock rates and higher sales for the following months. "Armed with this new knowledge, Kimberly-Clark executives went to the Food Lion category management team and established a

---

Databases versus Data Warehouses

Although they sound similar, databases and data warehouses serve two very different purposes for organizations. Databases are commonly used with business applications for the storage or operational and transactional data. It is not usually data that will be kept long term, but is used either by the business applications (such as an ERP system) to process transactions, or by the accounting information systems to prepare daily, weekly, and monthly financial reports. Any data within these databases that is required to be kept on a long-term basis (i.e., after the monthly reporting cycle ends) is archived in separate databases for retrieval.

Data warehouses may store much of the same types of data (transactional and operational data), but also can store other various forms of information a business collects during its operations. The purpose of a data warehouse is to present a large source of data that can be analyzed to give management a better understanding of the business, its operations, or the marketplace. Results gained from data warehousing and data mining are valuable to the internal decision-making processes within an organization.

virtually identical promotion and decided to increase store allocation quantities according to the new knowledge. As a result, the sales for the October promotion were 167 percent higher than the sales for the September promotion, with the out-of-stock rate dropping down to just above 10 percent" (Walsh, 2009).

KNOWLEDGE DISCOVERY FROM DATABASES

Data and information have become the basis for decision making in many industries. Organizations are collecting very large amounts of information about their customers, products, markets, employees, and their manufacturing, distribution, and marketing processes. Advances in database technologies, data storage capabilities, and processing power, as well as reduction in storage and computing costs, has enabled organizations to capture and store data quickly and more efficiently. In addition to the technological changes, a radical shift in consumer and social trends has made individual data easily available. An individual browsing the Internet or using social networking tools leaves a digital footprint with each and every activity. Data about an individual is collected every time he or she makes an online purchase, places a phone call, sends an e-mail message, or uses a credit card. Today, both corporations and the public sector also have access to information from real-world observations, made possible by the growing prevalence of radio frequency identification (RFID) tags, sensors, online cameras, and global positioning systems, as well as information from shared data banks and the Internet. Thanks to the advancement of wireless and mobile technologies that tap and

---

Nonprofit Knowledge Creation at the Salvation Army

It is important for organizations of all types to manage their knowledge, and this is true for those in the nonprofit sector. The Salvation Army is just one example of a nonprofit organization that has begun to realize the value of managing knowledge within a distributed organization. Cost savings is one driving force to its KM project, as any dollar saved can be put back into its charitable operations.

Most of the data collected originates from individual stores, call centers, or the website. Much of the information required is logistical in nature, which includes scheduling the pickup of donations and ensuring they arrive at the warehouse and eventually the right store. A big part of the organization's "business" is the Christmas Kettle Campaign, and they track locations of the kettles, who will staff the kettle, and how productive each volunteer is; they can then determine the most productive places to locate the kettles.

Keeping track of clients who require the organization's services is also an important use of organizational knowledge. Based on requests from stores or the Internet, it can ensure it is meeting clients' needs and providing them the services they require.

All of these sources of data are combined to create a holistic picture of the Salvation Army's operations. The organization can determine what areas of its services are working well, and in what regions of the country. Resources can be shifted to improve areas that are lacking in money or service quality. Because statistics developed for for-profit organizations would not be as useful for the Salvation Army, it developed its own measures to monitor its business and to create information for decision makers who eventually guide the organization's direction. It has found that the more knowledge it can generate regarding the workings of the business and its impact on its clients, the more effective the organization can be in satisfying its mission of helping those who need help (Wiess, 2008).

share information, ubiquitous access with real business benefits is near reality. Consequently, **knowledge discovery from databases (KDD)** and **business intelligence (BI)** have become extremely critical in addressing the problem that the digital information era has made a reality for organizations: data overload.

Organizations capture data on a daily basis to collect information on business activities and the environment, increase efficiency, and provide valuable services to customers and stakeholders. Traditionally, organizations have relied on people to analyze and interpret the data and convert it to knowledge that can be used to make useful business decisions. These analysts publish reports that contain their interpretations about market trends, customer behavior, and other topics. The reports generated are then used for decision making and strategic planning. However, the sheer volume of data now makes manual analysis completely impractical and unsustainable. KDD is concerned with the development of processes and techniques that can be leveraged to make sense of the data. The KDD process addresses the basic problem of mapping low-level data (which is typically too voluminous to understand and digest easily) into other forms that might be more compact (e.g., a short report), more abstract (e.g., a descriptive approximation or model of the process that generated the data), or more useful (e.g., a predictive model for estimating the value of future cases). The goal of KDD is to understand the data collected by the organization, and use this understanding to create new and valuable organizational knowledge.

Figure 4.4 illustrates the activities that KDD encompasses (Fayyad, Piatestsky-Shapiro, and Smyth, 1996).

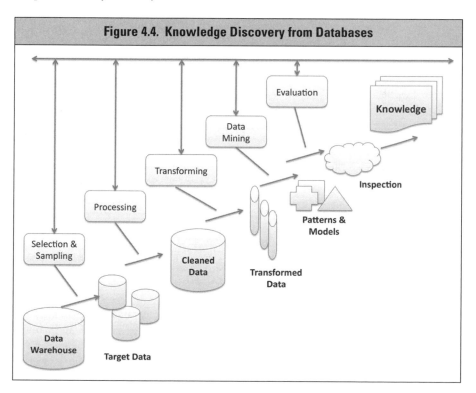

Figure 4.4. Knowledge Discovery from Databases

- *Data selection*: The extraction from a larger data store of only the data that is relevant to the data mining analysis. This data extraction helps to streamline and speed up the process.
- *Data preprocessing*: Data cleansing and preparation tasks that are necessary to ensure correct results. This phase typically includes eliminating missing values in the data, ensuring that coded values have a uniform meaning, and ensuring that no spurious data values exist.
- *Data transformation*: Converting the data into a two-dimensional table and eliminating unwanted or highly correlated fields so the results are valid.
- *Data mining*: Analyzing the data using an appropriate set of algorithms in order to discover meaningful patterns and rules and produce predictive models. This is the core element of the KDD cycle.
- *Interpretation and evaluation*: While data mining algorithms have the potential to produce an unlimited number of patterns hidden in the data, many of these may not be meaningful or useful. This phase is aimed at selecting those models that are valid and useful for making future business decisions.

Data Mining in the Health Care Industry

The health-care industry has moved to the practice of evidence-based medicine, a method that is proven effective for evaluating care techniques in medicine. To improve care and reduce costs, many organizations have begun to actively collect and manage data on their health-care operations in order to create evidence or knowledge of what is the most effective means of treating patients.

Hospitals can generate enormous amounts of data on patients, treatments, medicines, and administrative activities; therefore they require a robust system to ensure the accuracy and completeness of the data collected. They must utilize advanced software systems that can also interpret and analyze the data in order to create knowledge on the health-care setting. Finally, these systems must be able to present the knowledge in such a way that it is absorbed and used by the professionals responsible for caring for patients. Accuracy and ease of interpretation are key success factors in any data mining products.

Data mining can also play a role in actively searching for problem situations and alerting doctors. The safety of patients is critical, and these systems can monitor both the status of patients and the prescribed treatment to ensure no mistakes are made. Dashboards can be made available to doctors and nurses, summarizing everything from current patients' statuses to long-term trends seen in the hospital that can allow for targeted training or supply purchasing to cope with any outbreaks that may be starting. By creating a greater understanding of the health-care environment and providing accurate knowledge to the primary caregivers, medical data mining systems can improve the care and outlook for patients, as well as the overall operations of hospitals (Gerver and Barrett, 2006; Toman, 2009).

Business Intelligence represents a category of applications, technologies, and concepts for gathering, storing, analyzing, and providing access to data to help business users make better decisions. At a high level, BI technologies can be classified in two groups. The first, query reporting analysis, is a query-based analysis that is used to determine what happened in the business over a given period of time. BI solutions that are query based are usually manually operated and time consuming. Online Analytical Processing is an example of query-based BI. The second group, intelligent analysis, involves use of clever algorithms to perform a more intelligent analysis of data than the query-based approach. Intelligent analysis is able to spot patterns or relationships in the data that can help provide answers about what might happen to the business in the future. Data mining is an example of intelligent BI. Thus data mining is the name of a group of intelligent BI methods as well as an important stage in the KDD process.

Types of KDD

Organizations use many forms of KDD activities to create knowledge. Advances in image mining, acquisition and storage technology have led to tremendous growth in very large and detailed image databases. These images, if analyzed, can reveal useful information to the human users. Image mining deals with the extraction of implicit knowledge, image data relationship, or other patterns not explicitly stored in the images. Image mining is an interdisciplinary endeavor that draws upon expertise in computer vision, image processing, image retrieval, data mining, machine learning, databases, and artificial intelligence (Hsu, 2002).

Text mining, sometimes referred to as text data mining, refers to the process of deriving high-quality information from text. Text mining usually involves the process of structuring the input text (usually parsing, along with the addition of some derived linguistic features and the removal of others, and subsequent insertion into a database), deriving patterns within the structured data, and finally evaluating and interpreting the output. Text mining is an interdisciplinary field that draws on information retrieval, data mining, machine learning, statistics, and computational linguistics. The difference between regular data mining and text mining is that in text mining the patterns are extracted from natural language text rather than from structured databases. For example, JetBlue uses text analytics technology to parse through e-mails and feedback from customers to classify them as "detractors," "neutrals," or "promoters." This classification helps JetBlue develop programs to increase customer satisfaction and minimize churn (attrition). Choice Hotels also uses text analytics software to sort through surveys from thousands of customers each day. The software flags positive and negative feedback and then correlates the feedback with the facility where the customer stayed. This allows for a fast response from the customer service team. At a global level, this practice also enables managers to spot trends and identify problems. For example, they saw that although noise complaints were not one of the most frequent issues, they were one of the most severe because customers with these complaints were the most likely to say that they would patronize another hotel brand for future stays (Stodder, 2010).

Similarly, **web mining** is the application of data mining techniques to discover patterns from the websites and other information sources on the Internet. Web mining can be divided into three different categories depending on the goal of analysis: web usage mining, web content mining and web structure mining (Srivastava, Desikan, and Kumar, 2002). For retailer Barneys New York, web mining provides the ability to discover online customers' buying patterns and precisely target their communications. Sheldon Gilbert, the developer of Proclivity, the system that Barneys uses, says, "I'm a pattern hunter, so I created a system that was looking for patterns and was adaptive and self-learning" (Cohen, 2008).

Web usage mining is the application of data mining techniques to discover usage patterns from web data in order to understand and better serve the needs of web-based applications. Usage data captures the identity or origin of web users along with their browsing behavior on a website. This analysis can be classified further depending on the kind of usage data considered: web server data, application server data, and application level data. For example, Amazon.com uses data about the web usage gathered by the prospective customers' actions on the web page to provide a personalized customer experience. A host of Web mining techniques—such as click-path analysis or associations between pages visited—are used to improve the customer's experience during a "store visit." Knowledge gained from web mining is the key intelligence behind Amazon's features such as instant recommendations, purchase circles, and wish-lists.

Web content mining is the process of extracting useful information from the contents of web documents. Google offers Google News, a service that integrates news from the online versions of newspapers and organizes this knowledge categorically, making it easier for users to read their preferred sources of news. It seeks to provide the latest information by constantly retrieving pages from news sites worldwide that are being updated on a regular basis. The key feature of this news page, like any other Google service, is that it integrates information from various web news sources through purely algorithmic means, and thus does not introduce any human bias or effort.

Web Content Mining for Early Detection of Swine Flu Outbreak

Web content mining can be used as an early alert system to identify disease outbreaks. By crawling the web, aggregating related content, and identifying patterns, organizations are able to identify potential threats. In the case of the recent swine flu outbreak in Mexico City, a Seattle-based company called Veratect was able to identify the problem early on and alert the CDC of its findings. Veratect commented that it was able to detect the outbreak "by monitoring and analyzing the flow of social media traffic along with more official reports" (Madrigal, 2009). Similarly, the outbreak was pinpointed by web content mining tools including "the Google.org-backed data scraping tool, Healthmap, and a network of health professionals, ProMED..." (Madrigal, 2009).

Finally, web structure mining can be regarded as the process of discovering structured information from the web. This type of mining can be further divided into two kinds: hyperlink and document structure based on the kind of structural data used. PageRank is Google's metric for ranking hypertext documents based on their quality. The key idea is that a page has high rank if it is referenced (usually via hyperlink) by many other highly ranked pages. Therefore, the rank of a page depends upon the ranks of the pages pointing to it. This process is done iteratively until the rank of all pages is calculated.

Examples of Data Mining Techniques

At their core, data mining techniques focus on uncovering latent patterns among large data sets. One can employ a wide range of techniques to uncover patterns among data sets in order to create valuable knowledge for the organization.

Artificial Neural Networks

Utilizing neural networks is one of the most sophisticated data mining methodologies. Neural network techniques emerged from research in artificial intelligence (AI)— specifically, attempts to mimic the fault-tolerance and capacity to learn of biological neural systems by modeling the low-level structure of the brain.

Neural networks attempt to mimic a neuron in a human brain, with each link described as a processing element (PE). A processing element processes data by summarizing and transforming data using a series of mathematical functions. One PE is limited in ability, but when connected to form a system, the neurons or PEs create an intelligent model. The simplest form of neural network consists of three layers of PEs: input layer, hidden layer, and output layer (Patterson, 1996).

The neural network is then taken through a process called training, which involves modifying the strength, or weight, of connections from the inputs to the outputs. Training repeatedly, or iteratively, exposes a neural network to examples of historical data. The output generated is continuously compared with the target output in the historical data and the deviation between them is used as feedback to modify the weights. Training continues until a neural network produces outcome values that match the known outcome values within a specified accuracy level, or until it satisfies some other stopping criteria. The number of inputs, hidden nodes, and outputs and the weighting algorithms for the connections between nodes determine the complexity of a neural network, its accuracy, and the time it takes to create the neural network. The neural network can then be used to predict outcomes by supplying it with a set of input data or to detect unknown relationships between a set of input data and an outcome.

Neural networks are commonly categorized in terms of their corresponding training algorithms: supervised neural networks and unsupervised neural networks. Supervised neural networks are built using the training methodology just described and can be used to predict outcomes. Unsupervised neural networks employ training algorithms that do not make use of desired output data. They are used to find structures in the data, such as clusters (groups) of data points, or one-dimensional or two-dimensional relationships among the data. It is up to human users to interpret or label the groups in some meaningful way.

Neural networks are very good at pattern-recognition and pattern-matching tasks. This makes them useful for decision-support problems involving multiple variables and noisy or incomplete data. Many common business problems can be posed as pattern-recognition tasks.

Data mining through the use of neural networks has many practical applications. For example, a significant portion of online fraud occurs in the form of credit card chargeback fraud, which results in chargeback fees to the tune of $20 to $45 per transaction for Internet retailers. To address the problem, these retailers are leveraging screening technologies that use detailed neural network models to calculate and assign a score to each transaction based on individual cardholder habits and debit card industry usage. The neural networks have been developed by from studying millions of transactions, both valid and fraudulent; the objective is to determine which factors are most indicative of a fraudulent transaction and which are most indicative of a valid transaction (MacMillan, 2009).

In another example of neural network use, Standard & Poor's is using historical data to predict future outcomes on the stock market. The company's Neural Fair Value 25 portfolio uses a neural network model to search 3,000 stocks in that group for the 25 that it thinks has the greatest likelihood of appreciating in value. The neural model projects which stocks will see success in the next six months, basing these predictions on the factors present in the most successful stocks for the last six months. The model went through a "training period" to adjust key inputs and fine-tune its rate of error. A year after its inception, the NFV 25 had risen 30.7 percent, beating its benchmark, which was 15.5 percent for the S&P 500 index (Andrews, 2006).

Overall, data mining through neural networks has the ability to represent both linear and nonlinear relationships, and to learn these relationships directly from the data being modeled. Traditional linear models are simply inadequate when it comes to modeling data that contains nonlinear characteristics. Furthermore, neural networks are useful in chaotic situations because they have a high tolerance for noisy data as compared to other data mining methods (Kasabov, 1996).

Decision Trees

Decision trees have become popular as an approach to knowledge discovery and data mining. Given a large set of data, decision trees enable the tracing of decision paths, or rules, that lead to a certain outcome. Decision trees are able to produce human-readable descriptions of trends in the underlying relationships of a data set and can be used for classification and prediction tasks. These trees utilize squares and circles to depict actions that can be taken by managers. Squares represent discretionary decisions that a user can make. These are connected to other squares that represent all the available distinct outcomes of the decision. Circles are used to show in discretionary circumstances or external events that could occur and potentially result in uncertain outcomes. Each path that can be followed along the decision tree, from left to right, leads to some specific outcome. The decision tree begins at the root node and branches into leaves (leaf nodes) that represent different outcomes. The leaves further branch into more leaves (Rokach and Mainmon, 2008).

Decision trees are helpful in complex multi-stage decision problems, when you need to plan and organize a sequence of decisions and take into account how the choices made at earlier stages and the outcomes of possible external events determine the types of decisions and events at later stages. The appeal of decision trees lies in their relative power, ease of use, robustness with a variety of data and levels of measurement, and ease of interpretability. Decision trees are developed and presented incrementally; thus, the combined set of multiple influences (which are necessary to fully explain the relationship of interest) is a collection of one-cause, one-effect relationships presented in the recursive form of a decision tree.

A decision tree is created using an algorithm that splits the data set into an inverted decision tree. To build the decision tree, training data is fed to the algorithm. The algorithm begins at the root node of the tree and poses a classifier question that creates the branches and leaves based on the answer to the question. Thus the decision tree represents a series of questions. The quality of a question at any node is determined by how well the question differentiates among the target classes. Each question determines what follow-up question is best to be asked next. At each lower level node from the root, whatever question works best to split the subset is applied. This process of finding each additional level of the tree continues. The tree is allowed to grow until you cannot find better ways to split the input records. Typically, the top level of the decision tree is readily reproduced; however, at lower levels of the decision tree, training results and validation results tend to deviate. As error (deviation) rates climb the decision tree, the stability and reproducibility at the lower branches deteriorate. When deterioration begins, it is time to stop growing the tree and select a sub-tree consisting of the higher branches that are more stable (de Ville, 2006).

Many examples of successful decision tree data mining exist. In the direct marketing field, the telecommunications giant Bell Canada uses decision tree software to better understand customer preferences and the factors that influence the sale of a particular offer. Analysts feed the customer data to the decision tree software:

> By looking at the tree from the top and then down each "branch," we can quickly discover what factors help to "split" customers who bought long distance from those who did not. Equally important, we find Knowledge-STUDIO very adept at discovering how different factors interact. For example, suppose "Region" was an important factor at the top of the tree. If Region A showed twice the sales rate as Region B, that would be important. If within Region A we could further find a branch (for example, high overseas callers) that showed four times the sales rate, then that interaction of Region and high overseas calling would be an important factor to consider in the final model. (Comeau, 2001: under "Product Functionality")

Risk management operations have also utilized decision trees in their data mining and decision-making processes. When the baby-products company Gerber faced a choice about whether to eliminate polyvinyl chloride (PVC) from its products in response to an inquiry by the U.S. Consumer Products Safety Commission (CPSC), Gerber was faced with the choice of taking action before the CPSC issues its report, or waiting to see what recommendations the report would outline (Buckley and Dudley, 1999). Gerber used a decision tree weighed the costs of changing its manufacturing practices against the potential fallout from a mandatory recall. The company ultimately decided not to wait for the release of the CPSC report, but to proactively change its practices in the hope that it would provide a competitive advantage against others in the field.

Decision trees have many distinct advantages over other methods of data mining. Data preparation for a decision tree is limited. Other data mining methods often require data normalization, and dummy variables need to be created and blank values to be removed. Furthermore, it is possible to validate a model using statistical tests, neural nets, and other techniques. This makes it possible to account for the reliability of the model. Finally, this model has proven to be robust and perform well with large data sets in a short time frame. Large amounts of data can be analyzed using personal computers in a time short enough to enable stakeholders to take decisions based on its analysis.

KNOWLEDGE CREATION TO SUPPORT INNOVATION

Peter Drucker famously stated that every organization needs to develop only one core competence, and that is innovation. Through the generation of new knowledge and ideas, companies offer new products and services to stay ahead of their competition, satisfy their customers, and remain viable over the long term. **Innovation** can be defined as the use of new knowledge to offer a product or service that is in demand by an organization's customers or patrons. The innovation is an idea, thing, procedure or system that is perceived to be new by whomever is adopting it (Rogers, 1995). Organizations promote innovation by allowing their knowledge workers to create new knowledge and directing it toward the organization's core activities.

Innovation has strategic significance for organizations for a variety of reasons. It allows organizations to compete in new markets with differentiated products and services. This allows for the extension of business lines, brands, and the diversification of business activities. It helps keep pace with the ever-changing demands of customers by understanding their needs and wishes, and then creating solutions to satisfy those requests. When new technologies emerge, the organization can take advantage of these new tools in order to maintain its position within the industry, or possibly surpass its competition through the creation of a competitive advantage. Other times, innovation allows for a competitive advantage to be sustained over a longer period of time by creating knowledge in order to understand the business environment and form strategies that will lead to business success. Overall, organizations innovate to survive as any lapse in innovation activities presents an opportunity for their competition.

There are two common types of innovations. In the first, known as an **incremental innovation**, new knowledge is created by directly building on previous knowledge in order to improve or alter a product or service. It is usually referred to as competence enhancing and does not alter the business, industry, or related strategies. Microsoft's Office and Windows products are examples of an incremental innovation. Every one to two years a new version is released and even though many improvements and new features are contained in these products, the change or impact they have on organizations is minimal and not "game-changing." **Radical innovations**, on the other hand, are built on new knowledge that is substantially different from any existing knowledge and that in fact renders existing knowledge obsolete. These innovations can "destroy" the existing competencies of an organization and demand that new strategies be created in order to manage the resulting change. The replacement of the vacuum tube with the transistor was a radical innovation: it created new products and industries and changed not only how businesses operate, but also how people go about their daily lives.

One question that organizations continually seek to answer is why an innovation becomes popular or diffuse throughout a marketplace or society. Innovation diffusion is the process by which an innovation is communicated through certain channels over time to members of a particular social system. Innovations do not sell themselves, and in many cases superior innovations have not been able to replace older, more accepted standards. Rogers (1995) identified five variables that affect the rate of diffusion for innovations. The perceived attributes of an innovation reflect how the consumer or adopter views the innovation and its inherent value. These may include the relative advantage it can provide over older products; how compatible it is with existing systems and work processes; how complex it is to learn; how easily it can be tried or proto-typed, including how affordable a trial may be; and how easily it is used as observed by the adopter and others. The type of decision presented to the adopter will also affect whether the innovation is accepted. Is the use of the new innovation optional, or is it being mandated by a higher authority (such as a government regulator or supervisor)? Is it a decision that can be made by an individual, or does a collective group need to make the final decision, and does that decision require consensus?

The communication channels used to promote and advertise the innovation impact its adoption rate. Different people and organizations pay attention to different media and influences, so the communication channel must be compatible with the targeted user of the product or service. The extent, efforts, and resources committed by the change agent to promoting the innovation are also important. How many television commercials, print advertisements, news articles, promotional giveaways, product placements, and word-of-mouth mentions will be created in order to sell the idea of the innovation? Finally, the nature of social system in which the innovation is being introduced is quite influential. Some groups adopt innovations very readily, such as technology- and gadget-focused people, teenagers, and creative individuals. Other groups such as the elderly are quite reluctant to undergo change and may not see the value of the innovation as easily as others.

In order to be innovative, organizations must create new knowledge. They must either create or acquire the core knowledge that is common among their peers or industry members and is required to operate within their business and economic environment. This knowledge provides no competitive advantage but is a necessity for operating. Advanced knowledge is needed in order to enable competitive viability and differentiate their knowledge base from other similar or competing organizations. This is what begins to create differences in products, services, and ultimately the organizational strategy. Innovative knowledge is the most valuable knowledge to an organization; it enables an organization to take a lead position within a marketplace and significantly differentiate itself from others, possibly creating a sustainable competitive advantage. This type of knowledge can change how businesses compete and can take time for others to understand and acquire.

These three forms of knowledge can be created or acquired by organizations through different means. Many organizations with vast resources are capable of creating dedicated research and development departments or entire organizations. Others are left to create knowledge through "learn by doing" activities that focus on capturing knowledge that is created through daily work routines and distributing it at an organizational level. Many times outside sources are capable of creating knowledge for an organization. Universities and their resident scientists often work close with corporations to create new ideas and knowledge. Other organizations are willing to partner with organizations to jointly create knowledge and share the benefits. Customers can work closely with organizations to co-create knowledge in order to improve the products and services they use. Finally, luck is often a source of new knowledge which, even though it cannot be planned for or controlled, can benefit an organization.

An emerging method to sourcing knowledge involves looking beyond the organization to large groups of people, customers, or stakeholders. The idea that valuable knowledge is contained in large groups was initially suggested by James Surowiecki (2005), who examined how bringing together many small pieces of knowledge can add up to larger and more valuable knowledge that can be used by an organization. **Crowdsourcing** has become a popular term referring to polling vast amounts of people in order to gain a small piece of their knowledge, then analyzing the knowledge as a whole in order to determine what the crowd knows. Social media has been able to facilitate this type of knowledge creation through its ability to reach out to many people in varying networks to gain their information. An organization can now ask a question on Twitter and wait for its followers to respond. It can be challenging to create meaning out of thousands, if not tens of thousands of responses, but technology and information retrieval systems can assist with this process. The Obama administration and the White House have tried such tactics by posting bills and early drafts of legislation in order to gather feedback from the public. People are able to leave comments on what they have read, and those comments are available for the administration to analyze in order to create knowledge on how the public might perceive new legislation.

Authors have argued that just by listening to crowds, markets, or customers, organizations can gain many valuable insights that can help them design or market products. Li and Bernoff (2008) have examined how organizations can identify and listen to the "groundswell" of knowledge that can emerge regarding a specific topic, product, or organization. Different demographics are capable of expressing their ideas en mass, and through social media organizations are now connecting with significant knowledge that is created from the bottom up. In fact, by not only listening but communicating with or even creating their own groundswell, organizations have found that they can gain valuable marketing knowledge that factors into the success of a product. LEGO, the manufacturer of popular children's toys, was able to listen to and work closely with its user communities to understand groundswells that affected its products. By identifying the International LEGO Users Group Network, they listened to expert users' opinions and ideas on new products to understand who was buying their products and how they were being used. Through the creation of LEGO Ambassadors, they were able to more closely connect with the user community and have people responsible for listening to the groundswell knowledge that was related to LEGO toys. Some users were even invited to participate in LEGO design sessions, and then they communicated their experiences back to the user base. LEGO was able to increase brand awareness and loyalty by listening to the knowledge of customers, and interacting with them via electronic and personal methods in order to create new marketing knowledge.

Recently the question of how organizations naturally become innovative has arisen. How an organization develops the capabilities to create new knowledge and eventually generate valuable innovations is strategically important. Because knowledge creation begins with the individual, much attention has been placed on creativity and encouraging people to develop an environment where new ideas are generated.

Creativity is the generation or production of ideas that are both novel and useful. The concepts of *novel* and *useful* are difficult to define and may vary for individual organizations. The key point is that the new knowledge created must add value to an organization's processes, products, services, and customers. Creativity can be viewed as the first step in innovation, as innovation is simply the successful implementation of creative ideas. Not all new ideas and knowledge should be recognized as creative. Novelty for novelty's sake is also not considered creativity, as most often the reason for encouraging creativity is the development of new and useful knowledge that has value for an organization. Effective problem solving is not creativity, as problem solving and decision making in organizations usually follow recognizable patterns and utilize existing knowledge that the organization has previously created or acquired (Choo, 2006). An exception is when knowledge regarding new alternatives to the problem or solution must be formed, and the resulting knowledge is novel to the organization. Once again, these ideas may be applied differently in different organizations, as the organizational culture may dictate which creative activities are acceptable and which are considered non-value added, or wastes of corporate time.

As creativity is very similar to creating new knowledge, many of the challenges are similar when encouraging knowledge workers to express their creativity. Motivation, both intrinsic and extrinsic, is important because people cannot always be creative for the sake of being creative. Their intrinsic motivation must be dominant and drive the creative nature of individuals. This is a challenge for organizations that cannot pay people to simply be creative for eight hours a day. It is important to address the culture, environment, and nature of the work in order to encourage creativity. Many people are creative during conscious thought, but also within unconscious thought. When people comment on how they woke up in the middle of the night with a great idea, it is because their subconscious was active during sleep and has generated new knowledge. The challenge is for organizations to get their employees to recognize creativity from unconscious thought, and incorporate this knowledge into innovation activities. Finally, the affective experience or mood of the employee will affect their ability to be creative. Research has shown that happy people are more creative, suggesting that happy employees will exceed at creative work.

Many times, the results of creative thought challenge existing knowledge and the status quo. Organizational cultures can either stifle this creativity by not accepting or recognizing the opposing thought, or embrace it and try to understand the implications for the organization. Often the structure, culture, and leadership in the organization will have a strong influence over creativity. The individuals' work products will be strongly influenced by factors such as whether creative actions are required or optional, whether there is time pressure involved, the influence of knowledge networks and social influences, and the degree of risk in the activities.

Creativity is encouraged within groups. Here, it is important to ensure that groups have an adequate level of diversity to bring new and unique knowledge to the creativity process and avoid the traps of groupthink. For this reason the addition of new members to a group can stimulate creativity among others and alter the path of the group. Four aspects of the group can determine how creative it will be in creating new knowledge:

1. It should be help-seeking in order to break through barriers and creative blocks, and be receptive to assistance when solving problems.
2. The idea that the group is also help-giving allows it to assist other groups within the organization and allows for new interactions, different perspectives, and new knowledge to permeate the group.
3. Reflective reframing allows multiple iterations and reworking of the knowledge, allowing for building upon previous work and taking new and creative directions.
4. Finally, reinforcing all the activities that the group undertakes allows for the organizational values and positive knowledge activities to echo throughout the group's work.

Organizations that can encourage and leverage creativity at both the individual and group levels experience three key benefits. They create the ability to accelerate new product development, which generates a competitive advantage where the competition has a difficult time keeping up with the organization. For example, Google takes a nontraditional and unique approach to product development. While a traditional software company tends to release new products or features in big waves that are separated by several years, Google launches a flurry of product features or new innovations on a weekly or monthly basis. The core philosophy behind Google's product development/ knowledge creation approach is to try a bunch of ideas and see what survives based on feedback from the end users. Overall innovation activities within an organization also become accelerated, creating new processes and the ability to exploit emerging technologies. Japanese companies such as Canon and Honda have become very successful by using a unique approach to knowledge creation. The centerpiece of the Japanese approach is the recognition that creating new knowledge is not simply a matter of "processing" objective information. Rather, it depends on tapping the tacit and often highly subjective insights, intuitions, and hunches of individual employees and making those insights available for testing and use by the company as a whole.

Rapid technological innovation combined with globalization has created a level playing field for worldwide commerce, and subsequently an extremely competitive environment. As organizations are no longer able to rely on internal resources for knowledge creation and are increasingly turning to partners to accelerate the process, creativity assists in linking the knowledge activities of the internal employees and external partners. Most of these partners have expertise and knowledge that is expensive or time consuming for the organization to acquire internally, so therefore the organization benefits from the introduction of the new knowledge into the organization in a timely and efficient manner. Many consultants, specialists, and experts have developed very narrow yet deep knowledge in a specific area that can be temporarily acquired by an organization in order to quickly inject knowledge into the organization. The use of such knowledge workers has changed the nature of competition by providing organizations of varying sizes and wealth with the opportunity to gain expensive knowledge for their use. This is a reflection on the notion that knowledge has become one of the key factors in an organization's competitiveness and that knowledge is primarily resident in individuals. Organizations must find ways to not only gain this individual-based knowledge, but also employ these individuals and bring them inside the organization boundaries in order to acquire and use their knowledge. The knowledge economy differs from past economic movements in the transient nature of employees who move themselves and their knowledge freely between organizations. Through accelerating new product development, innovation, and enabling knowledge to be acquired from third parties, creativity is an important core competency for any organization competing in a dynamic environment.

Referencing in the Crowd

Libraries have the goal of improving knowledge creation within their communities. They often do this by educating patrons about where they can find information and knowledge in order to answer a question or solve a problem. This has traditionally been a face-to-face process where the patron must be at the library and interact personally with the librarian.

Recently, libraries have begun to offer virtual reference services, or the ability to use technology such as chat or video conferencing. From the comfort of home, users can ask a librarian a question as long as they have a connection to the Internet. In a distributed reference model, a person is not restricted to his or her local library but can ask a reference question to an expert in a library from any location. Or these questions can be posed to many experts if the source of the best knowledge is not known (as in a crowd of experts). For example, a patron with a medical question can ask a librarian at one of the country's top medical school libraries, or a patron who has a question on the history of a town or county can connect with a local librarian resident in that town or county and ask their question. If patrons do not know the best source of the knowledge they are seeking, services can be used to interpret the subject matter of the question and direct the request to the relevant group of experts who would be able to answer the question. This eventually allows for access to materials and knowledge well beyond users' geographical boundaries.

This new conceptualization of library reference service may have an impact on the structure of libraries. Will it be possible to have libraries focused on very specific subject matter, with experts located within those libraries, yet the ability to serve a global group of patrons? Can universities focus their library collections, especially in times of limited resources, and rely on the services of other partner libraries for subjects that may not be central to the university's studies? And can users now gain access to information and the knowledge of librarians no matter their academic affiliation or location?

We see collaborative processes similar to this on the Internet every day. Photo sites allow users to tag photos with their own tags or labels, allowing a person to upload a photo and determine the subject of the photo based on the tags that are applied. Comments sections in blogs can lead readers to other references or contain discussions of questions posed by readers and answers posted from knowledgeable sources. These concepts are now being applied to traditional question and answer forums such as the library in order to make reference service more distributed and collaborative.

BARRIERS TO KNOWLEDGE CREATION

Knowledge creation unfortunately is not automatic. Organizations need to be aware of the major challenges that impact the effectiveness, and efficiency, of knowledge creation.

Individual Challenges

The creation of knowledge is a human activity. Therefore, along with the benefits of this being an individual centric task there are many challenges that are also presented to individuals (and their relevant organizations). Barriers that are present when people attempt to transfer or receive knowledge are often the biggest challenge to effective knowledge creation and discovery. Similar to other knowledge management processes, people must be motivated to be involved in knowledge creation activities. Organizations have the resources to use both extrinsic and intrinsic motivators to encourage employees to integrate knowledge creation in daily routines (Szulanski, 2000). Many of the resources to encourage creation routines are difficult to measure from a management perspective, and therefore are not adequately utilized. The axiom "if it can't be measured, it can't be managed" applies here, and knowledge's mostly tacit nature prevents many traditional management methods from being applied.

Appropriability refers to the ability of the owner or creator of knowledge to receive a return equal to the value of the knowledge created. Explicit knowledge easily and instantaneously becomes available to the recipient and hence is also generally non-appropriable. Tacit knowledge is not readily available for consumption unless the owner of this knowledge is able to appropriate value or has the right incentive to share the knowledge. The organization needs to build the right incentive system to enable appropriability and sharing of tacit knowledge. Consulting company Booz Allen Hamilton represents a classic case of how appropriability was a major roadblock to knowledge sharing. The company was initially structured as a loose affiliation of partners. Partners serviced their own clients under what was little more than a shared administrative structure and brand name. Partners were rewarded for the revenue they brought to the firm. Therefore, there was little incentive for partners to share knowledge, share innovations across partnerships, or help other partners build profitable client relationships. Learning tended to occur at the individual and client team level, stimulated by particular engagements. While some informal networks existed, there was no explicit mechanism for sharing new insights beyond individual offices. The organization established a new partner-compensation system that would better align partners' incentives with the strategic interests of the firm. In place of highly variable individual bonuses, partners would each receive a uniform percentage bonus on their base compensation, depending on the overall results of the firm. Base compensation was in turn determined according to a combination of seniority and contribution in the institution on five dimensions of which revenue generation was only one element. This change along with other initiatives helped develop a culture of knowledge sharing at Booz Allen (Apostolou, 1999).

Organizational Challenges

Knowledge creation and discovery are critical to enable an organization to improve productivity, collaboration, and innovation. Organizations often invest a great deal of resources in knowledge management initiatives. Research has shown, however, that not all knowledge management projects succeed, and in fact some studies report that about 84 percent of knowledge management projects fail (De Long and Fahey, 2000). Many of these failures can be related to organizational barriers to knowledge creation, including the organizational culture.

Culture, which includes the underlying subcultures, shapes assumptions about how knowledge is defined and what knowledge types are worth managing. For example, a printed circuit-board design team was tasked with capturing lessons learned in its role in the product development process, which was a core process for the company. But the group's members were so concerned with being able to account for their time in the government-funded work that they initially refused to reflect on their experiences and develop lessons learned. The barrier to creating this new knowledge was removed only when the knowledge manager found an administrative accounting code suitable for labeling time used for extracting lessons learned (Leonard and Dixon, 1994).

Culture defines the relationships between individual and organizational knowledge, determining who is expected to control specific knowledge, as well as who must share (or hoard) knowledge. Culture embodies all the unspoken norms and rules of how knowledge is to be distributed between the organization and its individuals (Choo et al., 2006). Culture dictates what knowledge belongs to the organization and what knowledge remains in control of individuals or subunits. When people are asked to put their knowledge into an organizational knowledge system, they can perceive that they lose ownership of knowledge they alone had previously controlled. Often, an organization's culture will influence individual knowledge ownership, encouraging people to refuse to share their knowledge, even as the organization pursues a business strategy that requires individuals to share what they know.

As well, culture creates the context for social interaction that determines how knowledge will be used in specific situations. Cultural "ground rules" shape how people interact and have a major impact on knowledge creation. Four project managers at NASA noted that cultural barriers, such as reluctance to share negative lessons for fear that they might be criticized as being bad managers, were preventing learning and new knowledge creation. Managers began to work towards changing the culture of the organization so that employees would admit honestly not only when they were successful, but when they failed and understood why (GAO, 2002).

Finally, culture shapes the processes by which new knowledge is created, legitimated, and distributed in organizations. Knowledge ultimately assumes value when it affects individual behaviors, decision making, or strategy and is translated into action. In order for this to be accomplished, the internal process must support not only the creation of knowledge, but also its use. In the 1980s, Ford's market research department produced what it viewed as new knowledge in the form of marketing projections that the minivan would be a huge success as a new product in the automobile market. However, Ford's executives, particularly in the finance department, challenged the validity of this new market knowledge, labeling the minivan concept as untested and risky. In this case, the subcultures involved in negotiating the validity of the new knowledge failed to agree and act on the importance of the insights. As a result Ford's competitor, Chrysler, went on to capture this major new market.

Organizations need to embrace the notion of integrating knowledge creation into work routines and practices. Knowledge creation should be viewed not as a separate activity from day-to-day jobs, but as a complementary activity to how an organization conducts its business. A common challenge in organizations that create knowledge is how to capture and retain this knowledge in order to disseminate it to the appropriate parts of the organization. Knowledge capture is essential for organizations that rely on knowledge workers to bring knowledge into the organization and wish to encourage internal knowledge flows. This challenge has been addressed by organizations with mature project management methodologies that have recognized the importance of capturing knowledge gained through the execution of a project. During the project life cycle, there are many instances when the opportunity to capture knowledge arises. Throughout the process, knowledge management systems in conjunction with project management software can assist in the capture of explicit knowledge. Community-based initiatives where project managers or members gather to discuss issues and lessons learned also assist in transferring project knowledge (Bresnen et al., 2003). Implementing procedures to allow for the documentation of knowledge throughout the project prevent employees from forgetting important details that may have significant impact on other projects. In the postmortem phase, project groups can use both traditional reports and stories to assist members to convert the tacit knowledge gained into transferable explicit knowledge (Desouza, Dingsoyr, and Awazu, 2005). By encouraging employees to document what they know, and shifting reward mechanisms such that this knowledge creation activity is not viewed as administrative work, organizations can encourage the creation of knowledge through ensuring it is captured throughout daily routines and practices to enable knowledge sharing between functional areas and project groups.

Technical and System Challenges

In addition to the human and organizational barriers, technology intended to facilitate knowledge creation and discovery can in some cases add barriers if not properly designed and implemented. Many times a lack of common knowledge infrastructure appears when different groups adopt different technologies for knowledge sharing. Knowledge resides in the organization, but is created and exists in distributed silos. Therefore, in spite of significant explicit information being available within the organization it cannot be leveraged in knowledge creation projects. Standard company-wide architectures for knowledge management systems become critical in order to ensure the sustainability and scalability of KM efforts.

In some cases, organizations rely solely on technological assets for knowledge creation activities. "The biggest misconception that IT leaders make is that knowledge management is about technology" (Kulkarni, Ravindran, and Freeze, 2005: 309). Any knowledge management initiative must be a multidisciplinary effort and integrate people, processes, and technology. The knowledge creation cycle is a multidisciplinary effort that depends on organizational learning, sharing habits, and changes to culture; in other words, not just IT. It should be noted that in some cases knowledge management technology is unsuccessful in driving adoption as it is difficult to understand

and use. The focus should be on the people, with technology providing a foundation for their activities.

With any knowledge initiative that involves technology, training becomes a critical success factor in eventual system deployment. Some research has suggested that employee training has the strongest correlation with a successful KM implementation (Hung et al., 2005). Training ensures employees understand the new system and the processes associated with its use. User adoption is essential for success, and training is the primary way to prevent refusal or apathy by employees.

Environmental Challenges

Many of the overarching barriers to knowledge creation experienced by organizations arise from aspects of its economic, political, legal, market, and geographical environments. Some environments pose greater challenges to knowledge creation than others. For example, the technology industry experiences rapid growth in product innovation and technology, and this disruption poses higher knowledge creation barriers, as they must continually keep up with new knowledge that can have a substantial effect on the knowledge they are using and creating. As a new technology replaces existing technology, established organizations are forced to not only quickly acquire knowledge about the new technology but also revamp their internal knowledge base, employee skill sets, and processes. The threat of not being able to stay ahead of the technological disruption and fend of new entrants emerges. A further example has occurred with the growing popularity of cloud computing, a method of storing information and harnessing the processing power of external computing through the Internet. Cloud computing allows organizations to use the wide reach of the Internet for connecting with service providers and accessing applications, data, and other technology. Microsoft is faced with the challenge of not only redesigning its software products for use in the cloud but also retraining its employees to build and sell cloud services. Organizations in industries such as manufacturing or health care see a slower pace of change and hence lower barriers to knowledge creation (Bass, 2010). Agencies such as the government and other law-creating organizations have a direct effect on the knowledge activities of the organization. New laws that may affect privacy, intellectual property, and employee factors can impact not only the people engaged in knowledge creation projects, but also the strategy and return on equity of knowledge creation.

New and emerging regulations may differ vastly across countries and regions. An organization that intends on expanding to multiple geographies must acquire knowledge regarding the unique laws of each region and also keep its knowledge base updated as these regulations evolve over time.

CONCLUSION

The creation of knowledge is essential for the survival of any organization. Fortunately, knowledge creation occurs at many levels and through different activities within an organization. Individuals are the primary creators of knowledge, as they identify, acquire and use new knowledge in their daily routines and job functions. Their interaction with corporate knowledge and their experiences within and outside the organization provide them with the ability to combine different sources of knowledge to create new knowledge that is valuable and beneficial to the organization. They collectively form groups, teams, and projects where their interactions with others create synergies, tensions, and new actions that result in new knowledge for the organization. Collaboration is an important factor in combining existing knowledge (both tacit and explicit) to create new knowledge.

Organizations often employ dedicated resources for providing innovation and new knowledge. These resources and functions research, experiment, and develop new knowledge that leads to new products, services, processes, and technologies. It is these new and unique resources, which provides organizations a competitive advantage that they use to remain competitive. It becomes their responsibility to continually refresh these new innovations in order to stay ahead of their competitors.

Technology has offered many new tools for encouraging knowledge creation. Social media and Web 2.0 applications, data warehousing tools, and knowledge discovery from databases activities all allow for the transformation of data and information into knowledge. They rely on vast sources of data and complex relationships to bring together resources that create knowledge for the organization. Much of this knowledge may not be possible without the use of these tools by organizations.

As organizations continue to compete with rivals, search for new sources of growth, and embrace innovation and new technological advances, they will strive to increase their knowledge creation capabilities. With the goals of developing better products and services, pleasing customers, acting on better knowledge to support decisions, and the creating robust and leading strategies, knowledge creation will only increase in its importance to individuals, groups, organizations, and the larger economy.

Recap: The Major Points for Knowledge Managers to Consider When Creating Knowledge

1. Knowledge creation is primarily a human process.
2. Technology can facilitate knowledge creation, but it cannot replace people.
3. A supportive environment is needed for new knowledge to be produced.
4. Tolerance for risk and failure is needed, as not all new knowledge will be usable or valuable.
5. Creative people require flexibility in their work, and a balance between work and life.
6. The more people build relationships and interact, the more new knowledge is created.
7. Bridging distances and boundaries between people is crucial for encouraging interactivity and knowledge creation.
8. Individuals and groups both can create valuable knowledge, but must be managed differently to accommodate the preferences of individuals or the dynamics of groups.
9. Looking beyond the organization and its people for sources of new knowledge is essential. Think about customers, potential customers, stakeholders, local communities, government organizations, and other groups.
10. Problems are opportunities to encourage knowledge creation. Allow employees to tackle problems with their creativity and not be bounded by previous actions.

DISCUSSION QUESTIONS

1. Think of situations where you created knowledge mindfully (consciously) and mindlessly (unconsciously). What do these episodes tell you about how the environment influenced the knowledge creation? Do you think you can articulate and repeat the process of knowledge creation when doing so mindfully and mindlessly?

2. What are the various ways that an organization can create new knowledge? When is it most appropriate to utilize each method?

3. What are the key challenges faced by organizations who rely on creating knowledge to maintain their competitiveness? What are the strategies available to them to overcome these challenges?

4. Creating knowledge is essential for effective decision making. How does accurate and useful knowledge affect a manager's ability to make successful decisions?

5. What limits does technology have in helping people create knowledge? Can a situation exist where it would be advisable not to use any technological resources to assist in knowledge creation? Why?

6. What is the relationship between creativity and innovation? How do organizations encourage both of these activities in order to create new knowledge?

7. If employees and people are the key creators of knowledge, what can an organization do to encourage knowledge creation by individuals? How do these ideas specifically help knowledge workers become more creative?

8. Consider an organization that is implementing a strategy where the development of new ideas, products, and services are crucial to its future success. What methods are available to it that will connect people, encourage social interaction, and help form knowledge relationships that will facilitate the creation of new knowledge?

9. What are the advantages of bringing individuals together in groups or teams in order to encourage new knowledge creation? What are the risks?

10. Knowledge creation in very large organizations with many financial resources can be accomplished through extensive research and development, dedicated scientists and innovators, and the purchasing of external knowledge. What options are available to small organizations, nonprofit organizations, and those without the resources or capabilities to dedicate to full-time knowledge creativity?

11. Can social media tools and services help an organization's employees to create new knowledge? Give some examples of how a specific tool can assist a group of employees trying to develop a new service for customers/patrons.

12. Think of some examples of data that an organization collects on a daily basis, or through its routine business operations. How can KDD and business intelligence extract valuable knowledge from this data? Who in the organization might benefit from this knowledge?

13. Why are some organizations more creative and innovative than others? Why do some organizations lead their industries in the creation of radical new products and services, and others are left to react and try to catch up?

14. There are many sources of knowledge residing external to the organization that can be combined with internal knowledge to create new knowledge. What are

some of these sources, and how can an organization connect with these external sources in order to facilitate the flow of knowledge?

SUGGESTED READINGS

Desouza, K., T. Dingsoyr, and Y. Awazu. 2005. "Experiences with Conducting Project Post-mortems: Reports versus Stories." *Software Process Improvement and Practice* 10: 203–215.

Fayyad, U., G. Piatestsky-Shapiro, and P. Smyth. 1996. "From Data Mining to Knowledge Discovery in Databases." *AI Magazine* 2: 9–37.

Leonard, D., and N. M. Dixon. 1994. *The Organizational Learning Cycle*. New York: McGraw Hill.

Li, C., and J. Bernoff. 2008. *Groundswell*. Boston: Harvard Business School Press.

Nonaka, I. 1994. "A Dynamic Theory of Organizational Knowledge Creation." *Organization Science* 5, no. 1: 14–37.

Smith, S., and S. Paquette. 2010. "Creativity, Chaos, and Knowledge Management." *Business Information Review* 27, no. 2.

REFERENCES

Alavi, M., and A. Tiwana. 2002. "Knowledge Integration in Virtual Teams: The Potential Role of KMS." *Journal of the American Society for Information Science* 53, no. 12: 1029–1037.

Andrews, W. 2006. "A 'Neural' Approach to the Market." *Business Week*, May 2006. http://www.businessweek.com/investor/content/may2006/pi20060508_776926.htm.

Apostolou, D. 1999. "Managing Corporate Knowledge: A Comparative Analysis of Experience in Consulting Firms." *Knowledge and Process Management* 6, no. 4: 238–254.

Axon, S. 2010. "Facebook Will Celebrate 500 Million Users Next Week." Mashable. http://mashable.com/2010/07/17/facebook-500-million/.

Bass, D. 2010. "Microsoft Risks Margins as Office Business Fights Off Google." *Business Week*, February 17.

Brehmer, B. 2005. "The Dynamic ODA Loop: Amalgamating Boyd's OODA Loop and the Cybernetic Approach to Command and Control." Paper presented at the Tenth International Command and Control Research and Technology Symposium, McLean, VA.

Bresnen, M., L. Edelman, S. Newell, H. Scarbrough, and J. Swan. 2003. "Social Practices and the Management of Knowledge in Project Environments." *International Journal of Project Management* 21: 157–166.

Brown, J. S., and P. Duguid. 2001. "Knowledge and Organization: A Social-Practice Perspective." *Organization Science* 12, no. 2: 198–216.

Buckley, J., and T. J. Dudley. 1999. "How Gerber Used a Decision Tree in Strategic Decision Making." *Graziadio Business Review* 2, no. 3.

Choo, C. W. 2006. *The Knowing Organization*. 2nd ed. New York: Oxford University Press.

Choo, C. W., C. Furness, S. Paquette, H. van den Berg, B. Detlor, P. Bergeron, et al. 2006. "Working with Information: Information Management and Culture in a Professional Services Organization." *Journal of Information Science* 32, no. 6: 491–510.

Cohen, Arianne. 2008. "Barneys and Friend." Fast Company, May 1. http://www.fastcompany.com/magazine/125/barneys-and-friend.html.

Comeau, B. 2001. "ANGOSS Grows Decision Trees for Bell Canada." *Information Management*, July. http://www.information-management.com/issues/20010701/3615-1.html.

Conner, K. R., and C. K. Prahalad. 1996. "A Resource-Based Theory of the Firm: Knowledge Versus Opportunism." *Organization Science* 7, no. 5: 477–501.

De Long, D. W., and L. Fahey. 2000. "Diagnosing Cultural Barriers to Knowledge Management." *Academy of Management Executive* 14, no. 4: 113–127.

De Ville, B. 2006. *Decision Trees for Business Intelligence and Data Mining: Using SAS® Enterprise Miner*. Cary, NC: SAS Institute.

Desouza, K., Y. Awazu, and J. Y. Kim. 2008. "Managing Radical Software Engineering: Leverage Order and Chaos." *International Journal of Technology, Policy and Management* 8, no. 1: 22–40.

Desouza, K., T. Dingsoyr, and Y. Awazu. 2005. "Experiences with Conducting Project Postmortems: Reports versus Stories." *Software Process Improvement and Practice*, 10, 203–215.

Fayyad, U., G. Piatestsky-Shapiro, and P. Smyth. 1996. "From Data Mining to Knowledge Discovery in Databases." *AI Magazine*, 2: 9–37.

GAO (Government Accountability Office). 2002. "NASA: Better Mechanisms Needed for Sharing Lessons Learned." GAO, January 30. http://www.gao.gov/new.items/d02195.pdf.

Gayton, J. 2008. "Academic Libraries: 'Social' or 'Communal'? The Nature and Future of Academic Libraries." *The Journal of Academic Librarianship* 34, no. 1: 60–66.

Gerver, H., and J. Barrett. 2006. "Data Mining-Driven ROI: Health Care Cost Management." *Benefits and Compensation* 43: 1–5.

Goh, A. L. S. 2005. "Fostering Innovation through Knowledge-Centered Principles: A Case of Singapore Airlines." *International Journal of Knowledge Management* 1, no. 4: 73–90.

Hsu, W. 2002. "Image Mining: Trends and Developments." *Journal of Intelligent Information Systems* 19, no. 1: 7–23.

Hung, Y., S. Huang, Q. Lin, and M. L. Tsai. 2005. "Critical Factors in Adopting a Knowledge Management System for the Pharmaceutical Industry." *Industrial Management and Data Systems* 105, no. 2: 164–183.

Inmon, W. H. 1992. *Building the Data Warehouse*. New York: John Wiley.

Kasabov, N. K. 1996. *Foundations of Neural Networks, Fuzzy Systems and Knowledge Engineering*. Boston: MIT Press.

Kraft, M. 2006. "The Use of Blogs in Medical Libraries." *Journal of Hospital Librarianship* 6, no. 1: 1–13.

Kulkarni, U., S. Ravindran, and R. Freeze. 2005. "A Knowledge Management Success Model: Theoretical Development and Empirical Validation." *Journal of Management Information Systems* 23, no. 3: 309–347.

Leornard, D., and N. M. Dixon. 1994. *The Organizational Learning Cycle*. New York: McGraw Hill.

Li, C., and J. Bernoff. 2008. *Groundswell*. Boston: Harvard Business School Press.

MacMillan, R. 2009. "FBI: Internet Fraud Complaints Up 33 Percent in 2008." IT World. Last modified March 30. http://www.itworld.com/security/65408/fbi-internet-fraud-complaints-33-percent-2008.

Madrigal, Alexis. 2009. "Tracking Internet Chatter Helps Spot Swine Flu Outbreak." Wired, April 27. http://www.wired.com/wiredscience/2009/04/swinefluchatter/.

Mitchell, R., and S. Nicholas. 2006. "Knowledge Creation in Groups: The Value of Cognitive Diversity, Transactive Memory, and Open-Mindedness Norms." *The Electronic Journal of Knowledge Management* 4, no. 1: 67–74.

Nickerson, J. A., and T. R. Zenger. 2004. "A Knowledge-Based Theory of the Firm: The Problem-Solving Perspective." *Organization Science* 15, no. 6: 617–632.

Nonaka, I. 1994. "A Dynamic Theory of Organizational Knowledge Creation." *Organization Science* 5, no. 1: 14–37.

Nonaka, I., and N. Konno. 1998. "The Concept of 'Ba': Building a Foundation for Knowledge Creation." *California Management Review* 40, no. 3: 40–54.

Nonaka, I., and H. Takeuchi. 1995. *The Knowledge Creating Company*. New York: Oxford University Press.

Oinas-Kukkonen, H. 2005. "Towards Evaluating Knowledge Management through the 7C Model." Paper presented at the 12th European Conference on IT Evaluation, Dublin, Ireland.

Ostrow, A. 2010. "Twitter Hits 20 Billion Tweets." Mashable. Last modified July 31. http://mashable.com/2010/07/31/twitter-hits-20-billion-tweets/.

Paquette, S., and C. W. Choo. 2008. "Towards a Theory of Customer Knowledge Use: The Role of Knowledge Quality and Accessibility." Paper presented at the Administrative Sciences Association of Canada, Halifax, Nova Scotia.

Paquette, S., and L. Moffat. 2005. "Corporate Portals for Supply Chain Collaboration." *Journal of Internet Commerce* 4, no. 3: 69–94.

Patterson, D. 1996. *Artificial Neural Networks*. Singapore: Prentice Hall.

Rogers, E. M. 1995. *Diffusion of Innovations*. 5th ed. New York: Free Press.

Rokach, L., and O. Mainmon. 2008. *Data Mining with Decision Trees: Theory and Applications*. Hackensack, New Jersey: World Scientific Publishing Company.

Simon, H. A. 1976. *Administrative Behavior: A Study of Decision-Making Processes in Administrative Organizations*. New York, NY: Free Press.

Smith, S., and S. Paquette. 2010. "Creativity, Chaos, and Knowledge Management." *Business Information Review* 27, no. 2: 118–123.

Srivastava, J., P. Desikan, and V. Kumar. 2002. "Web Mining: Accomplishments and Future Directions." Paper presented at the U.S. National Science Foundation Workshop on Next-Generation Data Mining, Baltimore, MD.

Stodder, D. 2010. "How Text Analytics Drive Customer Insight." *InformationWeek*, February 10. http://www.informationweek.com/news/software/bi/showArticle.jhtml?articleID=222600276.

Surowiecki, J. 2005. *The Wisdom of Crowds*. New York: Random House.

Szulanski, G. 2000. "The Process of Knowledge Transfer: A Diachronic Analysis of Stickiness." *Organizational Behavior and Human Decision Processes* 82, no. 1: 9–27.

Toman, B. 2009. "Data Mining to Redesign Critical Care Services." Mayo Clinic. http://discovery sedge.mayo.edu/critical-care-data-mining.

Walsh, J. 2009. "POS Data Sharing Enables Kimberly Clark and Food Lion to Become Indispensible Partners." *Journal of Trading Partner Practices*, Spring. http://image.smythsolutions.com/emailBlasts/JTPP/Spring%2009/Articles/TPM/JTPPSpring09JWalshPOSData.html.

Wiess, T. 2008. "Salvation Army CIO Uses IT to Support Non-Profit." *Computerworld*. Last modified April 30. http://news.idg.no/cw/art.cfm?id=9E483831-17A4-0F78-3100624E902 C955E.

5

Knowledge Organization

Scott Paquette

OBJECTIVES

- Discuss the different methods and tools available for organizing knowledge.
- Review the evolution of knowledge organization, including the influence of technology over organizational practices.
- Understand the key elements in a knowledge organization strategy.
- Discover the challenges to knowledge organization, especially those surrounding tacit knowledge.
- Illuminate the role of knowledge markets in organizing knowledge, as well as other trends for the future.

INTRODUCTION

Organizations have progressed considerably in creating mature processes for identifying, creating, and acquiring knowledge. The advent of the knowledge economy has demanded that corporations recognize the value knowledge brings to their employees, business processes, and strategies. In order for any activities requiring knowledge to be effective, the knowledge held by an organization must be accessible. This demands that organizations rely on their ability to organize their knowledge so it is retrievable by the appropriate individuals.

Once acquired, knowledge often needs to be categorized. Knowledge organization is an essential part of knowledge management for several critical reasons. First, seldom is knowledge valuable only at the instant it is created. Ideally, from an organization's point of view, knowledge should be able to be reused multiple times. Reuse of knowledge (as will be discussed in greater length in Chapter 7) is one way in which the organization can amortize the cost of creating knowledge and gain value from it. To be successful for reuse, knowledge needs to be accessible and retrievable. For knowledge to be used effectively and efficiently, the collection of knowledge within the organization must be well structured.

Second, organizing knowledge enables one to see the big picture—that is, connect the dots. Context preservation is essential for knowledge, as without context, knowledge may just be information. Organizing allows us to connect related knowledge nuggets into categories or classes, so that we can analyze them as a group. In the context of tacit knowledge, through knowledge classification we will be able to connect individuals who have similar expertise, interests, etc. Third, organizing knowledge helps us to take a global view of "what we know" and "what we do not know." At the organizational level, this can point to knowledge gaps, critical deficiencies, and dependencies, all of which may help us better plan for and conduct knowledge management. Without having a systematic way of viewing an organization's knowledge, a strategy cannot be developed to acquire needed knowledge or leverage existing knowledge.

The consequences of not organizing knowledge in a manner that leads to retrieval and use can be severe. In 1995, Barings Bank of England went bankrupt as a result of $1 billion in unauthorized trading losses. The report from the Bank of England stated that a number of warning signs were present, including internal audit reports regarding controls over trading accounts and warnings from exchanges on possible trades that violated exchange rules. The knowledge that would have prevented the collapse existed internally and externally to the bank, but it was not received by the appropriate decision makers in order to avoid the failure (Choo, 2005).

This chapter takes as its starting point the various dimensions of knowledge that were explored in Chapter 2 to examine the problems of knowledge organization. Traditional methods used to organize knowledge as seen in libraries, database management, the World Wide Web, and Internet business will all be described. Top-down and bottom up (emergent) methods of organizing knowledge will be discussed as well, including those that utilize social media technologies. This chapter will primarily focus on the organization of explicit knowledge artifacts; however, attention will also be given to the organizational challenges surrounding tacit knowledge.

It is important for organizations to spend resources and effort in managing and categorizing the knowledge that exists within the boundaries of the organization. The fundamental objective of organizing knowledge is to allow for its retrieval. The costs of creating or acquiring useful knowledge are significant, so it is crucial that employees have the skills and the tools to allow them to retrieve the appropriate knowledge when it is required. They require such knowledge to act in their daily routines and job tasks, but also to understand the knowledge the organization possesses regarding a problem situation. We first discuss why organizing knowledge is difficult, and the obstacles faced by knowledge managers when attempting to organize their knowledge. The roots of knowledge organization will be traced through its foundations in library science up to today and the influence of the Internet. The next section discusses the theoretical roots of classification, and how libraries, databases, and online tools have expanded our needs and understanding of knowledge organization. Following a theoretical discussion of organization methods for knowledge, we will examine more practical methods of how organizations establish knowledge organization processes. Through comparing many diverse forms of organization practices, we will apply these methods to the ever-changing business environment faced by knowledge managers. Next, we will highlight the issues and challenges to organizing knowledge, and how new challenges are emerging with the advent of new networking and knowledge-based applications. We then explore a rather unique approach to organizing knowledge—

the creation of knowledge markets. Finally, we will comment on the future of organizing knowledge, and what lies ahead for companies who are searching for new and innovative organization methods for their information and knowledge.

EVOLUTION OF KNOWLEDGE ORGANIZATION

Knowledge exists in many forms in many areas within the organization, which can make it difficult to locate. The problem is further complicated when the organization lacks a comprehensive strategy for organizing knowledge, and many small, ad-hoc systems exist that prevent sharing knowledge beyond these local organizing schemes. It is essential that organizations avoid feudalistic approaches to knowledge organization, and instead establish common systems across the organization that eliminate boundaries to knowledge flow, allow employees from any department to access vital knowledge in other areas, and establish a common classification scheme that is accepted and used by all employees in finding knowledge.

Traditionally, organizations resorted to corporate information repositories, or libraries, in order to establish a centralized knowledge function. Before the proliferation of computers and the advent of digitization, organizations generated a tremendous amount of explicit knowledge in the form of paperwork, and this paperwork required people to administer it in order for it to be accessible to employees within the organization. Commonly this paperwork would be stored in a central location that was accessible only to employees located near the corporate library, who still had to go through the corporate librarian to access the materials. The challenge of knowledge tied to a physical artifact is that it is limited in how it can be distributed and in the number of people who can simultaneously possess the knowledge. Furthermore, physical knowledge assets require procedures to store, catalog, and control access in order to ensure the knowledge is locatable and not lost.

Many organizations deemed an in-house library the solution to their document control challenges. Librarians trained in traditional methods of librarianship became stewards of the organizational memory that resided in physical form. A central repository of documents was established so that employees could search for and use documents under the guidance of the librarian, records manager, or institutional archivist. This centralized approach allowed for appropriate control over the collection, one common and understood system for cataloging, and a balance between storage and version control. Yet this approach had limitations because it relied on one method for access and retrieval and employees with different needs were not easily supported (e.g., employees in different geographic locations).

Organizations must establish a system that preserves the historic corporate record of the organization by archiving knowledge. In order to learn from past successes or mistakes, organizations must retrieve the knowledge they have created in the past and understand this knowledge in today's context. A corporate archive can become an effective tool for teaching new employees about business operations and reminding current employees of past actions. By documenting and archiving business processes, they become available to many departments in a geographically dispersed organization and create a bridge between offices or departments in order to encourage knowledge sharing from the corporate repository.

Organizing knowledge has emerged as an important aspect of knowledge management. Today's organizations have moved away from a top-down, controlled structure that relies on management and senior leadership to dictate knowledge behavior and practices and create routines for employees. Now, more democratic and dynamic forms of knowledge organization are practiced in which the creation of knowledge practices resides at the lower levels of the organization. Knowledge workers are capable, curious, and creative people who enjoy the challenge of new responsibility. They are able to gain a strong understanding of their work environment and develop knowledge organization practices that best fit their organization. Therefore, smart organizations have realized the potential of delegating knowledge organization to lower levels to facilitate more efficient organization practices.

In the past, organizations would design knowledge structures to be fairly static and fixed over time. Examples are the databases found in many legacy systems that remain in use today. The original designers did not foresee many of the changes and new requirements needed by organizations, and utilized a design that was very rigid and difficult to change. However, over time we have learned that the flexibility and adaptability of organization systems and applications is a key design factor for these systems that allows the organization to adapt to its ever-changing business environment. This is not simple, as we cannot possibly envision all types of knowledge sources at the design stage. New frameworks to assist the designers of applications have been developed that recognize the idea of emergent knowledge processes which are difficult to define, yet must be considered by organizations when planning for the future (Markus, Majchrzak, and Gasser, 2002).

ON ORGANIZING KNOWLEDGE

The Difficulty with Knowledge

Organizing the knowledge that exists within a corporation and across the organization is difficult due to the dynamic nature of knowledge. Previous chapters have discussed the many types, forms, and channels that the organization uses to manage knowledge; creating a system that will be able to organize these vast types of knowledge presents challenges for both people and technology.

Most organizations create a system that will categorize their known types of knowledge in order to generate some degree of organization. Not included in this activity are the unknown forms of knowledge that exist but are not easily identifiable, or the forms that have not yet been identified. Tacit knowledge presents a further obstacle, as it is not easily identified, codified, or locatable, all traits necessary for organizing knowledge.

Consider the differences between designing a traditional information system and a knowledge management system. Information systems are capable of dealing with easily defined and codifiable information that can be used to generate reports or create new information for decision makers. The users are clearly identified during the development period, and the information types can be well defined in order to design the user interfaces, database structures, and reporting formats. A knowledge management system is presented with many more obstacles, as knowledge cannot simply be broken down into a form that translates directly to systems engineering documents. In most cases the format it will be received in or used is not known, nor are the potential senders and receivers. Further, knowledge changes in many unpredictable ways based on shifts in an organization's internal and external environments. Knowledge cannot be easily separated from its owner, especially tacit or sticky knowledge. Because separating knowledge from its context can alter its meaning or employees' perception of the knowledge, relying exclusively on systems to manage this knowledge is not recommended. The paradox of dealing with knowledge as a social construct in a technological environment can make certain design requirements of knowledge-based systems very difficult to implement (McDermott, 1999). The conflicts that arise when organizing knowledge, rather than information mirror these systems design challenges. The role of knowledge managers in organizations is to discover new and innovative ways to deal with these challenges in order to create an organized set of knowledge that is identifiable, transferable, and usable by individuals.

The Library Approach: The Historical View of Organizing Knowledge

Over the past centuries, we have seen a progression of how knowledge is organized by organizations. The idea of organizing information and knowledge originated with libraries, which have been the primary keepers of a society's information for centuries. Before the advent of public libraries and other public information resources, there was little need for standardized systems for organizing information and knowledge.

The Beginning of Libraries and Organizing Knowledge

As libraries first emerged in the public sphere, they were often not like the open and accessible structures we know today. Information was controlled by a small and select group of people who acted as a barrier between information and the general public. For example, in medieval times, books and resources were chained to lecterns or shelves in order to control distribution. Some libraries would allow borrowing, but their lending practices were controlled by certain churches, which limited patrons' access to collections. Other libraries, including libraries on some of the first university campuses, would not allow anyone but trained librarians to enter the stacks and handle books. Any requests for access to information resources would need to be considered and approved by the librarians (Putnam, 1962). Therefore, since the volume of information was extremely small and only a few individuals had access, they could install and use their own methods for organizing the codified information. Books sorted in alphabetical order by author, title, date published, or even date received by the library would be quite common. Knowledge organization was not standardized, but rather local and personalized.

A shift in knowledge organization occurred in 1876 when Melvil Dewey created his categorization scheme for books based on subject matter. The purpose was to allow libraries to not only to be more open with their information, but also to create an organizational method that could be shared with other parts of society. The following high-level taxonomy of subjects (Rowley and Hartley, 2008) was created and is still in use today by over 95 percent of libraries in US schools, and over 200,000 libraries worldwide (Weinberger, 2007).

000	Computers and General Reference	500	Natural sciences
100	Philosophy & Psychology	600	Applied sciences
200	Religion	700	Arts and recreation
300	Social sciences	800	Literature
400	Language	900	History and biography

This system was a much-improved evolutionary step over the personalized or random systems as it could be understood and used by the public, therefore allowing a new level of access to mass audiences assuming they could gain the initial access to the materials. Harris defined one of the important duties of a library as classifying their information, or to "determine the exact class to which the book belongs, to place it where it can be found again at once when inquired for" and "to open to the scholar seeking information the entire resources of the library" (1870: 114). However, Dewey's approach was and still is not without many faults, which reflect the problems of using such as standardized in different contexts by many different people.

For example, the **Dewey Decimal System** is based on the metric system: it has ten sections with ten subsections each, and uses decimal points to further subclassify books. One item (or book) must fit only one of these categories, and cannot be classified into multiple locations, due to the restrictions imposed by the physical nature of books. Furthermore, the use of numbers implies a hierarchy; although there is no such hierarchy, many assume that subjects appearing first are more significant than those that occur in the lower numbers.

Other social problems emerged from a system developed in the 1800s by a British scholar, which did not reflect a global view of information. The religious books and languages section (represented by the 200s by Dewey) allocates number 200 to 289 for Christianity, and only 290-299 for what he labeled "other religions." Two major religions in the world, Judaism and Islam, were only allocated one number each, which is disproportionate to their following. A similar problem occurs when we examine how the system organizes languages. The Ural-Altaic, Paleosiberian, and Dravidian languages have their own number (494), yet the Chinese language is not allocated its own number!

Finally, the problem of flexibility and the ability to expand the system is also clearly illustrated by the Dewey Decimal System. Computers and technology are sorted under the 001—the general information section, and not the applied sciences label (found as the 600s). There is a simple explanation for this decision, as computers were not invented nor imagined in the 1800s; therefore, no number was assigned to them. By the time we required the classification scheme to accept computer books, the 600 section was full. Therefore, the 001 label, which had been left open to include "everything else," was utilized to include these information items in the classification scheme (Weinberger, 2007). Many of the traditional organizational systems assume that the categories must be hierarchical to best represent the information, and the idea is to create the one best classification system that will serve all purposes (Miksa, 1988). Libraries attempted to utilize such a categorization scheme, but with the advent of knowledge digitization and the Internet later realized the limitations inherent in their system.

The Database Approach to Organizing Knowledge

Organizations have relied upon methods created for database design and management to organize their knowledge. Many companies rely heavily on their systems to execute their information and knowledge strategies, and therefore the technology often determines how knowledge is classified and organized. Although many databases are designed with flexibility and portability in mind, the requirements to achieve such goals in data management often vary from those required for effective knowledge management.

Database design works with two basic concepts, entities and relationships (Zhang and Salaba, 2009). For example, when designing a database for a school, entities could be students, faculty, classrooms, and courses. Relationships link entities together, such as students' enrollment in courses or the use of classrooms for courses. This creates a relational database model, which is then used by data and system architects to begin designing the storage aspects of the system (Chen, 1976). The conceptual scheme is created, which describes the data to be stored based on the relational data model (Ramakrishnan, 1998).

A relational database design is similar to creating a system for organizing knowledge, as it is a framework for categorizing and organizing data in a system (i.e., in the same way that a classification scheme is meant to categorize and organize knowledge). Standards are defined for data names, formats, and documentation in order to ensure consistency, quality, and searchability of data.

However, database design principles are based on the notions of fixed data types, non-dynamic data structures, and easily categorized and defined data types. Much of the design process for databases involves defining data at the lowest level, in order to generate a very specific description of the requirements for handling the data. Knowledge cannot be subjected to such a procedure, as it cannot be removed from its context and reduced to simple elements. These characteristics of typical organizational data are not shared with organizational knowledge, and therefore systems used to classify knowledge demand higher degrees of flexibility, adaptability, and user focus.

The World Wide Web Approach to Organizing Knowledge

Other technologies have helped the practice of knowledge organization evolve. The Internet and the World Wide Web (WWW) have given us a tremendous source for information and knowledge. They have also presented a challenge for those who wish to organize knowledge such that it is categorized, sorted, and easily retrieved by information systems. The constant influx of new webpages and information has required a shift in how we view the process of knowledge organization. No longer can each new information item be labeled and categorized amongst a standard scheme that would be useful to users around the world.

The Internet is a collection of large amounts of information that is derived from people with varying interests, beliefs, positions, cultures, traditional knowledge, and expertise. These differences in creators and users make it challenging to organize its information in such a way that will be understood and used by a global user base.

The only true taxonomy of websites is created through the domain registry process, where the users have the opportunity to classify their sites based on the domains they choose to house the site. The .com domain is traditionally used for business, the .org domain is for other organizations (many nonprofits), and the .edu is used for educational institutions in the United States. Nine top-level domains were originally defined for use in the 1980s when the system was created. Countries also have their own domain extensions (e.g., .ca for Canada, .uk for the United Kingdom) based on ISO-3166 country abbreviations. Although the creation of domain names is controlled by the Internet Corporation for Assigned Names and Numbers (ICANN), many other countries and organizations would like to see a more internationally represented organization control this aspect of the Internet (Mueller, 2002). This system is self-controlled and relies on individuals to correctly place a site in the most appropriate domain.

In the early years of the WWW, many organizations tried to create a directory of websites, and in fact a few people tried to publish books that were the yellow-pages of the WWW, listing websites on a physical document! The most popular online directory was *Yahoo!*, which created a tree-structure directory for searching the web. It allowed users who were looking for a particular site to browse others that were listed in the same category, similar to how one would browse books on the shelves of a library. As expected, the maintenance of such lists and directories became unmanageable as use of the web exploded and millions of new websites were being created every day. Also, it suffered many of the same problems the Dewey Decimal System has with its confined structure.

The Internet has moved from a knowledge source that individuals and organizations tried to control and organize into a disorganized information and knowledge store. From its use of hyperlinks to its unprecedented growth, it has become impossible to organize such as vast and diverse knowledge source. These attributes of the Internet have given rise to companies such as Google, which tries to bring the appearance of organization through its complex and multifaceted search tools. By striving for accuracy and relevance in searching the Internet, Google attempts to present the user with structured and organized search results that can be easily understood and used. The properties of digitized knowledge present many obstacles to organizations. However, smart organizations and corporations have used these challenges to their advantage.

The Amazon.com Approach to Organizing Knowledge

We can look beyond technologies and point to new forms of organizations that have created new methods of knowledge organization. Amazon.com began as a bookstore, and a bookstore is not entirely different from a library. Each deals with books as a source of knowledge, and attempts to organize these sources based on not only author and title but also the subject matter of the book. Both strive to provide the best access to information possible. Libraries want users to find the knowledge they are seeking, and Amazon wants customers to find the books they want (and related books) in order to drive purchases and generate revenue. However, when it comes to organizing the books available that the public can view and search through, Amazon has the distinct advantage as it does not deal with physical goods until an order has shipped, whereas the library must have physical goods organized, in public view, and searchable in order to create information access.

Amazon can digitally place any product it sells in many sections, allowing multiple searches to be successful. A book for children on the life of baseball great Babe Ruth can be categorized as a children's book, a sports book, a baseball book, a biography, and a book on American history. A library might have to make the decision to categorize it as a baseball book and place it in the sports section (796), or as a biography and locate the physical book in the biography section (940). Theoretically, the multiple labels for one book should make it easier to find and, therefore, more accessible to the public. Other types of products such as movies, music, or toys can be classified in a similar, flexible manner. Furthermore, when searching on Amazon.com, you are often presented with not only the product you wanted to find, but also additional information:

- Other books by the author/artist/actor
- Other related products
- Recommendations based on your search
- Customer reviews of the products
- The ability to search within the text of the book, not just the bibliographic metadata

Amazon's system uses the notion that similar items should be classified together. However, similarity is not a quality found in a particular item; instead it exists in the relation between items. Many argue that any two items can be found to have aspects that are similar, depending on the flexibility of the categorization scheme (Broadfield, 1946). Therefore, in Amazon's case, it relies on the triangulation of many algorithms that search **metadata** on both the customer and the products in order to improve its accuracy. This is an attempt to replace the human element required for organizing information. All of this information provided to the user when searching for books is not only to help them find the book and knowledge they want, but also to help them find other related information that may be valuable (Weinberger, 2007). It is akin to browsing the shelves of a library, but much more efficient and powerful.

THEORETICAL ASPECTS OF ORGANIZING KNOWLEDGE

Methods for organizing knowledge have a rich heritage that was initiated in the field of library and information science. Many of the advanced concepts for handling and sorting knowledge used today can be traced back to procedures created for the management and operation of libraries. The concepts originating from library science are important to understand when organizing traditional and dynamic forms of knowledge.

Classifications of Knowledge

As part of the process of organizing knowledge, we must have an understanding of the knowledge in order to interpret its meaning and understand how it would be used in an organization. To go beyond matching a piece of knowledge with another, an individual must understand not only the knowledge and its context, but also the taxonomy scheme being used. Since knowledge can usually be classified through various means, the person who is organizing the knowledge must be able to defend how exactly they organize the knowledge. It is not a task that is easily automated, as judgment plays a significant role in interpreting knowledge and categorization methods (Mai, 2010). Table 5.1 describes common characteristics of classification methods.

In order to organize the knowledge that organizations possess, they need to develop *classification* methods or taxonomies that are explicit, available to those who created and those that will use the system, and designed to be compatible with both the users and the knowledge. A **classification** can be defined as "a spatial, temporal, or spatio-temporal segmentation of the world," and therefore a classification system can be viewed "as a set of boxes (metaphorical or literal) into which things can be put to then do some kind of work" (Bowker and Star, 1999: 10). Most classification systems rely on the creation of categories that define the relationships between knowledge items. By arranging knowledge in a systematic way, these systems provide an overview of the field covered, and make the retrieval of one knowledge object possible without searching through the entire collection. An example of such a categorization system is the menu bar found on most software applications that arrange functions into categories such as file operations, edit operations, viewing operations, and so on. Therefore, a classification scheme is simply the systematic arrangement of a list of items in order to make the items practical to use and easy to retrieve. Typical classification schemes consist of schedules, or a listing of the subjects that depicts their relationships; a notion, or a code using numbers and/or letters that are used to arrange the subjects within the schedules; and an alphabetical index that makes finding terms within the schedules much easier. An effective classification scheme should be consistent, with unique classificatory principles in use. The categories are mutually exclusive, and the

Table 5.1. Characteristics of Classification Methods	
Characteristic	**Description**
Rely on categories	• Rely on the creation of categories, which define the relationship between knowledge items
Provide schedules and indexes	• Provide schedules that list the categories or subjects that are described within the system • Provide indexes such as an alphabetical listing of subjects to assist in navigating the system
Use notation systems	• Include notation systems such as numeric codes that provide a shorthand to describe categories and subcategories (e.g., Dewey decimal notation)
Support mutual exclusivity	• Ensure that an item can be classified in only one category and subcategory in the system
Provide for exhaustivity	• Ensure that the system is complete so all intended objects can be classified and classified accurately

system is complete so all intended objects can be classified and classified accurately (Bowker and Star, 1999).

Classification schedules are divided into *subclasses* in order to more accurately define the knowledge being organized. Two approaches exist for this type of division. Top-down, deductive procedures that divide a large group into smaller groups, and those small groups into even smaller groups are known as **enumerative classification** approaches. This is a hierarchical approach that does not allow for complex relationship structures, or can encourage the extreme subdivision of classes where these subjects created become too narrow. The second approach, **faceted classification**, constructs schedules from an inductive or bottom-up procedure. This requires extensive experience and familiarity with the knowledge being organized in order to create accurate and meaningful subjects, however, it is a more flexible system that can be maintained with some ease (Rowley and Hartley, 2008).

Knowledge taxonomies are groups of concepts arranged in a hierarchy and can be represented in a graphical depiction to reflect the concepts and relationships amongst those concepts in either a particular field or one organization. **Knowledge dictionaries** list key concepts and terms that are used within the taxonomy to allow for its use by members of the organization. In a taxonomy, the higher the concept is placed, the more generic the concept is. Conversely, the lower placed concepts are very specific instances of the high level concepts. Taxonomies are built upon the idea of inheritance, which implies that lower level concepts inherit properties of the concepts found immediately above them. This creates a "parent-child relationship" as properties of the parent are passed along to the child. All organizational stakeholders should be in agreement with the knowledge taxonomy in order to prevent ad hoc changes and variations to occur. These alterations can have a negative effect on the taxonomy's ability to effectively assist in knowledge retrieval (Dalkir, 2005).

The process to classify knowledge as part of a knowledge organization project is quite straightforward. The first step is to analyze the subject, whether relying on the knowledge itself or outside sources and metadata. Secondly, utilize the classification schedule that has been identified as the most appropriate and examine the summary tables and work downward through the schedules. These are the classifications that can be used for the knowledge being organized. If the knowledge falls between multiple disciplines, then recognize the class as the discipline that receives the greatest emphasis or use schedules that provide instructions for classifying interdisciplinary works. In many cases, a precise order for the subjects will have to be determined, which can be complicated when two independent themes are present. Finally, review the classification work to ensure that moving upwards in the hierarchy leads one from the knowledge through the appropriate subjects (Rowley and Hartley, 2008).

Classifying Knowledge with Organizations

Organizations have deployed a multitude of approaches to classify knowledge. One approach is to classify knowledge by its *value proposition* (Desouza and Awazu, 2005). Consider the following case: is the knowledge of how to fix a broken toaster or knowledge of the best vintage for French Bordeaux as valuable as bioengineering within the context of a pharmaceutical firm? The obvious answer is no! While valuable, the knowledge of how to fix a toaster or what wine to drink during dinner does not generate value at the same level as knowledge of bioengineering within a pharmaceutical organization. Now, consider another case: the information technology division of a financial firm. The firm has two employees, both of whom have knowledge of Java (a programming language), but one has more than ten years of experience within the financial sector, whereas the other has ten years of experience spread evenly across the manufacturing, government, healthcare, and financial sector. Which employee is more valuable to the organization? More specifically, which employee has knowledge that is more valuable to the financial firm? In most cases, the answer is the employee with deeper experience within the given industry. Why? The employee with deeper industry experience will be better placed to apply his/her knowledge of programming to realize value for the organization. Another way to think about the question of value is as follows: if you had to lose one of the two employees, who would be the easier one to replace? While it will be easy to hire someone with generic Java programming skills (most students who graduate with an undergraduate degree in computer science will have these skills), it will be a greater challenge to find someone who has knowledge of programming information systems work within the financial sector.

As the two brief illustrations show, the ability to classify knowledge based on the value proposition is vitally important for organizations. To this end, one classification scheme that we have found helpful is to adopt the resource-based view (RBV) that has been used extensively in the management domain (Barney, 2001; Barney, Wright, and Ketchen Jr., 2001). The RBV has been used as a framework to help organizations focus on resources that have competitive value. Resources are evaluated based on their Value, Rarity, Inimitability, and Non-substitutability (VRIN).

- *Value*: The first question to ask is, "Does the knowledge have value to the organization?" If the answer is yes, then it is a candidate to be managed. If no, then exerting effort and resources to manage it may not result in any organizational value (and may actually negatively impact the organization, as resources that are expended towards its management could be used for other productive purposes).
- *Rarity*: The second question to ask is, "Is the knowledge rare?" If it is, then you must manage the knowledge, as its loss might prove costly for the organization. Knowledge that is rare needs to be identified as such. In the case of rare knowledge that is in an explicit format, consider a rare book in the library: access to it should be limited and the artifact must be handled with care. In the case of tacit knowledge, sources of knowledge that is rare need special attention, as in the case of experts or individuals with long tenure within an organization.
- *Imitatability*: Third, ask, "Can the knowledge be imitated?" In the context of explicit knowledge, the simplest manifestation of this is in the ability to duplicate the artifact. In the case of a rare book or an original video recording or even a valuable photograph, the question of reproducibility through copying becomes important. If the knowledge artifact can be copied (both from a technical perspective, but also from a legal and ownership perspective), then it is in an organization's best interest to make copies so that it can be accessed in an

efficient manner and also to protect itself against loss. In the case of tacit knowledge, if the knowledge can be imitated, then it will be in the organization's best interest to train and transfer this knowledge to other individuals within the organization. Similar to the rationale for making copies in the case of explicit knowledge, this reduces the dependencies of the organization on the singular sources that possess the tacit knowledge.

- *Non-substitutability*: The final questions is, "If the knowledge artifact is lost, can another knowledge artifact be substituted on its behalf?" This question focuses attention on whether there are alternatives for the knowledge artifact, in the case of explicit knowledge, or individual, in the case of tacit knowledge. If there are none, then the artifact or the individual deserves the greatest amount of attention in terms of knowledge management. In the case of explicit artifacts these need to be protected with the strictest regiments. Consider the case of the well-protected secret of the Coca-Cola formula or how artifacts are protected in museums. In the case of tacit knowledge sources, these individuals are well-protected within the organization. These individuals are recognized for their unique knowledge, expertise, and skills. They are given the freedom to develop these further, and mobilize them towards the benefit of the organization. Incentives through compensation and other mechanisms (such as freedom to choose which projects they work on) are provided to entice them to stay with the organization. For example, in Microsoft, individuals who meet these characteristics are given titles such as Technical Fellows. Microsoft outlines the value of this designation as follows: "The special designation of 'Technical Fellow' is an acknowledgement of the key role a technical leader plays in driving intentional innovation, in alignment with Microsoft's business strategies, which in turn impacts the high-tech industry overall. A Technical Fellow's technical vision, expertise and world-class leadership is commensurate with that of a corporate vice president focused on business leadership. These individuals are instrumental in developing and driving technical strategies for Microsoft and the technology industry" (Microsoft, 2011).

Taken collectively, the criteria of value, rarity, inimitability, and non-substitutability can help an organization to direct resources to manage knowledge. A knowledge nugget or source that meets all these characteristics should be the primary concern of the knowledge manager, as they represent the knowledge assets that are the most valuable.

Knowledge Relationships

Knowledge, whether tacit or explicit, does not exist in isolation from other knowledge. This concept of **intertextuality** states that relationships between knowledge and knowledge sources should be established in order to make connections between different yet connected knowledge sources. These relationships can be different types, including:

- *Equivalence relationships*: Exist between exact copies or replicas of a document or work, and include photocopies or digital reproductions

- *Derivative relationships*: Items modified from the original item, which may include differing versions, editions, or revisions
- *Descriptive relationships*: The relationship between the original work and a description of that work, including commentaries and critiques
- *Accompanying relationships*: Two works that augment each other, and extend an original work
- *Sequential relationships*: Bibliographic items that continue or precede one another, such as sequels or series (Rowley and Hartley, 2008)

The Need to Establish Knowledge Relationships

Establishing relationships between pieces of knowledge is critical so that a complete set of knowledge can be made available when creating strategies or making important decisions. In 1998, Bridgestone/Firestone Inc. was forced to recall more than 6.5 million tires due to accidents caused by treads separating from the tire cores. This caused a public relations nightmare for the organization, as it was discovered that evidence existed in many forms that the tires had structural problems and should have been recalled at an earlier date. Reports from insurance firms to the National Highway Traffic Safety Administration and observances by Ford Motor Co. in other countries regarding similar problems existed, but were not made available to those who required such knowledge to make a decision regarding recalls. If Bridgestone/Firestone had established the ability to classify these pieces of knowledge as having a relationship to each other, a better understanding of the problem would have been generated and this knowledge could have been used to make better decision regarding the recalls (Choo, 2005).

One reason why knowledge relationships are important is to enable for visualization of the knowledge space. Put another way, how do you see the big picture by connecting the various knowledge elements? As in the tragic case of the failure of the US intelligence agencies to connect the dots on various knowledge elements that signaled an impending terrorist attack, the ability to see the forest beyond the trees is vital. Knowledge visualization is a key capability that organizations are trying to master. There are many approaches toward this end. The most simplistic of these is tools such as mind map, which is a document that represents words, ideas, and knowledge in a structured or organized picture. This knowledge is presented in a nonlinear manner to encourage the brainstorming approach to idea formation. It appears as a web or tree structure where ideas are linked together in order to solve problems, outline a design, or create an individual expression of creativity. Other approaches include techniques such as social network analysis (as described in Chapter 6, "Knowledge Transfer") that helps us visualize where expertise resides within the organization. More traditional techniques include creating knowledge directories within the organization that can be used to find individuals and collections of individuals who have expertise on given projects or those that work on specific projects. By keeping track of not only the knowledge that was created or gained by the project, but who received the knowledge and experience, an organization can then apply this knowledge again by assigning the knowledgeable people to different projects which encourages knowledge sharing throughout the organization. These ideas closely mirror the database approach to organizing knowledge, which was discussed earlier in the chapter.

Metadata for Knowledge Representation

Much of the work associated with identifying and classifying knowledge is represented in the *metadata* that is created regarding the knowledge. Metadata is simply defined as "data about data," or the description created about the knowledge. Metadata is structured in order to aid individuals or technology in the identification, retrieval, and manipulation of the knowledge. It is a form of knowledge representation, but is not intended to replace or substitute for the original knowledge.

Metadata has several purposes in organizing knowledge. Firstly, it provides a clear description of the resource so an inventory of knowledge can be created. This is useful for organizations that have quality standard requirements to document what knowledge is available, or for knowledge management programs focusing on locating knowledge within the organization. Metadata supports resource discovery across multiple platforms in the organization. Whether the individual is searching via an intranet or a knowledge management system, metadata will provide direction for their search. Many content management functions that oversee online content, whether internally and/or externally, require metadata to manage document lifecycles, ownership, and modification or version history records. Particular to digital resources, metadata can provide the means to declare ownership of intellectual content and verify the authenticity of a document. This is quite useful when information resources are used in legal and contractual situations. Finally, metadata acts as an enabler for the transfer of knowledge between information systems, and allows for much of the interoperability between different organizational systems. Metadata supports knowledge that is being passed between systems by allowing the receiving system to make sense of the knowledge and understand how to use it. Many systems supporting supply chain management use metadata to label the goods and materials being shipped between organizations by tagging item descriptions with metadata that allow for the receiving organization to directly input the received goods into its inventory system.

When storing the metadata of knowledge in organizations, the major issue is the preservation of context. For example, if you speak multiple languages, you will know that words and phrases may not translate exactly across language barriers and some-times it is hard to appreciate jokes that are not in your native language. Similarly, knowledge is context sensitive and the users of knowledge need to be informed of the context in which the knowledge was generated and the context for its use. To this end, several things are important for knowledge managers. First is to store details of who created the knowledge, as the source of a particular knowledge nugget will play a vital role in receiving more details about the knowledge artifact or encouraging future knowledge flows. Moreover, sources will also impact how people will use the artifact (this issue is discussed in greater length in Chapter 7, "Knowledge Application"). Second, it is essential to store details on the context under which the knowledge was created (e.g., was the knowledge created to solve a particular problem, was it the out-come of a random discovery, etc.?) For example, in research the results of experiments are valuable only if they can be compared across studies, and to do so there must be enough knowledge available about the studies to ensure that they can be replicated and fairly compared. Moreover, for individuals, an organization will need to know that the knowledge they are seeking originated in similar or near-similar contexts for it to be applicable. Context for knowledge can be stored by encapsulating details of the problems that the knowledge is purported to solve, the conditions under which the knowledge was created and what its implications might be, and storing other caveats such as areas for future development.

Finally, details on how to use the knowledge artifact need to be managed. For example, one might think of having expiration dates (like those found on milk cartons) for knowledge artifacts—these would indicate when the knowledge artifact is obsolete. Similarly, like prescription drugs, one can think of storing details on when a knowledge artifact should be used and what some of its adverse consequences might be, and who to contact if these materialize. Also, details such as which other knowledge artifacts are related to the given nugget would be valuable. Obviously, these are applicable only for explicit knowledge artifacts. In the case of tacit knowledge artifacts, metadata can include things such as best times and mediums to contact the knowledge source, or prior projects the knowledge source worked on.

DIMENSIONS AND METHODOLOGIES FOR ORGANIZING KNOWLEDGE

Organizing Knowledge Using a Top-Down Approach

Most organizations employ a top-down method when organizing their knowledge. Managers or the senior personnel who have responsibility for information in the organization develop the categorization schemes and organization methods that are reflected within the organization's information systems. The approach taken by most individuals who design knowledge-based systems in organizations is one that has its roots in the design of databases, where hierarchical structures were most often used. This approach was translated into methods for organizing other knowledge contained within the organization, including the codified knowledge most commonly found on corporate intranets. Like the approach Yahoo! took when first attempting to organize websites found on the emerging Internet, organizations created tree structures for categorizing and storing knowledge on intranets, as they assumed this was the easiest format for employees to locate and acquire the documents, reports, presentations, and other information. The assumption was made that people search for knowledge the same way they would search for data within a large corporate database. This proved to be incorrect; many cases have been written about the failure of intranets to become successful knowledge repositories and a platform for organizational memory (Detlor, 2004; Ruppel and Harrington, 2001). Intranets designed with poor organization methods quickly became information junkyards and repositories of unused knowledge.

Top-down approaches to organizing knowledge can be effective within the right context. In many cases it is in organizations' best interests to classify and organize their knowledge:

- *By source*: Not only does this method allow for easy retrieval if you know the author of the document, it will group multiple instances of a person's codified knowledge together, creating a profile of what they know which can be representative of the tacit knowledge they possess.

- *By form*: This method makes storage in a knowledge-based system easy because the different forms of knowledge can easily be grouped and accessed together; however, most users do not search for this classification, and it does not group similar items together.
- *By impact*: If the organization can devise an accurate measure to reflect the impact of the knowledge, then this form of classification will illuminate the types of information that are used in the organization, and who is creating knowledge that is impactful.
- *By risk*: As the notion of risk management permeates organizations, classifying knowledge in order to support the management of strategic and operational risks can have wide benefits throughout the organization, especially in support of decision making.
- *By value proposition*: Once again, if an acceptable metric for quantifying the value knowledge can provide the organization can be implemented, then organizing knowledge by its value to the users and the entire organization can help identify a focus for knowledge management.

A centralized top-down control structure to organizing knowledge allows the organization to use a controlled indexing language (or vocabulary) to describe the subjects. Control is important for consistency since the terms which will be used are defined, the relationships between those terms are exact, and therefore searching becomes much more efficient. The opposite of controlled vocabularies are natural language vocabularies, where the author, title, and citation indexes are all derived from system terms. Using the full text in indexing produces a very detailed index (Rowley and Hartley, 2008).

The knowledge manager has an important role to play in this organizing approach because much of the strategy and guidance for identifying, classifying, and organizing the knowledge must come from the top. Managers will have to define the procedures (such as the procedures for dealing with nonroutine forms of knowledge), the scope of the knowledge to be organized, and the classification scheme to be used. And if the classification scheme is unique to the organization, managers will have to determine how it will be developed. Any knowledge organizing activities will fall under the realm of knowledge management, so ensuring that organizational knowledge can be integrated into existing knowledge management systems (where applicable) and that the emphasis is on the improved ability of employees to retrieve and use knowledge become the responsibility of a knowledge manager.

Organizing Knowledge Using a Bottom-Up Approach

As knowledge becomes more social, so should the methods used to organize knowledge. Although traditional classification systems have demonstrated authority by their status within the organization, and many of them still endure charges of bias and politics, new classification schemes must be developed in order to maintain the trust of the users. The bias of an organizational system can be one of its most prevalent problems (Mai, 2010).

As social media and crowdsourcing methods have become recognized in the corporate world, these tools have been applied to the organization of knowledge. Through the realization that for some knowledge it is not required to have a centralized control mechanism for the classification schedule, this control has been disseminated to the public or users of the knowledge. Not only can resources and time be saved through "employing" users to create a system, they will also exert effort in applying the system they create and classifying individual items. Users can be very close to the knowledge they use and may also have tacit knowledge regarding the subject matter or the resource that the organization does not have. Therefore, given the ability to apply this tacit knowledge in organizing knowledge, they can enrich the organization's understanding of the knowledge and create a system that is more customized, usable, and understood by similar individuals. These updates in some cases can occur in real time depending on the technology being used (such as many social media services), allowing for ongoing monitoring of the content.

Two of the most popular implementations of socially organizing knowledge are YouTube and Flickr. These sites allow users to post their respective videos or pictures online to share with the general public or a select group of users. They can also allow anyone to assign a tag or subject label that describes the content of a picture or video. As video and pictures do not share the ability to be automatically indexed or cataloged by technology with textual items, these service providers are overcoming the technical challenge of classifying the knowledge depicted in the visualizations by allowing large groups of users to complete the work. Tagging involves either generating a new classification or label, or selecting a label from a predetermined set of categories and applying it to an image, video or other knowledge product.

Other examples of bottom-up organizational endeavors emerged from the need to organize very large amounts of knowledge that could be done only through human judgment. As NASA used satellites and robotics to map the surface of Mars, it generated an enormous amount of information on the surface of the planet, including structures of craters and other rock formations. The goal was to have all formations classified under a system developed for astronomers studying other moons and planets. Since it was not possible to allocate enough resources to this massive categorization project, NASA turned to the public. A website called "Be a Martian" (http://beamartian .jpl.nasa.gov) was established to allow volunteers to participate in mapping features of the surface or counting craters. Here, basic tagging principles allowed users to have fun and earn virtual badges while creating valuable knowledge for NASA scientists.

Some problems can occur with this approach. The expertise and knowledge of the organizers cannot be predetermined, so the quality of classification work can vary greatly, depending on the population performing the work. Tags may not be mutually exclusive, or may be very redundant if users have the ability to create their own tags. Perceptions, biases, and politics may also come into play when users exercise their own judgment in organizing knowledge. Finally, technology or other systems must be used to coordinate such large-scale efforts in order to ensure completeness and direction of the work.

Although this is a noncentralized approach to organizing knowledge, a knowledge manager will still have an essential role to play in the bottom-up management of knowledge. The scope of the knowledge to be organized must be defined, and strategies as to how to effectively engage the user or broader community must be developed. Sometimes "seeding" the category list will set implicit guidelines and standards for other users to follow. A strategy for launching and initially supporting the organization work should be developed. More important, procedures for handling conflicts and unexpected events will have to be devised to ensure that those participating in the organizing of knowledge receive reciprocal value for their efforts. Determining how to review and evaluate the results of the organizing work will be important, as a balance must be struck between too much revision and control, and leaving inconsistencies or inaccurate classifications intact.

MANAGING KNOWLEDGE IN PROJECTS[1]

Globalization is quickly eroding the number of companies that enjoy and can protect a "home turf" advantage. As telecommunications and free-trade zones work to homogenize the rules and standards of engagement in geographically dispersed markets, companies must compete for any and all opportunities. This implies having the ability to put the best available team on a project. One benefit of having a larger, global organization is the ability to call on a deeper, more diverse talent pool to form project teams. But organizing globally dispersed resources can be challenging as distances, work habits, and cultures all act to inhibit group cohesion and productivity. By viewing knowledge acquired by organizations through a project lens, they can better manage and organize the knowledge gained and used from the execution of projects. Table 5.2 summarizes the types of knowledge that exist within projects in organizations.

A project management framework offers an increasingly used set of tools for planning and organizing work. A well-designed knowledge management system should take into consideration the types of projects, formal or informal, that an organization engages in and understand the knowledge management requirements for those projects.

Table 5.2. Types of Project-Related Knowledge	
Type	**Description**
Knowledge about projects	• High-level information about projects (metadata) such as project descriptions, cost estimates, and schedule information, which is useful to decision makers across the organization
Knowledge from projects	• Lessons learned and innovations that occur as part of project initiatives, and which the project team should ideally capture and make available to other project teams
Knowledge in projects	• Knowledge that is required to execute the project; systems and tools are required so that teams members can manage and manipulate this knowledge

Understanding how work is accomplished and the specific business processes will provide additional guidance as to the best structure and core features a knowledge system should offer.

Turner (1993: 8) defines a **project** as "an endeavor in which human, material and financial resources are organized in a novel way, to undertake a unique scope of work, for a given specification, within constraints of cost and time, so as to achieve beneficial changes defined by quantitative and qualitative objectives." Projects have moved from being simple phenomena to manage to more complex entities that span geographical locations, multiple occurrences, and different organizational affiliations. Evaristo and Fenema (1999) proposed a typology of projects, based on two dimensions: the number of locations (single versus multiple) and the number of projects (single versus multiple). The traditional structure is a single project in a single location, although multiple projects running at one location (colocated programs) are now typical within organizations. A distributed project is a single endeavor being conducted by individuals from multiple locations. Finally, the most complicated scenario is multiple projects conducted at multiple locations. Complexities can be attributed to managing multiple interdependencies across time, space, and projects. Organizations engage in multiple forms of these projects on a regular basis. The challenge for organizations is to ensure that knowledge is managed within, and across, the various projects. This challenge is exacerbated when we think of global, and distributed, projects.

Knowledge about projects includes project descriptions, cost, and schedule information, artifacts normally aggregated by organizations that formally recognize the "project" as a basic unit of business operations. However, many companies adopt the project model for task execution and do capture or aggregate the information about their operations. This can lead to a lack of understanding of where the organization is heading strategically or how it could improve its own performance. It is important to discover what systems are currently collecting this type of knowledge and consider exposing that knowledge through your knowledge system to decision makers. In many instances a simple understanding of costs and scope for certain types of activities can improve decision making in other areas of the organization.

Knowledge from projects creates multiple artifacts that are developed over the course of a project's lifecycle. The lack of rigor around capturing lessons learned and process innovations conducted for the sake of a specific project are major sources of knowledge loss and, thus, operational efficiency in corporations. However, the capture, formatting, and organization of such artifacts take time and effort, not to mention the time and effort required to search through large repositories of knowledge artifacts that may or may not support task execution. Care must be taken to consider what knowledge is useful to capture and to make available to other project teams. Knowledge systems should be designed so that capture and organization of such artifacts is easy and that the process for doing so fits as seamlessly into a project team's normal workflow.

Knowledge in projects is comprised of the work break down structures, the team calendars and available resources required to execute the project itself. Knowledge systems should provide tools so this knowledge can be managed and manipulated by team members. When catering to distributed project teams, providing a variety of collaboration features enables project teams to overcome geographic distances and time separations with tools that match both their work requirements and personal working preferences. However, not all members of a project team will feel comfortable with new tools. Variety should be balanced against simple training options and guidance on best practice for using tools in specific types of situations. Such guidance will assist the organization of knowledge collected in the process of collaboration, making transfer of such knowledge from the context of a team to the rest of the organization more efficient.

After surveying an organization's operations and gaining an understanding of the work routines and business processes utilized, including what knowledge from other locations employees use, the overall topography of a knowledge management system for global use can be designed. The topography of the system will dictate the natural flow of knowledge. When configured properly, it will facilitate the flow of relevant knowledge across key organizational boundaries while mitigating the risk of information overload through keeping some knowledge purely local.

Approaches for Managing Project Knowledge

Client-Server Model

As depicted in Figure 5.1, a client-server approach to knowledge management provides a central repository for organizational knowledge. Individual agents in the organization access the knowledge base for retrieval and update purposes. In this approach, individual employees or groups in the network request and publish knowledge to a central server. Clients cannot own the resources on the server. They are allowed to use them, but control of the knowledge and the processes which manage that knowledge are held centrally.

Centralized configurations are useful when project teams perform similar forms of work. This model also enables system managers to filter and control the volume and

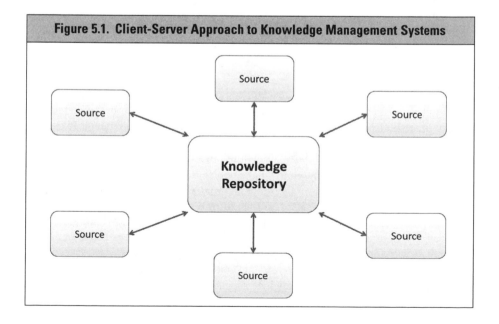

Figure 5.1. Client-Server Approach to Knowledge Management Systems

quality of content available to the rest of the organization. A company pursuing a global organizational strategy would prefer this type of system as minimal direct interaction between operating nodes and project teams ensures maximum standardization across many groups' processes, procedures and the work product.

There is often resistance to contributing to such a centralized repository. Stein and Ridderstrale (2001) discuss three reasons why people resist sharing knowledge. They include fear of retaliation or penalties imposed by the business for stepping outside of dictated norms, monopolization, the feeling that knowledge is power and by sharing knowledge one loses power, and restrictions such as the lack of ease of contribution and the lack of control over the knowledge once contributed. These systems often don't allow for less formal working spaces where employees can develop new ideas and get feedback from trusted colleagues before posting to the central repository. This has certain advantages for enforcing work protocols and standards, and also the ability to strictly control the quality of content that is made available to the organization, but it must be rationalized against both the organizational strategy and work styles actually being employed in each operating division.

Another key advantage of a centralized system approach is the ability to create and control the categorization scheme for all of the knowledge collected. As discussed previously in this chapter, such a scheme makes knowledge discovery more efficient as users learn to expect what types of knowledge are stored in what section of the system and are able to increase the speed of their task execution based on this learning. The drawbacks to a centralized organizational scheme include the amount of time and energy required to properly categorize contributions. Additional features can be added to enable ranking mechanisms to indicate relevance and for end users to be able to develop more personal "views" of the information, which allows individuals to apply their own "sense making" to the repository structure. However, the overall value proposition of centralized configurations remains to enhance control over content quality and organization by a central entity and an enhanced ability to enforce organizational standards to knowledge management processes.

Decentralized Approach

At the opposite end of the spectrum, as depicted in Figure 5.2, a peer-to-peer networking model allows each node to act as both a client and a server. As such it can access content directly from other nodes in the network and also publish content, making it available for any other group within the organization. Peer-to-peer computing is enhanced by the current availability of mobile devices, and ad hoc meetings can be easily arranged to clarify assumptions, make decisions, or justify previous decisions.

As individuals gain control over their own knowledge repositories, they are less likely to view sharing of knowledge as a threat to their own status and will be more likely to make contributions. Similarly, with the absence of any centralized standards for formatting, content quality, or other contribution protocol, the concerns about retaliation are dramatically reduced as are perceptions of restrictions.

There is a downside to such systems if content quality and version control are important issues. Distributed systems lend themselves to multiple versions and variations on knowledge artifacts, leading to an increase in innovation but not necessarily

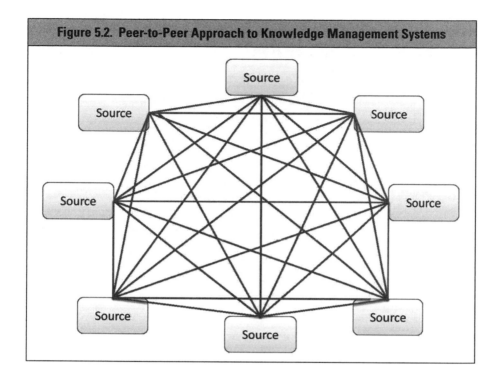

Figure 5.2. Peer-to-Peer Approach to Knowledge Management Systems

precision. They also lead to dissociation between the original knowledge source and the knowledge that gets used. In many organizational cultures the inability to assign credit for the genesis of an idea is less important. In others, it is critical. Another problem these types of configurations often have is in enabling the discovery process. Unlike a centralized repository, users have little or no idea how to find particular categories of information. Searching and browsing activities often result in too many results with too little immediate relevance to the task at hand.

However, the lack of a centralized organizational scheme is partially overcome by the natural tendency of people to seek and share what they feel is valuable. This tendency can be enhanced by employing "business intelligence" tools that enable end users to rate and tag useful content. Such functionality enables a more democratic process for establishing organizational best practices and also provides an audit trail to trace useful work products back to the roots of their creation. For companies such as Google that thrive on innovation and a first-to-market strategy, the speed and intensity of collaboration enabled by such systems more than overcomes the lack of a centrally controlled repository.

Hybrid Approach

A hybrid model as depicted in Figure 5.3 is used to realize the benefits of both the centralized and decentralized approaches while mitigating the downsides of each. In this model, a central repository is used to store and organize knowledge about projects. This is considered "authoritative content" that the organization recognizes as valid or

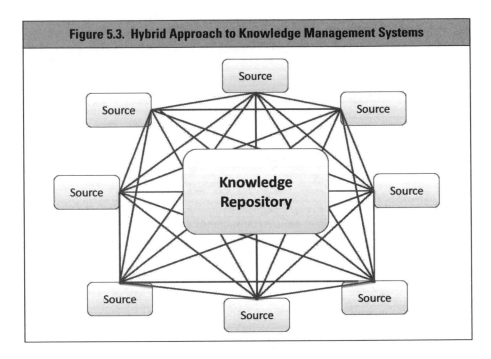

Figure 5.3. Hybrid Approach to Knowledge Management Systems

a best practice. However, the end users of the system are allowed to collaborate directly and to manage working knowledge, or knowledge required to execute projects. These areas allow for decentralized control and low barriers to contribution. When working knowledge is deemed to be significant enough to share with the rest of the organization, it is transferred to the central repository for review and publishing.

Social Tagging and the Traditional Library

The concept of social tagging, or giving crowds and the general public the ability to create metadata for information is becoming popular with the advent of Web 2.0 technologies. Services such as Delicious and CiteULike are representative examples of how a social classification system can easily be put into action in order to organize a set of knowledge. Social tagging can also be used by more formal institutions to create methods for organizing knowledge. The University of Pennsylvania's academic library system has developed a service called PennTags, which allows students to tag books and other information resources with their own search terms (Steele, 2009).

The decision to experiment with such an innovative system to organize their codified information products was described as "external systems weren't able to capture links to most library resources, including our OPAC or journal article search engines. Additionally, we recognized that a system of this kind would provide a nice light-weight way to build flexible data models for each project. So, for example, we can use the backend of the PennTags system as a way for librarians to produce research guides, as the basis of a video reviewing system, and to add user-created content to our catalog" (Farkas, 2007: 143).

Hybrid Knowledge Organization at Parsons Brinckerhoff

Parsons Brinckerhoff (PB), a 14,000-employee civil engineering firm, recently deployed a hybrid system. PB's knowledge system is divided into three zones, each with its own rules for content management. The first zone is for authoritative content and can be considered the central repository for the purposes of illustrating our model. By default, all content in this zone is accessible globally to the organization and must pass through some form of review and vetting process by a centrally designated subject matter expert (SME). This zone is governed by a globally standardized navigation and content organization structure to ease content discovery.

The second zone is dedicated to formal project teams and department teams to govern as they wish. They can create repositories for working documents or restricted content. Although these areas can be exposed to the global search capability within the system, users know when they discover content in these areas, that it has not necessarily been vetted or reviewed by SMEs. They are, however, organized roughly by organizational structure, allowing for a shared logic to be applied when browsing for content. The third zone is dedicated to individual employee use. In these areas employees have full control over the content and tools in use. These areas can be used to manage content for daily task execution, to facilitate ad hoc collaboration across departments or geographic boundaries. The content here is regulated only by the general standards of corporate conduct. They can be personalized to match whatever logic scheme or workflow best suits the individual employee at any particular time. Collaboration spaces created within this zone have a time limit, encouraging collaborations that take on a protracted lifespan and thus should be governed by a more formal structure to be moved to the second zone.

PB's system is a classic hybrid allowing for highly decentralized control of working content, or content managed within projects and tasks, highly centralized control of vetted and approved content about and from projects and combinations in between. Blogs, wikis, discussion boards, lists, and content libraries can be deployed in any of the zones; however, the management of each of these tools is governed by a slightly different set of rules. Users are free to move from one zone to another, but they are also made aware of the differences in the treatment of content and rules for collaboration in each.

Allowing users to socially create their own organization classifications encourages further knowledge discovery of the content of the knowledge, and possibly the transfer of tacit knowledge that is accessible only through the individuals using the system. Systems such as PennTags can prove useful also to the librarians who are traditionally responsible for creating the more formal structures of classification, who were able to view the socially created tags of the difficult-to-capture tacit knowledge. Farkas (2007) outlines how social bookmarking can be used as a professional tool for librarians to learn about developments in various fields that they serve, by activities such as creating groups within an externally hosted tool like Delicious, and sharing links to relevant resources.

The introduction of social organization methods to the traditional library setting can improve how patrons use the library and acquire knowledge. A primary concern that has emerged is that most online library catalogs are lacking in comparison to the usability of popular search engines, most notably Google. Even the so-called better online catalog interfaces are considered cumbersome in comparison to the search and retrieval functions offered by more general use search engines. Casey (2007) argues that while librarians might understand and even find true value in the organization of the library catalog, the needs of library users and the general public are quite different depending on the context of the knowledge. For them, having to deal with the different interfaces to access different materials is perceived as a hassle and poor design, and many user-centered features are simply absent in the design. A list of factors that would improve the usability of modern library systems includes relevancy ranking, clean interface, spell-checking capabilities, faceting, true basic search field, advanced searching, full-text searching of all holdings, professional reviews, similar searches (recommendations), user-added tags, customer reviews, blogs, an option to allow reputation ranking, an aggregated rating system, suggest to friends link (via email), RSS feeds, and a citation creator for various formats. The complexity of the library catalog offers unique challenges to those tasked with organizing information. In order to organize knowledge in such a manner that it is easily accessible to a wide group of users, libraries must seek new and innovative solutions that challenge traditional organization and classification methods.

A taxonomy created through social means will always have to clear the obstacle of trust. How can we evaluate organization methods based on how well the user population trusts its ability to correctly identify, organize, and locate knowledge? Mai (2010) suggests five criteria: credentials of the people who created the system, the track record of the organization scheme and the people who created it, the reputation of the organization and people for creating reputable classifications, how other people accept and use their classification, and whether it has a similar classificatory structure as other trusted schema. A layperson using an organization method may not have the knowledge required to utilize these criteria, and therefore the organization method must be clearly trustworthy to those who are not subject experts. Trust can either come from use of the system over time, or through the trust previously established in the relationships between the user and the organization that presented the classifications (Goldman, 2001).

Specific Issues with Organizing Tacit Knowledge

Many of the knowledge organization techniques discussed in this chapter are clearly applicable to common forms of explicit knowledge found in companies. When knowledge is well defined, visible to employees, and codified so that it can be transferred between individuals, it presents few challenges to those attempting to incorporate it into a knowledge organization system. However, many challenges occur when working with the tacit knowledge that exists in companies. As mentioned earlier, tacit knowledge is difficult, if not impossible, to separate from the individuals who possess it and the context in which it exists. Therefore, techniques to organize tacit knowledge must be centered on the individual.

Organizations must first identify the tacit knowledge in their internal environments. This can be done through the summarization of human resources data, or employee surveys that ask employees to rate their knowledge in particular fields, with particular technologies, of customers they deal with, and so on.

Once a good understanding of the scope of the tacit knowledge in the organization has been created, knowledge managers can then utilize many tools to categorize and locate this knowledge. The focus remains on knowledge retrieval, so ensuring that people know "who knows what" becomes important. Technologies that can analyze social networks, or build knowledge maps (including cognitive maps) and depictions of knowledge networks can serve as guides for people searching for knowledge that remains in a tacit form. Nontechnical methods such as cross-training and rotation programs, education events, and knowledge fairs can not only help introduce people to the knowledge that exists in their organization, but also the people who possess the knowledge. This creates social relationships that may prove useful in the future for retrieving tacit knowledge.

ORGANIZING KNOWLEDGE AS MARKETS[2]

Going beyond the organizational view of knowledge, we can look at knowledge in a larger context by understanding how multiple individuals, organizations, or industries can manage their knowledge. One way is through the creation of a knowledge market as a device for managing widespread knowledge.

A market can be defined as a collection of buyers and sellers who interact to exchange goods and/or services. Markets are systems of exchange (Biggart and Delbridge, 2004). Exchanges can be either altruistically or economically motivated. Altruistic motivations lead to unequal exchanges; this is where one entity (individual or organization) exchanges services with another entity for no cost (or at a cost that is miniscule in economic terms compared to the product or service being delivered). Volunteer organizations and nonprofit organizations fall under the umbrella of altruistic markets. Economic markets, on the other hand, are governed by equality; that is, all parties involved in an exchange must contribute some resources to the transaction. History tells us that economic markets started out under the barter system—trading goods for goods. Individuals exchanged the products they produced for those that they needed but could not produce. For example, a farmer would exchange wheat for wool. Over time, markets moved to a price system. This was made possible through the emergence of currencies. Currencies provided individuals with a common unit on which to govern exchanges. The governing dynamics of markets have changed very little since the days of currencies. However, what has changed is the behavior of buyers and sellers given the advancements in information technology.

The term electronic market has been used to denote markets that are conducted or facilitated using technology. Most commonly such markets are found on the Internet. Examples of such markets are Amazon.com and eBay. Before electronic markets, we were restricted to make purchases locally. Today, we can purchase goods from around the world using the Internet. In the past, buyers had limited information on the market, but today we can search for numerous products, make comparisons, negotiate with multiple sellers, and then make the purchase within minutes. While the Internet has dramatically improved the way markets operate, the fundamentals hold true: to make a profit, sellers need to charge a price that is higher than their cost of producing and is lower than the purchaser's intended utility for the goods or services. Electronic markets are facilitated using technology. They are set up on platforms such as the Internet or its many variants such as intranets or extranets. The markets, however, retain the human elements; the traditional aspects of making a purchase such as searching, negotiating, exchanging payments, and receiving the product and service are preserved. A buyer can engage in the same kinds of behavior through the use of various technologies, the only difference being the increased speed of conducting these processes in electronic markets. For instance, the use of intelligent search agents on the Internet can help a consumer find products that meet given specifications and negotiate a purchase price.

We define **knowledge markets** as the logical space where buyers and sellers can engage in the exchange of knowledge products and services. It is important to note that we are concerned here with a logical space and not a physical space. An example of a logical space is the Internet; physical space is the office building. Due to advancements in information technology, knowledge markets just like electronic markets can be housed exclusively in a logical space. Having the market be housed in a logical space has several advantages. The first is that market participants do not need to meet physically at a location. This opens up the avenue for global participation of buyers and sellers. The second benefit is that the market can operate 24/7/365. In addition, electronic markets are cost efficient when compared to operating a physical market. Table 5.3 summarizes the types of knowledge markets.

Knowledge markets can be classified based on the market maker. The market maker is the entity responsible for setting up the market. Having the requisite infrastructure, inviting buyers and sellers, and determining the rules of the market are all the tasks of the market maker. We can have three types of market makers: private organizations, consortiums, and third parties.

Internal Knowledge Markets

An organization can create an internal knowledge market, thus playing the role of a market maker. Participation in the knowledge market is controlled by the organization and is restricted to the organizational members. Internal knowledge markets are created

Table 5.3. Types of Knowledge Markets	
Type	**Description**
Internal knowledge markets	• Participation is controlled by the organization and is restricted to the organizational members. • Employees submit ("sell") knowledge to internal systems and acquire knowledge ("purchase") from other employees; the currency can include actual credits/charges to departments or points-based rewards that can be redeemed by employees.
Consortium-based markets	• These markets are formed by partner organizations to achieve common goals through exchanging knowledge, such as best practices. • The consortium acts an independent organization and functions as the manager of the market.
Third-party knowledge markets	• An independent organization seeks to bring together buyers and sellers for exchange of specific kinds of knowledge (e.g., Keen.com). • This model is ideal when you have a large number of individual buyers and sellers who have limited resources (i.e., the cost per transaction is small, and the third party profits through economies of scale).

to provide a means for employees to exchange knowledge. They also are a viable means to address concerns about getting employee participation, providing incentives, valuing knowledge, and creating dialogue between employees.

Fujitsu, in fact, developed an internal knowledge market for engineers spread over Japan where producers of knowledge set prices for their registered knowledge and users pay for them upon download (Yoshimura, 1996). When system engineers (SE) "knowledge providers" register their knowledge in the system, they set the price of the knowledge registered. When a "knowledge seeker" chooses a knowledge document, its price appears. If the knowledge seeker decides to purchase the knowledge, the price of the knowledge document, plus a shipping and handling fee, is charged to the knowledge seeker's department. If the knowledge is available in an electronic format, it is sent via e-mail. If not, a fee for paper copies is charged, as well. The department where the knowledge provider belongs receives revenues from the sales generated from knowledge exchanged. Infosys has also implemented a similar knowledge market called K-Shop (Ramasubramanian and Jagadeesan, 2002). Employees can submit research papers, project experiences, and other types of knowledge goods through a website. When a document is submitted to the K-Shop, experts review the document and, if found suitable, publish it. The reviewer and author are compensated via knowledge currency units (KCU). Each reader of the document must pay a certain number of KCUs for utilization of the document. KCUs can be redeemed for cash and other gifts. The use of KCUs helps entice users to participate actively in the knowledge market.

Consortium-Based Markets

Consortiums are organizations that collaborate to achieve common goals. Consortiums can play the role of market makers in order to allow knowledge exchanges between the various partner organizations. Unlike with internal knowledge markets, consortium-based markets seek to stimulate knowledge flows between organizations rather than within organizations. Trading partners own their knowledge and exchange it in the market. The consortium can be viewed as the manager of the market. Consortium-based markets are ideal when a group of companies belonging to a given industry can jointly collaborate on an endeavor. The consortium acts as an independent organization. Hence, it does not show favoritism to any of the founding members, yet it serves a viable means to restrict membership to those organizations that are chosen and approved by the founding members.

In 2000, DaimlerChrysler, Ford Motor Company, and General Motors jointly created a single business-to-business supplier exchange, called Covisint (http://www.covisint .com/). Covisint enables raw material suppliers, original equipment manufacturers, and the retailers to interact in a holistic manner by facilitating connection making, communication between trading partners, and also collaboration. While Covisint is not a pure knowledge market, it does allow for knowledge exchanges. Much of the knowledge exchanged is supplementary to the movement of physical goods and services. Shop.org, the online presence of the National Retail Federation, is another consortium based knowledge market. Shop.org is devoted exclusively to helping established retail organizations exchange lessons learned, case studies, and marketing and intelligence reports, on a wide range of issues dealing with multichannel retailing.

Third-Party Knowledge Markets

We can also have knowledge markets that are managed by third parties; here membership will be open to participants meeting a specified criterion. A third-party market maker is an independent organization that seeks to bring together buyers and sellers for exchange of specific kinds of knowledge. Third-party market makers must earn revenues to cover their expenses of setting up the market and to make a profit. Keen.com, a knowledge market, connects individuals seeking advice on a wide array of topics with experts in the domain. Individuals can search for experts in a wide assortment of topics, ranging from personal relationships to astrology. Once an expert is identified, the buyer is connected via a telephone call to the expert for exchange of knowledge. The buyer is charged a fee per minute for the duration of the telephone call. Keen.com takes in a commission based on the duration of the call. Ingenio.com is a similar knowledge market that connects individuals seeking advice on business and professional matters. Third-party run markets are ideal when you have a large number of individual buyers and sellers who have limited resources yet would like to interact. The market takes advantages of economies of scale. Each buyer and seller pays only a small fee to the market; the trick is to attract enough traffic so that the cost of the market is covered. There are two types of third-party markets: all-in-one and focused markets. All-in-one markets are akin to eBay.com. Here, you can find sellers offering a wide array of goods and services. Focused third-party markets, as the name implies, are focused on a select product and service category. For example, Ingenio.com is focused on the exchange of management and business knowledge. Third-party markets are also popular in the arena in intellectual property exchanges. TechEx (http://www.techex.com) is a business-to-business knowledge market for technology licensing in the biomedical industry, conceived at Yale University's Office of Cooperative Research. The market brings together various technology and research providers such as universities, research and development labs, and private researchers, with technology purchasers and licensees such as government and business organizations. The market acts as matchmaker between the various parties to facilitate the commercialization of research and innovation.

Components of the Knowledge Market

In addition to the market maker, we have buyers and sellers, rules of the market, and the market space that make up the components of the knowledge market.

Knowledge Buyers and Sellers

Buyers and sellers interact in the market for the purposes of facilitating exchanges. Buyers are the recipients of knowledge products and services from the sellers. Membership into the market as either a buyer or seller is a function of the type of market—internal, consortium, or third-party.

In the internal knowledge market, the market maker allows its employees access to the market. Depending on the sophistication of the internal knowledge markets, each member might have different access to goods being exchanged in the knowledge market. Such an arrangement is common in highly sensitive organizations such as defense departments; here, each member will need to possess a security clearance to access specified knowledge artifacts.

In a consortium market, buyers and sellers are screened by the existing members of the consortium before being allowed into the market. The role played (a business partner, vendor, supplier, purchaser, etc.) by the organization will determine the type of access they have to the market. For instance the supplier view of the market will be very different than what a purchasing organization will see.

UClue as a Third-Party Knowledge Market

Third-party markets are the most dynamic in terms of membership. Most third parties allow members to switch roles between a knowledge provider and a knowledge purchaser depending on the transaction being conducted; moreover, members may join and leave the organization at will with little cost. Third-party markets may or may not pre-screen buyers and sellers. Screening of knowledge providers is aimed at evaluating whether they have the requisite skills and know-how they claim. UClue is a third-party knowledge market, originating from the now abandoned Google Answers. This market helps users find answers to their questions, for a fee ranging from $10 to $400. A knowledge provider (the researcher) will search for the information and knowledge requested by the buyer. When they find it, they will post it to UClue and will notify the buyer. The buyer is then charged a fee for the answers. UClue, the market maker, carefully screens the knowledge providers (the experts) who are responsible for answering users' questions.

Third-party markets may also screen buyers for their ability to pay for goods and services provided. Some third-party markets screen the knowledge products being traded in the market. All knowledge products representing ideas that are traded on Ideaexchange.com are put through a quality assurance process by the representatives of the company. Only if they pass this screening are they allowed to be traded on the market.

It is important to note that buyers and sellers can be human or artificial. Human buyers and sellers are employees or individuals; artificial buyers and sellers are electronic agents who conduct transactions on behalf of their human principals (Maes, 1994, 1995). Intelligent agents are popular in all fields of commerce. For example, we can have intelligent agents that search for products based on a given set of purchase parameters. Similarly, we can have an agent who negotiates a price based on our price and demand elasticity. As the Internet becomes more sophisticated we can expect to see an exponential rise in the number of automated (artificial) agents who engage in electronic markets, knowledge markets being no exception.

Knowledge Market Space

So what exactly constitutes the space of the market? Consider the traditional bazaar, *souq*, or mall. In these market settings several salient features are present. First, there is some notion of organization. In a department store, for example, all kitchen items are lined up in one aisle, while all clothing goods are in another. This facilitates buyers having quick access to products, creating a friendly shopping experience. Second, most malls have a map or a directory that helps in navigation. A person who is new to the mall or needs to find a specific store can consult this and traverse the marketplace. Without it, buyers will have increased search times and poor shopping experiences. Third, a mall's environment is highly conducive to retaining buyers within its confines for large durations. Malls have benches, restrooms, fountains, and entertainment, all of which contribute to increasing its "stickiness" factor. Finally, the market also enforces rules that buyers and sellers must follow. Sellers will be punished if they sell defective material or engage in cheating of customers; similarly, customers cannot steal material from the buyers or use fraudulent currency.

The knowledge space of the organization must have similar features to a traditional market space. Knowledge products and services should be presented in an organized manner. The layout of the logical space, most commonly a website, should be user friendly. Users should find it easy to navigate the space and get to where they want to go. The content of the knowledge space must be laid out in an appropriate manner. Consider the UClue site. The design of the logical space is simple when it comes to aesthetics, yet it is one of the easiest to navigate through. The site allows users the functionality to search for knowledge questions based on popular categories and genres. The more well designed a website, the greater the chance that users are going to have an enjoyable experience, and greater is the likelihood that they will come back to the website. Users should also be allowed to personalize and customize their views of the market. Customization and personalization helps users navigate the website in an efficient and effective manner (Spector, 2002). Moreover, it allows them easy access to items that interest them. Knowledge markets should also have avenues to foster dialogue between the various players of the market. The use of discussion forums, chat rooms, electronic discussion lists, and bulletin boards can all be used to engage users to share their feedback on the market experience, engage with other users, and provide the market maker with suggestions on how to improve the market. One of the most important components of the market space is the help function. Users must have ready access to help in times of despair. An effective and efficient help function can do wonders for improving the quality of user experience; an ineffective help function can cause grave harm to user morale and result in users leaving the site. A help function is a knowledge provider—knowledge is provided to users when they encounter a problem in the market. Users should be allowed to search through a FAQ to find answers to routine queries; they must also have the option of interacting with a live customer service or help assistant via live chat, e-mail, or even telephone. Just as the knowledge market is open for business 24 hours, so must the help function be available without interruption. It is also important to answer queries posed by users in a timely manner, or they will leave the market.

The market maker, buyers, sellers, rules, and space are the components of the knowledge market. Any market, including a knowledge market, must help support the basic trading process. The various activities of the trading process include search, pricing, payment, and authentication (Kambil and van Heck, 2002). The search process is comprised of all activity involved in identification and comparison of trading opportunities by buyers and sellers. Next in the process, pricing includes the discovery, negotiating, and agreement of prices for products. The payments process occurs when both the funds and goods (being the knowledge) are exchanged between the buyers and the sellers. Finally, the last process is the authentication process, which occurs when the buyer verifies the quality (or accuracy) of knowledge sold and the resulting credibility of each of the parties involved in the transaction is determined. The trading process of a knowledge market is very similar to trading goods in a traditional market, so we will not explore this topic further. We will move on to discuss some of intricacies and peculiarities of a knowledge market, beginning with the nature of knowledge products and services.

Knowledge Products and Services

Drawing on the economics literature, we can classify products and services as being search, experience, or credence. *Search* goods and services are those for which value can be determined prior to purchase. *Experience* goods and services are those for which value can be determined only after purchase. *Credence* goods and services are those for which value cannot be completely determined even after the purchase because buyers do not possess necessary skills and abilities to judge credence qualities. The classification of goods and services into these categories has important bearings on how they are accounted for in knowledge markets.

Search goods and services are the most basic in nature. A consumer understands the nature of these items and can make value judgments before committing to a purchase. History with the product and service is one reason why consumers can make pre-purchase judgments. If you are familiar with a brand of beer, such as Heineken, every successive bottle of Heineken you purchase is a search good. You know the value before you shell out the money. Similarly, if you frequent a local barber for your haircuts, you are engaging in purchasing a search service. Due to your history with the barber you know the value of the service.

Experience goods are those that need to be tried before we can make a value judgment. Going to a new restaurant or purchasing a resort vacation are examples of experience goods and services. Unless we actually indulge in the good or service, we will not be able to value it appropriately.

Credence goods and services are the most difficult to make value judgments on for two main reasons. First is verifiability: the idiosyncratic nature of credence goods makes it difficult to determine their value. Second, when compared with experience and search goods, credence goods may seem to be riskier purchases. Here is where the "fame" of the seller as previously having satisfied the buyers may provide differences in perceived value.

In knowledge markets, search goods are also very basic in nature. They are easy to understand and limited in scope. If we would like to purchase a basic piece of software code that computes the sum of 100 numbers, we are purchasing a search knowledge product. We know the value of the knowledge prior to using it. Search knowledge services are also basic in nature and normally involve a history between the seller and the buyer. For example, if you need to get a document edited and hire the services of an editor with whom you have a history, then you are purchasing a search knowledge service. Going back to the case of UClue, when a knowledge seeker (the buyer) posts a query to the expert (the seller), the buyer must attribute a value to the potential answer. This value is the price the buyer is willing to pay for the answer; the price can range from $10 to $400. Most of the knowledge requests here can be considered as meeting the characteristics of search, as the buyer must be able to estimate the value. The distinction between experience and credence knowledge goods and services is a difficult one to make. The distinction is dependent on the knowledge possessed by the buyer. If the buyer has expertise in the area in which goods or service are sought, they can be characterized as experience; otherwise, they will be categorized as credence. As an example, after reading a FAQ about maintenance of a computer, a buyer who is a veteran computer expert will easily determine the value of this document. In this context, the explicit knowledge is an experience product. However, if the same FAQ was used by a computer novice, he/she would not be able to gauge its full value; in this context, the explicit knowledge is a credence good. A similar line of reasoning applies to services. If you are knowledgeable about accounting and tax accounting, you will be able to gauge the value of services provided by a tax accountant, signifying an experience service. On the other hand, if you do not possess accounting knowledge, you have just consumed a credence service.

Search goods and services are the easiest to manage. The buyers understand the nature of these items and as long as the market provides them with legitimate information regarding the details of the product or service offering, informed decisions can be made. On the other hand, experience and credence goods require a bit more effort. The market needs to provide more information than what is required by search products and services. Information will help lower the initial anxiety associated with making the purchases, as it reduces the uncertainty associated with the transaction. The buyers need to be able to estimate the quality of the product and service offering. Moreover, they also need information to evaluate the abilities of the knowledge sellers. Information needed to evaluate the product and service is most commonly provided via rating systems, mechanisms that allow past purchasers to rate their satisfaction with the knowledge good or service. In addition to providing answers to standardized questions such as "rate how satisfied you were with the purchase," the purchaser can also provide detailed comments on what was liked and disliked. The market needs to make such information available to future potential purchasers. If buyers are not satisfied with the knowledge they received, the market maker must provide them recourse to resolve the matter. This can be handled via several mechanisms. UClue prescreens the knowledge providers. The market provides the knowledge buyer with a satisfaction guarantee: a buyer can ask for a refund should they not be satisfied with the knowledge provided. Ideaexchange.com also prescreens the knowledge products offered for sale in the market, vouching that the goods provided meet quality standards.

In addition to rating the knowledge artifact, many markets allow the purchasers to rate the knowledge seller. Many times, a knowledge seller will offer multiple products and services. Rating systems for products and services are apt at capturing feedback on the individual goods and services that were purchased, but do not provide direct feedback on the seller. Knowledge sellers can be rated based on, for example, how quickly they delivered the service or good, or how they handled customer queries.

This information will help buyers for whom the good or service being purchased is a credence product. In knowledge markets, ratings and feedback provided by the community help to certify that the seller can create and deliver a product or service of acceptable quality. UClue has an interesting mechanism to providing incentives to knowledge sellers to deliver high quality products. Knowledge buyers pay an agreed-upon price for their knowledge request; however, they are also encouraged to pay something extra as a tip. Knowledge purchasers pay a tip to show their appreciation. In some knowledge markets, a knowledge seller can be banned from the market if there are repeated complaints of poor service. In other markets, the knowledge buyers are reminded to always check the past comments and history of the potential knowledge provider before committing to a transaction.

Information content of the markets is an important consideration one must bear in mind while constructing the knowledge market. As a rule, more information is almost always better than no information. However, for it to be useful, the information provided on the sellers and buyers must be of integrity, validated, and trustworthy.

THE FUTURE OF KNOWLEDGE ORGANIZATION

The resources that organizations use for managing and organizing their knowledge must continually adapt to the new forms and increasing amounts of knowledge that is acquired. Systems used to organizing both tacit and explicit knowledge are required to be constantly updated as organizations seek to learn new concepts, work with new customers, and modify their corporate strategies as they attempt to obtain new competitive advantages (Alavi and Leidner, 2001).

New technologies will always be available for organizing knowledge, but it is important to consider what novel value is provided by these systems and how well they will be able to adapt to an unpredictable future. Recent developments in knowledge management now require systems to work with many sources of external knowledge, including knowledge received from social media technologies. Many organizations have begun to connect with their customers through services such as Twitter and Facebook, where knowledge can be acquired from interacting with users. This knowledge may be valuable, but it is difficult for an organization to retrieve and use based on the enormous volume of information within these systems. The developers of new technologies must find a way to interpret the knowledge in order to determine what knowledge applies to the organization, and organize this knowledge so it can be retrieved and used by employees in their daily operations. This is just one example of how automating the classification and organization of knowledge can be done with technology, which in some cases serves as a predecessor to human involvement.

An emerging problem in the field of organizing knowledge is developing ways to organize tacit knowledge so it can be made available to people across an organization. Since much tacit knowledge cannot be codified or easily identified, knowledge managers must find new ways to assist people in connecting to other people's tacit knowledge (Cavusgil, Calatone, and Zhao, 2003; Paquette and Xie, 2010). Here is an opportunity for the non-technological solutions that an organization develops to assist in organizing a valuable source of knowledge. Having people connect with other people has always proven to be the best way to encourage tacit knowledge sharing, and this social inter-action leads to organizational methods that can help identify tacit knowledge for others to use. Knowledge managers should continually be thinking about connecting people within their organization, and attempting to organize how they connect based on classifications of the knowledge needed by the organization's employees.

In the future we will see the continual reduction of the importance of physical documents, as new improvements in digital conversion and reading technologies are created. Many legal precedents are being created to allow for the use of digitized documents in contracts and other litigious situations (Beecher, 2006; Dearstyne, 2006), which allows less paper to be archived for future purposes. Employees have been adjusting to less paperwork in their own lives, as seen by the popularity of e-readers and other e-book devices. These shifts in society's view of paperless work can be leveraged by organizations that will try to use only electronic information in order to simplify the knowledge that they need to organize.

Because of the ease of digitizing information and making it available through knowledge management systems and enterprise-wide systems, many organizations have started to move away from explicitly classifying and organizing the information with the intention of making searches more efficient, and instead have concentrated on the search process and tried to gain efficiencies in how people search for knowledge. Some companies have expressed the view that it is easier to "dump everything into one big pile," or store everything in a common database or knowledge store, and perfect the search algorithms that are used to find information. This is the principle that underlies how Google searches the vast scope of the Internet in order to retrieve relevant knowledge. Although there are some technical advantages to be gained if the vast majority of the knowledge is stored in a codified digital form, this method may prove practical for only data and information, not knowledge. Knowledge, in its many forms used by organiza-tions, is very complex and does not often lend itself to efficient organizing via technical means. Many pieces of knowledge are unique and require human interaction within a social sense to be interpreted and organized accurately. Although we have excellent systems designed to perform full-text searches of books and documents, we have a long way to progress before technology can interpret knowledge that is contained in codifiable form, or not codified and resident in the people, organization and corporate culture.

Numerous ideas discussed within the field of personal knowledge management (PKM) have implications for organizing knowledge. PKM examines how knowledge processes operate at the individual level, where employees and knowledge users create processes to manage their own personal stocks of knowledge (Wright, 2005). Many arguments exist that individuals are closest to their own knowledge, and therefore are the best at organizing and managing their knowledge in order to maximize its value. As such, companies looking to develop and adapt their knowledge organization techniques can examine personal knowledge management techniques that have been developed in their organizing when requiring new ideas and organizing processes. By moving these activities from the individual to the group or organizational level, organizations can take advantage of innovations created by individual employees in order to improve company-wide knowledge organization processes.

A final challenge that will need to be addressed by companies stems from their ever-increasing use of knowledge gained across different contexts, from new domains or interdisciplinary sources. This knowledge can be quite different from more standard forms of knowledge used by organizations; therefore, it poses many challenges to those knowledge managers attempting to organize it based on the organization's existing schemes or technology. By extending their reach when acquiring knowledge from new external sources, organizations are acquiring knowledge from new sources in novel forms that may have compatibility issues with the knowledge already existing within the corporate boundaries. Knowledge managers need to ensure that the classification and organization methods employed in the organization are flexible enough to incorporate this new knowledge and integrate it into the organization's existing knowledge base. In most cases, knowledge that is considered interdisciplinary or originating from a new context is quite valuable to the innovation capabilities in an organization; therefore, it is essential that knowledge organization activities consider how to generate value from this knowledge.

CONCLUSION

The earlier chapters of this book focused on fundamental aspects of knowledge management: identifying useful knowledge, acquiring or creating the knowledge needed, sharing the knowledge throughout the organization, and storing the knowledge through the use of technology and human means. The underlying strategy of these knowledge activities is to find value in knowledge and ensure the right people have access to the knowledge they need to excel in their jobs.

Finding knowledge, whether tacit or explicit, can be difficult unless the organization has a strong knowledge organization strategy and mature classification and organizing practices. If employees are expected to access knowledge in order to perform their jobs, the onus is placed on the organization to ensure they have not only the tools in place to give them access, but knowledge organized in a manner that facilitates easy retrieval. Companies have used many approaches to organizing knowledge, including processes similar to those used by traditional libraries, companies operating primarily on the Internet, and organizations that have exploited the properties of digital knowledge to create new organization techniques.

In order to organize knowledge, it must be understood well enough to be classified into groups, or taxonomies. This process may produce either metadata regarding the knowledge or a classification scheme that can be used for all knowledge within or used by the organization. Many times, this work relies on determining relationships between different pieces of knowledge and using this understanding to compare and contrast knowledge until accurate categorizations can be distilled. The entire process of organizing knowledge can be directed from a top-down approach, where a central function or group has control over the categories, relationships, and terms for classifying knowledge, or a bottom-up process that relies on users of the knowledge to apply their own experience in order to generate classifications that accurately reflect and organize the knowledge. Organizing the knowledge has required, and will continue to require, many different strategies, utilizing varying methods and technologies. However, organizations must organize their knowledge and adapt their organizing methods to a dynamic business environment in order to realize the full potential that knowledge brings to their organization.

Recap: The Major Points for Knowledge Managers to Consider When Organizing Knowledge

1. The better knowledge is organized, the more likely it will be reused by others, saving the time and expense of recreating the knowledge.
2. Organizing knowledge enables one to see the big picture of the organization, and connect the dots between related knowledge sources.
3. As knowledge has evolved, so have our methods for organizing knowledge. Good knowledge classification systems are built to be flexible and adaptable to new forms of knowledge.
4. Many of the early systems for organizing knowledge were bound by the tangible, physical form that knowledge took (such as a book). Newer systems are able to take advantage of the digitization of knowledge and create new ways of organizing knowledge for users.
5. The fundamental trend in the evolution of knowledge organization methods is to allow for customization and control by the user. Organization schemes want to move away from the "one model fits many" idea, toward adapting the system to a particular user's needs.
6. Many organizations tend to organize knowledge around its place within the business, such as its value, rarity, imitatability, and non-substitutability.
7. The relationships that exist between knowledge and knowledge sources is an important idea to understand, as it will help the knowledge manager link related knowledge sources together. It helps determine what sets of knowledge are complete, and what knowledge gaps exist.
8. Although traditionally organized in a top-down approach, new methods of bottom-up knowledge organization are emerging, such as crowdsourcing classifications, folksonomies, and social tagging.
9. Tacit knowledge is difficult to organize due to its intangible nature and that it cannot be unattached from its source. However, by organizing the sources of tacit knowledge an organization can begin to understand what tacit knowledge it possesses and where it is located.
10. Knowledge markets are one system that can be used to classify and organize knowledge from an economics perspective. They can both identify and value knowledge by creating a market for such knowledge.

DISCUSSION QUESTIONS

1. Organizing knowledge helps us know what knowledge we possess. How is this similar to creating an inventory of an organization's knowledge assets? Why is it different?
2. What are the advantages of an organization centralizing its approach to organizing knowledge? What are the disadvantages? What types of knowledge are organized best under a centralized approach, and what types may be missed?
3. When an organization decides on a system to organize its knowledge, it has to determine how flexible to make the system. What options are available to ensure all forms of knowledge can be adequately identified and classified by the system?
4. What tools are available to help with organizing tacit knowledge? Think of both technical and nontechnical solutions.

5. What are the benefits of allowing users to create the categorization scheme for organizing knowledge? Does this practice of social tagging have any drawbacks?
6. What benefits do knowledge markets provide organizations that are attempting to organize their internal knowledge?
7. Many new approaches to organizing knowledge have been driven by new technologies or organizational forms. Can you think of any emerging technologies or new organizations that may present new methods for organizing knowledge?

NOTES

1. This section draws heavily on a previously published article: Desouza, K.C., and J.R. Evaristo. 2004. "Managing Knowledge in Distributed Projects." *Communications of the ACM* 47, no. 4: 87–91.
2. This section draws heavily on a previously published article: Desouza, K.C, and Y. Awazu. 2004. "Markets in Know-How." *Business Strategy Review* 15, no. 3: 58–65.

REFERENCES

Alavi, M., and D. Leidner. 2001. "Knowledge Management and Knowledge Management Systems: Conceptual Foundations and Research Issues." *MIS Quarterly* 25, no. 1: 107–136.

Barney, J.B. 2001. "Is the Resource-Based Theory a Useful Perspective for Strategic Management Research? Yes." *Academy of Management Review* 26, no. 1: 41–56.

Barney, J.B., M. Wright, and D. J. Ketchen, Jr. 2001. "The Resource-Based View of the Firm: Ten Years After 1991." *Journal of Management* 27, no. 6: 625–641.

Beecher, S. 2006. "Can the Electronic Bill of Lading Go Paperless?" *International Lawyer* 40, no. 3: 627–648.

Biggart, N. W., and R. Delbridge. 2004. "Systems of Exchange." *Academy of Management Review* 29: 28–50.

Bowker, G. C., and S. L. Star. 1999. *Sorting Things Out: Classification and Its Consequences.* Cambridge, MA: MIT Press.

Broadfield, A. 1946. *The Philosophy of Classification.* London: Clive Bingley.

Casey, M. 2007. "Library Catalog 2.0." In *Library 2.0 and Beyond*, edited by N. Courtney. Westport, CT: Libraries Unlimited.

Cavusgil, S. T., R. J. Calatone, and Y. Zhao. 2003. "Tacit Knowledge Transfer and Firm Innovation Capability." *Journal of Business and Industrial Marketing* 18, no. 1: 6–21.

Chen, P. 1976. "The Entity-Relationship Model: Toward a Unified View of Data." *ACM Transactions on Database Systems* 1, no. 1: 9–36.

Choo, C. W. 2005. "Information Failures and Organizational Disasters." *Sloan Management Review* 46, no. 3: 8–10.

Dalkir, K. 2005. *Knowledge Management in Theory and Practice.* Burlington, MA: Elsevier Butterworth-Heinemann.

Dearstyne, B. 2006. "Order in the Court? Records Management and Electronic Data Discovery." *Records & Information Management Report* 22, no. 6 1–14.

Desouza, K., and Y. Awazu. 2005. "Segment and Destroy: The Missing Capabilities of Knowledge Management." *Journal of Business Strategy* 26, no. 4: 46–52.

Detlor, B. 2004. *Towards Knowledge Portals: From Human Issues to Intelligent Agents.* Norwell, MA: Kluwer Academic.

Evaristo, J. R., and P. Fenema. 1999. "A Typology of Project Management: Emergence and Evolution of New Forms." *International Journal of Project Management* 17, no. 5: 275–281.

Farkas, M. G. 2007. *Social Software in Libraries*. Medford, NJ: Information Today.

Goldman, A. I. 2001. "Experts: Which Ones Should You Trust?" *Philosophy and Phenomenological Research* 63, no. 1: 85–110.

Harris, W. T. 1870. "Book Classification." *Journal of Speculative Philosophy* 4: 114–129.

Kambil, A., and E. van Heck. 2002. *Making Markets*. Boston: Harvard Business School Press.

Maes, P. 1994. "Agents that Reduce Work and Information Overload." *Communications of the ACM* 37, no. 7: 30–40.

Maes, P. 1995. "Intelligent Software." *Scientific American* 273, no. 3: 84–87.

Mai, J.-E. 2010. "Classification in a Social World: Bias and Trust." *Journal of Documentation* 66, no. 5: 627–642.

Markus, M. L., A. Majchrzak, and L. Gasser. 2002. "A Design Theory for Systems that Support Emergent Knowledge Processes." *MIS Quarterly* 26, no. 3: 179–212.

McDermott, R. 1999. "Why Information Technology Inspired but Cannot Deliver Knowledge Management." *California Management Review* 41, no. 4: 103–117.

Microsoft. 2011. "Microsoft Technical Fellows." Microsoft.com. Accessed March 11. http://www.microsoft.com/presspass/exec/techfellow/default.mspx.

Miksa, F. 1988. *The DDC, the Universe of Knowledge, and the Post-Modern Library*. Albany, NY: Forest Press.

Mueller, M. L. 2002. *Ruling the Root: Internet Governance and the Taming of Cyberspace*. Boston: MIT Press.

Paquette, S., and B. Xie. 2010. "The Relevance of Elderly Technology Users in Healthcare Knowledge Creation and Innovation: A Case Study." Paper presented at the Hawaii International Conference on System Sciences, January 5–8.

Putnam, G. 1962. *Books and Their Makers in the Middle Ages*. New York: Hillary Press.

Ramakrishnan, R. 1998. *Database Management Systems*. Boston: McGraw-Hill.

Ramasubramanian, S., and G. Jagadeesan. 2002. "Knowledge Management at Infosys," *IEEE Software* 19, no. 3: 53–55.

Rowley, J., and R. Hartley. 2008. *Organizing Knowledge: An Introduction to Managing Access to Information*. 4th ed. Burlington, VT: Ashgate.

Ruppel, C. P., and S. J. Harrington. 2001. "Sharing Knowledge through Intranets: A Study of Organizational Culture and Intranet Implementation." *IEEE Transactions on Professional Communication* 44, no. 1: 37–52.

Spector, R. 2002. *Anytime Anywhere: How the Best Bricks-and-Clicks Businesses Deliver Seamless Service to Their Customers*. Cambridge, MA: Perseus.

Steele, T. 2009. "The New Cooperative Cataloging." *Library Hi Tech* 27, no. 1: 68–77.

Stein, J., and J. Ridderstrale. 2001. "Managing the Dissemination of Competencies." In *Knowledge Management and Organizational Competence*, edited by R. Sanchez, 63–76. Oxford: Oxford University Press.

Turner, J. R. 1993. *The Handbook of Project-Based Management*. Maidenhead, Berkshire, England: McGraw Hill.

Weinberger, D. 2007. *Everything Is Miscellaneous*. New York: Times Books.

Wright, K. 2005. "Personal Knowledge Management: Supporting Individual Knowledge Worker Performance." *Knowledge Management Research and Practice* 3, no. 3: 156–165.

Yoshimura, K. 1996. *Network Renaissance*. Tokyo: JMAM.

Zhang, Y., and A. Salaba. 2009. *Implementing FRBR in Libraries: Key Issues and Future Directions*. New York: Neal-Schuman.

6

Knowledge Transfer

Scott Paquette and Kevin C. Desouza

OBJECTIVES

- Convey the importance of knowledge sharing in organizations.
- Provide an understanding of a basic knowledge transfer process, and the many variations and forms of transferring knowledge.
- Describe the importance of social networks and social media technologies in transferring knowledge.
- Illustrate how organizations look beyond their boundaries for important knowledge.
- Examine the obstacles and barriers to transferring knowledge.

INTRODUCTION

An organization's ability to transfer knowledge among its employees, functional areas, and geographic locations is a key determinant of the success of its knowledge management initiatives. In order for knowledge to be utilized once it is created, thereby providing value to the organization, it must be shared with colleagues, teammates, and coworkers. The sharing and transferring of knowledge is vital to knowledge management.

Some forms of knowledge are very easily transferred. Codified knowledge such as best practices, charted business process, rules and regulations, and policies and procedures can be captured and distributed to many members of an organization through multiple channels. It is this form of knowledge that technology-based knowledge management systems can handle with ease and which becomes a foundational element for any KM program. Other knowledge, the more tacit and non-codifiable knowledge that exists within people, is much tougher to externalize and share, and it is this knowledge that many KM programs focus their non-technology based efforts on.

Knowledge transfer strategies have multiple goals involving the facilitation of both types of knowledge. They attempt to connect professionals across functions, platforms, and geographic distances. These connections assist in the formation of knowledge networks that help people establish relationships for knowledge sharing. The standardization of professional practices and acceptance of stewardship responsibilities are both enhanced by knowledge transfer, as knowledge specific to a profession can be disseminated throughout a practice, spanning organizational and industry boundaries. Sharing of best practices through the documentation allows organizations to learn from others, avoid mistakes, and identify valuable knowledge that has a common use throughout the organization. Finally, reducing "time to talent," or the time it takes to get new employees trained through both explicit and tacit knowledge sharing can enhance and accelerate training for new employees, who will be able to demonstrate their value to the organization more quickly when codified knowledge sources are accessible, in addition to identifying and connecting with experienced personnel to assist them in tacit knowledge transfer.

Recently, the notion of knowledge sharing, especially as facilitated through social media and other Web 2.0 technologies, has come to the forefront of many knowledge management strategies. The rise of these knowledge management systems has not only corporations and organizations, but society as a whole reevaluating how they can use such technologies to improve their knowledge transfer processes. These technologies were readily adapted by individuals and are commonly used in their personal lives, and corporations now must determine how to integrate these technologies into their business operations.

Three shifts in knowledge management, though, have placed a greater emphasis on an organization's ability to transfer knowledge. First, there has been a shift from one expert being the primary source of knowledge to acknowledging that everyone engaged in work tasks is in possession of knowledge. The notion of a common knowledge base for a practice allows more advanced learning and innovation to occur. Advanced knowledge transfer capabilities are needed in order to disseminate this knowledge beyond the individual level to larger groups, teams, and communities. Knowledge transfer processes should be designed to involve multiple individuals at multiple levels of experience (e.g., novice, advanced, new, experienced). Second, knowledge has moved from residing in disconnected individuals to being embedded in groups or communities. Organizations must ensure they have the capability to communicate to the entire group, not relying on one individual in order to transfer knowledge. Further, identifying knowledge that could reside in numerous places or be held by a variety of people requires the capability to easily search and locate valuable knowledge. This emphasizes the need for networks and social technologies to manage knowledge at the group or societal level. Third, knowledge can no longer be viewed as a stable commodity or asset that is easily managed by an organization. It is now recognized as dynamic and constantly changing, requiring any knowledge activities to be flexible, adaptable, and forward thinking in their design. Knowledge transfer capabilities and technologies must be nimble, adaptive, portable, and flexible in order to ensure the organization can adapt to a changing environment and not be constrained by out-of-date capabilities.

Ensuring efficient and effective knowledge transfer within an organization is a key component of an organization's knowledge management strategy and activities. Creating the network connections between employees and external knowledge sources is critical to infusing knowledge into an organization's core competencies. Understanding the unique factors that motivate and facilitate knowledge sharing is the first step in creating a knowledge supportive culture throughout the organization.

This chapter will present concepts, technologies, and challenges related to the transfer of knowledge by individuals in an organization. The following section will elaborate on knowledge transfer by describing the knowledge transfer cycle, examining the various types of sources and recipients who participate in transferring knowledge, and discussing how these offer many forms of knowledge transfer within organizations. Next, the ever-changing role of technology and its impact on individuals in knowledge transfer activities is described, including the emerging role of social media in knowledge sharing. Knowledge transfer does not occur only within an organization, but quite often across organizational boundaries. This section illustrates how knowledge flows between organizations and external entities such as customers and stakeholders, including the unique strategic and operational challenges that this form of knowledge transfer presents. The final section of this chapter presents barriers and challenges in both individuals and the organization that prevent knowledge from being transferred freely.

Solving Global Challenges through Sharing Knowledge:
The Bill and Melinda Gates Foundation

The impact of knowledge sharing among large groups of people is not limited to those organizations in the private sector. This is one strategy applied by the Bill and Melinda Gates Foundation, an organization whose goal is to influence large change and improvements around the world (such as reducing poverty or improving health) through scientific discovery and innovation. They work closely with scientists from around the world to not only develop new solutions to global problems, but share this knowledge with other scientists, communities, governments, and nongovernment organizations in order for the knowledge to have the greatest impact. Historically, much of the "Western world's" scientific knowledge was not transferred well to developing and emerging nations, causing a large divide in the economic and health resources available. Now, this knowledge is being infused into these communities in order not only to help the people, but to teach and train them about population growth, economic opportunities, disease prevention, and healthy living. In return, the foundation sometimes gains significant knowledge from these indigenous populations that can contribute towards the developed world's understanding of their cultures and enrich its knowledge of science and the world.

THE KNOWLEDGE TRANSFER CYCLE

Direct Transfer between Source and Destination

Every transfer of knowledge has five essential components that create the environment for knowledge sharing. This concept follows the Shannon-Weaver Communication Model (Bishop and Cates, 2001). See Figure 6.1 for a graphical depiction of a typical knowledge transfer process.

There must be a source, which initially possesses the knowledge, and a recipient, who will receive the knowledge. It is important that both the knowledge source and recipient are willing to transfer the knowledge. If the source is not willing to or capable of sharing its knowledge, or the recipient is not willing or able to receive the knowledge, then the transfer will not occur.

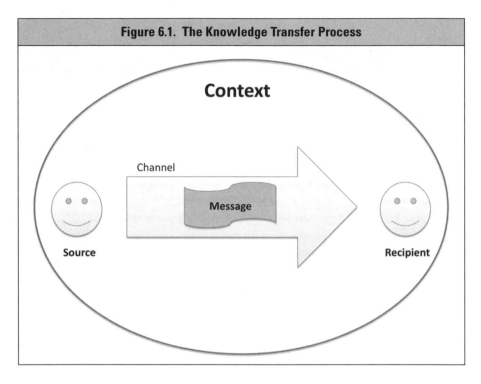

Figure 6.1. The Knowledge Transfer Process

Besides the knowledge, the two most important components of any knowledge transfer are the source and the recipient. Knowledge flows between different forms of entities, including individuals (humans), technology (machines), and organizations. Human to human transfers are the most common, and happen on a daily basis. Here, both explicit and tacit knowledge is transferred in both professional and social settings. Key to this transfer is the existence of a social connection between the individuals. It is here that social media technologies have had their greatest influence in their ability to create new connections, maintain weak connections, and further strengthen well-established ties.

Human to machine transfers involve the externalization of knowledge where individuals attempt to codify or imbed their knowledge into a system. The goal of this transfer is to take knowledge that is difficult to share and convert it into knowledge that can be transferred more widely throughout an organization. In this case, the individual must have access to the technology and know how to use it effectively in inputting and sending the knowledge to others. Machines can also transfer required knowledge using corporate networks in order to span organizational boundaries. For example, many organizations that rely on sharing information about inventory, demand, and sales utilize enterprise resource planning (ERP) systems that must be able to communicate with each other. This communication is dependent on technological standards that allow data and information to flow seamlessly between different systems. Organizations also have nontechnical knowledge transfers between one another, relying on individual employees to initiate the exchange. Professional groups, industry organizations, and other external groups can play a major role in facilitating knowledge transfers between different, and sometimes competing, organizations.

The source and the recipient are connected through a channel that allows the knowledge to be transferred. The channel is not always a physical medium, but can be a virtual space, shared mindset, or environment that allows for the knowledge to be transferred. This is similar to Nonaka's concept of "ba," a condition required for the creation of knowledge (Nonaka and Konno, 1998; see Chapter 4 for an in-depth discussion). However, more common channels are physical. Technology is a common channel that could include a computer network, the Internet, or applications designed to assist people in transferring knowledge. Physical spaces can be designed to allow for knowledge transfer. In the workplace, locating teams, functional areas, and people who perform common or complementary tasks in close proximity will allow them to share knowledge. Break rooms, meeting room, and areas designed for people to meet (either formally, or through serendipity) can increase the flow of knowledge in organizations.

Different forms of channels have varying abilities to transfer knowledge, a concept known as media richness. Many knowledge management systems are capable of handling great amounts of explicit knowledge or vast distances. Other personal channels like meetings, mentoring sessions, and informal get-togethers allow for great tacit knowledge sharing between people. For example, e-mailing ideas and advice to a colleague might transfer a great deal of explicit knowledge and possibly some amount of tacit knowledge, but having a face-to-face conversation with him or her would increase the amount and richness of tacit knowledge that is exchanged. Knowledge managers must be able to recognize the differences in channels and the types of knowledge that are being exchanged in order to select the most appropriate channel and maximize both explicit and tacit knowledge sharing (Daft and Lengel, 1986).

More than just ideal physical assets or design is required for knowledge to be transferred. For tacit knowledge, people need to have a similar set of traits in order for the transfer to occur. For example, they must speak a similar language or have the capacity for translation. They must understand the concepts of the knowledge being transferred, or have the absorptive capacity (Cohen and Levinthal, 1990) to be able to identify the knowledge, realize its importance, and have the desire to receive it. This notion includes the idea that a social relationship can form the channel for knowledge transfer. Tacit knowledge is transferred much more easily if the source and the recipient have a social connection or belong to a common social network, which allows for social interaction and activity that assist in knowledge sharing. Many knowledge management systems and applications strive to connect people by allowing employees to identify their social networks; find people who have similar interests, projects, or responsibilities; and bring them together to create the channel to transfer knowledge.

The central element of knowledge transfer is the actual knowledge. For knowledge to be transferred, it must be possessed by the source and be in a form that can be received by the recipient. In some cases the transfer is very intentional, and the knowledge is known to both the source and recipient. In many other instances, one or both of the parties involved may not be aware that they have or need the knowledge, or that the knowledge transfer has in fact occurred. For example, while socializing with colleagues, a colleague may not be explicitly talking about work, but another colleague may be the casual recipient of cultural knowledge, or knowledge of what the organizational culture is like within a particular part of the organization. This may be reflected by how this person refers to other employees, superiors, and the work environment. However, whether intentional or subconscious, this knowledge transfer requires all of the important elements.

Noise Interference

A perfect transfer of knowledge would occur if the message is received by the receiver exactly as the source had intended. However, in reality this rarely occurs because other information or knowledge, commonly referred to as noise, gets added to the message. Noise introduces errors into the knowledge system that increase the uncertainty of the information, or create difficulties for the receiver to receive the knowledge accurately.

Three forms of problems occur when noise interferes with a knowledge transfer:

1. Noise can influence how accurately the knowledge is received. Without an accurate transfer, the recipient is not able to decode and act upon the knowledge.
2. Semantic errors occur when the knowledge does not accurately reflect the source's intentions or original knowledge. The recipient must be able to precisely receive the message in order to use the recipient's own knowledge to understand and interpret it.
3. Finally, noise can create errors by preventing the recipient from gaining the true context and meaning of the message.

These errors may not prevent the message from being received or even interpreted correctly, but it will inhibit the knowledge from having the desired effect on the recipient. Knowledge transfer not only is an action in itself, but also intends to influence the actions and behaviors of others. Therefore, the message must be consistent with the recipient's beliefs, cultural values, and experiences. If these are not in alignment with the source's message, the resulting noise will prevent the knowledge from having the desired result.

The final element in knowledge transfer is the context in which the knowledge is being transferred. This context can have a strong impact on the knowledge itself, and helps the recipient understand the knowledge being received. Context can be viewed as either static or dynamic. The static context of information reflects those items, such as a person's date of birth, that do not change over time and are not influenced by external events. Dynamic context causes knowledge to be highly variable and can be influenced by changes in relationships, switching organizations, or changing geographic locations. As much as information and knowledge are considered dynamic assets, in reality most knowledge is contained within a static context. However, the emphasis is placed on the more valuable knowledge that resides in a dynamic context and consumes more effort and resources to manage. Knowledge in a static context can be transferred directly from users, while in a non-static context this knowledge is often obtained through more indirect means, such as environmental sensing and scanning (Henricksen, Indulska, and Rakotonirainy, 2002). Furthermore, a dynamic context can prevent changes to established knowledge networks and procedures that will have to be identified and acted upon to resume effective knowledge transfer. For example, changes in links between individuals within a network can occur, and those links would have to be either reestablished or substituted with new links. This assumes that the knowledge desired is resident in multiple people and the links can be recreated or modified. Furthermore, it also assumes that the knowledge has not undergone a significant transformation and will require a different system structure to be transferred.

Through a Human or Machine Intermediary

Knowledge transfers are not always conducted directly between a source and recipient. **Intermediaries** can play an important role in the transfer process. They can be technical assets such as knowledge management systems or other information communication technologies. Technological intermediaries are effective at bridging boundaries such as geography, language, or differences in practice.

Human intermediaries assist in knowledge transfer by bridging knowledge networks or creating connections between individuals. They may act as translators of data that others may not be able to access or understand, and create useful and targeted knowledge for others. For example, an important issue in the management of government knowledge is the question of what government data should be open to the public. Many argue that just making large data sets accessible to anyone will increase government transparency and allow citizens to gain access to important government knowledge that they technically own. Others argue that creating a direct transfer from government to citizens will not work on its own, as knowledge intermediaries will be required to process, interpret, and draw identifiable knowledge from this data. In this case, human intermediaries become important for knowledge transfer between large governmental organizations and the general public by allowing knowledge to flow over multiple barriers.

An intermediary, whether human or technological, represents one extra "hop" that the knowledge must take in order to reach its intended recipient. Some intermediaries simply pass the received knowledge on, and others prepare the knowledge for reuse by the recipient by indexing, sanitizing, summarizing, packaging, or translating the knowledge. These actions can either add clarity to the knowledge through customization, or create distortion through incorrect or biased interpretation. Distortion reduces the accuracy and therefore the value of the information to the recipient. The more intermediaries or "hops" involved in the knowledge transfer process, the greater chance that distortion will occur. When the knowledge transfer process or network is created, the ability of more intermediaries to disseminate the knowledge versus the rate of distortion must be considered.

When using intermediaries to encourage knowledge sharing, the organization must realize the implications intermediaries have on knowledge security. The more people who come in contact with the knowledge, the greater the chances that a leak could occur, allowing unauthorized access to the knowledge. Many hops in the knowledge transfer process also present more opportunities for the knowledge to be intercepted en route to the recipient. Greater security will be required along those network paths that extend to many individuals. An organization's ability to trust the intermediary is very important to ensure the knowledge is received properly, handled in way that maintains the integrity of the knowledge, and transferred only to the intended individuals.

Distributed Knowledge

McDermott (1999) acknowledges that knowledge is something that is constructed in a social setting, as individuals create a shared memory through their actions. When people converse, their views, ideas, and perspectives can be altered based on new knowledge received. This social constructivist perspective argues that the context is important to the knowledge being shared, which distinguishes it from documents and other knowledge that is separated from people (Dalkir, 2005). Tsoukas (1996) views the organization as a distributed knowledge system, which implies that knowledge is resident in people, in different forms (explicit versus tacit), in different technologies, and cannot be wholly known or gathered at one time. This forces organizations to deal with uncertainty in their planning and decision making, since an incomplete set of knowledge may be the best knowledge they can acquire. Knowledge within the organization is constantly changing through internal and external interactions, requiring the knowledge and practices governing that knowledge to be constantly redefined over time. Therefore, managing knowledge across a distributed context is an emergent process that must adapt to the organization's needs, people, and external environment.

Organizations have become adept at leveraging distributed knowledge through the identification and utilization of innovation networks. Having knowledge reside in many people (or many organizations), yet being capable of coordinating this knowledge to

---

Sharing Project Knowledge When Developing Software

An interesting context to examine how project teams in organizations share knowledge is the practice of creating software products. Here, it can be seen how different forms of knowledge rely on different vehicles to be shared among people working on the same project. For example, it is important for social interaction to occur between the developers in order for them to feel comfortable in sharing their valuable knowledge. Formal meetings are an excellent venue for exchanging explicit knowledge; therefore they can be valuable at various stages of the project. Organizations should try to ensure these meetings are cross-functional to allow for knowledge to flow across functional boundaries. Personal networks are a key channel for the sharing of tacit, or experiential, knowledge, especially between developers with much experience and those who are new to the organization or to software development. In fact, some research has shown these networks become more valuable as the perception of the value of formalized meetings decreases.

Many organizations implement a document sharing system or other technical project management software to encourage developers to share what they know. However, sometimes not all documents are stored in such a system, and not all departments use systems like these equally. Many times, developers use these knowledge systems only when there are formal requirements to do so. Therefore, organizations must ensure that the system is truly a cross-functional or cross-departmental system with standards. The system should be integrated into how the developers work so that they do not consider knowledge sharing to involve burdensome administrative work. Finally, one important piece of knowledge that all developers need is the ability to answer the "who knows what?" question. Any tools or mechanisms that can be put in place to allow them to know their fellow employees or project workers improves their knowledge of their colleagues' abilities and saves them time in locating knowledge required to complete their work (Kautz and Kjoergaard, 2007). Many of these factors and ideas can apply to other contexts besides software development, and managers responsible for project teams can learn many similar lessons to those in the software development industry.

come together in a collaborative work sense, has enabled organizations to develop large networks of knowledgeable people in order to create new knowledge. Technologies and flexible organizational structures have bridged geographical distances to allow different people to work together on projects that require diverse knowledge inputs. For example, the open source software community relies on knowledge transfers between distributed people to create new programs that can be used by all. In many cases the entire set of collaborators do not know each other personally, but are able to bridge these gaps in their network to work together and collaboratively build new products. Another example can be found at Penguin Books, which initiated a project in conjunction with the BBC to bring teenagers together to create new works of fiction. Selected young writers were trained by professional writers, and they became editors of the collaborative work. Online authoring tools similar to wikis are used to allow teenagers from across the United Kingdom to contribute their ideas, with the end product being a novel consisting of many multimedia aspects including text, video, audio, and pictures. The finished story is a product of the contributions of many teenagers from across the country, yet it is one cohesive work of fiction.

Real-Time Knowledge Transfer (Synchronous) or Delayed Transfer (Asynchronous)

Depending on the situation, the technologies involved, and the needs of both the sender and recipient, knowledge transfer can occur in either a real time (synchronous) mode or a delayed (asynchronous) mode. Most electronic forms of knowledge transfer initially were asynchronous such as sending e-mail, posting documents on an intranet, and viewing static websites. As Internet technologies matured, bandwidth increased, and users became more sophisticated, synchronous transfer has become more widely used. Instant messaging, online chats, video conferencing and Internet telephony all help facilitate real-time knowledge transfer. Furthermore, it is very difficult to transfer tacit knowledge through asynchronous means unless the tacit knowledge can be externalized into a codifiable form. Real-time transfer is the preferred method for transferring valuable tacit knowledge; therefore, it has been the focus of many new technologies and services.

As technologies become ubiquitous in everyday life, expectations have increased for real-time, instantaneous responses to communications. People have constant connectivity to the Internet and access to their e-mail via cell phones and smartphones. More businesses are open 24/7, and the pressure to react to electronic messages is ever increasing. For example, to remain competitive, salespeople try to be responsive to their customers' needs and requests, which places an additional burden on their daily responsibilities. Although these knowledge transfer activities are important and valuable to the organization, they present a source of additional stress to individuals.

Individuals respond to different forms of knowledge transfers in different ways. In asynchronous or delayed knowledge transfers, there may be time to craft the message, choose the appropriate channel, increase the accuracy of the message receipt, and spend more time interpreting the message. Conversely, in real-time communications, we have less time for the transfer process and therefore rely on routines and experiential knowledge when reacting to the received knowledge. This leads to different preferences on the type of knowledge transfer preferred. Technologies are excellent for capturing and preserving delayed transfers such as e-mail, as they are usually received in a codified form. However, newer technologies are now able to archive and retrieve real-time communications for future use, such as instant messaging, and full phone and teleconference conversations. Organizations want to preserve this transferred knowledge both so that parties not involved in the exchange can learn from it, and also to save resources by having the transfer occur once.

As knowledge management activities become more embedded in everyday activities, the time we have to pay attention to the important information and knowledge becomes a scarce commodity. Attention is the time one has to perform concentrated mental engagement on a particular item of information. Individuals become aware of much of the information in their daily routines, and through a mental narrowing activity they decide what information will receive their attention. These decisions affect information behaviors. People rely on their ability to screen out noise and unimportant knowledge, but overload can still occur when too much knowledge is received. Individuals can also be overloaded by unimportant knowledge, which will drown out the more important knowledge that is being transferred.

Forms of Knowledge Transfer

An important concept when understanding the knowledge that is possessed by an organization, **common knowledge** can be thought of as the knowledge that is learned by performing an organization's daily business routines, processes, and procedures. Each individual organization will have its own common knowledge, and this will distinguish it from other organizations in its industry. The effective management of this common knowledge can assist in creating a competitive advantage for the company that may be very hard to duplicate by rival firms. Common knowledge is transferred within an organization through five forms of transfers: serial transfer, near transfer, far transfer, strategic transfer, and expert transfer (Dixon, 2000). See Table 6.1 for a summary of the different forms of transfers.

Serial transfers occur when knowledge has been gained by part of the organization in one setting, and it is transferred to another part of the organization in a different setting. Usually this process takes the knowledge experienced by a team and moves it into the public space, making it available to other teams. It is knowledge describing an action that can be both repeated and learned by other members of the organization. Either explicit or tacit knowledge may be transferred, but in both cases, the knowledge stems from experience. For example, many organizations hold post-project review meetings where they discuss a recently completed project, the results, and lessons learned throughout the process. These lessons can be documented and shared with other project teams that can use this knowledge in the management of future projects. In this transfer, technology can be an asset: it bridges geographical distances and allows various units of the organization to communicate. Most often, this transfer relies on formal and established knowledge networks to disseminate the knowledge, but in some cases informal networks and transfers can enrich the knowledge transfer.

Near transfers facilitate the transfer of explicit knowledge that has been learned through the repeated process of performing certain actions. This type of knowledge

Table 6.1. Five Forms of "Common Knowledge" Transfers	
Type of Transfer	**Description**
Serial	• Knowledge gained in one area is transferred for use in another part of the organization in a different setting. • This may be explicit or tacit knowledge. • Technology can be an asset by bridging geographical distance.
Near	• Near transfers facilitate the transfer of explicit knowledge that has been learned through the repeated process of performing certain actions (i.e., forming best practices). • Knowledge is easy to describe, or codify, and can be well-supported in KM systems and disseminated in the form of e-mail, a new policy document, or a posting on a corporate intranet.
Far	• Far transfers involve knowledge related to non-routine tasks. • The transfer comprises mainly tacit knowledge. • Individuals (employees) are needed in order to establish connections to disseminate the knowledge.
Strategic	• Strategic transfers involve knowledge related to a non-routine task that deals with work at a strategic level (impacting large areas of the organization). • The transfer comprises mainly tacit or experiential knowledge. • This type may require multiple, high touch, complex transfers.
Expert	• Expert transfers involve knowledge related to non-routine problems; transfers can occur when one part of the organization is seeking help from another. • Dissemination requires collaboration and interaction of heterogeneous set of individuals and dynamic teams, which should be supported by either technologies or the management structure of the organization.

can be easily replicated as it refers to a task that is routinely and sometimes continually performed by employees. Quite often this knowledge becomes the basis for best practices that can be shared through a knowledge management system or another electronic communications system. The knowledge is easy to describe, or codify, and can be understood by other teams or employees. An example is when the engineers notice a flaw in the company's product during a routine test procedure and correct it. They can document this problem, specify when it would occur during what specific test, and explain what the correction should be. This knowledge can then be disseminated to other test engineers in different locations in the form of email, a new policy document, or a posting on the corporate intranet. Knowledge management systems and their ability to store and transfer knowledge are important to this form of transfer. They are able to represent many forms of knowledge, create connections between individuals, and expand professional networks such that all knowledge can be shared more efficiently. An intermediary's ability to receive the explicit knowledge and codify it in a manner that promotes sharing becomes a critical factor in how well this knowledge transfer works.

Far transfers differ from near transfers as the knowledge is related to a nonroutine task or a situation that does not normally occur during the course of business. It is usually tacit knowledge that has been learned from an action, and the organization wishes to ensure that other teams that might encounter a similar situation receive this knowledge. In order for this form of transfer to occur, the organization must have technology or other methods in place to facilitate the sharing of tacit knowledge. It is preferable that the team or group of employees that discovered the knowledge have connections with other peers within the organization, but if not this transfer will have to establish those connections. Therefore, it is important to know who requires similar common knowledge and how to connect with those people. For example, a salesperson may encounter a customer who is not similar to other clientele or has unusual needs that the organization has not encountered. If the salesperson or team develops a method of marketing the company's products or services to such a customer, they have created valuable knowledge that other sales teams may find useful. In this case, a sales meeting or other formal sales function would offer the opportunity to share knowledge in person and facilitate the far transfer of this situational knowledge. As this transfer mainly is comprised of tacit knowledge, the networks an individual has established enable that employee to disseminate the knowledge. The social challenges that can inhibit knowledge transfer apply to this form of transfer, including corporate politics. Far transfers deal with knowledge that is not easy to pass between a recipient and a source; therefore, connections and relationships that have been established are crucial to ensuring this knowledge is disseminated adequately.

When a team receives knowledge that arises during a nonroutine task or that occurs infrequently yet deals with work at a strategic level, a **strategic transfer** can assist them in transferring this knowledge to others. The knowledge usually impacts large parts of the organization, such as lessons learned during disaster scenario planning. Most often, this form of transfer is used when tacit or experiential knowledge is involved, and involves many face-to-face meetings or the formation of knowledge network connections. Here it is important that individuals can interpret the knowledge and its meaning at a strategic level, and understand the value to the entire organization. Many times, this transfer indicates the need for further transfers of tacit knowledge, and may require many complex transfers due to the wide-reaching nature of the knowledge.

Finally, **expert transfers** facilitate the transfer of knowledge related to unusual or nonroutine problems, and occur when one part of the organization is seeking help from another. This transfer deals with non-documented or non-codified knowledge that requires connections in order to be transferred, and it relies on the organization's ability to bring different people together in order to share knowledge. The result of this activity may be that even more knowledge is created in order to solve the existing problem. The organization should have structures in place to allow the formation of ad-hoc or dynamic teams consisting of heterogeneous sets of individuals who can work together in order to share their experiential knowledge. This type of transfer occurs frequently in new product design and development activities, where knowledgeable individuals from various product and business groups come together to create a new product that fills a particular gap in their product lines, or solves a certain problem for a client (Dixon, 2000). The organization must have a fairly strong understanding of what knowledge is resident within the organization, and who possesses it. Knowledge systems such as knowledge directories and corporate yellow pages can assist in establishing who will participate on the team. When these teams are virtual or have members from different locations, their collaboration and interaction should be supported by either technologies or the management structure of the organization.

Intentional versus Unintentional Knowledge Transfers

Most of the discussion surrounding knowledge transfer has assumed that both the source and recipient of the knowledge are motivated and intent on transferring knowledge. However, this is not always the case. Many knowledge transfers are accidental or unintentional and can have both positive and negative consequences.

Knowledge can be accidentally shared with others through leaks or mistakes by the organization. External leaks usually have negative consequences for the organization, as the knowledge may be proprietary and confidential. A proper information security management program is essential to ensure that, as the organization builds networks and relationships that extend across the organizational boundary, the knowledge being released into the environment is beneficial and valuable to the organization.

Knowledge sharing by snooping also occurs regularly in an organization. People by their nature are curious, and tend to look for knowledge even when it may not necessarily be intended for their receipt. Employees may slow down as they are walking by meeting rooms to listen to conversations, hear exchanges through the thin walls or cubicles, or come across documents with knowledge that is not intended for them. Organizations as a whole also participate in snooping as a form of competitive intelligence when seeking knowledge about their competitors. Not all knowledge is made public or available through sources such as legal and financial filings or the Internet. In order for an organization to truly understand the activities of its competitors and their significance, it can try to learn as much as it can from competitors by searching for clues to their activities, strategies, or other metrics. For instance, some companies have been known to count cars in a rival's parking lot in order to estimate the number of employees, and whether the organization is growing or laying people off. It is important to recognize the line between legal snooping activities and illegal corporate espionage. An organization must act ethically and morally when snooping for external information and also must ensure it has an understanding of the laws which surround such activities.

Finally, much knowledge is shared within an organization through serendipity, or unintended sharing. Organizations with formal and mature knowledge management programs are quite adept at creating an environment and circumstances where employees can come together and share knowledge in order to either create new knowledge or realize other benefits of knowledge sharing. However, often knowledge is shared unintentionally, just through an incidental conversation. Providing common meeting areas such as lunchrooms or break rooms, or planning social activities that involve employees who do not normally work together, can result in not only new relationships and the extension of existing social networks, but the unexpected yet valuable transfer of knowledge. For example, in one organization, the sales department and accounting departments did not normally interact through their daily business routines. Yet at one company barbeque that was held weekly in the summer, some employees from these two departments were talking and realized that information received by the accounts receivable people was valuable to the salespeople. Ultimately, they recognized that these two departments are the only two customer touchpoints in the organization, and they were privy to knowledge about the customers that was not available to other departments. Furthermore, they could compare observations and ideas from interacting with customers that helped the sales people learn more about current and potential targets. From attending a barbeque and casually talking, these departments began a knowledge transfer that was continued well after the incidental activity and provided numerous benefits to the organization.

Social Networks for Knowledge Transfer

A key tenet in the social sciences is that people are part of thick webs of relationships and interactions. The importance of social interaction in the knowledge transfer process points to the need to identify, create, and leverage social networks. These networks consist of individuals or groups that are connected through personal or professional relationships. It is through these networks that explicit and tacit knowledge can flow from one individual to another. For some forms of knowledge to flow freely, the source and recipient of the knowledge must have social contact, as opposed to an asynchronous online connection. They will have to know of each other's existence, know what knowledge each possesses and has the ability to share, and share a common channel through which the knowledge will flow (Golbeck, 2007). In organizations, this can be as simple as coworkers talking over their lunch break, participating in a lunch-and-learn session, or attending more formal activities such as meetings, conferences, or formal training sessions.

Social network analysis is one technique to understanding the connections and relationships between people. It involves both mapping and measuring relationships between people, groups, organizations, or other knowledge sources. A map is created with nodes representing the people or groups, with links illustrating the relationships or knowledge flows between the nodes. Nodes can represent any entity in a network such as individuals, business units, or companies, which allows for different levels of analysis. This attempt to visually depict complex human systems can assist an organization in answering questions such as where its knowledge comes from, who shares knowledge with whom, how heavily people depend on the organizational structure for knowledge sharing, and what role technology plays in creating and maintaining these relationships.

There are many underlying themes to social network analysis. First, it attempts to identify the types of ties that exist between network members. Similarities regarding two connected members within the network are examined, such as geographic location, membership in the same communities, clubs, associations, and whether they share similar attributes such as gender, political affiliation, or age. Social relations also describe the type of tie, and whether there is a kinship (i.e., they are members of the same family); other relationship such as friendship; formal reporting relationship at work; identifiable affective relationship; or cognitive tie (such as knows well or knows about). The flows that identify the connection can also be used to determine the type of tie, such as whether the individuals are connected via information flows, resource flows, or monetary flows. The strength of the tie between nodes is an important measurement, and can be defined as the time, emotional intensity, intimacy, or reciprocal services between two nodes, which are referred to as either strong or weak. The stronger the tie, the more likely that knowledge will flow freely between the two nodes (Alavi and Kane, 2008). The technology available to the individual, including social media tools, can help determine the strength of the ties.

The collective ties within a network can be examined to determine the network's density, or the ratio of actual ties to the number of possible ties within a network. The effect of network density on knowledge sharing is debated. Some studies have shown dense networks have a greater flow of knowledge; others have argued that a sparse network gives nodes access to a greater diversity of knowledge sources, enriching the knowledge that can be received. Individuals in sparse networks are less likely to be connected with similar people, diversifying the available knowledge base.

Social network analysis also studies the nodes (or individuals within the networks) themselves to see how characteristics of the nodes affect the entire network. The perceived (or actual) influence of the node on the network, the position within the network of the node, and its proximity to being central to the network help determine the importance of the individual to the network. This reflects the concept of centrality and has a direct influence on the effectiveness of the individual's knowledge sharing activities. If the node (individual) has many short paths to other individuals, for example, the node may be very adept at transferring knowledge to others (Borgatti et al., 2009).

Finally, the influence the network wields on its environment is an important issue. If the network is strong and capable of achieving its goals and objectives, it might become a powerful piece of the organizational structure. A network's ability to control valuable assets, such as knowledge, may determine the success and influence it can develop within an organization. As organizations rely more heavily on knowledge as a resource, the social networks and individuals within those networks who manage knowledge efficiently will become prominent within an organization.

Social network analysis is used within knowledge management to identify the relationships between people and map the knowledge that flows in the context of these relationships. It helps an organization understand who possesses important knowledge, which nodes (people or groups) are able to connect with individuals who have knowledge, how the connections are made, whether intermediaries are used, and how strong a tie is necessary in order for knowledge to flow. Barriers or structures that impede knowledge transfers can be identified by determining who is not sharing knowledge with others. The nodes of the network can be defined at both the individual and the departmental levels of the organization in order to better understand knowledge flows. For instance, once the organization has determined which individuals or groups have close contact with customers, it can track the knowledge flows from these people to see where customer knowledge flows within an organization. If it is not flowing to important groups such as new product development, the company may not be using this knowledge to innovate products that the customers are demanding. The organization can then encourage people with this important external knowledge to connect with new internal departments to ensure everyone has a connection to the customer.

Organizations manage social networks in either an active or a passive manner. Active management involves the intentional engineering of certain network features and characteristics in order to facilitate knowledge transfer. This can be accomplished through the use of boundary spanners, boundary objects, gatekeepers, information brokers, and intermediaries. Passive network management assumes that networks form based on the characteristics of the organization, and therefore the organization makes no direct attempts to alter the networks.

Conducting Social Network Analysis

When analyzing a social network within an organization, the goal is to answer the following questions:

1. Who knows whom, and how strong are the relationships?
2. How well do people with relationships know the knowledge that the other possesses, including their skills and experience?
3. Where does knowledge originate regarding important topics or tasks that the employees perform?
4. What resources are available and are used to gain knowledge about important questions or problems?
5. What organizational resources help connect people, strengthen relationships, and share information and knowledge?

These questions can be answered through surveys, interviews or a combination of both methods. The following steps are usually typical of the social network analysis process (Dalkir, 2005):

1. Identify the scope of the analysis project and determining the individuals or groups that will be analyzed. This step should include a definition of the characteristics of the network and why these people are similar.
2. Clarify the objectives of the project, including what hypotheses and questions will be answered, and how this new information will help the organization in its knowledge management, decision making, operations, and strategic activities.
3. Identify the tools that will be used to collect information, including any survey questions, interview protocols, or software aids.
4. Carry out the actual data collection activities.
5. Use a software mapping tool that will construct the social network and display it in a descriptive visualization.
6. Perform the analysis of the results, which may include the impact of this particular network on knowledge management activities, including knowledge transfer. Any changes or actions that may occur based on this analysis can also be identified.
7. Continue social network analysis activities to either expand the process to other areas of the organization, or update previously mapped networks to identify changes.

KNOWLEDGE TRANSFER THROUGH TECHNOLOGY

Historically, organizations relied on social interaction and the exchange of codified information in order to transfer knowledge. Key methods of sharing knowledge among employees included meetings, training and seminars, conferences, and social activities for tacit knowledge, and formal documentation procedures, archival processes, and information databases and repositories for explicit knowledge.

During the 1990s, the acceptance of personal computers and corporate networks helped to foster the notion that technology has an important role to play in knowledge management, and specifically in facilitating knowledge transfer. An example is the popularity of Lotus Notes, an e-mail and database collaboration tool that allowed employees to share codified information. Intranets and portals became the cornerstone for knowledge management systems. They were all-encompassing knowledge systems intended to assist knowledge workers in the creation, sharing, storage, and use of knowledge. They had specific functionality designed to increase the flow of knowledge within organizations. Most were used in the transfer of explicit knowledge through shared databases and document repositories that could be easily searched by employees. Other functions and tools attempted to encourage tacit sharing through the identification of knowledge and where it resided. Knowledge directories or "KM yellow pages" were a source where employees could search for different skills, experience, and knowledge, and find individuals who may possess the knowledge. The goal was to create a place where employees could ask the question "Who knows what?" and be given an answer. However, most knowledge directories relied on individuals to identify themselves and their knowledge, which often turned out to be problematic. Employees would either overstate their knowledge to increase their reputation, or underreport their experience to avoid being pestered by many requests for help.

Today, organizations depend on a robust technological infrastructure for knowledge transfer. E-mail has become keystone to all electronic knowledge distribution. Other business applications have become integrated into employees' daily routines and processes, and daily work routines cannot be performed without them. The importance of technology availability and uptime has become predominant, as large amounts of money can be lost when an organizational system fails to operate.

Many of the popular trends in business are in creating new opportunities for knowledge transfer facilitated by technology. The globalization of business requires strong communication capabilities across offices and countries. Global business relies on the ability to transfer knowledge to and from the home country in order to standardize work, work collaboratively, and utilize virtual teams. The continued dominance of the knowledge economy means businesses must be able to create an environment that attracts and retains knowledge workers. This will require creating an environment where knowledge activities are supported by the latest technology in order to allow these workers to create and use knowledge. The need for collaboration within and beyond corporate boundaries is driving organizations to use knowledge systems with social and collaborative functionality that can promote innovation and creativity.

As companies recognize the value of tacit knowledge and the role social networks play in the creation and acquisition of tacit knowledge, they are employing new technologies in order to connect people together with the goal of sharing valuable knowledge that is difficult to codify. Social media tools have grown in prominence based on their noncorporate use, but now organizations are examining these tools to consider how they can be used to share knowledge and create value.

In the early stages of this shift to these different technologies, organizations have realized Web 2.0 technologies assist in not only expanding one's knowledge network, but also maintaining weak ties to many similar people with complementary interests. They are excellent at facilitating lateral knowledge transfers across organizational

---

Global Knowledge Sharing at IKEA

With over 250 stores in 35 countries, IKEA is the largest global retailer of furniture. Despite its size, IKEA does not have a formal knowledge management strategy; however, it has successfully integrated many knowledge sharing ideas and methods into its standard business processes. IKEA focuses on not only sharing knowledge within different locations, but also transferring this knowledge globally.

Creating a knowledge-sharing culture starts at IKEA when employees first join the organization. Their initial training covers the importance of knowledge and sharing it with colleagues. Many senior employees attend the training sessions to describe their experiences in order to begin the transfer of their tacit knowledge. IKEA also shares best practices developed in various locations via its intranet, which is accessible to employees around the world. The intranet supports IKEA's philosophy of career-long learning by providing new and updated courses for the many types of employees. The employee manual also reflects IKEA's view of knowledge sharing, stating, "As an IKEA employee you are willing to share your knowledge and experience with all IKEA employees" (Jonsson and Kalling, 2007: 167). Employee rewards and promotions are partially based on how well employees share their knowledge through formal and informal mechanisms.

One challenge IKEA tries to overcome is learning about local cultures when entering new markets. Many times the knowledge it has stored in its organizational memory is not applicable to new cultures or nationalities. Therefore, the organization creates the absorptive capacity to gain knowledge from the new environment and apply it to how IKEA works. The company strives to maintain its goal of "One IKEA" by rewarding knowledge sharing between employees in order to increase its overall organizational learning and global competitiveness (Jonsson and Kalling, 2007).

---

boundaries, but may not be as effective with top-down knowledge sharing. The richness of one's knowledge network directly affects one's ability to identify, acquire, and use knowledge; so the expansion of individual and professional networks can help an organization create and acquire valuable knowledge.

The rise of technology use within organizations has greatly helped knowledge sharing. Not long ago, knowledge was codified in physical documents and stored within a room full of paper files. To become accessible to the organization, an employee had to physically go to the room, locate the required documents, and search for the exact information he or she needed. Corporate librarians had the responsibility of maintaining the organization of such collections and responding to requests from employees for information. This assumes, of course, that the information had been (or could be) codified and had been properly documented, cataloged, and stored. The advent of networked computers within organizations allowed this codifiable knowledge to be digitized and shared by other networked employees. Soon applications such as intranets and portals emerged with the intent of assisting in the storage and location of knowledge. More recently, the emergence of social media and Web 2.0 technologies and their adoption by corporations has extended the ability of organizations to not only share codified explicit knowledge, but create and maintain knowledge networks that allow for the transfer of tacit knowledge. Although technology alone cannot deliver successful knowledge-sharing capabilities, and therefore effective knowledge management strategies, it can be an important facilitator in an organization's knowledge activities and contribute to a culture that supports strong knowledge transfer activities and processes (McDermott, 1999).

Building a Knowledge-Sharing Culture

Building and sustaining a knowledge-sharing culture within an organization is very difficult, as changing an organization's culture is slow, challenging, and often intractable in large organizations. Many unique organizations foster their own cultures, which can dictate the norms, rules, and accepted actions for many aspects of the organization, including knowledge management. One example of an organization that was successfully able to change the culture surrounding its knowledge management practices is Sarkuysan, a Turkish manufacturer of copper products.

Sarkuysan values four key concepts within its corporate culture: storytelling, trust, continuity, and loyalty. These are supported by both a commitment by management and the organizational reward system. Storytelling is embraced by continually describing the rich traditions and heritage of the company through newsletters and at corporate functions, including a yearly banquet. Continuity is ingrained through the practice of promoting within the company and allowing employees to create a lifelong career by moving through various areas of the organization. Low turnover and no layoffs have helped maintain this value. Loyalty is encouraged by investing in employees and training them constantly through their lifelong careers. By treating the employees well and showing its appreciation, Sarkuysan gains their loyalty throughout their career. Finally, trust must be earned by consistent and good actions over a period of time. Trust must be built not only between the company and its employees, but also their customers and stakeholders such as shareholders.

These cultural values assist in the creation of a knowledge-promoting company. Storytelling encourages knowledge sharing which allows tacit knowledge of previous experiences and situations to be commonly known and shared with new members of the organization. Continuity promotes low turnover rates; therefore, the company retains employees with valuable experiential knowledge. Loyalty and trust promote an environment where employees feel safe and rewarded for sharing what they know with others, often trying to improve of the organization, and not just themselves.

By leveraging its unique and strong organizational culture, Sarkuysan was able to develop a corresponding knowledge culture that encourages knowledge sharing among its employees. The alignment of its organizational and knowledge strategies was key to fostering an environment where employees naturally share what they know with others in order to perform their jobs better, thereby enabling the organization's ability to utilize its knowledge (Nayir and Uzuncarsili, 2008).

Social media tools that can be leveraged for knowledge sharing include blogs, wikis, social networking tools, podcasts and videocasts, and commercial tools such as Facebook, Twitter, and Digg. These tools can allow knowledge that includes unique personal views and perspectives to be shared with a wide audience. Those who follow an individual's social media creations can be identified as a following, or more formally as members of that individual's community. Personalized social media does have its challenges, such as quality and accuracy (which in many cases is subjective), security (whether outside sources can access this knowledge), and the notion that the knowledge must be continually updated and kept fresh.

Wikis are a form of social media tool that can allow many users to externalize their knowledge in a form that can not only be shared with others, but also augmented and combined with another individual's knowledge. By tapping into many unknown or difficult to access areas of the organization, a wiki can solicit contributions from a diverse group of employees and allow them to share knowledge through creating their own wiki spaces. The opportunity to control how the knowledge is presented and shared with others often gives employees a sense of responsibility and ownership. However, for wikis to be successful, they must reach a critical mass of users who create and share knowledge within this forum. The organization will also have to deal with the question of how controlled the wiki is. Are employees free to share whatever knowledge they wish, or will ground rules exist on how the wikis can be used? Furthermore, the correction process must be articulated in order to have a plan to deal with disputes, disagreements, and conflicting knowledge. Finally, wikis may disseminate significant knowledge throughout the organization, but they do not ensure that everyone participates in transferring their knowledge to others. Freeloaders are always a problem for knowledge systems because they do not contribute to the pool of knowledge available.

Although the use of social media seems very promising in facilitating the transfer of knowledge between individuals or groups who may not necessarily have natural connections within the organization, it poses many challenges for management. Before an organization launches any social media tool, it will have to determine how to handle the following questions if and when they arise:

1. What if employees use their blogs to post hate speech or to harass a fellow employee?
2. What if blogs are used to denigrate the organization itself, air petty complaints, or allege that its leadership and strategy are misguided?
3. What if arguments break out in a discussion forum and the conversation descends into name-calling and flame wars?
4. What if people fill up their employee profile pages with pictures of their pets and vacations?
5. Will people just use social networking software to plan happy hour, rather than to complete their work?
6. If the information on these platforms really is valuable, won't it be harvested and sold to the highest bidder?
7. How can we ensure that these technologies do not make it easier to deliberately or inadvertently leak confidential knowledge to the outside world, including competitors?
8. How can we ensure that these technologies will not make it easy for information to leap over our internal boundaries or violate policies, industry regulations, or legal requirements?
9. If we give up tight control over our intranet's content, how can we possibly avoid running afoul of all potentially relevant regulations and laws around information sharing in all the places we do business?

KNOWLEDGE TRANSFER OVER BOUNDARIES

Functional Boundaries

Knowledge transfer is inherently difficult to achieve within an organizational context due to the social and structural barriers. When two people want to share their knowledge, they must overcome boundaries that divide the channel on which the knowledge flows. **Boundary objects** (Carlile, 2002; Star, 1989a, 1989b) are used to span these boundaries

Social Media and National Security

Social media use is not limited to only individuals and corporations. An initiative by the United States government encourages employees of the Central Intelligence Agency (CIA), the Federal Bureau of Investigation (FBI) and the National Security Agency (NSA) to network through their own social media network. **A-Space** (for Analytic Space) is a Facebook-type platform that allows individuals from the three agencies to connect together and share intelligence information on similar subjects that might not normally leave one agency's boundaries. For example, each agency can contribute its knowledge to the section that tracks al Qaeda movements in the Middle East, creating one central and complete knowledge base of the intelligence focused on that subject. New ideas, theories, and information can be shared in a collaborative workspace where analysts come together to create new meaning and knowledge out of many smaller pieces of knowledge. Analysts are often unaware that their counterpart exists in different agencies, and this tool will assist in linking them together in order for them to share knowledge on a similar topic. Even video can be added in order to present a multimedia approach to sharing knowledge. A-Space is a heavily secured private network and is not available to the public.

The information is organized in "compartments," which means that an analyst studying the Russian military may not have access to reports regarding terror threats in Southeast Asia. However, these connections can be made through a streamlined request process in order to assist in linking knowledge that may not normally be considered related. A-Space has access to the information on Intellipedia, the wiki-based intelligence system that allows analysts to construct internal web pages on intelligence matters and contribute their knowledge in an open dialogue (Shaughnessy, 2008).

Many believe that this initiative stems from the 9/11 commission report that examined knowledge sharing between various federal security agencies and determined inadequacies in both the culture and structure of sharing knowledge with other organizations. A-Space encourages knowledge sharing by allowing analysts and other intelligence employees to create connections with their external counterparts. Asking questions of colleagues is a central theme of this technology, encouraging individuals from separate organizations to build cross-agency networks, gain situational awareness, and hold discussions on interpreting the knowledge. Even if the result is finding flaws in their data or reasoning, this is a valuable contribution to the collective knowledge (Dixon, 2009).

and allow knowledge to flow. These objects are not necessarily physical objects, but devices used to enable both the course and the recipient of the knowledge to connect and share knowledge. Boundary theory describes three forms of boundaries and boundary objects that individuals must overcome in order to share knowledge. Table 6.2 summarizes the forms of boundaries and boundary objects.

Table 6.2. Three Boundaries That Prevent Knowledge Transfer	
Type of Boundary	**Description**
Syntactic	• The knowledge source and recipient do not share a common language (i.e., syntax).
Semantic	• Common language capabilities exist between sender and receiver but they are unable to communicate or represent the deeper meaning to create common understanding.
Pragmatic	• The knowledge is foundational and rooted in action; thus, the context becomes very hard to communicate without doing the action.

The first type of boundary that prevents knowledge transfer is a **syntactic boundary**, which exists when the knowledge source and recipient do not share a common syntax for communicating or representing the knowledge. Simply put, if they do not speak the same language and cannot understand each other, knowledge cannot be transferred. Syntactic boundary objects allow people to understand the language basics and create a communication platform that both source and recipient can use to understand each other. For example, when an organization faces major changes and revises the metrics that describe organizational performance, it must ensure that any new metrics can be applied to the work that the organization performs, and processes and procedures can be reflected in these metrics. The syntactic objects are the new metrics that reflect the dynamic workplace and can communicate knowledge of the operations to the executive level in order for them to make well-informed decisions.

Semantic boundaries are those that prevent two employees from having the means to learn about differences and dependencies in their work. This recognizes that although the knowledge source and recipient are syntactically compatible and are speaking the same language, interpretations or understandings of the knowledge may vary, making collaboration difficult. In some cases, this barrier is augmented when employees originating from different cultures transfer knowledge amongst themselves and their cultures give them a different interpretation of the knowledge. Semantic boundary objects allow the source and recipient to go beyond just a syntactic understanding of the transferred knowledge, and give them the ability to provide a deeper meaning and understanding that is common to both. An organizational example is when knowledge is transferred between different functional areas of an organization. In communications or written documentation, the new product development area may use language, terms, or jargon that can be confusing or misinterpreted by the sales area. When planning a new product launch, the sales team must have an understanding of the new product, its design, and who the target customers would be. However, if the specifications and documentation of the new product are very technical in nature, its functionality and uses may not be clear. A document or description of the product in a language that can be understood by not only the sales team, but also the customer, would serve as a boundary object to ensure the knowledge is accurately transferred between the two groups.

The final boundary type, **pragmatic boundaries**, reflects that knowledge can be "practice-based" and rooted in activity or action. Much knowledge, especially tacit knowledge, is created in practice or during the act of performing a job. This context becomes very hard to communicate without a foundation of knowledge that is rooted in that particular act. In order to span such a boundary, pragmatic boundary objects attempt to facilitate processes where individuals can jointly create and share their knowledge through action. For example, in many trades and crafts, people learn their profession not just by taking courses and reading books on their job, but completing an apprenticeship program where the novice spends time working alongside an expert in the field in order to transfer knowledge that is difficult to codify or externalize into explicit knowledge. By being embedded in a practice and incorporating observation and action into their training, they are able to transfer a more complete set of knowledge encompassing the knowledge needed to learn about their profession.

Managing Tacit Knowledge at the Allianz Group

Although tacit knowledge is very difficult to transfer and manage, it is the most valuable knowledge possessed by a firm. The Allianz Group, a financial services organization with offices in 70 countries, recognizes the importance of tacit knowledge to its business through the use of international expert teams. These teams are managed by a team manager and have a defined set of performance targets, produce reports on best practices within the organization that are shared globally and help create recommendations to assist in problem solving of many different units and functional areas. Much of their knowledge is also shared through workshops where they interact with other Allianz employees and share not only explicit, codified knowledge, but also tacit knowledge of their experiences within the organization. These workshops also assist in the creation of knowledge networks across functional and geographic boundaries.

To extend the success of these workshops, Allianz created centers of competence to further facilitate tacit knowledge transfer across international groups. For example, it found companies or teams that had deep knowledge and expertise in one area of the business such as direct insurance. These companies or teams would then provide support to other companies that required a knowledge infusion on the topic, and could also be involved in training staff, provide codified knowledge in the form of documentation, or act as consultants on a project or decision. These centers have provided significant value to the organization, including one instance where a center worked with a local company to improve overall sales performance in the company's broker distribution channel. A detailed assessment of the processes and routines used by the channel combined with the existing competence and skills of the individuals led to an improvement in training and hiring methods, which eventually resulted in improved sales. By recognizing the difference tacit knowledge can have on an organization's people and operations, Allianz has mobilized knowledgeable and experienced people to share their tacit knowledge to benefit other individuals and the entire firm (Spies, Clayton, and Noormohammadian, 2005).

Although it is often argued that knowledge management, and particularly knowledge sharing, is the responsibility of every employee, there are some key individuals who facilitate the flow of knowledge over boundaries. These individuals sit at the cusp of the boundary and are able to identify important knowledge and transfer it into their organization or group based on their knowledge networks and ability to connect and translate other knowledge sources. Tushman (1977) describes two types of these facilitators as either gatekeepers or liaisons. **Gatekeepers** act as filters and provide the services of identifying knowledge external to their organization, determining how to acquire that knowledge, and bringing that knowledge into their organization. In this role, they act as a filter and can not only facilitate the flow of knowledge into the organization, but also block other knowledge from being acquired. This is an essential aspect of their role because, by placing a judgment on the value, usefulness, and necessity of the information, they can help to prevent information overload from external sources. However, like all knowledge management roles performed by individuals, they are susceptible to bias and other decision-making heuristics that can prevent them from allowing needed information to cross the boundary. Finally, gatekeepers begin the process of transferring the external knowledge to other internal members of their organization. They must possess additional knowledge of who the right recipients are for this knowledge and what channel is best to distribute the knowledge.

Liaisons are the second type of boundary spanners; their principal role is to identify and create the connections to outside knowledge sources that are necessary for their organization to find and transfer knowledge. Through the development of both professional and social networks, they learn where valuable knowledge exists and how to acquire that knowledge. Examples are those employees who are members of professional associations and trade associations, have worked for competitors or in other industries, or have connections to government and regulatory bodies. For example, in the financial industry many senior hires come from professional services firms, such as accounting and consulting firms. This is advantageous for an organization because these individuals have strong links to their profession, and can be a conduit to acquiring information from outside the organization. Professional accounts are very active within their professional body, which ensures a professional network is maintained, and supports learning on new auditing and tax issues. If an organization has a question regarding a new tax law and its consequences on the organization's financial operations, having an accountant with ties to the profession can expedite the knowledge transfer. That person can easily contact colleagues, other accountants, or the professional body to gain information on the tax changes, including opinions on its larger consequences to a company's operations or strategy. This knowledge may not be available to organizations that do not have a liaison connected to the accounting profession.

Organization and the External Environment

Organizations have realized that not all valuable knowledge is located within the boundaries of the firm. More often, they are required to look to the external environment for knowledge that may be possessed by nonemployees, such as customers. Customers possess knowledge that may provide new insights, innovations, and ideas not necessarily found inside the organization. Their understanding of the marketplace, the organization's products, and perhaps competitors' products can be valuable to an organization in a competitive business (Joshi and Sharma, 2004; Slater and Narver, 1995; Urban, 2004). By utilizing existing relationships and channels, an organization can connect to its customers and establish a knowledge sharing partnership that is extremely difficult for its competition to duplicate (Prahalad and Ramaswamy, 2000). Customer knowledge may provide an organization with new knowledge assets and relationships which may help establish a competitive advantage in its marketplace.

Customer knowledge is quite different from customer information, which can be considered as name, address, purchase history, and so on, as customer knowledge is the knowledge residing within an organization's customers, as opposed to the information about these customers (Davenport, 1997). Customer knowledge allows an organization to convert its customers from passive recipients of products and services into partners that generate and cocreate knowledge (Gibbert, Leibold, and Probst, 2002). The goal is to facilitate the acquisition, sharing, and further creation of knowledge residing in customers to add value for both the organization and its customers. Direct interaction or strong relationships with the organization are required in order to allow this knowledge to flow. This can be quite a challenge, considering it requires companies to overcome many obstacles to facilitate knowledge sharing and transfer amongst their own employees, let alone have their customers provide them with valuable knowledge.

Knowledge derived from customers is most likely contained within a two-way flow of knowledge that creates value for both parties. Examples can be consumer preferences of new product features, new uses for current products, knowledge derived from joint research and development, design improvements from suppliers intended to reduce the cost of manufacturing, and knowledge regarding trends within the business environment. An important aspect of customer knowledge is that it is knowledge owned not by the organization, but by others who may or may not be willing to share such knowledge.

In order for an organization to identify, acquire, and use external knowledge from customers, it must have not only the systems and people who are capable of connecting with their customers, but the internal processes and abilities to use this knowledge. Furthermore, the customers must be motivated to share their knowledge. An organization must be able to convince customers that it is to their benefit to teach the organization what they know about the products, services, and the industry in order for a two-way flow of knowledge to be created.

Many companies are actively involving their customers in marketing and innovation activities. For example, Google posts beta versions of new products on its Google Labs site, where customers can try out new search tools. Customers give feedback on their experience, ideas, problems that might have occurred while using the product, or general impressions of the product. Developers receive this feedback directly and incorporate the customers' knowledge into the product design (Desouza et al., 2008). Similarly, Healthcare Alarm Systems connects with customers, doctors, and other health-care providers through its extensive sales force in order to not only improve on the design of its products, but also discover new and innovative uses for them in the health-care field. Internal marketing and product development employees shadow salespeople during sales calls in order to learn about their products from a customer perspective, and transfer that knowledge into the organization in order to share with their colleagues (Paquette and Choo, 2008). Both of these examples illustrate how organizations can create a two-way flow of knowledge to transfer knowledge from their customers into the organization.

Customers also share knowledge with themselves independent of the organization, and companies can tap into the knowledge repositories to transfer external knowledge to their internal operations. The Harley-Davidson Motor Company has a very active customer base that shares knowledge on routes and excursions, as well as knowledge of the product and Harley experience. A community of both experienced and novice riders has come together in order to share knowledge about a product for which they are quite dedicated. Harley-Davidson can listen to these interactions between customers and learn about their perceptions, opinions, and ideas about their bikes and incorporate this knowledge into new designs or marketing materials (Desouza and Awazu, 2005).

National Boundaries

Knowledge sharing has its challenges when crossing not only organizational boundaries, but also national boundaries. An emphasis on the global nature of business has required many organizations to ensure efficient and effective knowledge transfers between different nations and cultures. Multinational enterprises exist because they can use knowledge gained from being in multiple countries to create a competitive advantage, rather than being situated in one country and simply exporting their goods or services to other parts of the globe. For this organizational structure to be successful, the company must be able to effectively transfer knowledge across the globe.

Global knowledge sharing faces two key challenges. The first challenge is being able to span vast geographic distances while transferring both explicit and tacit knowledge. Explicit knowledge that can be electronically codified is easily disseminated through corporate knowledge management systems such as intranets. However, organizations strive to ensure that any tacit knowledge does not stay in another country, as this knowledge may be more valuable to strategic decision making. Ensuring that knowledge systems can connect people beyond national boundaries will greatly enhance any knowledge activities.

Second, many barriers to sharing knowledge globally arise due to differences in cultures. These cultures can be location based (e.g., different offices developing their own organizational subculture) or nation based (e.g., different national cultures). Both types of cultures perform knowledge work in varying and sometime conflicting ways. Culture can determine how a group of employees looks for knowledge, values and filters different knowledge types, and shares (or hoards) its knowledge. Recognizing how different cultures view knowledge is an important knowledge management activity that requires understanding, compromise, and respect. For more information on knowledge management in a global context, see Chapter 8.

Globally Transferring Knowledge at BMW

Many organizations face challenges when sharing knowledge internally, and these challenges are greatly augmented when they must share knowledge globally with other company units. Although organizations traditionally focus on the flow of knowledge from the head office and to subsidiaries in a global context, it is also important to transfer the knowledge gained locally in different units to the head office where decisions and strategy are formulated. In the case of BMW, the company also considers the flow between the different local units important, in order to consistently build its brand and disseminate its marketing message on a global scale.

BMW worked to overcome several barriers to knowledge transfer. Cross-culture issues such as differing languages were addressed by ensuring the different units had a high level of autonomy when managing their knowledge. The company had to ensure that the network connections between employees in different offices were strong and well maintained. Many in-person events were staged to create connections among the employees, and the use of cross-functional or cross-national teams also played a part in creating strong network ties. In many cases, these formed formal network ties that provided structure for the employees to connect and share knowledge.

In order to makes sure that knowledge shared within BMW's networks was used, the organization addressed the issue of absorptive capacity: the ability of its people to recognize, understand, and absorb the new knowledge into their work practices. Training went above and beyond operational knowledge to ensure the organization could work with knowledge originating from different local markets. Instilling adaptability in how people learn and where the knowledge originates meant that people got used to different knowledge and tried accepting the knowledge for their daily routines.

BMW recognized the existence of valuable knowledge in the local regions of its global offices, not only for head office use but also for use by other offices. Although geographically distributed, knowledge managers recognized many common barriers to knowledge transfer, including cultural, network, and learning barriers. By addressing each of these and establishing procedures and methods for sharing knowledge, knowledge flows on a global scale were created to enhance the work of the local offices (Schleimer and Riege, 2009).

KNOWLEDGE TRANSFER ISSUES AND CHALLENGES

Transferring knowledge between individuals is not an easy process. In fact, many have regarded knowledge sharing as an unnatural, political, and challenging activity. In order to complete a successful knowledge transfer, both the source and the recipient must overcome many obstacles and barriers. The most common obstacle is that the individual does not know the knowledge exists, or where it can be found. This is very common in large organizations where codified knowledge can have many locations and be inaccessible through technology. This problem becomes even more prevalent when the knowledge is tacit, and the individual must know who possesses the knowledge. To transfer the knowledge, a relationship between the source and the recipient must also be present; otherwise, they may not be able to share knowledge. Knowledge can be regarded as *sticky*, which means it is difficult for the source to pass along. This can be due to many factors, such as lack of available transfer channels, politics and culture, lack of motivation to transfer, or simply because the knowledge itself is not an easy asset to pass along due to its context specificity and stickiness.

Knowledge Stickiness

Szulanski (2000) examined the notion of knowledge stickiness, and determined that four types of stickiness can be applied to knowledge:

1. Initiation stickiness occurs when people may not be able to recognize new opportunities to transfer knowledge. Even if they identify an opportunity to add value by sharing their knowledge, they might not know how to start the transfer, have the relationship to connect to the other person, or have the technology to make the transfer possible.
2. Implementation stickiness deals with the challenges that occur while two individuals are attempting to share knowledge. These can be problems specific to the transfer such as communication gaps, misunderstandings of the knowledge, technical difficulties, or legal and regulatory barriers.
3. Ramp-up stickiness poses another transfer challenge, as even though the knowledge may reach the intended recipient, it takes time and effort for the recipient to fully understand the knowledge and its context. Partially due to absorptive capacity and also because people need time to fully comprehend new knowledge, unexpected problems of learning new knowledge or performing a new knowledge activity delay the benefits of the knowledge from being realized.
4. Integration stickiness challenges the recipient of new knowledge to integrate the knowledge into their activities and routines in order to continually receive value from the new knowledge. Here the individual wants to avoid only a one-time benefit of the knowledge and receive continual benefits that may occur from changing how they work or how they adapt to the knowledge of a new environment. Once again, the timeliness of receiving the knowledge benefit is important and requires individuals to get up to speed quickly and fully recognize what the received knowledge means, how it applies to them, and how they can use it on an ongoing basis.

Underlying any transfer of knowledge is the assumption that both the source and recipient are motivated to transfer the knowledge. Motivation resides naturally in people, but needs to be stimulated in order for it to affect their behavior. Extrinsic motivation occurs when individuals can satisfy needs indirectly, such as through monetary compensation. Extrinsic motivation is created through aligning the employee's monetary and other basic needs to the goals of the organization. For example, paying employees a bonus for a defined amount of knowledge transferred into a knowledge management system would be considered a form of extrinsic motivation. On the other hand, intrinsic motivation occurs through activity done for one's immediate need or satisfaction. Here the activity or behavior is valued for its own sake and is self-sustained. In organizations, this form of motivation may be achieved through satisfying, fulfilling, or challenging work.

Two categories of factors create motivation in people. Hygiene factors are those that may be required for motivation, but their absence will certainly create job dissatisfaction. These can include such things as supervision, organizational policies, good working conditions, adequate compensation, peer relationships, and job security. The second, motivator factors, may not necessarily always be present but their presence increase motivation and job satisfaction. Opportunity for achievement, recognition, the substance of the work, responsibility, advancement, and personal growth all contribute positively toward job motivation.

In many cases, it is assumed that intrinsic motivation has a positive influence on employees and their contribution to the organization. It is a requirement for activities that require a high level of creativity and innovation, increases the speed of learning (time to talent), and enables the sharing of both explicit and tacit knowledge. However, employees must be coordinated as a collective to perform in a goal-oriented way. This is essential for any activities (including KM processes) that are aligned toward the organizational strategy and goals. Allowing intrinsic motivation to direct the actions and behaviors of employees can have unexpected or even unwanted outcomes. Changing intrinsic motivation is also more difficult than motivation emphasized though a "control and reward system." When determining what tasks you want to motivate your employees to undertake, it may be very difficult to assign explicit rewards to intrinsically motivated routines.

One factor that can influence the success of the knowledge transfer is the absorptive capacity of the recipient. In order to receive knowledge, the recipient must share a common base of knowledge with the source and be able to understand the knowledge. For example, organizations often bring their product developers and engineers together with marketing staff when designing new products. It is assumed that the marketing people have knowledge about what customers are demanding and how that can be reflected in new products. The engineers are the people who will design the products, so sharing this market knowledge is essential for developing a product that customers will buy. However, many times these two groups have trouble communicating based on their knowledge and skills. The engineers may try to convey knowledge regarding a technical aspect of a product's design, and the marketing people do not have the basic technical knowledge or comprehend the engineering knowledge. Customers might demand features on a product that are not technically possible or are cost prohibitive to build, yet the engineers cannot explain the technical reason to the marketing employees. In order to prevent this trap, the organization must establish a shared set of common knowledge and ensure that its employees have a broad set of skills that can be learned through formal means such as training courses, or spending time in other departments. Many courses attempt to bridge these gaps, with titles such as "Finance for Non-Financial Managers" or "Introduction to Marketing for Technical Employees." Their goal is to build the absorptive capacity in employees so they are able to receive knowledge from a wider group of internal individuals and collaborate together.

Organizations must realize that even though they may establish knowledge transfer procedures, policies, and the technology and structure to support knowledge transfer, other factors can impede an individual's desire or ability to share knowledge. For example, culture is a major factor in determining the behaviors of individuals in organizations, including their willingness to share knowledge. Many organizations have cultures that promote knowledge hoarding, and people may not feel comfortable in sharing knowledge. A culture of trust is essential; some individuals feel it is risky to display their knowledge to others, as the result might be disagreement or being told they are wrong. Organizations must be very aware of how their culture influences knowledge management activities, including employees' willingness to share their knowledge.

Organizational politics can impede knowledge sharing. If the notion is prevalent that knowledge is power and sharing knowledge results in losing power that only they possess, individuals will be less likely to give up their power, and hence their knowledge. The more knowledge intensive an organization becomes, the less likely its members will be willing to share the valuable commodity of knowledge. Therefore, politics will emerge when others try to acquire knowledge possessed by others. For example, a consultant with technical knowledge that is not possessed by any coworkers may gain the reputation as being the local expert with this technology and be rewarded with his or her choice of assignments involving the technology. If the consultant were to share this knowledge with other employees, the consultant's power would also become distributed and others would be able to compete for choice of assignments. Therefore, from a political standpoint, it would be in the consultant's best interest to keep the knowledge to himself or herself. This notion goes against the best situation for the organization, which would be for the consultant to train multiple employees in order to ensure the knowledge is shared.

Transferring knowledge may not always be in an organization's best interest. Much of an organization's strategic knowledge can be considered confidential or proprietary and should not leave the boundaries of the organization. Other knowledge such as marketing plans, customer knowledge, and product designs are also not meant to be transferred externally. In some industries, especially in the financial sector, federal regulations prevent knowledge sharing between some internal areas. In their efforts to encourage knowledge sharing by their employees, organizations must also be cognizant of what knowledge cannot or should not be shared.

Organizations must recognize their desire to make knowledge available within an organization to the right people, while ensuring that the knowledge only reaches the intended employees. Opening systems and the use of technologies such as wikis may initially seem like a good KM strategy, but these knowledge resources must be treated like any other information system and have the proper security and controls in place. For example, if supply chain partners are allowed to access inventory and sales data through an intranet (in essence creating an extranet), the organization must ensure that access to the intranet does not lead to access to other internal systems. This is important since many organizations use their intranet as a basis for a portal that links all internal systems together. Furthermore, when accessing ERP systems that connect many of the functional areas of an organization, the company must ensure that an external partner is not granted access to all the ERP modules and data, only the ones that are not confidential. Even allowing external access to an internal system opens up one more access point in the information network that can be exploited by an intruder. Systems that span boundaries and link the organization with external companies, partners, or customers must be adequately secured, as giving access to these internal systems can lead to unintended knowledge sharing if tight access controls are not enforced. Although knowledge transfer is an important part of an organization's strategy, knowledge managers must always define who should have access to the knowledge and, more important, who should not.

Although many issues and challenges exist for knowledge managers (see Table 6.3 for a summary of these challenges), their focus should remain on ensuring the right knowledge is accessible by the right employees, at the right time. By engaging corporate leadership, allocating resources as needed, and employing new technologies and social

Table 6.3. Summary of Obstacles to Knowledge Transfer	
Obstacle	**Effect on Knowledge Transfer**
Not being aware of the existence of knowledge	Prevents the transfer from being initiated
Not being aware that there is a need for knowledge	Prevents any action, including knowledge transfer
The nonexistence of, or gaps in, the relationship of the source and recipient	Causes no knowledge or incomplete knowledge to be transferred
Knowledge takes time to be transferred	Knowledge may be transferred, but not in a timely manner
The knowledge that is received may not be useful to the recipient	Although the knowledge transfer occurs, no value is realized from the activity
No motivation exists for the knowledge transfer	The source does not initiate or the recipient does not complete the knowledge transfer
The recipient does not have the absorptive capacity to receive the knowledge	The transfer may not occur, or the knowledge may be interpreted incorrectly
The organizational culture does not support knowledge sharing	Individuals will be reluctant to request or respond to a knowledge transfer request
Strong organizational politics impede knowledge transfers	Individuals will be reluctant to request or respond to a knowledge transfer request
Regulation or structure blocks knowledge flows	Knowledge cannot be transferred
Information security parameters are not defined adequately	Knowledge transfers are accidentally blocked, or too much knowledge is shared

media tools, an organization can position its knowledge to improve work practices, decision making, and strategy formulation.

CONCLUSION

Many factors such as technology, reduced organizational barriers, and an awareness of the importance of knowledge to an organization are changing how companies view and transfer knowledge. A shift has occurred from having a few experts as the primary source of knowledge to having everyone engaged in work tasks that involve the identification, creation, and acquisition of knowledge. Knowledge activities now encompass everyone in an organization, and the responsibility to be involved in the transfer of knowledge is distributed beyond only a few experts.

Through expanded knowledge networks, integrated knowledge work processes, and an emphasis on group or community knowledge, all employees at all levels of the organization are expected to share a fundamental level of common knowledge. This shift is also reflected in a second change, where knowledge has gone from being resident in individuals to being embedded in groups or communities. Social media technologies are leveraging this level of knowledge in an attempt to disseminate knowledge through distributed knowledge networks. Our base of common knowledge is becoming greater as organizations and technology make the process of knowledge transfer easier and integrated into our daily routines.

Knowledge has transformed from a stable commodity to a dynamic and ever-changing asset. This presents many challenges to organizations that rely on efficient and effective

---

**Recap: The Major Points Knowledge Managers Need to Know
When Facilitating Knowledge Sharing**

1. Ensure appropriate and effective communication channels between sources and destinations of knowledge.
2. Ensure a diverse set of channels is available to accommodate the various forms of knowledge and knowledge transfers.
3. Have both open and secure channels available to employees.
4. Routinely survey social networks within organizations to identify blocks, overload on certain nodes, the need for more boundary spanners, and the opportunity for technologies to assist the human element, and look for new sources of knowledge that can be integrated into the network.
5. Determine regularly if new communication channels are needed or if certain sources and destinations need to be connected.
6. Create the appropriate incentives to promote knowledge sharing across boundaries.
7. Encourage people to look beyond organizational boundaries and seek knowledge that can be transferred into the organization from external sources.
8. Coordinate with training and development departments to determine the common or foundational knowledge that every employee must possess to ensure knowledge transfers are effective.
9. Survey the employees to determine their perceptions on the knowledge-sharing environment. Is it safe, open, encouraging, rewarding?
10. Look for ways to support informal, accidental, or serendipitous knowledge sharing amongst employees who may not work together or in the same department.

knowledge transfers. Knowledge managers must continually review their knowledge strategies, programs, and activities to ensure they meet the needs of the employees. Managers must further ensure that their knowledge programs are aligned with the strategy of the organization and continue to support the changing goals and objectives with their knowledge transfer capabilities. The move away from codified, recorded knowledge to tacit and experiential knowledge ensures that people, technology, and a dynamic business environment all have major effects on the knowledge that we use in our personal and professional lives.

DISCUSSION QUESTIONS

1. What are the important elements required for the transfer of knowledge? What is the role of the knowledge manager in procuring, facilitating, and managing these elements?
2. Knowledge transfers can rely on either humans or technology to improve the flow of knowledge. What are the advantages and disadvantages (or limits) of each for an organization creating a knowledge strategy based around the sharing of information?
3. What advice would you give an organization that is contemplating using social media technologies to improve knowledge sharing? What are the benefits and risks of using these tools within an organization?
4. Is unintentional knowledge sharing good or detrimental to an organization? Is it something that should be encouraged or prevented?
5. Sharing knowledge with other people is a very personal act. What do you require in order to feel willing and comfortable in sharing your knowledge with others? How can organizations create an encouraging and safe environment for people to share their knowledge?
6. Consider the example of a company that wants to ensure the knowledge its sales staff receives about customers is shared with other internal departments, such as marketing, finance, and new product development. What barriers to knowledge flow will it encounter? What boundary objects can be used to span these boundaries?

SUGGESTED READINGS

Alavi, M., and G. C. Kane. 2008. "Social Networks and Information Technology." In *Knowledge Management: An Evolutionary View*, edited by I. Becerra-Fernandez and D. Leidner. London: M.E. Sharpe.

Carlile, P. 2002. "A Pragmatic View of Knowledge and Boundaries: Boundary Objects in New Product Development." *Organization Science* 13, no. 4: 442–455.

Dixon, N. M. 2000. *Common Knowledge: How Companies Thrive by Sharing What They Know*. Boston: Harvard Business School Press.

Szulanski, G. 2000. "The Process of Knowledge Transfer: A Diachronic Analysis of Stickiness." *Organizational Behaviour and Human Decision Processes* 82, no. 1: 9–27.

REFERENCES

Alavi, M., and G. C. Kane. 2008. "Social Networks and Information Technology." In *Knowledge Management: An Evolutionary View*, edited by I. Becerra-Fernandez and D. Leidner. London: M.E. Sharpe.

Bishop, M. J., and W. M. Cates. 2001. "Theoretical Foundations for Sound's Use in Multimedia Instruction to Enhance Learning." *Educational Technology Research and Development* 49, no. 3: 5–22.

Borgatti, S., A. Mehra, D. J. Brass, and G. Labianca. 2009. "Network Analysis in the Social Sciences." *Science* 323: 892–895.

Carlile, P. 2002. "A Pragmatic View of Knowledge and Boundaries: Boundary Objects in New Product Development." *Organization Science* 13, no. 4: 442–455.

Ciabuschi, F. 2005. "On IT Systems and Knowledge Sharing in MNCs: A Lesson from Siemens AG." *Knowledge Management Research and Practice* 3: 87–96.

Cohen, W. M., and D. A. Levinthal. 1990. "Absorptive Capacity: A New Perspective on Learning and Innovation." *Administrative Science Quarterly* 35, 1: 128–152.

Daft, R. L., and R. H. Lengel. 1986. "Organizational Information Requirements, Media Richness and Structural Design." *Management Science* 32, no. 5: 554–572.

Dalkir, K. 2005. *Knowledge Management in Theory and Practice*. Burlington, MA: Elsevier Butterworth–Heinemann.

Davenport, T. 1997. *Information Ecology: Mastering the Information and Knowledge Environment*. New York: Oxford University Press.

Desouza, K., and Y. Awazu. 2005. "What Do They Know?" *Business Strategy Review* 16: 41–45.

Desouza, K., Y. Awazu, S. Jha, C. Dombrowski, S. Papagari, P. Baloh, et al. 2008. "Customer-Driven Innovation." *Research Technology Management* 51, no. 3: 35–44.

Dixon, N. M. 2000. *Common Knowledge: How Companies Thrive by Sharing What They Know*. Boston: Harvard Business School Press.

Dixon, N. M. 2009. "How A-Space Is Shaping Analysts' Work: DIA Knowledge Laboratory." Defense Intelligence Agency Report, June 22. http://conversation-matters.typepad.com/A_Space_Study.pdf.

Gibbert, M., M. Leibold, and G. Probst. 2002. "Five Styles of Customer Knowledge Management, and How Smart Companies Use them to Create Value." *European Management Journal* 20, no. 5: 459–469.

Golbeck, J. 2007. "The Dynamics of Web-Based Social Networks: Memberships, Relationships, and Change." *First Monday* 12, no. 11. http://firstmonday.org/htbin/cgiwrap/bin/ojs/index.php/fm/article/view/2023.

Henricksen, K., J. Indulska, and A. Rakotonirainy. 2002. "Modelling Context Information in Pervasive Computing Systems." *Pervasive '02 Proceedings of the First International Conference on Pervasive Computing*, 167–180). Berlin: Springer-Verlag.

Hoover, J. N. 2007. "U.S. Spy Agencies Go Web 2.0 in Effort to Better Share Information." *Information Week*, August 23. http://www.informationweek.com/news/internet/showArticle.jhtml?articleID=201801990.

Jonsson, A., and T. Kalling. 2007. "Challenges to Knowledge Sharing Across National and Intra-Organizational Boundaries: Case Studies of IKEA and SCA Packaging." *Knowledge Management Research and Practice* 5: 161–172.

Joshi, A. W., and S. Sharma. 2004. "Customer Knowledge Development: Antecedents and Impact on New Product Performance." *Journal of Marketing* 68: 47–59.

Kautz, K., and A. Kjoergaard. 2007. "Towards an Integrated Model of Knowledge Sharing in Software Development: Insights from a Case Study." *International Journal of Knowledge Management* 3, no. 2: 97–120.

McDermott, R. 1999. "Why Information Technology Inspired but Cannot Deliver Knowledge Management." *California Management Review* 41, no. 4: 103–117.

Nayir, D., and U. Uzuncarsili. 2008. "A Cultural Perspective on Knowledge Management: The Success of Sarkuysan Company." *Journal of Knowledge Management* 12, no. 2, 141–155.

Nonaka, I., and N. Konno. 1998. "The Concept of 'Ba': Building a Foundation for Knowledge Creation." *California Management Review* 40, no. 3: 40–54.

Paquette, S., and C. W. Choo. 2008. "Towards a Theory of Customer Knowledge Use: The Role of Knowledge Quality and Accessibility." Paper presented at the Administrative Sciences Association of Canada.

Prahalad, C. K., and V. Ramaswamy. 2000. "Co-Opting Customer Competence." *Harvard Business Review* 78, no. 1 (January-February): 79–87.

Schleimer, S., and A. Riege. 2009. "Knowledge Transfer Between Globally Dispersed Units at BMW." *Journal of Knowledge Management* 13, no. 1: 27–41.

Shaughnessy, L. 2008. "CIA, FBI Push 'Facebook for Spies.'" CNN. Last modified September 5. http://www.cnn.com/2008/TECH/ptech/09/05/facebook.spies/index.html.

Slater, S. F., and J. C. Narver. 1995. "Market Orientation and the Learning Organization." *Journal of Marketing* 59, no. 3: 63–74.

Spies, M., A. J. Clayton, and M. Noormohammadian. 2005. "Knowledge Management in a Decentralized Global Financial Services Provider: A Case Study with Allianz Group." *Knowledge Management Research and Practice* 3: 24–36.

Star, S. L. 1989a. "Institutional Ecology, 'Translations' and Boundary Objects: Amateurs and Professionals in Berkley's Museum of Vertebrate Zoology." *Social Studies of Science* 19, no. 3: 387–420.

Star, S. L. 1989b. "The Structure of Ill-Structured Solutions: Heterogeneous Problem-Solving, Boundary Objects and Distributed Artificial Intelligence." In *Distributed Artificial Intelligence*, edited by M. Huhns and L. Gasser, vol. 2: 37–54. Menlo Park: Morgan Kauffman.

Szulanski, G. 2000. "The Process of Knowledge Transfer: A Diachronic Analysis of Stickiness." *Organizational Behaviour and Human Decision Processes* 82, no. 1: 9–27.

Tsoukas, H. 1996. "The Firm as a Distributed Knowledge System: A Constructionist Approach." *Strategic Management Journal* 17(Winter Special Issue): 11–25.

Tushman, M. L. 1977. "Special Boundary Roles in the Innovation Process." *Administrative Science Quarterly* 22, no. 4: 587–605.

Urban, G. L. 2004. "The Emerging Era of Customer Advocacy." *Sloan Management Review* 45, no. 2 (Winter): 77–82.

7

Knowledge Application

Chen Ye with Kevin C. Desouza and Scott Paquette

OBJECTIVES

- Discuss how an organization gains value from knowledge management efforts if it can systematically use and reuse knowledge to further its goals and objectives.
- Present the critical issues that one needs to pay attention to when deploying knowledge to meet the needs of decision makers.
- Demonstrate the application of knowledge within organizations through citing current examples and cases.

INTRODUCTION

For an organization, the ultimate goal of managing knowledge is to increase profit by improving the efficiency of operations, increasing the quality and quantity of innovations, and enhancing competitiveness. However, the desired benefits cannot be achieved without knowledge collected being effectively applied within the firm. Therefore, members at all levels of the organization need to make a systematic effort to utilize the knowledge available at different points of their activities, such as decision making. In reality, various social, organizational, and individual barriers exist between knowledge producers and knowledge consumers, leading to nonutilization, under-utilization, or misuse of knowledge. Bridging the gap between knowledge generation and application is one of the main challenges of knowledge management. Successful companies often reap the reward of consistent and systematic knowledge application and achieve sustained competitive advantage. For instance, Apple's application of its knowledge of the consumer technology market, in design and marketing departments, led to a series of products with wide acceptance by the consumers, and remarkable value generated for its shareholders. IBM also demonstrates the significance of knowledge application, through its decade-long efforts in deploying technologies that allow its consultants to find and reuse intellectual assets.

This chapter mainly addresses the strategies and impacts of knowledge application on business organizations. That is not to say knowledge application is inconsequential to other types of organizations. On the contrary, educational institutions, police departments, political parties, charitable foundations, government agencies, military branches, and the like can all better serve their constituents with more effective knowledge application. Whether the goal is enhancing student learning or defeating the enemy, we can benefit from integrating knowledge from a full spectrum of sources and putting it into better use. The Memphis Police Department, for instance, reduced serious crimes by 31 percent by deploying an analytics system codeveloped with University of Memphis and IBM. The system evaluates the citywide incident patterns and predicts criminal hot spots, allowing the department to take proactive actions accordingly and curtail further crimes (ebiz, 2010). Alameda County Social Services Agency saves 11 million dollars of taxpayer money by using a business analytics system to identify fraud and eliminate duplicate work among the cases filed by its 250,000 clients (IBM, 2010).

Traditionally, knowledge is considered to be possessed by a limited number of experts who usually specialize in a narrowly defined area. It falls on the shoulders of these domain experts to act as agents of knowledge application when work tasks call for their expertise. The circle of influence of these experts and their knowledge are often limited by physical and organizational constraints. It is not uncommon for a financial analyst working on the first floor to spend days researching a certain tax code from the state of Illinois, without knowing that the accountant working on the third floor has extensive experience with Illinois tax laws. Today, most organizations compete in increasingly complex environments influenced by regulatory, economic, and global factors. A large amount of knowledge is constantly being generated when fast turnarounds in decision making have become essential for survival. From the organizational perspective, the silos of functional units are being broken down and the lines between different job titles are being blurred. These trends lead to an increasing reliance on each individual, as opposed to a few experts, to be an effective knowledge worker. This process resembles the democratization of knowledge that has helped to spread knowledge to the masses in modern history. As stated by Larry Sanger, Wikipedia cofounder, "Professionals are no longer needed for the bare purpose of the mass distribution of information and the shaping of opinion" (Sanger, 2007). In other words, the democratization of knowledge in a modern organization both demands and empowers individual members to be effective knowledge creators and consumers.

Furthermore, the sphere of knowledge application has been expanded to involve stakeholders outside of many organizations. For example, some companies are leveraging consumer-driven innovations for developing new products and services. Such crowdsourcing strategy depends on hundreds and thousands of customers using their individual intellectual capital to provide the company with valuable ideas and suggestions.

Knowledge can also be applied in a peer-to-peer fashion. Many companies host web forums that allow customers to post questions and answer each other's questions, bypassing internal members of the organization. Such disintermediation not only expedites knowledge application, but also allows knowledge that may not yet exist in the organization to be identified for potential use. Take the case of a user who purchased a new software application may run into a rare incompatibility issue with an obsolete hardware component on her computer. The supposed experts, the technical service personnel from the software vendor, may be able to provide only a generic response related to software-hardware incompatibility; while another user who has encountered and solved the same problem before might be able to provide the precise solution. When a user provides a useful solution, knowledge is also being collected and preserved; it is ready to be reused when other users seek a solution to the same problem later on.

In our discussion we have not delved into the role of information and communication technologies (ICTs). Many of the developments in knowledge management depend on ICTs and the Internet: from the computer systems that allow coding and storage of vast amount of knowledge objects, to advanced algorithms that power the search engines for speedy discovery of knowledge artifacts. Recently, technologies have emerged to play more than a utility role in a knowledge system. These systems are technology-driven and fully automated, removing the need for human agents. One example of such a system builds on **self-service technologies (SSTs)**. SSTs allows individuals to complete service transactions, such as checking out at a grocery store or printing a boarding pass at the airport, through interactions with software-based interfaces. SSTs are especially suitable for handling highly repetitive transactions following simple and explicit procedures. Other technologies act as enablers of new approaches for applying knowledge. For example, GPS and RFID technologies have enabled the pinpointing of individuals and goods, leading to more and more innovative location-aware services. Some of these services such as bus locators allow humans to make better informed decisions. Others combine the location information with existing knowledge and the real-time decision-making capability of computer software. It is no longer science fiction for a software agent embedded in a digital sign to recognize and greet a consumer passing by, and recommend a nearby store based on her past purchasing habits.

In this chapter, we present different strategies for an organization to use knowledge, with an emphasis on how computer technologies can be integrated with human strategies to achieve better knowledge reuse under different situations. We then discuss a number of issues pertaining to motivating human knowledge workers, as individuals and as team members, to reuse knowledge. Detailed descriptions and recommendations on self-service technologies, a prime example of technology-enabled knowledge application, are provided. We conclude the chapter with discussions on the business value impact of knowledge application, including our recommendations on how business value can be measured and monitored.

HOW KNOWLEDGE IS APPLIED

Knowledge cannot be applied without an agent that analyzes a problem, selects pertinent knowledge from available sources, and utilizes the knowledge to devise a solution. Only humans have traditionally played the role of the knowledge user. Advances in modern technology have created knowledge application strategies where machines substitute for, or more often supplement, human decision makers. In order to select the most appropriate strategy for a specific problem domain, one needs insight into both the advantages and disadvantages of human and machine decision making, as described in the sections that follow. Table 7.1 outlines the strengths and weaknesses of human and machine agents.

Table 7.1. Strengths and Weaknesses of Human and Machine Agents		
	Strengths	**Weaknesses**
Human	• Ability to adjust to unusual or unpredictable events • Domain knowledge • Understanding of the context of decisions • Qualitative evaluation	• Limited cognitive ability to evaluate all options • Time constraints • Psychological biases such as sunk-cost, confirming-evidence, and overconfidence
Machine	• Ability to rapidly perform complex calculations with accuracy and consistency • Ability to summarize, reduce, and compress a large quantity of data • Immunity to physical and emotional effects	• Inability to recognize nuance and interpret unpredictable events • Ignorance of useful knowledge encoded in the details, leading to suboptimal outcomes

Humans Strategies

Human agents such as domain experts are still the most important users of knowledge, especially of tacit knowledge. Compared to machines, human decision makers have a number of key advantages including creativity, flexibility, domain knowledge (Bruggen, Smidts, and Wierenga, 2001), and qualitative evaluation (Blattgerg and Hoch, 1990). Meehl's broken-leg problem is an interesting example of human experts' advantages. In this example, the task of predicting whether a person would go see a movie on a given day is assigned to both a human judge and a mathematical model, with the knowledge that the person has just broken one of his legs. The mathematical model outperforms the human decision maker when the broken leg was not disclosed. On the contrary, only the human judge is able to accurately predict that the person is not likely to attend a movie with a broken leg (Meehl, 1954). This example illustrates that human experience allows a human decision maker to understand and consider rare conditions such as a broken leg much better than a mathematical model. Furthermore, the social capital possessed by an individual in a community is also an important factor in knowledge application. The interpersonal connections that build on trust and empathy could be the most useful facilitator of knowledge transfer from one individual to another.

People still remain the best decision makers based on their ability to understand the context of the decision, and adjust their decision processes to unusual or nonpredictable events. Insurance companies have developed very complex systems to perform underwriting of new policies for people applying for car or home insurance. Many of these systems have created the opportunity to receive insurance quotes instantaneously and online. As long as the policy details and the applicant conform to normal expectations and no surprising facts are stated in the application, knowledge systems have become quite proficient at adjudicating the policy and creating a quote for the premiums. For example, a request for a quote from a married 35-year-old woman with two kids who owns a minivan is a common, known request and can be easily handled by an automated system. However, this process breaks down when information is presented to the system that varies greatly from historical precedents or normal conditions as defined by the designers of the system. A 16-year-old boy, with little experience and two traffic violations, who drives a Porsche would be an unusual case that would not fit into the algorithms of the decision-support system. In this situation, human employees, who will utilize their tacit knowledge, experience, and judgment to correctly price the policy, must underwrite the policy.

CALL and the US Army

The Center for Army Lessons Learned (CALL) is a military intelligence unit dedicated to the collection and application of knowledge for the US Army (Chua and Lam, 2006; CALL, 2011). According to its mission statement, CALL strives to increase collaboration between individuals and the Centers of Excellence (CoE) to enrich mission success through providing expertise and experience on the battlefield. It also attempts to refine the army's methods for training, and leader development, through the management of knowledge (Chua and Lam, 2006). To accomplish its goal, CALL relies on a pool of subject matter experts for the collection, analysis, and dissemination of observations, insights, and lessons learned. These experts are well trained and highly experienced personnel drawn from units across the Army. They are responsible for carrying out CALL's unique knowledge application process consisting of four steps. First, CALL carefully selects events for observation that are most likely to yield valuable knowledge for future operations, and develops a set of learning objectives for each event. Once an event is selected, teams of data collectors are assembled and deployed to observe the ground operations, collect useful data, and conduct analyses. Each team member is a specialist with in-depth knowledge in one or more areas such as ground combat or local culture. In combination, the expertise of all team members constitutes a comprehensive coverage of all areas relevant to the mission, ensuring meaningful observation and understanding of the event. The observations gathered are sent back to CALL to be interpreted by a separate group of experts known as the analysts. After soliciting and reviewing feedback from other knowledgeable personnel around the army, the analysts construct lessons learned based on their analyses and interpretation of the observations. These lessons are subsequently released to the intended audience through electronic channels such as e-mail and the web, and archived in the CALL database. Units that receive these lessons, either at their own request or as the result of a mass distribution, will put the knowledge into use by acting on the recommendations. In short, the CALL knowledge application process relies heavily on human experts for the collection, creation, dissemination, and application of knowledge.

While human nature provides inimitable advantages, it also presents a number of issues. Limited cognitive capability of an individual undermines her ability to explore all options as a decision maker. Such limitation is referred to as bounded rationality (Simon, 1982). The time constraint imposed on human decision makers in real-life situations further exacerbates this problem, as they are forced to use simplified decision strategies and forgo useful information (Payne, Bettman, and Johnson, 1993). Furthermore, humans are subject to a number of systematic biases such as anchoring, sunk-cost, confirming-evidence, overconfidence, prudence, and recallability traps (Alpert and Raiffa, 1982; Fischhoff, 1982; George, Duffy, and Ahuja,, 2000). Take sunk-cost as an example. Someone who is planning a vacation purchased a nonrefundable air ticket. He learns later that there is a travel package deal which could reduce the overall cost of the vacation. However, he may not take advantage of the newly gained knowledge and book the package, simply because he is reluctant to lose the money he has already paid for the air ticket. His human emotion prevents him from taking the course of action that is optimal according to logic.

Behavioral theories suggest that some of these biases could be deep-rooted in human psychology and very persistent. Theory of cognitive dissonance posits that people intuitively focus on information that supports their point of view, due to the need for self-justification. Such a tendency can take the form of the conforming-evidence bias. Many real-life stories of wrongfully convicted people reveal that some police detectives tend to ignore the conflicting evidence once they have established a prime suspect for a case. In the business sector, decision makers can easily fall into similar traps by cherry-picking only knowledge that supports their preexisting views.

The Shuttle Disasters

After the space shuttle Columbia was destroyed during reentry on February 1, 2003, the Columbia Accident Investigation Board (CAIB) determined that the immediate cause of the disaster was a piece of insulating foam peeling off from the external fuel tank during the launch (Reuters, 2004). The foam struck and punctured a hole in the leading edge on Columbia's left wing. The hole allowed hot gases to penetrate the interior of the wing during the re-entry into the Earth's atmosphere, destroying the support structure and leading to the disintegration of the shuttle. The CAIB's report, however, indicated that the root cause of the tragic accident was more of a human and organizational error than a technical one. Debris shedding from the external tank was a well-known problem to NASA. It had caused minor damage on prior shuttle flights. Over time, management became overconfident with the insignificance of falling debris. When NASA engineers observed the impact of the foam on the wing during Columbia's ascent, they warned management of the potentially severe consequence of the damage, and made requests for high-resolution imaging of the shuttle in orbit, as well as astronauts' visual inspection of the left wing. However, key decision makers repeatedly disregarded the warnings and declined the requests based on their imperfect knowledge of the risk associated with the incident. In addition, management believed that nothing could be done regarding the damage, while later investigation revealed that realistic options to avoid the catastrophic event did exist. CAIB also noted that the factors behind the Columbia disaster are strikingly similar to those behind the Challenger accident 17 years earlier. In the case of Challenger, NASA managers dismissed the warnings from the engineers about the danger of low temperatures prior to the launch, which caused the infamous failure of the rubber O-rings that eventually led to the shuttle breakup (McEntee, 2011). CAIB concluded that the same organizational culture and flawed decision-making process was largely to blame for both shuttle disasters.

Although much research has been done on how to diminish the effects of these biases through warnings, feedback, and trainings, human decision makers cannot fully eradicate the distortions that are ingrained in their minds. Recently, the field of behavioral economics has begun to examine questions such as these, in order to determine when human characteristics cause people to not follow expected norms and make decisions that may not be economically optimal (Ariely, 2008).

Machine Strategies

Given the shortcomings of human decision making, computer-based **decision support systems (DSS)** are designed to alleviate the burden of human decision makers. Several generations of DSS have evolved over the past few decades. In addition to the obvious immunity to physical and emotional effects, one fundamental capability of these systems is performing very complex computations. Therefore, they are often used to summarize, reduce, and compress a large quantity of original data into chunks which are manageable for human minds (Marakas, 1998; Desouza, 2002).

One specialized group of DSS, **executive information systems (EIS)**, is capable of aggregating relevant data throughout an organization and presenting a highly condensed summary to senior executives. Decision making at the top level requires that reliable and accurate insights on the state of the entire company be available in a timely fashion. However, traditional information gathering processes requires data to be collected and aggregated along layers of organizational hierarchy, across different business units, leading to critical decisions being made based upon inaccurate and outdated information. An EIS integrates internal and external information generated and stored by computer systems and applications across the company, and presents key statistics such as financial ratios or sales data in real time, using easy to use user interfaces. With such systems, key decision makers can constantly monitor the performance in areas of interest, spot anomalies and identify trends, and make rapid responses.

Today, EIS has evolved into business intelligence (BI) systems that perform sophisticated analytical and statistical processing, and present variables of interest, often referred to as key performance indicators, on a dashboard. The dashboard contains graphic representations of different key performance indicators in arrangements similar to the instrument panel of passenger vehicles. It can be accessed from a variety of computing devices including mobile devices. Users at various levels of the organization can use the dashboard to view relevant information and make speedy and informed decisions. AstraZeneca, the global biopharmaceutical organization with over $3 billion annual spending on research and development, implemented a business intelligence solution to provide visibility to project performance to users around the globe. Managers, research scientists, and therapeutic experts all have access to a consolidated view of project schedule, cost, and resources, resulting in improved project performance and reduced time to bring new treatments to the market.

A DSS's reduction of original data, due to its use of mathematical models and computer algorithms, presents its own problem. In the process of condensing all available information into a snapshot presentable to a human decision maker, a DSS typically leaves out a large number of details. While this approach helps to improve the decision-making efficiency, it may also reduce effectiveness of the decision making. When important details are hidden, useful knowledge encoded in the details is ignored, leading to suboptimal outcomes. This is particularly true when a DSS tackles a problem with a high level of uncertainty (entropy) (Desouza et al., 2004).

In recent years, social media—web-based applications that enable interactive dialogues and exchange of contents—have gained significant popularity. Assisted by sophisticated analytic tools, social media has emerged as a new decision support technology. An example of how social media technology is enabling decision making can be found through an examination of emergency and disaster management by companies. In an emergency situation, decisions that have a significant impact on the organization must be made very quickly and with confidence. The information and knowledge available to

---

Larry Ellison and NetSuite

NetSuite Inc. is a computer software company cofounded by Larry Ellison, the iconic founder and CEO of Oracle Corporation, in 1998 (BusinessWeek, 2006). Ellison had long desired the ability to monitor the pulse of the vast sales organization at Oracle in real time. However, the existing technologies at that time could not accommodate his vision. He had to rely on phone calls to get the latest sales figure from managers, and tolerate that data was usually out of date by the time it reached him. Therefore, one of the first tools developed by NetSuite was a web-based dashboard system that provides a company's executives a real-time view to its sales performance, aggregated from data extracted from the information systems throughout the enterprise. Before long, both Ellison and Zachary Nelson, CEO of NetSuite, became avid users of the dashboard. Ellison would access the dashboard in the comfort of his private yacht during his vacations, examine up-to-the-minute performance of NetSuite, and exchange views with Nelson. The NetSuite dashboard not only presented aggregated performance to the top executives, but also enabled access to the specific details for each salesperson, including individual sales leads and even individual email messages. Ellison used the system to keep a close watch on the top potential deals before the end of each quarter. He would access the dashboard multiple times a day, and step in to close the deal himself when he saw the need. Such intervention from the top executives was certainly not always welcome by all those affected. At both Oracle and NetSuite, there were salespeople who resisted the dashboard with actions such as withholding their sales leads, and there was criticism from privacy advocates. However, Ellison and Nelson were unfazed, as they believed the benefits of the dashboard far outweighed its shortcomings. Their companies have joined a long list of renowned organizations that use similar systems to provide their executives instant access to key business information.

---

the decision makers plays a crucial role in their ability to react to a dynamic and unusual event, as well as the processes for decision making. Organizations can use Social media to quickly gather information on the situation, retrieve archived knowledge that may help with coping with the emergency, and expedite communication links between employees and outside agencies. During the 2010 Haitian earthquake, the US military was in a position to coordinate relief efforts and direct the flow of aid to the island. Air Force staff at the Pentagon had to react quickly to a volatile and uncertain scenario, and found that using social technologies such as wikis improved their access to information. Social media facilitated knowledge sharing and decision making in two ways. First, it increased knowledge reuse between staff members to provide current information for decisions. Previously, the majority of knowledge was shared during formal briefings, but now each staff member had complete visibility into how his or her colleagues were managing knowledge and using this knowledge in their decisions. This included gaining access to their sources, identifying when different functions were working on the same problem from different ends (something that occurs frequently), and finding materials that could easily be repurposed for other needs. Another major advantage of social media was that it allowed the military to bypass or eliminate formal liaison structures used previously to share knowledge between different agencies. Besides translating knowledge from one domain to another, the liaison's most valuable function was brokering knowledge sharing requests. Typically, the problem was not so much that staff in one agency were not allowed to access knowledge from another, but that it would be difficult in practice for them to know who, what, where, and how to access that knowledge. Social media facilitated this awareness and improved the quality and the timeliness of decisions (Yates and Paquette, 2011).

Most decision support systems are effective in organizations as they bring a standard-ized process to organizational decision-making activities. For certain sets of decisions that require consistency and accuracy, the best decision process can be encoded into the system for employees to follow. Historical codified knowledge can be included in the system to provide users insight with previous cases and insights that they might not be aware of, yet this knowledge still resides in the organization. Timeliness can also be an advantage of automated systems that can perform routine analysis very quickly compared to managers and other employees. Once the system has proven itself to be accurate in the decision support it provides, the level of review and requirements for additional scrutiny by humans will decrease, improving its efficiency even more.

Human-Machine Strategies

Drawing on the strengths and weaknesses of the human-centered and machine-centered approaches, one can clearly see the potential for integrative strategies. In fact, a complementary approach, combining a DSS with human experts' judgment and intu-ition, has consistently outperformed either a human expert or a DSS alone (Blattberg and Hoch, 1990; Hoch and Schkade, 1996). Many theories also exist to explain the benefits of integrating human practitioners and computational models (Little, 1970; Einhorn, 1972). Table 7.2 summarizes examples of human-machine strategies.

Table 7.2. Examples of Integrated Human-Machine Strategies		
	Description	**Important Considerations**
Machine (DSS) makes final decision	• Human practitioners provide informational inputs to the DSS, which calculates the solution.	• High-quality inputs are required from human experts (i.e., contextual understanding and domain knowledge). • Before fully accepting the machine solution, human decision makers need to ensure the validity and completeness of input data, confirm that the DSS is functioning appropriately, and verify the final decision using common sense.
Expert measurement + mechanical combination	• Human practitioners use qualitative skills to develop component solutions. • Machine combines decision elements to generate an overall solution.	• This is appropriate for highly qualitative problems with multiple underlying dimensions (i.e., there is sufficient complexity that human combination could be error prone).
Humans make final decision	• Humans make independent judgments using their experience and evaluate system-generated solutions. • Humans choose whether to compromise, accept, or reject the system-generated solution.	• Humans make compromises by assigning weights for each decision based on context. • Before accepting the machine solution, human decision makers need to ensure its validity through automated and commonsense checks.

One of the main considerations in applying an integrative human-machine strategy is whether the primary decision-making role should reside in the human experts or the DSS. Depending on the answer, human-machine strategies can be classified into two categories:

- Strategies for situations where the DSS plays the primary role
- Strategies for situations where the practitioner plays the primary role

Strategies in the first category rely on the DSS to make the final judgment for a given problem. The quality of the output from a DSS depends not only on the accuracy of its mathematical models, by also on the quality of the inputs it receives. Therefore, we can take advantage of the human strengths, including qualitative evaluation and richer domain knowledge, by letting human practitioners provide informational inputs to the DSS. Higher quality inputs from human knowledge workers will lead to better results from the DSS, thus achieving a combination of the human strengths and machine strengths.

Human inputs to a DSS can take various forms at different stages, depending on the decision-making strategy employed by the DSS. For data mining systems, selection of data inputs is one process where human practitioners' advantages can be utilized. Computer programs excel in mining a large quantity of data to extract useful patterns. However, identifying and selecting a good subset of the original data from which to perform the modeling is critical to a data mining project, and it is often the weakest link of a computer system because it requires strong contextual understanding and domain knowledge. Therefore, involvement of domain experts is one of the critical success factors for a data mining system (Hirji, 2001). When domain experts act as gatekeepers for data inputs, their domain knowledge is passed to the computer system.

In addition to excelling in addressing quantitative issues such as data mining, human-machine strategies can also be advantageous in solving highly qualitative problems. A highly qualitative problem is often solved via a divide-and-conquer approach, by decomposing it into multiple underlying dimensions. Once these component dimensions, which are still qualitative, are solved individually, the solutions can be combined to form the final judgment. The traditional, human-centered approach puts both the decomposition and the combination stages in the hands of human experts. However, human experts are error prone because they might inadvertently or knowingly omit one or more of the underlying dimensions during the evaluation or the combination process. Moreover, calculation errors might occur when they combine individual evaluations into an overall one, even if evaluations for the underlying dimensions are accurate. To combat these human errors, the "expert measurement + mechanical combination" approach was proposed (Einhorn, 1972). While still relying on human experts to develop the individual evaluations to the underlying dimensions, the evaluations are fed into a mathematical model to generate an overall solution, effectively combining the human experts' strength in qualitative evaluation and DSS' strength in computation and consistency.

Human inputs can also be beneficial when a computer solves certain types of complex problems. It is well documented that for many complex problems such as voice and image recognition or playing board games, a computer system is often incompetent or inefficient despite its immense computational power. The inefficiency is due to the fact that a DSS employs very primitive strategies compared to human problem solvers. On the contrary, human beings are very proficient in solving certain complex problems, despite having very limited computation ability. Hence, we could integrate human beings' thinking strategies into a DSS by allowing domain experts to provide procedural or strategic inputs to the DSS. In practice, such a strategy may be difficult to apply because the strategies and heuristics used by human beings are often considered hard to emulate with traditional computer algorithms. One possible solution is to supply the DSS with a collection of partially solved problems that can greatly reduce the time it takes the computer to search for the optimal solution. Computer chess programs, for example, often rely on a database of endgames solved by human players to devise a winning plan. Another possible solution is presented in decision calculus (Little, 1970), which describes a methodology that combines human expertise and mathematical models to solve a particular problem. Successful application of decision calculus requires extraction of human experts' problem-solving strategies, and represents the strategies using formulas. These heuristic and experiential formulas can be combined with mathematical and statistical models in a DSS. On the one hand, such an approach reduces the need for complex analytical models that are difficult to construct and hard to understand by human managers. On the other hand, it also benefits from the consistency of extracted formulas compared to relying solely on human experts whose performance may fluctuate from task to task.

An example of advancing organizations through the combination of human and system decision support has recently been implemented by many environmental and climate change scientists. Traditionally, quantitative data on the natural environment and how it has been changing over the past decades has been collected through electronic sensors and measurements. For example, the monitoring of crop growth and food production in Africa has relied primarily on remote sensing technologies (Brown, Paquette, and Ross, 2008). From this data, information regarding the environmental situation is created, and decisions are made based on this information. Food growth and production data is normally provided to international aid and development agencies in order for them to allocate relief supplies. However, recently the human element of conducting science has proven useful to verifying the accuracy and augmenting the detail of such scientific data collection. Through the use of people's tacit knowledge and observations, this qualitative knowledge can be applied to the electronically gathered data in order to improve the decisions made by governments, organizations, and local communities (Brown and Paquette, 2009). In Africa, local community members can verify remotely sensed data for accuracy, and can also provide new qualitative measurements such as local government support, security, economic information, and indications of environmental changes. This blend of quantitative data from instruments and qualitative data from local community members has also been employed to understand the climate changes occurring in the Arctic. An example is the indigenous populations who rely on the ice along coastlines in Alaska for hunting and fishing in the winter months. Traditionally, satellite images and physical ground measurements of the ice have been employed to understand the composition, thickness, and physical properties of the ice. Recently, local community members and their elders have been contributing their expertise and knowledge gained from a lifetime of relying on the ice for their food. They are able to predict the stability and types of ice that will form based on their knowledge of the environment and sea conditions. This knowledge is useful to scientists who would not normally have access to such valuable tacit knowledge (Paquette, 2010; Trainor and Paquette, 2011).

Unlike human-machine strategies that place the final decision-making authority on the computer system, strategies that integrate a DSS into human decision making are much more commonplace. In most real-life situations, such as in a hospital where an expert system is used to help diagnose patients, the final decision is the responsibility of human experts, with a DSS playing a supporting role. There are three possible approaches of integrating a DSS into human decision maker's decisions: compromising, total acceptance, and total rejection. Both a DSS and human experts are capable of solving many problems independently. To reach a compromise between the independent solutions from the two sources, the human experts will determine weights for each solution based on decision contexts. For example, less weight should be assigned to the solution from a DSS, if it is newly introduced with little proven track record.

In some situations, human decision makers may not be able to reach their own conclusions due to various constraints such as time or information processing capabilities. In this case, a total acceptance or total rejection of the DSS solution may be necessary. Before fully accepting the machine solution, human decision makers need to ensure the validity and completeness of input data, confirm that the DSS is functioning appropriately, and verify the final decision using common sense. Otherwise, full rejection of the machine solution is warranted, and the entire process should start over after the errors in the DSS are identified and corrected.

THE CHALLENGES OF KNOWLEDGE REUSE

Regardless of the strategies organizations choose to apply, they should recognize that reusing existing knowledge will not solve all problems. The goal of knowledge reuse is to combine existing expertise and insights with new information to form an optimal solution. In this process we might find it necessary to adjust or even reject existing knowledge, especially knowledge that is time sensitive or context dependent, and create new knowledge. For example, a company might have noted that the majority of customers in an emerging market can only access the Internet using slow dial-up connections. However, the access condition could be vastly improved in a few years, and any e-business operations built on the presumption need to be amended or redesigned to reflect the new condition. Blindly applying existing knowledge could stifle creativity and innovation, and undermine the opportunity to find new ways of looking at problems.

In Chapter 4, we discussed the use of communities to encourage knowledge exchange and application. One issue that could undermine the effectiveness of such effort is free-riding. While individuals are motivated to contribute knowledge due to various intrinsic and extrinsic factors, there will always be those who only consume without giving back. The 80/20 phenomenon is often observed when it comes to knowledge contribution in communities, where 80 percent of the knowledge is contributed by 20 percent of the members. Therefore, to encourage full participation, contributors should be rewarded with proper incentives and recognitions.

HUMAN-KNOWLEDGE APPLICATION

What Drives Consumption of Explicit Knowledge?

The majority of reusable knowledge in an organization is explicit knowledge. These knowledge artifacts represent a strategic asset for the organization. Like any asset, this knowledge needs to be deployed and utilized effectively before the organization can gain competitive advantage from it. While the benefits of knowledge management are strategic and organizational, reaping these benefits requires each individual to actively and constantly seek and apply knowledge objects in accomplishing his or her daily tasks. However, research has suggested that many organizations are under-achieving in knowledge reuse due to lack of cooperation from the knowledge workers (Desouza, 2003; Davenport, Thomas, and Desouza, 2003). Hence, it is critical to understand the factors that drive consumption of explicit knowledge at the individual level. See Table 7.3 for a list of factors that contribute to knowledge use and reuse.

As discussed in Chapter 5, depending on whether a potential consumer has the expertise to judge the value of a knowledge object, explicit knowledge can be either an experience or a credence good (Desouza, Awazu, and Wan, 2006). It is difficult for consumers to judge the quality of an experience good until they have actually consumed it. When the piece of explicit knowledge is within the consumer's domain of expertise, he or she will be confident in assessing the value of the knowledge product. Thus, the decision on consumption will be based mainly on the consumer's evaluation of salient characteristics of the knowledge object itself. On the other hand, when the consumer is a novice and lacks the expertise to judge the value of the knowledge object, he or she

Table 7.3. Factors Contributing to Knowledge Use and Reuse	
Factor	**Description**
Expertise of user	• When the knowledge is within the user's domain of expertise, the user will use his or her own judgment to apply the knowledge.
Expertise of producer	• When the knowledge is outside the user's domain of expertise, he or she will base the decision to apply the knowledge on the trustworthiness and reputation of the producer.
Ease of use	• Less complexity and effort will increase the likelihood that knowledge is applied.
Perception of relative advantage	• If individuals perceive a relative advantage, such as economic gain or social prestige, they will be more likely to use knowledge.
Perception of risk	• Perception of risk will discourage individuals from using a knowledge object.

will form the decision based on evaluation of the trustworthiness and reputation of the knowledge producer instead. Therefore, two groups of considerations could influence an individual's consumption of explicit knowledge. For the knowledge producer, an individual is more likely to apply knowledge from a source he or she perceives as credible. Here credible means someone can be trusted as a competent, reliable, and honest knowledge provider. In addition, a user is more likely to trust someone with a closer relationship, and therefore to consume the knowledge artifacts.

As to knowledge products, research on innovation adoption has long found users prefer products that are less complex and easier to use, and those that provide relative advantage over other alternatives. Relative advantage is the gain, such as increased economic profitability or social prestige one expects to receive from accepting an innovation (Rogers, 1983). To a potential user, new knowledge is an innovation. Less complexity and more relative advantage of a knowledge product, as perceived by the individual, will therefore promote the use of it (Desouza, Awazu, and Wan, 2006).

In addition, a consumer has to bear a certain amount of risk when using a knowledge object. Knowledge is usually provided without guarantees, and the consumer is fully responsible for both positive and negative outcomes from reusing the knowledge. The consumer may also be unable to determine whether a knowledge artifact is an experience or credence good. Overall, a high risk evaluation will discourage the consumer from using knowledge.

Knowledge Reuse for Teams

In the previous section, knowledge application was viewed from the perspective of a single organizational member. Knowledge workers are typically organized into work groups or teams, collaborating on tasks and projects. Therefore, no discussion of knowledge application is complete without thoughts given to these organizational contexts. This section discusses how team dynamics influence knowledge reuse.

To a knowledge consumer in an organization, one of the most important considerations is the presence of multiple knowledge spaces. A knowledge space is a logical or physical location that houses knowledge objects (Desouza, Awazu, and Tiwana, 2006). Knowledge spaces range from a database storing explicit knowledge pieces to people's minds where tacit knowledge resides. Desouza, Awazu, and Tiwana (2006) discussed three distinct knowledge spaces: private, quasi-public, and public. Each individual has a knowledge space that hosts his or her own private knowledge. Through the collaborative work which individuals perform in teams, quasi-public spaces emerge. Lastly, a global, public knowledge space is available to all members of the organization.

Through their study of 25 software development organizations, Desouza, Awazu, and Tiwana (2006) discovered that reuse of knowledge in the public space, which is the main goal of organizational knowledge management initiatives, depends on the level of expertise of a knowledge consumer. Compared to novices, experts are much less likely to search the public space for a knowledge piece missing in their private spaces. Much of this tendency stems from their beliefs that any knowledge they lack is unlikely to be available in the public space, or that they can do a better job creating the knowledge on their own.

Similar to experts, "expert teams," or permanent teams that have worked together for a long duration on similar projects, rely less on public knowledge space. In such teams, the repeated interactions between the members bring a convergence of their knowledge space and search strategies. Such convergence eventually leads to self-reinforced usage of team knowledge space and, to a certain degree, the exclusion of the public space. On the contrary, members of a transient team formed only for completing a single project, are more likely to seek, discover, and reuse knowledge artifacts in the public space.

One cautionary note should be mentioned: as groups engage in decision making, they can become trapped in what has been termed **groupthink**. During group or team sessions where knowledge is being introduced in the decision-making process, individuals can begin to act in homogeneous and nonindividualistic patterns, leading to the suspension of critical thinking and moral judgment. Too often groups attempt to remain cohesive and in total agreement, rather than explore all options fully through introducing external, conflicting, and challenging information into their decision making (Janis, 1982). It is critical that those leading the consideration of decisions ensure that members act as individuals. Leaders should remain impartial, encourage outside opinions and expertise, encourage working in subgroups that can be altered, and provide the opportunity to reevaluate decisions.

Organizations must also be aware of how knowledge is used throughout the organization, and be deliberate in encouraging consistent application of knowledge in similar activities. The problem of aligning departments and subdivisions of the organization in

---

IDOM

IDOM SA provides professional services in engineering, architecture, and technical and managerial consulting (Aramburu and Sáenz, 2007). Based in Bilbao, Spain, IDOM employs more than 2,500 professionals in 11 countries in America, Europe, and Africa. The company is structured as an association of professionals rather than a traditional hierarchical organization, and it is wholly owned by about 200 individuals who have reached partner status. IDOM views knowledge as a strategic asset, and fosters a deep-rooted culture of collective learning, knowledge sharing, and knowledge application among the professionals. As stated in the company's formal strategy, "Technological innovation, understood as the conversion of knowledge into the improvement or creation of new services, products or processes, is aimed towards the improvement of internal processes and the application of new technologies to the clients' products and processes" (Aramburu and Sáenz, 2007: 74). Such culture is embedded and enforced throughout the management systems and organizational policies and routines, and embracing it is a requirement for each individual. In IDOM, transient project teams are formed for specific projects, which are the basic organizational units of the company. It is within these teams that individuals exchange, combine, and utilize tacit knowledge as a social process, and organizational learning takes place. Middle managers who are responsible for assembling and leading these teams are trained to exemplify a cooperative spirit and motivate knowledge transfer among team members. Additional mechanisms are also in place to encourage knowledge sharing and application. For example, experts in specific fields are required to design and conduct training sessions to transfer their expertise to other parts of the organization. Furthermore, values such as collaboration, desire to help, and transfer of knowledge are included in the professional expectations at each level in IDOM. As such, sharing and exploitation of knowledge are integrated into the assessment and career development mechanisms of the organization.

order to have coherent and consistent operations working towards a common strategy is crucial for the success of the organization. Knowledge sharing regarding activities is a necessity between departments in order for everyone to know what the others are doing, which can prevent duplication of efforts or the repeating of previous errors. In some cases, one department's action can negate another's success; therefore removing barriers to knowledge transfer is strategically important.

USE OF EXTERNAL KNOWLEDGE

In Chapter 6, the concept of customer knowledge was introduced as an important source of knowledge that originates from outside the organization. Customer knowledge is derived from direct interaction or relationships. It is potentially more useful and labor-intensive than *customer information* because it resides in humans and requires other intelligent humans to identify this knowledge and apply it to their daily routines (Davenport, 1997).

Instances of customers providing knowledge to an organization typically do not happen with one large idea or major revelation. Instead many smaller pieces of information or knowledge collected over some time are pieced together by the organization to create relevant and valuable knowledge. This implies the need for strong, consistent, and repeated interactions between the organization and the customer over a period of time that slowly create knowledge capable of influencing strategic and marketing decisions. It takes time to build customers' trust and establish strong relationships with customers that are capable of facilitating knowledge sharing, further illustrating the need for long-term relationships that help identify and acquire customer knowledge.

In many situations, the types of customer knowledge available to the organization are determined by the structure of the industry and market, which in turn influence the types of knowledge available to the firm. They vary in the forms and strengths of relationships that are formed between companies and customers, and in product-customer relationships where some customers can easily become lead users (e.g., commonplace, low-tech products) and some do not have the foundational knowledge to reach this level (e.g., high-tech products or products that are complicated to use). Lead users are defined as those users of a product or service who face the needs of a marketplace well before more typical users and are positioned to gain a significant benefit from using the product or service to gain a solution to those needs (von Hippel, 1988).

The perceptions and beliefs surrounding how knowledge is structured or how to identify customer knowledge influence the types of customer knowledge available to an organization. The perception of the quality of the knowledge is central to this notion. Any customer knowledge received by the organization must either have had perceived quality on the surface, or conveyed the potential of future usefulness. Otherwise, the firm does not keep it for present or future use. This quality must be evident to the organization especially when new knowledge conflicts with existing knowledge. The firm creates the means of reliably evaluating knowledge when it contradicted conventional wisdom, causing it to understand the limits that customer knowledge may have. Differences exist in the creation of internal and customer knowledge, including the inclusion of inherent biases and a lack of previous knowledge to build upon (Paquette and Choo, 2008).

TECHNOLOGY-ENABLED KNOWLEDGE APPLICATION: SELF-SERVICE TECHNOLOGIES

Technologies that enable humans to help themselves complete transactions, access information and knowledge, and connect to other knowledge sources are becoming commonplace. Self-service technologies (SSTs) are commonplace across many industries. SSTs can best be described as applications that enable the access, manipulation, and application of information and knowledge. The number one advantage of these technologies is that they lower the cost of operations by removing human agents from the process. Today, most airlines have reduced the number of check-in desk staff due to the kiosks and online check-in systems. In addition, airlines, such as United Airlines, have SSTs not only that allow for simple transactions like check-in or changing of seat assignments and getting on stand-by lists, but can also enable customers to get their new flight information and boarding passes in the case of their flights being cancelled. SSTs are appealing to deploy when dealing with processes that are simple in nature, can be easily structured, and have high volume of transactions.

In deploying SSTs, an organization is essentially changing the manner in which users complete transactions. First and foremost, this requires working toward showing users that completing a transaction through SSTs has the same outcome as dealing with a human agent. This requires building trust in the new mechanism to complete transactions accurately so users will switch between two substitutes (dealing with humans versus interacting with the SSTs to complete their transactions). In order for this to occur, the users will need to find that the technology alternative is compatible with their previous experiences in dealing with the human agents. For example, if the human agents used to ask for certain pieces of information to access an account, similar information should be required when accessing the SST option. In addition, it is good to keep as a measure of good standard to try and seek if you can meet the Turing Test, which assesses whether users can recognize if they are dealing with a human or a machine. If a human and machine are in a room and an individual interacts with their output only through a screen and cannot tell the difference, then you are dealing with an intelligent machine. For humans to feel comfortable dealing with SSTs as replacements for traditional human mechanisms, some level of intelligence must be present in the systems. SSTs must also be more effective and efficient than their human counterparts. When SSTs make fewer errors, or no errors, or are quicker to use than dealing with humans, they have a relative advantage as a mechanism to get transactions completed, providing an incentive to use them when compared to traditional channels. In addition to being compatible and having relative advantages, the SSTs must also have the same level of perceived security as their human counterparts. Perceived security is important as normally interacting with SSTs calls for exchange of information. Humans may not feel comfortable sharing their information through technologies if they do not have some sense of their security guarantees. Security and privacy guarantees and protective mechanisms are important aspects of SSTs design criteria.

The second important issue is the provision of support for users as they interact with SSTs. Ideally, the SSTs being deployed will be simple and intuitive so users can navigate through the process themselves in order to complete their transactions. Unfortunately, even the simplest technologies will require some level of support. The need for accessible and helpful support functions cannot be understated. Support functions need to be real-time so that users can have their queries answered while in the process of completing transactions. If users abandon a transaction due to frustration with the experience, they will not come back. Today, many SSTs that are deployed on the web will track the time that the user is taking to complete a transaction, and when it exceeds a given threshold will offer the user alternative help channels (e.g., through chatting with a human agent online).

KNOWLEDGE APPLICATION AND THE MEASUREMENT OF VALUE

Similar to technology-based business initiatives, a knowledge management program requires an organization to invest a significant amount of financial and human capital. For the application of knowledge, successful deployment of each of the strategies discussed earlier demands new hardware, software, and business processes. It is imperative for managers to ensure the expected payoffs for the resources invested in the KM program are achieved. Only when the business value created by knowledge application is measured with reasonable accuracy can managers assess the performance of their KM programs and communicate the benefits to upper management and other stakeholders.

While business value of information technology in general has attracted much debate in the academic literature, there has been scant discussion on how companies can accurately assess the performance of their KM initiatives and the business value created by these initiatives. In practice, many companies lack systematic approaches to measure the business value created by their KM programs. Therefore, the goal of this section is to provide a review of current research on business value of technology innovations, and then present a set of measures for business value created through knowledge application. We will also discuss the issues and strategies related to applying these measures.

The Impact of Technologies on Business Value

When businesses invest in any type of innovative technology, the technology is not the complete solution. Organizations expect the technology innovation to increase general business value. The business value of a specific function, practice, or strategy refers to its impacts on business performance of organizations. Researchers have applied various theoretical lenses and developed explanations for how new technologies may generate business value. Jacobides, Knudsen, and Augier, for example, argue that "other than capturing the value from innovative efforts through fending off imitators and achieving superior profitability, firms can also benefit from investing in assets that will appreciate" (2006: 1201). Building on their analysis of an innovator's role in its knowledge architecture, they concluded that firms stand to benefit from new technologies that balance the act of achieving better operating profit and creating wealth through investment in complementary assets which will appreciate in value.

Applying the lenses of the resource-based view of the firm, Melville, Kramer, and Gurbaxani (2004) present another approach to understanding business value creation through the application of innovative information technologies. Per the resource-based view theory, valuable resources that are rare, inimitable, and non-substitutable would lead to sustained competitive advantage for organizations. Technology and knowledge are examples of these types of resources. Combined with other complementary organizational resources, technology resources can lead to competitive advantage. However, the performance impacts of technology innovations exist at two levels: business process level and organizational level. Technology innovations first lead to better performance for individual business processes, such as procurement, inventory, and distribution. As a result, the gains in business process performance will aggregate and impact overall organizational performance. Therefore, we should expect to observe the performance impacts of technology innovations at these different levels.

The Difficulty in Measuring Business Value

In spite of the importance and desirability of accurately measuring business value of new technologies, it is difficult to accomplish in real life for a few reasons. First, there is usually a significant time lag before the benefits of new technologies come into effect. In today's business environments, senior managers understandably want to see a quick return on investment for every dollar they invest in any business initiative. However, the value of an innovative product, process, or service will take time to accrue. Before showing any positive impacts on business performance, due to its disruptive nature, a new technology may even introduce a short-term negative impact because of the resources it takes from other areas and the temporary interruption to business functions caused by its introduction. Second, at any given time many companies will be implementing multiple business initiatives simultaneously. Therefore, it is often unclear which factors contribute to the changes in business performance and to what degree. Such ambiguity results in difficulty in deriving accurate measures of business value. Third, value created by an innovation can be captured by consumers, or other companies in the value chain instead of the company that introduced it (Hitt and Brynjolfsson, 1996). Xerox, for example, invented technologies such as the Ethernet, computer mouse and graphic user interface, and laser printer. However, for various reasons it was not able to capture most of the business value brought about by these innovations. In addition, most companies operate in complex and ever-changing environments. Fluctuations in external factors, such as the overall economic climate, or the industry environment, will also impact the company's ability to reap the benefits of its innovations (Melville, Kramer, and Gurbaxani, 2004; Kwon and Watts, 2006).

Like any technology innovation, KM is also subject to the aforementioned issues. Implementation of a new KM system may require a certain level of business reengineering. Therefore, it could be disruptive to the users and groups involved. The impact of a newly implemented KM system will take time to materialize. When the impact is visible to the employees in the firm, it may be perceived as ambiguous due to the confounding effects of many internal and external factors. It is also challenging to derive measures from strategy and link these measures to KM activities. Often, a key target for measures is alignment, but this notion must be clearly defined with specific goals (Turner and Mionne, 2010). KM efforts typically impact the bottom-line performance indirectly through a secondary entity such as a process or a business unit. Therefore, the final impact on the bottom line can be derived only from the intermediary metrics. These difficulties, however, should not be taken as excuses for not assessing the business value generated by a KM program. Instead, they serve as cautions for managers responsible for assessing KM performance to avoid relying solely on a single category of business value measures.

Business Value Measures

As Table 7.4 illustrates, measures for business value of technologies may be classified based on two dimensions. This classification should not be viewed as aiming to find a best category of measures for the business value of KM programs; instead, we contend that business value is a complex issue and it is necessary to achieve a full picture of business value created by a KM system. As Chan (2000) discusses, there exists a great divide between both qualitative and quantitative measures, and individual and organizational measures of business value. In order to achieve an accurate assessment of the benefits of technology innovations, it is imperative to bridge such divides and use a more balanced perspective toward identifying business value. Such a proposition is in accordance with the balanced scorecard approach, which calls for "multiple aspects of performance, and operationalizing these with financial and non-financial measures that encompass both leading and lagging indicators" (Duh, Chow, and Chen, 2006: 942).

Productivity, Profitability, and Strategic Measures

Studies have shown that technology innovations can bring both productivity and profitability gains for organizations (Hitt and Brynjolfsson, 1996). Belderbos, Carreeb, and Lokshinb (2004: 1481) state that "labor productivity growth will be most affected by cost reducing innovation, while innovative sales productivity growth is more affected by demand expansion oriented innovation." Productivity concerns a firm or business unit's ability to convert inputs such as capital, labor, and raw material into outputs such as products and services for internal or external consumption (Hitt and Brynjolfsson, 1996). Profitability, on the other hand, focuses exclusively on a company's ability to achieve its ultimate business goal of generating profits for its owners. In addition, technologies bring long-term benefits such as a better business model, or the ability to adapt quickly to changing customer need. These benefits transcend the

Table 7.4. Measures of Business Value Created through Technologies		
	Qualitative	**Quantitative**
Strategic	• Competitive advantage • Inter-firm relationship • Response to change (agility) • Quality improvement • Improved customer relations • New business plans • Business model improvement • Organizational structure and process improvement • Product differentiation	• Number of new products • Percent of revenue from new products • Market value minus book value (goodwill) • Market value/book value (Tobin's q) • Market share • Price cost margin
Productivity	• Employee productivity • Employee skill level • Relative quality of products	• Revenue • Revenue growth • Capacity utilization • Inventory turnover • Cycle time reduction • Stockouts • Supply chain savings • Reducing operating costs • Labor productivity • Total factor productivity • Asset turnover • Sales generated by new to the market products per employee
Profitability	• Pricing power	• Return on assets • Return on equity • Return on sales • Return on invested capital • Total shareholder return • EBIT margin • Profit margin

more immediate considerations of generating higher output and achieving better bottom-line performance, and should be categorized as strategic measures of business value. Measures of business performance can be measures of profitability, measures of productivity, and strategic measures.

Measuring profitability is often mandatory as it focuses exclusively on a company's ability to survive and compete in a marketplace. To measure the bottom-line impact of knowledge application, accurate estimates of cost savings or revenue increases are necessary. In this case, the front-line managers who oversee day-to-day operations have the best understanding of how knowledge is monetized in specific functional areas such as product development or marketing. Once the dollar figures are estimated, calculations of the return on investment can be performed and aggregated to assess the broader impact of knowledge application at the organization level (Rivinus, 2007).

Measuring profitability alone is not enough. It is also necessary to measure the productivity gain of a KM program, because it represents the most immediate and direct benefits of a new technology. To a certain degree, measuring productivity counters both causal ambiguity and time lag issues in business value measurement. Increased utilization of knowledge is expected to bring measurable improvements to the productivity of those involved. For example, through the use of a KM system, the personnel in a technical service department are expected to reduce the amount of time it takes to satisfy a service request. As such, the percentage reduction of average service time per request, or the increase in average requests served per unit time are both reasonable metrics for measuring the contribution of knowledge application to the operation. Moreover, in knowledge intensive industries, increased knowledge exchange among employees could be considered a measurable productivity gain by itself. For example, Rivinus (2007) reported the use of social network analysis to visualize and measure the intensity of inter-department interactions, as a validation of the business value of the KM program at a global civil engineering firm.

Knowledge Management at Nike

Nike was founded by University of Oregon head coach Bill Bowerman and track athlete Philip Knight in 1964 (Stonehouse and Minocha, 2008). Over the decades it has achieved tremendous growth. It is the world market leader in the athletic shoe and sports apparel industry and a major supplier of sports equipment. It also operates the Niketown retail stores, and sells its product through an online store. Since Nike's early days, knowledge of customers has played a critical role in its success. As a professional coach whose trainees include over 30 Olympians and 24 NCAA champions, Bowerman has a strong passion for developing better running shoes for athletes and deep knowledge of the sport of running. Building on his understanding of runners' needs, he focused his design efforts on the thread pattern, overall weight, and fit with runners' feet, and developed a stream of successful high performance running shoes that are also more comfortable and durable. The rapid adoption of these shoes among well-known athletes, combined with the surging popularity of sports programs on TV, provided the company with an early boost in sales and brand recognition among the youth audience.

As Nike evolved into a global company with a growing product line and wider customer base, it paid even more attention to learning about and responding to its customers. While customer knowledge continues to drive product development, it also plays critical roles in other key areas of Nike's value chain. Based on its knowledge of youth culture, Nike adopted the slogan "Just Do It" for an advertising campaign in 1988, which soon became one of the best known slogans worldwide. Endorsement deals from carefully selected athletes such as Michael Jordan and Roger Federer and teams such as the Brazil national football team provide substantial enhancement to Nike's brand image globally. Nike also makes full use of its knowledge in collaboration with suppliers and retailers. Knowledge about technology and design helps the suppliers produce high quality products, and knowledge about the customers helps the retailers ensure availability of Nike products and promote them to the consumers. In summary, Nike's achievements in the global market can be attributed to its ability to leverage knowledge in three key functional areas: product development, marketing, and supply chain management.

In addition, KM managers have to keep strategic measures in mind because they symbolize the long-term benefits of better knowledge utilization. Strategic benefits such as improved agility or better product differentiation may not bring immediate improvements to an organization's top-line or bottom-line performance. However, they represent the potential to boost an organization's productivity and profitability over time, which is often the most valuable benefit for a KM initiative.

Singapore Airlines

With a fleet of more than 100 aircraft, Singapore Airlines (SIA) operates passenger and cargo flights to destinations on five continents from its main hub in Singapore. Temasek Holdings, the investment and holding company of the government of Singapore, holds more than 50 percent of the voting stock of SIA (Goh, 2005). As a small island country with scant natural resources, Singapore has a long-lasting commitment to developing an economy based on human capital and infrastructure. Over the decades the country has made substantial investments in information and communication technologies and pursued a national economic strategy with knowledge-driven innovations at its foundation. As one of the poster children of Singapore's knowledge economy, SIA is internationally acclaimed for its ability to achieve greater performance and generate value through knowledge-driven strategies and innovations.

To survive and succeed in the hypercompetitive commercial aviation industry with a limited domestic market, SIA has continuously sought to differentiate itself with superior customer service and innovative products and solutions in its international expansion. Central to SIA's customer-oriented strategy is the utilization of knowledge to create innovations. To this end, SIA has invested heavily in both advanced technologies and its employees to stimulate knowledge sharing. For example, it was among the first airlines to adopt the PROS revenue management system, which utilizes all sources of relevant knowledge such as network traffic flows, point-of-sale patterns, business policies, and alliance requirements in order to maximize revenue through better seat allocations, fare class structure, and sales promotions. SIA has also been relentless in improving its employees' knowledge application effectiveness through various training programs, even during business slowdowns. In addition to fostering internal knowledge sharing, SIA has built a knowledge collaboration network with suppliers, partners, and customers to identify strategic opportunities and support its strategic goals. For instance, to formulate its e-business strategy, SIA collaborated with IBM and conducted extensive research with customers, business partners, employees and management. The collective knowledge led to a number of service innovations, such as a 24-hour auto-ticketing machine that allows customers to buy their tickets from the machine using their credit cards. Through its partnerships with companies such as Discovery and Visa, SIA also gained insights to better understand, attract, and serve different groups of travelers. Moreover, SIA's institutionalized process of innovating from customer knowledge has led to initiatives ranging from adding adjustable "ears" in the headrests for neck support, to the launch of a new budget airline subsidiary catering to cost-conscious flyers. Overall, these knowledge-driven strategies help establish SIA as an industry leader in customer-oriented innovations, as evidenced in the numerous industry awards it has received. Not surprisingly, SIA also excels among its peers in tangible measures including market share and financial performance.

Qualitative and Quantitative Measures

Some measures of performance are objective, independently verifiable, and often derived from certain accounting or financial measures. Examples of quantitative measures include number of new products, revenue, and return on assets. Conversely, there are measures that are more subjective and harder to quantify as a concrete number. These measures capture outcomes that are important yet for which it is difficult to achieve an objective numeric assessment, such as customer satisfaction, agility, and pricing power. Although it is still possible to quantify these outcomes to a certain degree, such quantification has to rely more on people's perceptions, estimations, and guesswork than precise measurements. This distinction is similar to the classification of tangible and intangible measures (Hoogeweegen, Streng, and Wagenaar, 1998), or hard and soft measures (Chan, 2000).

In practice, quantitative measures are objective and involve less guesswork, require simple calculations, and are easier to perform. Since knowledge application strategies are typically technology-based, data collection, summarization, and reporting for quantitative measures can be automated using software applications as part of the system. These hard numbers are favored by top executives and shareholders, and they are also easier for comparing across different projects. Qualitative measures are subjective, and allow KM managers to assess the opinions of the individuals (employees, managers, senior executives, customers, or business partners.) who have the best understanding of the impact of knowledge utilization in their functional area. Applied appropriately, qualitative measures give managers a rich set of information mere numbers cannot provide. In addition, for certain measures, both quantitative and qualitative approaches are equally valid and valuable. For example, after implementing a KM system in a customer service department, determining how much consumers' satisfaction level has increased is just as important as measuring the improvements in average service turnaround time.

Assessing Business Value Impacts

In this section, we outline a number of steps that serve as a general guideline for measuring and monitoring business performance impact of KM initiatives:

1. *Set clearly defined goals for a KM program, both at the organizational level and at the business process level.* A successful KM initiative starts with a clear and consistent focus, aligned with the strategic mission and goals of the organization. Once the goals are clarified, they drive all subsequent activities of the KM program, including the selection of specific outcomes to be measured and monitored. It is also necessary to set appropriate goals for different levels of the organization. While the top-level goals lead to important organizational level measures, lower-level goals will guide the frontline managers to develop finer grained measures that are more likely to capture the direct impact of knowledge application to specific business units. A global conglomerate, for example, that deploys a new KM system in its consulting arm would be more likely to accurately measure the performance impact for that specific unit rather than the entire company.

2. *Select a mixed set of measures from different sections in Table 7.4 (p. 233), and develop a balanced scoreboard with both quantitative and qualitative measures, and choose strategic, productivity, or profitability measures that match the goals identified in the previous step.* Choosing the right mix of measures would largely depend on the business goals of specific KM programs. A company focusing on developing innovative products would expect its new products to bring additional

revenue and profit. A company competing on supply chain efficiency, on the other hand, would expect better profitability through cost savings. Depending on the business goals, a KM system may be introduced to support only a specific functional area such as inventory management, and some of the measures such as stock-outs are tailored for these specific areas. The measures listed in Table 7.4 exclude those that are specific to a narrowly defined industry. For example, patient mortality rates would be one of the most relevant measures for an expert system introduced in a hospital. Therefore, it is critical to involve the domain experts in selecting the right measures for any given system.

3. *Develop baselines for the measures prior to the implementation of the KM system, and monitor the performance impact of the new system at every stage of the implementation process.* The lag effect of value accruement means it is crucial to select an appropriate time horizon between inception and measurement. Although senior management understandably desire faster return on their investments, it is often difficult to predict when the contribution of a specific KM initiative would make it through the necessary processes and show up in performance measures. Therefore, for any measure managers choose to use, single point of time measurements will not be reliable. In addition, measuring and monitoring performance impacts should be an integral part of a KM initiative, starting with a baseline measure prior to the implementation, rather than an afterthought of a KM project. KM managers need to incorporate periodical performance assessments into their daily activities.

4. *Identify key stakeholders for the KM initiative, and communicate the meanings and results of the measures to the key stakeholders.* As discussed earlier, an important purpose of measuring business value is to communicate the benefits of KM initiatives to key stakeholders. Different stakeholders may have different vested interests in a specific system. A new web-based customer knowledge management system may stimulate different expectations from customer service personnel, marketing executives, the CEO, customers, and the shareholders. Continuous support from all the key stakeholders is one of the critical success factors for any KM program. It is therefore important to choose the right set of measures and communicate the results to all stakeholders.

5. *Close the loop by learning from successes, and more importantly, failures.* Like any new technologies, a KM program is inherently risky and not all initiatives succeed. Organizations should have a certain level of tolerance of failure when engaging in KM initiatives. A mature organization learns from its mistakes, and applies the knowledge and insights gained from past failures in its future endeavors. A failed project could lead to greater success down the road when such learning takes place.

COMPETITIVE INTELLIGENCE

Competitive intelligence (CI) assignments are commonplace in most organizations. Traditionally, CI assignments take the form of collecting, analyzing, synthesizing, and communicating information on targets of interest, most notably the competitors of the organization. These assignments normally involve scouring through the available public information on the target (e.g., from news releases, blogs, or industry press mentions) and then arriving at actionable knowledge on competitive moves and positions, areas of investment, and even senior personnel hires and transfers. More recently, CI assignments have even involved trying to access human sources (e.g., employees, business partners, customers) for information on the organization. Most of the time, these involve creative social engineering—deceiving individuals into sharing confidential information (Desouza, 2007) (see sidebar on Procter & Gamble).

Procter & Gamble: Garbage Surfing

In early 2001, the top executives of Procter & Gamble (P&G) found themselves in hot water when they discovered that their competitive intelligence gathering efforts on Unilever may have gone too far (ICMR, 2004). The two companies had engaged in fierce competition in many segments of the consumer goods market on the global stage. While P&G holds the lead position in the lucrative North American cosmetics and toiletries markets, Unilever had been fighting for a bigger share. It is within this backdrop that competitive intelligence managers at P&G hired a Cincinnati-based organization called The Ranch to conduct intelligence gathering missions on Unilever's hair care business. The operatives resorted to dumpster diving—rummaging through garbage bins on Unilever's property—to collect documents containing confidential information on business strategies. They also allegedly employed social engineering techniques by posing as market analysts, journalists, and students to Unilever employees in order to gain access to critical information. P&G executives decided to disclose the incident voluntarily to Unilever, and the two companies ultimately reached an agreement to settle the issue and avoided court battles. P&G reportedly returned over 80 documents to Unilever, and vowed that none of the information contained will be ever used to gain competitive advantages. P&G maintained that while the operation in question was against the company's business ethics standards, it had not broken any law, and was conducted without the knowledge of the top management. Since the incident, there have been intense discussions regarding the line between acceptable competitive intelligence operations and corporate espionage. The fact that Unilever was vulnerable to dumpster diving and social engineering, two of the best known attack vectors for computer hackers and corporate spies, also raised red flags on big corporations' preparedness to protect their competitive information.

Several important issues need to be considered when dealing with knowledge application in competitive intelligence assignments. First is the element of secrecy— much of the value of a competitive intelligence assignment comes from the fact that it is done in secret. Consider the case of government intelligence agencies, who suffer huge setbacks when their covert operations are uncovered by foreign entities. Preserving the element of secrecy allows an organization several choices as to how knowledge can be applied. An organization can choose to act on the knowledge and thereby consider designing and executing counter measures. This may be valuable if the organization realizes that a competitor is going to conduct actions that might have severe adverse consequences to its operations (e.g., the introduction of new products or services). In other cases, an organization may choose to stay quiet and simply continue to track the organization and its next moves. This is a viable strategy when there is a need to track an organization and study details of its moves. For example, in the case of a terrorist cell, there is a need to monitor the behavior of individuals to learn about where they are getting their funding or who are they cooperating with; acting on the information may result in immediate capture of a few individuals but may sacrifice the bigger goal of eliminating the overall organization. Hence, protecting information around knowledge application becomes a significant concern. The organization needs to restrict access to its calculated and potential actions, details regarding information collected, and its tentative conclusions.

Second is the issue of ethics. As the case of Procter & Gamble has shown, organizations can cross the line when they engage in competitive intelligence activities. It is important that actions be conducted in line with ethical considerations. Engaging in acts of social engineering or dumpster diving may lead to discovery of potentially valuable information, yet the cost of the information may be too great to bear if these unethical actions are uncovered.

Third is the issue of security. Just as any organization can conduct competitive intelligence activities, so can an organization become a target of such activities. It is hence vitally important that organizations take great care to ensure that sensitive information is protected. Adequate guidelines needs to be in place, and followed, on how to protect information. Details such as what information is proprietary, who should screen information before it is made publicly available, and how to secure sensitive information while it is in transit (e.g., taking materials to a customer) need to be spelled out. In most organizations, sensitive information is restricted to a select few individuals (e.g., senior executives and officers of the organization).

The goal of CI is to help the firm to make the right decisions that lead to sustainable competitive advantage. It can encompass a wide range of objectives depending on the company's competitive positioning in the marketplace. The objectives may address strategic-level issues such as a competitor's plans for developing new product lines, entering new markets, pursuing mergers and acquisitions, lobbying for favorable legislation, or forming strategic alliances. For managers who are on the front line, their concerns would more likely be tactical level intelligence such as a competitor's upcoming holiday promotions. In some cases, intelligence relating to a customer or a business partner could also be of interest (e.g., a potential supply glitch due to a major supplier's unsuccessful computer system upgrade).

To accomplish the objectives of CI, it has to be an organizational process embedded in every level of decision making. CI success requires sufficient organizational resources and full awareness of CI's role and benefits among all employees. Although a dedicated team (or an outside firm hired for this purpose) could perform the continuous monitoring and synthesizing of information more effectively, managers at different levels should be involved in assessing the company's strategies and operations, identifying the competitors, formulating and prioritizing the objectives, interpreting the discoveries, and acting upon the knowledge gained. The CI program also needs to be evaluated regularly for its effectiveness, with adjustments made to meet changing competitive landscapes.

A successful CI program provides a company with the knowledge and foresight to predict, instead of reacting to, the competitors' movements. It gives top management a clear picture of the threats and opportunities in the marketplace, and greater confidence in charting new strategies.

RISKS OF KNOWLEDGE APPLICATION

It is important for an organization to include its knowledge management activities under the umbrella of a corporate risk management program. In fact, knowledge management activities can augment an organization's risk management practices by providing complementary structure and practices to enterprise risk management. KM supports the identification of risks in an organization through the practice of encouraging knowledge sharing regarding business practices, including those activities that may be deemed risky. Knowledge creation can help with the analysis of risks by determining the significance and likelihood of operating and financial risks to which the organization exposes itself during its normal course of business.

It is important for businesses to be forward looking not only in their strategic planning and decision making, but also in how they manage risk. KM activities that identify possible future risks can lead to risk proactive management programs. Early warning and environmental scanning processes all act as radar for possible events in the business environment that create new risk for organizations. KM technologies can further assist in the identification and assessment of risk based on an organization's archived information, including history and knowledge regarding current and proposed business activities. Finally, communication of the risks and strategies throughout the organization can use knowledge management activities such as knowledge sharing and storage to ensure all employees are aware of risks and know how the organization manages these risks on an ongoing basis (Rodriguez and Edwards, 2010).

CONCLUSION

The organization's ability to apply its knowledge to critical business activities serves as the key link between the business goals of a KM program and its actual, realized benefits. The changing business and technology landscape leads to a variety of means by which knowledge can be utilized. While human experts and decision support systems are both viable agents for knowledge application, human-machine strategies combine the computation power and consistency of computer systems with the judgment and intuition of human decision makers. Such strategies also provide KM managers with flexibility in the precise roles humans and machines will play, and how their decisions are weighted to reach the final conclusion.

Regardless of the strategy applied, reusing knowledge inevitably requires the active participation of knowledge workers, typically organized in work groups in an organization. Therefore, KM managers also need to have a better understanding of human motivations and team dynamics as related to knowledge application, and incorporate such knowledge in the design of the KM system itself, along with the accompanying policies, procedures, and incentive structures.

Technological advances have brought fully automated software applications that are able to access, manipulate, and apply knowledge to serve customers. These self-service technologies replicate the entire service transaction traditionally performed by human agents. Advantages of SST include quicker service for the customers, lower costs for companies, and relief from highly repetitive tasks for the employees.

As knowledge application serves as the bridge between knowledge and realized benefits, continuous monitoring of business value impacts should be an integral and high-priority task in a KM program, rather than just an afterthought. Precise measures of the business value of knowledge are difficult to achieve in practice for a number of reasons, not the least of which is the intangible nature of the effects of knowledge. Nevertheless, a carefully chosen mix of business value measures that address the impacts at different levels, using different methods, will help managers assess the performance of their KM initiatives, and convey the benefits of knowledge management to key stakeholders. To reap tangible benefits from their knowledge, organizations must proactively apply knowledge using technological and organizational means to further their missions and goals. Successful companies will be those that can convert the full potential of their knowledge through establishing the means to have it effectively utilized by their employees.

Recap: The Major Points for Knowledge Managers to Consider When Applying Knowledge

1. Determining the mix of human and technological agents that will apply knowledge affects knowledge practices within the firm and the value generated by the knowledge utilized.
2. Technology can provide many advantages when working with large amounts of knowledge, but humans are still needed to interpret the results.
3. One way to increase the reuse of organizational knowledge is to capture knowledge created in teams, and share that knowledge with other teams who can learn from successes and avoid mistakes.
4. Managers need to look beyond organizational boundaries to find knowledge that resides externally to the organization, in customers, stakeholders, and communities.
5. Self-service technologies can go beyond saving organizations labor costs, and create a vehicle for the capture and dissemination of knowledge into the organization.
6. If the goal of knowledge management is to create value for the organization, then it is the responsibility of the knowledge leadership to measure the impact of KM and use this to direct the knowledge strategy.
7. Measuring the value for business derived from knowledge management activities can be difficult, but both quantitative and qualitative measures exist that go beyond financial considerations to illustrate the impact of knowledge on an organization.
8. Competitive intelligence is an important source of knowledge that can create a picture of the external environment from which a plan for the acquisition and use of knowledge can be formed.
9. The integration of knowledge management and risk management can lead to better enterprise risk mitigation, accurate predictions of future risks and consequences of actions, the means for communicating risk management techniques throughout the organization, and the monitoring of the entire organization for signs of risks.
10. The application of knowledge can rely on many technologies, strategies, and organizational structures, but it always is centered on the individual who uses the knowledge and creates value from this use.

DISCUSSION QUESTIONS

1. Can you give one specific example where you think a government agency or an organization in the public sector can improve its service through better application of existing knowledge?
2. What should an organization consider before deploying self-service technologies to replace human customer service agents?
3. After the shuttle Columbia disaster, the CAIB recommended an overhaul of organizational culture at NASA to prevent similar tragedies in the future. What would be your specific recommendations for NASA?
4. In what ways could we counter the effects of human biases in decision making?
5. What approaches can a large corporation take to encourage knowledge sharing and reuse across different business units?
6. What are the advantages of facilitating knowledge reuse using an online community? What are potential disadvantages?
7. Based on your own experience, what are the obstacles to reusing knowledge and how can they be overcome?
8. What should the manager of a KM program do when top management demands hard evidence that the resources invested in the KM program are creating value?
9. How does competitive intelligence differ from a traditional SWOT analysis?
10. Should a company use knowledge on a major competitor acquired through a source such as Wikileaks to gain competitive advantage? Why or why not?

REFERENCES

Alpert, M., and H. Raiffa. 1982. "A Progress Report on the Training of Probability Assessors." In *Judgment under Uncertainty: Heuristics and Biases*, 294–305. Cambridge: Cambridge University Press.

Aramburu, N., and J. Sáenz. 2007. "Promoting People-Focused Knowledge Management: The Case of IDOM." *Journal of Knowledge Management* 11, no. 4: 72–81.

Ariely, D. 2008. *Predictably Irrational: The Hidden Forces that Shape our Decisions.* New York: Harper.

Belderbos, R., M. Carreeb, and B. Lokshinb. 2004. "Cooperative R and D and Firm Performance." *Research Policy* 33: 1477–1492.

Blattgerg, R.C., and S. J. Hoch. 1990. "Database Models and Managerial Intuition: 50% Model + 50% Manager." *Management Science* 36, no. 8: 887–900.

Brown, M., and S. Paquette. 2009. "Short Term Emergency versus Long Term Development: Decision Making for Improved Outcomes." Paper presented at the Association of American Geographers Annual Meeting, Las Vegas, NV, March 22–27.

Brown, M., S. Paquette, and K. Ross. 2008. "The Use of Remote Sensing-Derived Biophysical Data for Early Warning of Food Security Crises: Evidence from FEWSNET." Paper presented at the SPIE Europe Remote Sensing Conference, Cardiff, Wales, September 15–18.

Bruggen, G.H., A. Smidts, and B. Wierenga. 2001. "The Powerful Triangle of Marketing Data, Managerial Judgment, and Marketing Management Support Systems." *European Journal of Marketing* 35, no. 7/8: 796–814.

BusinessWeek. 2006. "Giving the Boss the Big Picture." Bloomberg BusinessWeek. February 13. http://www.businessweek.com/magazine/content/06_07/b3971083.htm.

Chan, Y. E. 2000. "IT Value: The Great Divide between Qualitative and Quantitative, and Individual and Organizational, Measures." *Journal of Management Information* 16, no. 4: 225–261.

Chua, Alton Y.K., and W. Lam. 2006. "Center for Army Lessons Learned: Knowledge Application Process in the Military" *International Journal of Knowledge Management* 2, no. 2: 69–82.

Davenport, T. 1997. *Information Ecology: Mastering the Information and Knowledge Environment.* New York: Oxford University Press.

Davenport, T.H., R. J. Thomas, and K. C. Desouza. 2003. "Reusing Intellectual Assets." *Industrial Management* 45, no. 3: 12–17.

Desouza, K.C. 2002. *Managing Knowledge with Artificial Intelligence.* Westport, CT: Quorum Books.

Desouza, K.C. 2003. "Barriers to Effective Use of Knowledge Management Systems in Software Engineering." *Communications of the ACM* 46, no. 1: 99–101.

Desouza, K.C. 2007. *Managing Knowledge Security: Strategies for Protecting Your Company's Intellectual Assets.* London: Kogan Page.

Desouza, K.C., Y. Awazu, and A. Tiwana. 2006. "Bringing Use Back into Software Reuse: Four Dynamics," *Communications of the ACM* 49, no. 1: 96–100.

Desouza, K.C., Y. Awazu, and Y. Wan. 2006. "Factors Governing the Consumption of Explicit Knowledge." *Journal of the American Society for Information Science and Technology* 57, no. 1: 36–43.

Desouza, K.C., D. Thomas, Y. Zhang, and Y. Awazu. 2004. "Information Integrity in Healthcare Enterprises: Strategies for Mitigation of Medical Errors." *International Journal of Healthcare Technology and Management* 6, no. 2: 241–255.

Duh, R.-R., C. W. Chow, and H. Chen. 2006. "Strategy, IT Applications for Planning and Control, and Firm Performance: The Impact of Impediments to IT Implementation." *Information and Management* 43: 939–949.

ebiz. 2010. "Memphis Police Department Dramatically Reduces Crime Rate with IBM Predictive Analysis Software." ebiz.com. July 21. http://www.ebizq.net/news/12882.html.

Einhorn, H.J. 1972. "Expert Measurement and Mechanical Combination." *Organisational Behavior and Human Performance* 7: 86–106.

Fischhoff, B. 1982. "Debiasing." In *Judgment under Uncertainty: Heuristics and Biases,* 422–444. Cambridge University Press: Cambridge.

George, J.F., K. Duffy, and M. Ahuja. 2000. "Countering the Anchoring and Adjustment Bias with Decision Support Systems." *Decision Support Systems* 29, no. 2: 195–215.

Goh, A.L.S. 2005. "Fostering Innovation through Knowledge-Centered Principles: A Case Analysis of Singapore Airlines." *International Journal of Knowledge Management* 1, no. 4: 73–90.

Hirji, K.K. 2001."Exploring Data Mining Implementation." *Communications of the ACM* 44, no. 7: 87–93.

Hitt, L.M., and E. Brynjolfsson. 1996. "Productivity, Business Profitability, and Consumer Surplus: Three Different Measures of Information Technology Value." *MIS Quarterly* 20, no. 2: 121–142.

Hoch, S.J. and D. A. Schkade. 1996. "A Psychological Approach to Decision Support Systems." *Management Science* 42, no. 1: 51–64.

Hoogeweegen, M. R., R. J. Streng, and R. W. Wagenaar. 1998. "A Comprehensive Approach to Assess the Value of EDI." *Information and Management* 34: 117-127.

IBM. 2010. "Alameda County Social Services: Closing Service Gaps Through Better Use of Information." IBM.com. February 26. http://www-01.ibm.com/software/success/cssdb.nsf/cs/JSTS-7Z6QLF.

ICMR (IBS Center for Management Research). 2004. "Procter and Gamble vs. Unilever: A Case of Corporate Espionage." Case Study. http://www.icmrindia.org/casestudies/catalogue/Business%20Ethics/BECG036.htm.

Jacobides, M. G., T. Knudsen, and M. Augier. 2006. "Benefiting from Innovation: Value Creation, Value Appropriation and the Role of Industry Architectures." *Research Policy* 35: 1200–1221.

Janis, I. 1982. *Groupthink: Psychological Studies of Policy Decision*. Boston: Houghton Mifflin.

Kwon, D., and S. Watts. 2006. "IT Valuation in Turbulent Times." *The Journal of Strategic Information Systems* 15, no. 4: 327–354.

Little, J.D.C. 1970. "Models and Managers: The Concept of Decision Calculus." *Management Science* 16, no. 8: B466–B485.

Marakas, G.M. 1998. *Decision Support Systems in the 21st Century*. Englewood Cliffs, NJ: Prentice-Hall.

McEntee, P. 2011. "Ignored Before Challenger, Utah Engineer Heeded After Tragedy." *Salt Lake Tribune*. Last modified January 28. http://www.sltrib.com/sltrib/home/51130569-76/nasa-challenger-mcdonald-launch.html.

Meehl, P.E. 1954. *Clinical Versus Statistical Prediction*. Minneapolis: University of Minnesota Press.

Melville, N., K. Kraemer, and V. Gurbaxani. 2004. "Review: Information Technology and Organizational Performance: An Integrative Model of IT Business Value." *MIS Quarterly* 28, no. 2: 283–322.

Paquette, S. 2010. "Applying Knowledge Management in the Environmental and Climate Change Sciences." In *Encyclopedia of Knowledge Management*, edited by D. Schwartz and D. Te'eni, 2nd edition. Hershey, PA: Idea Group.

Paquette, S., and C. W. Choo. 2008. *Towards a Theory of Customer Knowledge Use: The Role of Knowledge Quality and Accessibility*. Paper presented at the Administrative Sciences Association of Canada, Halifax, Nova Scotia, May 24–27.

Payne, J. W., J. R. Bettman, and E. J. Johnson. 1993. *The Adaptive Decision Maker*. Cambridge: Cambridge University Press.

Reuters. 2004. "NASA Blames Application of Foam for Shuttle Disaster." *Los Angeles Times*, August 14. http://articles.latimes.com/2004/aug/14/nation/na-shuttle14.

Rivinus, C. 2007. "Demonstrating Value at Parsons Brinckerhoff." *Knowledge Management Review* 9, no. 6: 24–27.

Rodriguez, E., and J. Edwards. 2010. "People, Technology, Processes, and Risk Knowledge Sharing." *Electronic Journal of Knowledge Management* 8, no. 1: 139–150.

Rogers, E.M. 1983. *Diffusion of Innovations*. 3rd ed. New York: The Free Press.

Sanger, L. 2007. "Who Says We Know: On The New Politics of Knowledge." Edge. http://www.edge.org/3rd_culture/sanger07/sanger07_index.html.

Simon, H.A. 1982. *Models of Bounded Rationality*. Cambridge, MA: MIT Press.

Stonehouse, G., and S. Minocha. 2008. "Strategic Processes @ Nike—Making and Doing Knowledge Management." *Knowledge and Process Management* 15, no. 1: 24-31.

Trainor, S. F., and S. Paquette. 2011. "Data to Knowledge in Climate Science, Adaptation, and Policy: A Case Study of the Alaska Center for Climate Assessment and Policy." Paper presented at the Association of American Geographers Annual Meeting, Seattle, WA, April 12–16.

Turner, G., and C. Mionne. 2010. "Measuring the Effects of Knowledge Management Practices." *Electronic Journal of Knowledge Management* 8, no. 1: 161–170.

von Hippel, E. 1988. *The Sources of Innovation*. New York: Oxford University Press.

Yates, D., and S. Paquette. 2011. "Emergency Knowledge Management and Social Media Technologies: A Case Study of the 2010 Haitian Earthquake." *International Journal of Information Management* 31, no. 1: 6–13.

Part III

Building Knowledge Management Programs

8

Building Global Knowledge Management Systems

Kevin C. Desouza and Chris Rivinus

OBJECTIVES

- Explore the salient issues surrounding the design of global knowledge management systems.
- Understand new challenges presented by the global environment.
- Identify adjustments that are required for applying knowledge strategies in different countries.
- Discuss cultural issues that affect knowledge management and their support systems.

INTRODUCTION

In this chapter, we explore the topic of building global **knowledge management systems** (KMS). Businesses are now affected by many factors that change how they manage knowledge. These factors originate not just locally or domestically, but from global sources. **Global**, as defined in *Merriam-Webster's 11th Collegiate Dictionary*, means "relating to, or involving the entire world" or "of relating to, or applying to the whole." Therefore, designing global knowledge management systems involves designing a system that can cover, or is utilized by, all locations of an organization no matter where they are located on the globe. Geographic dispersion is, however, only one dimension of a global system (Evaristo, et al., 2004). Organizations are also divided into units, departments, teams, and other logical groups. Integrating these units and building a system that can address or relate to the needs of the diverse units is a further aspect of building global knowledge management systems. If a KMS is not designed to span global boundaries, the knowledge it supports would be shared only within each "locality," whether it be a physical location (such as a country or region) or a logical space (within a team, for example). It is therefore important to use a broad perspective when designing and implementing global knowledge management systems.

Designing a global knowledge management system requires gaining an understanding of different perspectives. The perspective used will define what is "local" and consequently what is "global." A local unit can be as small as a team or department that has clearly differentiating features or characteristics. For example, local cultures emerge within occupations or even departments and units within an organization. The manner in which the accountants of the organization work will be different when compared to engineers. Similarly, employees working in Mumbai will operate a bit differently than those working in Beijing or London (Cook and Yanow, 1993; Schein, 2004). Designing global knowledge management systems can be viewed as attempting to build an environment where knowledge flows transcend either physical (e.g., geographic) or logical (e.g., functions or teams) localities. To do so requires an understanding of why it is difficult to move knowledge from one location to another, and why some knowledge is utilized while some remains untouched. Global knowledge management programs wrestle with the need to balance between standardization (i.e., applying a vanilla-flavored approach to the entire organization) and tailoring systems to accommodate local nuances and innovation. Ideally, global knowledge management systems will ensure that they can take advantage of economies of scale and the interoperability that come with standardization, while trying to avoid imposition of a practice or process that disrupts productive local cultures and working styles.

To appreciate the challenge of building global knowledge management systems, consider a simple example: if there are three employees who speak English, Hindi, and Mandarin, how do they communicate and share knowledge? One option is to choose one of the three languages, say Mandarin, and teach the non-Mandarin speaking employees this language. Then the employees share a common language, which should facilitate knowledge sharing. But speaking the language and communicating with others effectively can be two very different skills. Native speakers rely on technical terms and jargon that are not always shared with others. Some direct translations simply will not make sense, akin to the problems of translating a joke from one language to another. Moreover, one will have to address the challenge of how to convince someone to learn another language. Choosing Mandarin might offend the Hindi and English speakers, as this may send the message that their languages are inferior or not as important. These are problems presented by language, which is only one syntactical barrier a global knowledge management system must overcome. Most organizations do not have a choice as to whether they will operate and compete globally, and the inability to facilitate global knowledge flows will result in an organization that is suboptimal, fragmented, and unable to compete in the marketplace.

We begin this chapter by exploring some of the reasons why careful design of global knowledge management systems is necessary. First, we explore the topic of globalization; the increase in connections between countries is one of the primary factors behind the need for robust global knowledge management systems. Second, we explore the concept of **culture**. We discuss three dimensions of culture: national, organizational, and occupational. Third, we explore two critical concepts that distinguish one locality from the next: distance and language. Given these foundational concepts, we then explore the various models used to build global knowledge management systems. Here, we explore three models used to facilitate knowledge management across the various geographical units of an organization. We then explore the management of knowledge in distributed projects and the elements that engage workers across various boundaries, whether they are geographic, functional, or both. We illustrate issues that organizations must consider when joining and participating in knowledge. Concluding the chapter, we will walk through critical issues that companies must acknowledge when designing global knowledge management systems.

THE EFFECTS OF GLOBALIZATION

Globalization, as described in a business context, usually connotes the growing inter-connections and interdependencies among nations. Therefore, we examine the question "is the world becoming more connected?" Or, as Thomas Friedman pondered, is the world becoming flatter? (Friedman, 2007). In this section, rather than providing an extensive overview of the literature on globalization, we examine two opposing views on the how the world is changing. One view assumes that the world is indeed become flatter, connected, and globally integrated. The opposite view holds that the world is still a long way from being closely integrated. This view holds that the gaps between the haves and the have-nots have not yet closed to a point where we can consider the world flat. Understanding both viewpoints is critical to building global knowledge management systems. See Table 8.1 for a summary of viewpoints on globalization.

Thomas Friedman's (2007) book *The World Is Flat* argued that due to advances in computing hardware, software, and telecommunication networks, the world was flat and the corporate playing field was becoming leveled in terms of global commerce and competition. Friedman highlights several **global flatteners** that have contributed to the leveling of the playing field, the most critical ones being:

1. The collapse of the Berlin Wall (signifying the end of the Cold War)
2. Emergence of Netscape (the first browser that enabled laypeople to connect to, and collaborate on, the Internet)

Table 8.1. Summary of Viewpoints on Globalization

Name	Description	Proponent/Author	Indicators
Flat world view	The world is becoming leveled in terms of global commerce and competition.	Thomas Friedman	• Global communication and collaboration increase (through advancements in technology such as the Internet). • Economic interdependence between nations increases (through trade, outsourcing, and off-shoring).
Spiky world view	The world is spiky, rather than flat, with the spikes occurring around geographic centers where there is clustering of talent, innovation, and creativity.	Richard Florida	• Skills, expertise, and infrastructure are unequally distributed. • Certain geographies have the skills base and resources to compete in global markets while others lack basic infrastructure.

3. Advancement of workflow software (computer-to-computer messaging and transactions giving rise to the electronic commerce, also called electronic business transactions)

4. Uploading (rise of Internet-based communities where online collaboration takes place through the sharing of electronic documents)

5. Outsourcing and offshoring (contracting work outside the organization and to foreign locations)

6. Optimized supply-chains (integrating production and distribution processes and outputs across organizational and national boundaries),

7. In-forming (rise of search engines and other information services that allow individuals to find and access information on topics of interest), and

8. Digital devices (global diffusion of information manipulation tools such as personal digital assistants, instant messaging, etc.).

These flatteners have lowered the cost for individuals and organizations to connect, share information, and collaborate. In addition, each of these flatteners has promoted access to information and knowledge that was previously not present, or where there were severe barriers that impeded access. The flatteners also allowed for leveling the intensity of global competition. It is hard to ignore how these factors have reduced barriers to information access and transformed global business (Friedman, 2007).

Another indication of how the world is becoming more interconnected is the trend toward **outsourcing**. Businesses are outsourcing not only manufacturing work, but also outsourcing knowledge work (e.g., software development, innovation, scientific research) at an increasing pace. Open-source communities that bring several hundred or thousand individuals together to collaborate on developing software products are also more commonly used for the development of new applications. It was the open-source movement that created Linux, the main competitor to the Windows operating system.

Many individuals have succumbed to the lure of Internet and social media services, and most employees would not be able to function as social beings without them. Electronic commerce, as demonstrated by the prominence of online giants such as Amazon or eBay, is well on its way to replacing a significant percentage of the brick-and-mortar shopping experience. Through platforms such as YouTube and Facebook, individuals can connect with peers across the globe and share information and knowledge. Consider the case of the 2009 elections in Iran. When demonstrations and riots broke out on the streets of Tehran and all over Iran, it was through channels such as YouTube and Twitter that the local Iranian populace shared firsthand reports of the events with the globe (Parr, 2009). All of these technologies have contributed to a more globally connected world, and one where we can access and connect to information from places which were not possible before.

Accessing information from distant corners of the globe is only one sign of our increasing interconnectedness. Another issue to consider is the increasing interdependencies among nations. It is commonly accepted that no nation can exist in isolation, and that events in one country will impact others. When there is a crisis in North Korea due to the threat of nuclear exercises, not only are its closest neighbors, South Korea and Japan, concerned, but countries including the United States, France,

Germany, and Russia are concerned as well. Similarly, when a crisis breaks out between India and Pakistan, not only are the citizens of those countries impacted, but businesses all over the globe begin to worry about the impacts on global business operations. To see the effects of how interdependent and interconnected the world is, consider the most recent global financial crisis. The crisis began with the collapse of the US subprime mortgage market in approximately July 2007. The ensuing collapse of the housing market in the United States had a ripple effect throughout the globe. Here are just a few of the effects:

- In 2007, Northern Rock, a medium-sized bank in the United Kingdom, asked for protection from the Bank of England. This would be the first among many global financial institutions to eventually either be bailed out by government (public) funds or collapse (HM Treasury, Bank of England and Financial Services Authority, 2007).
- The annualized rate of decline in gross domestic product was 14.4 percent in Germany, 15.2 percent in Japan, 7.4 percent in the United Kingdom, 9.8 percent in the Euro area, and 21.5 percent for Mexico during the first quarter of 2009 (Baily and Elliott, 2009).
- In October 2008, the banking system in Iceland, an economy dependent on the finance sector, collapsed and the government had to borrow money from the International Monetary Fund (IMF). This did not help the government's cause, and the entire government collapsed, beginning with the entire cabinet resigning and causing the prime minister to call for early elections in January 2009 (The Economist, 2008).
- African economies were not spared either. In May 2009, South Africa, the largest economy in Africa, fell into recession for the first time in 17 years. The South African economy shrunk by 1.8 percent in the last quarter of 2008 (France24, 2009).
- The poorest countries of the world had to battle a food crisis in 2008. Commodity prices rose to the extent that the world poorest people could not afford basic sustenance commodities. Massive demonstrations took place in at least 15 countries during the first half of 2008 (Shah, 2008).

Clearly the world has become more interdependent and interconnected. But, the question still remains, has the world become flat? Has the economic playing field become leveled? Can individuals, and organizations, across the globe identify the right resources and access them with ease? For example consider Johannesburg, South Africa. Finding Internet access similar to what one might expect in the United States or Europe is difficult, if not impossible. Internet charges are quite steep, especially by the standards of local South Africans, and even tourists experience these high communication costs. Internet fees are paid not only for time used, but also based on the amount of data downloaded. The availability of wireless Internet access is not as common as it is on the campuses of universities and schools in the United States. Now, if this is difficult to imagine, it becomes more striking when one realizes Johannesburg is one of the most advanced and economically developed cities in Africa! Conditions in this developed city far surpass those one might witness in more rural areas in South

Africa. Not far from Johannesburg in Tugela Ferry, the administrative and business center of the Msinga District, the situation could not be more different.

Globalization and Its Impact on Libraries and Museums

Libraries and museums are not immune to globalization. Today, the nature of libraries and museums is undergoing fundamental changes. The most obvious outcomes of the effect of globalization and technology advancement can be seen with how artifacts are acquired, stored, and even accessed by patrons. Libraries are acquiring greater amounts of their artifacts in digital format. It is common for patrons to preview documents online (through websites such as Google Books, http://books.google.com), download and even consume artifacts (e.g., journal publications) without ever stepping foot into the library. In addition, while in the past individuals were limited to local expertise of librarians and even the collections housed by the libraries, today, distance barriers have been surpassed through technological innovations. Consider the case of the ipl2 Consortium that emerged from a merger between Internet Public Library and Librarians' Internet Index. The consortium is "a global information community that provides in-service learning and volunteer opportunities for library and information science students and professionals, offers a collaborative research forum, and supports and enhances library services through the provision of authoritative collections, information assistance, and information instruction for the public" (ipl2 Consortium, 2011). Project such as the ipl2 Consortium are breaking down traditional geographic boundaries, and are even bringing experts, novices, and enthusiasts (volunteers) together for collaboration. Today, one can visit exhibits for major museums (e.g., The Field Museum in Chicago) online, go on interactive tours, and even exchange information about the experience online. Moreover, there is a shift taking place in the power structures. As an example, the Wing Luke Asian Art Museum (WLAAM) involves members of the community in designing special exhibits. This approach is in stark contrast to traditional settings where the curator holds the knowledge and designs the exhibit. The WLAAM involves community members in the entire life cycle of exhibit design through creation of Community Advisory Committees.

The Msinga District, located in the KwaZulu-Natal province of South Africa that has the highest rate of HIV infections in the world (Dugger, 2009), is one of the poorest communities in South Africa (Msinga Municipality, 2011). Not only do most people not have access to the Internet, they lack basic computers and software applications. Clearly, one can see that they might not see the world as a level playing field, or flat. Solving these problems in the context of an organization is often very expensive. Simple connectivity is often hard to come by in many developing countries, let alone high speed bandwidth. Attempts to deliver a certain minimum standard or accessibility and even certain functionality to all employees in a truly global organization can be problematic.

In addition, that a foreign subsidiary has been outfitted with proper technology by today's Western standards does not imply that the locals being hired know how to use it appropriately. Additional training and exposure to standards of practice will be required to bring levels and depths of participation in a knowledge system commensurate with a developed world employee base. It is important to acknowledge that the customers a local subsidiary is serving will have varying degrees of familiarity with online tool sets. Care must be taken not to assume that workflow can necessarily be streamlined in developing nations through the introduction of software or that participation in an online knowledge management system will be intuitive or even manageable. Simply providing access to technology is not sufficient; one must be able to ensure that those who are using the technology have the necessary knowledge, and infrastructure support, to take full advantage of the technology. This is where large disparities still exist across the globe; thereby preventing the development of a level playing field.

Several notable scholars, including Joseph Stiglitz, winner of the Nobel Prize in 2001, have leveled valid criticism on Friedman's (2007) work. Stiglitz argues that the gap between the rich and poor is continuing to grow, contributing to a world that is less flat. In an interview in *U.S. News & World Report*, he noted:

> I went to Moldova—a country whose gross domestic product had gone down 70 percent since the beginning of transition [from Soviet-era communism]. It was supposed to make the country richer, yet three quarters of the country's national budget was being spent on paying foreign debts. It got very emotional when the daughter of one of [our] associates went to the hospital, the hospital ran out of bottled oxygen, and she died. There was no oxygen in the entire country. They couldn't afford a stable supply of goods, in part, because their foreign exchange was being used to service the foreign debt. (Kingsbury, 2006: under "How Do We Approach Issues Like Third World Debt")

It is not expected that a hospital in a developed country would run out of essential medical supplies such as bottled oxygen. Economic disparity clearly makes the world uneven, and puts into question the idea of a level playing field. Pankaj Ghemawat presents a more balanced, and accurate, treatise on globalization (Ghemawat, 2007). Ghemawat illustrates the fundamental cultural, political, geographic and economic differences that need to be strategically managed if organizations are to be successful in conducting global operations. He notes that global indicators showing that the world is flattening are misleading, and instead points to patterns in telecommunications traffic as useful indicators. For example, the international share of Internet traffic has been decreasing, rather than increasing, indicating that the growth in telecommunications traffic is local rather than global. This suggests that that even though organizations have the capability to reach global destinations, most focus on their localities. Hence, while we do have global capability, our behaviors are still dominated by local concerns.

Consider another argument by Richard Florida that the key economic factors are talent, innovation, and creativity, which are not evenly distributed globally (Florida, 2008). His work provides evidence for a clustering effect. The world is spiky, rather than flat, with the spikes occurring around geographic centers where there is clustering of these key factors. Creative people and resources migrate to these clusters because they offer the best chance of success. This is one reason why many parts of the world lack the necessary knowledge and expertise to transform their living conditions. The economics on how knowledge, especially knowledge required for innovation and transformation, is distributed is far from being fair and universally accessible. In many parts of the world, access to even the most basic forms of knowledge (e.g., how to take care of one's health, and provide for one's survival) is not available.

While the world has become interconnected, and countries have furthered their interdependence, all people of the world do not have an equal playing field nor can they be treated as a homogenous set. Today, many parts of the globe have advanced due to the availability of information and communication technologies, which has allowed them to compete and thrive in the global markets. The most notable examples of these countries are India and China. Yet, there is still a large percentage of the globe for which globalization has not yet borne fruits. Disparities are wide, and access to even basic resources (like food and water) is hard to come by. Hence, getting access to technologies such as the Internet, or skilled expertise and knowledge, is not even a concern. Moreover, the world is far from being homogenous, and cannot it be treated as flat when it comes to global dealings. Cultures around the world are different, work settings and forms are heterogeneous, languages vary, and even distances matter. Appreciation for, and management of, these elements is critical to achieving global knowledge management.

CULTURE

Culture can be defined as follows:

> A shared set of assumptions, invented, discovered or developed by a group as it learns to cope with its problems of external adaptation and internal integration. It has worked well enough to be considered valid, and is to be taught to new members of the group as the correct way to perceive, think, and feel in relation to those problems. (Schein, 1991: 247)

Therefore culture is the set of shared expectations, norms, values, and beliefs that guide the behavior of organizations. Many organizations display a very strong culture with close ties between their members and a narrow scope of opinions and values. Others have a very weak culture that allows for a more heterogeneous population, individuality, and an acceptance of varying ideas and practices. Any culture can consist of multiple subcultures, which can follow the structure of organization, hierarchical roles, professions, geographic locations, or random collections of groups within the organization. The notion of **organizational culture** is important to organizations and their knowledge management practices. Culture can shape assumptions about what knowledge is important, mediate the relations between levels and functions, create a context for social interaction, and shape the creation and adoption of new knowledge (Choo et al., 2006).

Individuals identify with different cultures across the globe, and even within global locations differences in cultures exist (Geertz, 1973). For example, while there is much that binds Americans together and similarities can be seen across the United States, there are differences in practices, beliefs, and expectations between those who live along the East Coast in cities such as New York versus those who originate from the South in a city such as Huntsville, Alabama. These differences define how people think, behave, and evaluate behavior. Ultimately collaboration requires individuals to be compelled, somehow, some way, to interact. Because culture defines many of the conscious and subconscious motivations required for collaboration, understanding cultural nuances is critical to building global knowledge management systems. No matter the technology serving as the foundation for a knowledge-based system, emotional intelligence and cultural awareness must be constantly applied during its design, development, and implementation. Therefore, a global knowledge management system must be constructed through a combination of technology and human elements.

Culture plays an important role in collaboration. Different cultures, including cultural features such as language, develop among groups of people who interact to achieve their common goals. Regardless of whether the world is flattening, the digital age is only in its infancy in the context of the span of human history. For hundreds of thousands of years, humans have been collecting in relatively small groups and figuring out a way to interact, to cooperate and to share experiences they find meaningful. As generations have come and gone, they have helped evolve their cultural systems to adapt to new ideas, new environmental conditions, to boredom, etc. But they have also handed down to the next generation an increasingly rich and complicated combination of shared symbols, behavioral protocols, priorities, and valuation systems.

Bourdieu and Passeron (1990) identify a significant facet of what defines cultural behavior as **doxic**, or behavior based on values or priorities that are not explicitly thought through or even conscious (Bourdieu and Passeron, 1973, 1990). These value systems are deeply ingrained in our psyches and define our sense of what is intrinsically right or wrong. Humans have interacted in relatively isolated groups facing unique circumstances over thousands of years, so it is easy to see why there are such deep-seated differences about how cultures should behave. Many times these feelings are so entrenched that they appear to the individuals to be self-evident.

Culture not only is created and shared by groups collaborating and operating in isolation, but also causes groups to want to continue their isolated position. People from different cultures may become offended or mistrustful when others do not observe these norms. Cultural differences often provide relatively simple hurdles to collaboration which can be discussed consciously. However, many of the differences between groups of people are deep enough or subtle enough that discussing and resolving them can be both extremely difficult and painful. Therefore, in order to manage knowledge globally, it becomes very important to pay attention to the cultural differences among various groups within the organization. Cultural differences need to be understood and appreciated, and methods need to be devised to connect individuals who hold different cultural expectations and backgrounds—and for whom this difference affects how they contribute, store, search, and use other's knowledge.

In addition, managing knowledge relies on individuals feeling comfortable in their environments in order to share knowledge with others and also seek knowledge when the need arises. Ensuring that individuals who might come from different backgrounds or locations feel comfortable with the combined resulting culture is important to promote knowledge sharing. Failure to build a knowledge management system that is aligned with the culture of the workplace will lead to waste of resources; employees will abandon, or worse yet, misuse, the knowledge management system. The three most common levels to view information culture in order to understand these influences on knowledge use and knowledge management systems are national, organizational, and occupational culture.

National Culture

National culture includes the values preferences, behaviors, and norms that differentiate people from various countries across the world. National cultures are ingrained from birth. Who a person is culturally depends on where he or she was born, how he or she was raised, the influences of formal education, and the accepted norms and methods of interactions. National cultures bind individuals from a country, or region. Consequently, they also create challenges when people from different cultures work together. Expectations might be misaligned, norms might not be understood, and the intentions behind behaviors could be interpreted incorrectly. Hofstede presents, through his seminal work on national cultures, the five major dimensions of culture (Hofstede, 2001). Table 8.2 contains a summary of cultural dimensions.

1. *High versus low power distance*: This represents the extent to which powerful authorities are accepted within organizations and to which power is distributed unequally within the organization. Low power distance reflects the behavior of individuals within nations where there is less difference in power between the most powerful and the least powerful person. Most Western democracies are an example where ordinary citizens can be democratically voted into public office. In low power distance nations, the status of individuals in high, or powerful, positions is not simply accepted or revered. People are more likely to relate to

Table 8.2. Dimensions of Culture		
Dimension	**Description**	**Example**
Power distance	Represents the extent to which authorities are accepted within organizations and the equality of power distribution	Low power distance: • less automatic acceptance and respect for authority figures • less difference in power between the most powerful and the least powerful person
Individualism and collectivism	The extent to which the individuals are expected to develop their own identities in comparison to the importance of being part of a group and conforming to group norms	Collectivist: • group identification is emphasized; individuals are expected to put their personal aspirations second to the group goals
Masculinity and femininity	The degree to which values are preferred that are perceived as masculine versus feminine	Masculine: • cultures that traditionally value competitiveness, assertiveness, wealth accumulation, and ambition
Uncertainty avoidance	The degree to which uncertainty is tolerated	High uncertainty avoidance: • uncertainty and ambiguity are awkward and avoided (e.g., through rules of conduct)
Long-term vs. Short-term orientation	Preference given to short-term outcomes versus taking a longer-term view of the consequences of decisions and actions	Long-term orientation: • individuals place greater emphasis on how their actions are not only perceived in the present time, but also might impact those who came before them and those that will come after them

each other as equals and power status is arrived at through democratic means. In these settings, people with less powerful positions feel comfortable questioning the decisions, and decision-making process, of those in power, and contributing to debates and discussions as equals. Examples of countries that have low power distance are Australia and Denmark. On the other hand, in high power distance countries, people in power command authority and are revered. Power relations are adhered to during interactions. As a result, those in high positions in organizational hierarchies are seldom questioned or debated with. The less powerful simply accept, or choose no confrontation with, those in higher power positions. Examples of countries with high power distance are India and Malaysia. Power distance is not an objective measure, in that it is more based on how people in a country perceive the significance of power distances. Power distances play out in the propensity for individuals to question those in power, and even contradict or confront incorrect information from these sources. Consider briefly an exchange between a Malaysian project manager (PM) and an Australian engineer. The latter may feel it is very appropriate to openly question and challenge the PM. However, the PM may take very serious offense to this, interpreting it as an open challenge to his or her authority, as opposed to an opportunity for process improvement.

2. *Individualism versus collectivism*: This represents the extent to which the individuals are expected to develop their own identities, choose their own affiliations, and act for themselves, in comparison to being part of a group. In cultures where individualism exists, rewards are given to individual "heroes." In collectivistic cultures, on the other hand, the group is put before the individual. Individuals are expected to put their personal aspirations second to the group goals. The United States and the United Kingdom are examples of the most individualistic national cultures, while many Latin American and Asian cultures are more collectivistic in nature. Collectivist cultures promote and expect teamwork and individual sacrifice within the organizations. Teams are central to the functioning of these organizations, and seldom do individuals seek to outshine the team. On the other hand, in individualistic cultures, the organization often provides incentives for individuals to outshine their peers; the incentives to cooperate and share the glory are lower when compared to collectivist settings. This difference comes into play when trying to solicit knowledge contribution to your system. How do you incentivize people to contribute? In some cases people may respond well to individual recognition, where for others this could be embarrassing. In other cases it may be enough to simply mandate that contributions be made, where some may ask "Well, what's in it for me?"

3. *Masculinity versus femininity*: Although society is endeavoring to evolve beyond gender stereotyping, this framework distinguishes between "masculine-oriented" cultures that value competitiveness, assertiveness, wealth accumulation, and ambition, and "feminine-oriented" cultures that value relationships and quality of life. If two groups subscribing to different cultural backgrounds in this dimension try to collaborate, there is a chance that conflicts may manifest themselves in terms of different preferences for work methods and goal priorities. This can

easily be seen in how offices in different countries view overtime and vacation, and the stigma that is placed on individuals who either use their full allotment of vacation, or focus on accumulating many hours of overtime.

4. *Uncertainty avoidance*: Cultures that are high in uncertainty avoidance prefer to deal with anxiety and ambiguity through structured protocols such as rules. In these cultures, uncertainty not only is unwelcome but makes for awkward situations. On the other hand, cultures that have low uncertainty avoidance are not too concerned with anxiety and ambiguity; here, emergent solutions are used to resolve situations. Mediterranean and Latin American countries have been shown to have high uncertainty avoidance preferences while Americans and Chinese have been shown to have relatively low uncertainty avoidance.

5. *Long-term versus short-term orientation*: In long-term oriented cultures, preference is given to taking a longer-term view to the consequences of decisions. Therefore, the concept of persistence plays an important role. People do not simply forget or assume that one's actions are meant to influence only the present time. On the other hand, in short-term oriented cultures, people are more likely to consider their actions within shorter time frames; the inclination to focus on quarterly results in corporations in the United States is a great example of this orientation. Memory and past traditions play less of a role here. Most Asian cultures, especially China, Japan, and India, place greater value on the long-term orientation than their Western counterparts. As an example in the Japanese or Indian traditions, it is important to save face and avoid shaming a family. Individuals place great emphasis on how their actions not only are perceived in the present time, but also might impact those that came before them and those that will come after them.

Several caveats need to be kept in mind about these cultural dimensions. First, they cannot be used to generalize to all individuals within the specific geographical boundaries of a country. Personality and personal experience play a huge role in determining individual behavior. Indian college students exposed to the Internet and American movies, for instance, might subscribe to a short-term orientation and low power distance, while their parents' generation might have opposite preferences on the cultural dimensions. Even within a nation, differences in cultures can occur between regions. For example, people who live in major cities might have different preferences on the cultural dimensions than those living in rural areas. In major cities of India, for example, you are more likely to see the prominence of Western-style cultural values than the traditional value preferences. Second, some cultural characteristics may blur national boundaries and be present across a larger region encompassing two or more countries. Third, much of the research that generated the explanation for such differences across countries was done over 40 years ago, and it is not clear whether differentiated changes across clusters of cultures would have separated them further or, because of the globalization of communication, media and news phenomenon, started to coalesce in closer groups. It is still widely accepted, though, that there are differences in culture across large groups of individuals—and it is therefore imperative to not only be aware of such differences, but also prepared to manage with these differences in mind.

Organizational Culture

Culture also differs from one organization to another. Consider the differences between a military organization and Google's corporate headquarters. Organizational culture can be defined as the set of accepted values, ideals, expectations, norms, behaviors, and patterns of interaction within an entity. Different organizations will place emphasis on different things. For example, the United States Army will value discipline, sacrifice of self for country, respect for authority and chain of command, and selflessness. Google, on the other hand, values teamwork, innovation, problem solving, and collaboration. The values that an organization places on various ideals and objectives will dictate how people behave and interact within the organization. As a further example, in most law firms the cultural values dictate that winning is important. Rewards are given to those who win cases, sometimes even to the point of the ends justifying the means, at any cost. As a result, it is not surprising that law firms have a difficult time promoting a culture of knowledge sharing and collaboration. Simply put, these values do not make sense in the cultural reality of the organization. Rewards are given not to teams, but to individual lawyers, and other incentives (e.g., promotions to partnership in the firm) value the individual over the collective.

Organizational cultures are an important aspect of knowledge management as they determine the underlying behavior regarding how individuals will operate in an organizational setting. Similar to national culture, not every employee within one organization will subscribe to the predominant organizational culture. Those who do not follow the organizational values will have a greater challenge adjusting to and being part of the organization. However, they may be able to influence the culture through questioning the underlying norms, values, and assumptions, thereby hopefully making the organization alter its cultural preferences. Organizational culture plays a critical role during the hiring and initiation of new individuals into the organization. An individual might be extremely talented, capable, and perform at a high level at one organization, and then go on to perform poorly in another organization. The individual may simply hold a different value system or may interpret the meaning of behavior in a different way, which may impact his or her performance. This commonly occurs in sports, when a player who is a star on one team, fades away when he or she switches to another team. Two issues play into this: first, the player may not fit within the organization, and second, the organization might not be amenable to making changes to accommodate the nuances of the player. This illustrates why many organizations try to determine whether an individual will fit the cultural values of the organization. Table 8.3 contains a summary of factors that shape culture within organizations.

Within organizations, we can have different sets of cultures, or subcultures. As we will see in the next section, cultural differences might be based on occupations. Function, hierarchy, or age can define these subcultures. Baby boomers for example, are not inclined to multitask. Younger workers often thrive in knowledge-rich, multitasking environments. Newer generations are also comfortable exchanging information and knowledge in virtual environments. These employees have developed their own language and shorthand for facilitating online communications. For example, it is common for them to use syntax such as 4U (for you), LOL (laughing out loud),

Table 8.3. Factors Shaping Organizational Culture		
Factor	**Description**	**Example**
Values	The underlying values to which the organization subscribes	• The U.S. Army may value chain of command and discipline while Google values teamwork and collaboration.
Incentive systems	The behaviors and results that are rewarded or reprimanded by the organization	• An organization may emphasize individual results, while another organization may give rewards based on teamwork.
Hierarchy	The extent to which authority is gained through position and seniority	• Younger workers may confer respect based on demonstration of expertise within a domain, while older workers may expect to gain authority and respect through job position.

and BRB (be right back) during informal, or in some cases even formal, corporate communication.

The challenge facing organizations is not only how to bridge the cultural differences but also how to identify ways to ensure that all employees are suitably trained and equipped to become the future managers of the organization. Here is where friction normally occurs, as different cultures may possess opposing opinions towards what management is, and how it should be operationalized. For example, studies have shown that younger generations are not ready to immediately accept authority, but instead believe that authority and respect are earned through the demonstration of expertise within a domain (Barzilai-Nahon and Mason, 2010; Bylin, 2009). This is in stark contrast to the predominant norm shared by many older workers, who assume that authority is related to tenure and age. Learning styles also differ among these two generations, which makes group instruction difficult. Baby boomers are accustomed to learning through formal instruction such as courses situated in classrooms. Newer generations often learn best through their experiences, including experimentation and making mistakes. Knowledge flows, therefore, are not natural between these two age groups, and a global knowledge management system will need to carefully address this challenge.

Occupational Culture

Consider how people engaged in different professions go about their daily routines and job tasks. Engineers, personal trainers, police officers, and medical professionals all form their own rules, accepted behaviors, and means of handling knowledge. Cultures develop around occupations as these groups of professionals interact and work together to advance their discipline and their skills. Within an organization, different occupational cultures become clearly defined and one might be dominant over others. Understanding occupational culture is very important to encourage employees from different units (or who have different occupations) to collaborate. Different occupational cultures often use words to mean different things and create their own language, or jargon. Jargon, as we know, promotes speed of communication within groups as it targets very specific shared meaning. However, jargon also makes it difficult to foster intergroup communications because one group may not understand or even appreciate what the other one is saying. Similarly gestures and modes of communication might be different. For example, it might be acceptable for an employee to use informal language when talking with people the employee works with often, as meanings including the subtle nuances are easily transferred. However, if communication flows beyond one occupation, there is need for greater effort and care in the words and methods chosen for communication.

Different occupational cultures subscribe to distinct value systems, norms, and modes of interaction as all of these elements have been evolved over time to help them accomplish specific types of work. As a result, when trying to get individuals from different occupational cultures to collaborate, one has to understand what these are, and find common grounds or methods to bridge the differences. At a minimum, one has to make all parties understand the differences in the value systems and respect them. An illustration of this is the Federal Bureau of Investigation (FBI) in comparison to the Central Intelligence Agency (CIA). Prior to the tragic events of September 11, 2001, these two organizations seldom cooperated and collaborated (Desouza and Hensgen, 2003). The FBI operated domestically, whereas the CIA operated internationally. The two organizations have different missions, goals, and structures. Since 9/11, the two agencies have had to bridge many boundaries to knowledge flow and communication. They both may be branches of the US government, but they have many distinct differences. The FBI, as part of the Department of Justice, is a law enforcement agency that is in the business of dealing with incidents through the capture of evidence and the prosecution of criminals. The FBI operates in a reactive mode, as it becomes involved only after a crime has been committed. The CIA, on the other hand, is not in the business of building cases or prosecuting criminals. Its charter calls for being proactive and preventing threats before they materialize. It cannot sit back, wait for a terrorist threat to materialize, and then begin working on the identification of a terrorist. The occupational culture of the FBI calls for one to take care in preserving evidence, collecting evidence in a manner that can be presented in a court of law, and following rules (e.g., the acquisition of search warrants). The occupational culture of the CIA calls for covert operations, use of informants who need to be protected and whose identity cannot be revealed, and operations that may not be in keeping with the US Constitution. Today, through the use of job rotations (where an employee might serve time in both organizations) and joint task forces (teams involving members from both organizations), bridges are being constructed to foster understanding and mutual respect among employees of the two organizations.

Language

Languages matter across cultures (Desouza, 2005; Peirce Edition Project, 1982–2010). Words have meanings, but so do inflections in the voice, the cadence of a spoken sentence, and the accompanying gestures. Moreover, the modes of communication are diverse across cultures. When considering the design of global knowledge management systems, it is important to give attention to the concept of languages. Today, it is common to find multilingual websites, created to promote sharing of information with a diverse audience. These websites are rather basic in nature as they take static content, translate it, and then present it in the local languages. This is an acceptable solution if the sharing of information does not change on a regular basis and the intention is to promote simple communication as opposed to conversations. Communication is the passage of information from one entity to another (Daft and Wiginton, 1979). Conversations call for exchange of context-rich information between two or more entities. That means not only of text-based symbols, but a transmission of additional elements that round out intended meaning.

Language, shared perspectives, shared values, and behavior, are all irreducibly tied together (Saussure, 1916). Consider that several Native American cultures have no past tense in their traditional languages. Their cultural perspective did not require that such language structures be developed. Juxtapose this structure against the elaborate tense conjugation of English. Now consider translating a "Lessons Learned" document into such a Native American language. It can be done, but the expertise and time required to comprehensively convey the meaning intended in the original document is significant.

Because language is used on a daily basis, it influences how our brains develop, the concepts we are comfortable grappling with, the metaphors that make sense to us, and the way in which we process information. Written translation is often not equivalent to knowledge transfer. Verbal queues such as inflection, and voice strain, as well as visual cues such as facial expressions or body posture, help place expressions of language in context and provide deeper, more complex presentations. Some languages are considered "high context" languages and rely on shared understanding of circumstances and behavior to shape specific meaning. Others, including English, are considered "low context" and have more complicated rules built into the language itself to communicate specific meaning.

Often people who learn a second language originating from a similar culture have an easier time distinguishing the nuances of meaning that are not communicated with direct translations. Comprehension is enhanced if the individual is interacting with others from the same profession. The jargon and other language shorthand are more likely to represent familiar concepts or impart familiar value sets. But inevitably, only a true expert in a second language will have the skills required to capture full meaning. And this tacit knowledge is gained not just by understanding sentence structure and memorizing vocabulary, but by understanding the values and cultural perceptions in which the language has its roots and that provide the context for its use. It is therefore impossible to overcome the various communication barriers posed by multiple languages in organizations through technology solutions alone. A critical aspect of a global knowledge management system is the education of the users about the various cultures from which any bit of knowledge comes. Connecting users with content in a language they can understand is a good step. But connecting them to each other in real-time collaboration environments is the only way to close knowledge transfer gaps across cultural boundaries.

Building Knowledge Management Systems: The Value of an Incremental Approach

It is always safer and smarter to start small and grow a knowledge management initiative gradually, based on a string of discrete successes. While it is often true that improved knowledge management practices would increase the effectiveness of and/or impact almost any aspect of an organization's operations, rarely has a single, company-wide, "big bang" knowledge management approach lived up to that potential. Take the case of Accenture, the multinational consulting giant (Paik and Choi, 2005). With over 75,000 employees worldwide, all engaged in the packaging and selling of knowledge, there is no business model on earth that should be more driven and aligned with excellent knowledge sharing practices. But even here we see the best efforts to collect, tag, and organize pieces of knowledge gained in one area of the business for distribution to another that could really use it. Here they had a team of over 500 dedicated knowledge workers feeding a massive knowledge database that in many parts of the company became a staple of daily life. But in other areas of the company, particularly Asia, the system was abandoned in favor of local variations. Why? Language was a big issue. In spite of the official corporate language being English, it is difficult and time consuming to translate between the local language in which business is conducted and Accenture's preferred language. This and other cultural barriers led to a sense of alienation on the part of many managers in Asian countries. Failure to rectify that sense of alienation led not only to the managers developing and adopting their own knowledge system, but also led them to feel as if their knowledge and contributions did not count in the eyes of the rest of the company. The ultimate analysis of why the knowledge management efforts in Accenture fell short of the goals spoke to how a "one size fits all" approach just does not work. So how do you develop a system that is both cohesive enough to maximize knowledge sharing opportunities globally, while making it attractive and useful locally? One step at a time.

DISTANCE

A goal of knowledge transfer is full, context-rich communication and collaboration. The advent of modern computing ensures that our ability to interact with people in real time offers the possibility for mitigating the effects that physical distance imposes on communications. Unfortunately many employees report that e-mail, instant messaging (IM), videoconferencing, and webinars create the perception in the workplace that people are less connected. From the perspective of culture, language, dialects, and shared meaning are all developed with groups of people that interact on a daily basis. Communications that include exchange of words, tone of voice, facial expressions, body language, and shared experiences leads individuals to feel that there has been a more complete exchange of meaning through the interaction (Daft and Wiginton, 1979; Daft and Lengel, 1986). These context-rich interactions are accelerators for trust, a topic for further discussion in this chapter. Technology and knowledge systems that enable regular, consistent, context-rich interactions stimulate a deeper foundation for shared meaning and more complete knowledge transfer. Barriers to context-rich and regular interactions create distance between employees and inhibit collaboration.

Geographic distances are the most obvious and difficult types of distances to overcome as they create other forms of distances (Jarvenpaa and Leidner, 1998). Employees who do not share the same space, the same local events that affect their commute, the same cultural references, or the same local language simply have less in common with those who do share all of those elements. Technology enables people separated by geography to communicate, but culture always develops locally ensuring that barriers to full understanding of one another will be relatively great.

Another category of distance is time, which is often coupled with great geographic separation. This is most exaggerated in companies with offices on opposite sides of the world, such as New York and Hong Kong, where one employee's day is another's night. The disruption caused by late-night conference calls taken from home and the discipline to overcome time differences for regular collaboration can prove formidable when asking cross-regional teams to perform.

Separation between employees can happen even if they work in the same building or sit in adjacent offices. Although individuals are more likely to interact over a water cooler break or office social function, it is entirely possible that daily workflow will ensure that employees in close, daily, physical proximity never actually interact. The degree of rigidity to which employees are expected to hold to their assigned responsibilities and workflows is sure to either increase or decrease the cultural isolation between functional groups in the workplace.

Many times, distance created by workflow can be separated along lines of expertise. This occurs within the context of a small department or project team. But other factors can exacerbate the separation created between groups that hold certain expertise. As noted above, jargon and or highly technical subject matters can functionally separate groups within a particular discipline from others who work near them, or even rely on their work product. The status of an expertise within a business can also dictate their relative degree of isolation. IT professionals suffer through a negative aspect of this phenomenon all the time. Their work is highly technical, their communications filled with jargon and technical terms, and their skills, although essential, are not often viewed as a "core competency" of the company. Ironically, their work is the basis for overcoming many types of distance in an organization, but the nature of their work can easily breed isolation.

Addressing distance is the foundation for developing trust and fostering more effective knowledge exchanges between individuals and groups of individuals. It isn't necessarily geographic separation that creates distance; it is any process or structure that inhibits regular interaction with individuals who could learn from one another. All else being equal, the greater the distance—whether it is geographic, temporal, or functional/expertise—the greater the need to pay attention to how knowledge is transferred from one locality to another.

MANAGING KNOWLEDGE ACROSS BORDERS[1]

Designing a global knowledge management system that will achieve 100 percent knowledge transfer in all key areas of the organization is essentially impossible. Cultural barriers hinder the ability of an organization to achieve 100 percent efficiency when leveraging its existing knowledge resources. The objective should be to devise a system that can support and enhance the ability of the organization to achieve knowledge transfer around key strategic objectives. Understanding how the organization is approaching its global strategy leads to an understanding of what knowledge is most important to transmit and in what direction. This understanding is critical to shaping a system that will support organizational objectives and help in value realization and goal attainment.

Through lowered trade barriers, better technology, and exchange rate advantages, companies are able to reach across national boundaries in order to gain market share. With more companies entering foreign markets, simply establishing a subsidiary overseas modeled as an extension of the parent company is no longer satisfactory. Competitive advantage, in many cases, can only be maintained by the ability to establish foreign subsidiaries that are structured and managed in a manner appropriate to the market opportunity. Managing knowledge exchange across borders is a critical element to enabling an effective and coordinated global enterprise. Bartlett and Ghoshal (1989) described four organizational design strategies for competing in business endeavors across borders. Organizations can choose to pursue one or more of these strategies; each calls for different priorities and strategies for facilitating global knowledge sharing. See Table 8.4 for a summary of organizational design strategies for global enterprises.

A *multinational strategy* is one in which foreign subsidiaries run nearly autonomously. In this model, the parent or holding company is run as a loose federation. Subsidiaries set their own operating standards, have their own local brand recognition, and have a heavy hand in determining their own targets while the parent or holding company simply manages the profits or suffers the losses. Running autonomously enables subsidiaries to quickly respond to changes in local markets creating a first

Table 8.4. Design Strategies for Global Organizations		
Name	**Description**	**Strengths and Weaknesses**
Multinational	Subsidiaries are nearly autonomous, with control over decisions regarding their operations.	• Flexible and responsive because strategies and tactics are determined locally, where the actual work is being done • Difficulty in realizing efficiencies like shared administrative services, when each part of the organization is run differently
Global	The actions of the subsidiaries are heavily regulated and controlled by the headquarters or home office.	• Competitive advantage created through reputation and global brand strategy; economies of scale realized • Limited ability to respond to local market conditions
International	Subsidiary organizations take on core brand identity and are expected to adapt to meet local needs.	• Competitive advantage is created through reputation and flexibility is achieved through tailored delivery • Difficulty in balancing and prioritizing global and local objectives
Transnational	The identity of the parent company is defined by the activities of all the local subsidiaries.	• Ensures local flexibility while exploiting global efficiencies and diffusion of innovation • Difficulty in leveraging the activities of the local subsidiaries

mover competitive advantage. That flexibility, however, comes at a cost of efficiencies of scale that might otherwise be achieved by forcing subsidiaries to adopt global operating standards. It is hard to realize efficiencies like shared administrative services when each part of the organization is run differently. Private equity firms, for instance, may buy local business operations that are engaged in a specific core competency. The parent company supplies capital and some managerial support, but ultimately wants the business to develop as its own autonomous entity, possibly with an eye toward a later resale. If the private equity firm decided to standardize the branding or operational philosophy of its subsidiaries, they may lose their identity and appeal, reducing their customer base. This would offset any gains in operational efficiency that standardization would bring.

For a firm pursuing a multinational strategy, knowledge sharing occurs most frequently at the local level. The ability to facilitate knowledge transfer across normal business, national, or cultural boundaries may not be as important as intensifying collaboration within a single operating unit embedded within a single local geography. As the parent company is relatively hands-off in decision making, its need for transparency into the regional operations is limited and its need to transmit information across national boundaries will be narrow in scope. This type of business model employs a regionally commissioned and locally executed model for decision making. Therefore, strategy and tactics are determined at a local level of the company that is much closer geographically from where the actual work is being done. An effort should be made to provide exposure to the parent company about the regional efforts, but in summary format. An appropriate knowledge management system for this organizational strategy will focus on helping local employees find locally held intellectual property, capture and codify local innovations and will not focus on ensuring ease of knowledge flow and collaboration between local business units. Systems should be built using local languages and catering to local cultural norms and business processes to ensure maximum level of comfort and collaboration at the local level.

A *global strategy* is one in which the actions of the subsidiaries are heavily regulated and controlled by the headquarters or home office. This approach ensures achieving global efficiency through economies of scale and standards of service regardless of local conditions. Competitive advantage is created by the promotion of a reputation for the particular quality of service or product offered or a global brand strategy. It undermines the ability to respond to local market conditions, but relies on brand recognition and product standards to influence local buying habits. McDonald's restaurants are an example of this strategy. The fast food retailer's success relies heavily on consistency of experience for the customer, regardless of where the individual restraint is located.

For McDonald's, control of all aspects of the company's operations is critical. Key knowledge is assembled, refined and maintained almost exclusively at the parent level. Although there will be diversification at the local level to address local regulatory issues, sourcing concerns, and pricing differences, there is little room or need for local innovation. In fact, local innovation erodes the principle strategic objective of McDonald's products, namely global consistency. There is a strong need for local subsidiaries to understand the information and instructions they are being provided and to respond with only the specific information that is requested. Knowledge management strategies should focus on supporting a headquarters-commissioned and executed model of decision making, reducing barriers of the subsidiaries to understand the knowledge transfers of the parent company. Although knowledge management systems should have feedback channels, this type of system should focus heavily on the ability of the subsidiaries to receive timely knowledge and to understand its application in the organization. The knowledge management system employs either a dedicated team of translators or local geography to ensure that complete meaning is conveyed. Further, requirements for collaboration between local operations will be minimal as the flow of information is routed more exclusively to and from the parent organization.

An *international strategy* exploits a core knowledge base or set of processes defined by the parent organization. Subsidiary organizations receive these core elements and are expected to adapt them to meet local needs. In this strategy, the parent company holds key intellectual property or brand presence, but sales depend on the ability of subsidiaries to adapt these core elements for local conditions or interests. Competitive advantage is achieved through the balance of maintaining a strong core brand identity and locally tailored delivery or distribution of the product. Ernst & Young and other consulting firms rely on this model to deliver the quality of thought leadership that their name represents, applied and adapted to local conditions in each country where they operate.

Similar to the example of McDonald's, the knowledge management system for an international consulting firm must focus on information flows that support headquarters-commissioned and regionally executed strategies. This system, however, also needs to have strong support for elements of the strategy that are adapted at the regional level and for collaboration between local operations. For a professional services company such as Ernst & Young, sharing expertise, lessons learned and even work assignments between business units in different countries will often increase performance across the organization. This is a hybrid model where a strong focus on reception and understanding of headquarters-generated messaging must feed into environments that facilitate both intense local collaboration and work processes that facilitate collaboration with nonlocal teams. This type of system must clearly differentiate between channels for global knowledge flows and local knowledge flows and have a structure which differentiates and supports the objectives for each. Establishing this balance is often the most difficult aspect of implementing such a hybrid system. Providing employees access to too much information without helping them filter what is useful and what is simply noise for their daily work is just as debilitating for a company as not providing employees with required information. Information overload must be guarded against when opening up access to multiple sources of knowledge and expertise from the far reaches of a global organization.

A *transnational strategy* follows the notion "think globally but act locally," through dynamic interdependence between the parent and the subsidiaries. In this model, the brand identity of the parent company is composed of the activities of all the local subsidiaries. Organizations following a transnational strategy coordinate efforts, ensuring local flexibility while exploiting the benefits of global integration and efficiencies, as well as ensuring worldwide diffusion of innovation. Time Warner is an example of this model, as many global media and news companies rely on the activities at the local level to inform and improve the product being delivered throughout its worldwide distribution network.

A knowledge management system that supports this type of global strategy should be the flattest and most interconnected. Here the emphasis is on making the contributions of local business units as visible as possible. Web 2.0 and social media technologies are effective in these environments as employees look to harness and leverage the value that these unique and dispersed contributions offer. This is the best example of a "knowledge-driven company," where the knowledge contributions of those out in the field are recognized and valued as a core resource that drives the business. To that end, the structure of the knowledge management system that supports this strategy must emphasize social networking across distances and focus on multiple pathways to content discovery. Considerable effort must be made by the local participants to overcome the various language barriers involved, although motivation to do so may occur naturally.

There are three dominant strategies that organizations use when designing global knowledge management systems. These strategies describe how organizations plan and organize their knowledge management programs. Details such as who directs the knowledge management effort, how much flexibility local sites have in determining knowledge management programs, and how coordinated knowledge management efforts are across each geographic location vary depending on the strategy pursued. Each strategy maps to the global strategic postures of the organization described earlier in this chapter. See Table 8.5 for a summary of the strategies for designing knowledge management systems.

Table 8.5. Design Strategies for Knowledge Management Systems		
Name	**Description**	**Strengths and Weaknesses**
Headquarters-commissioned and executed	Headquarters is in charge of devising the knowledge management framework and implementing the program on a global basis.	• Large degree of uniformity and consistency in the processes across regions; economies of scale are secured • Local site has limited control over how knowledge management processes and technologies are used, which may impact quality of usage
Headquarters-commissioned and regionally executed	Headquarters decides on the overall framework by which knowledge is managed, and each region will then work within these constraints to tailor the KMS for local deployment.	• Achieves overall consistency while providing a degree of freedom for local sites to meet their unique needs • May not achieve full economies of scale
Regionally-commissioned and locally executed	Regional centers design the KMS from the bottom up.	• Allows for the greatest amount of customization and responsiveness in terms of building a knowledge management system that addresses local needs • Fails to achieve a connected and unified structure from a global point of view

Headquarters-commissioned and executed is the most rigid and uniform approach to global knowledge management strategies. In this model, the headquarters is in charge of devising the knowledge management framework, determining an approach, choosing appropriate processes and systems, and implementing the program on a global basis. Here, each local site has limited control over how knowledge management processes and technologies are used. This strategy aligns with the global strategy outlined by Ghoshal and Bartlett (1990). An example of this is Coca-Cola. While there might be slight modifications to meet local needs, there is a large degree of uniformity and consistency in how the product is created and sold across regions. Under this strategy, headquarters owns the responsibility for conceptualizing, designing, developing, and implementing the knowledge management. Consistency is ensured through the organization, and economies of scale are secured.

Headquarters-commissioned and regionally executed is where the headquarters remain responsible for the overall strategic direction of the knowledge management program, but a degree of flexibility is afforded to local offices that operate within a regional space. For example, the management at the centralized headquarters could choose the overall framework by which knowledge is managed, select the type of technology support that the organization will employ (e.g., a specific vendor system), and possibly instruct how knowledge should flow across localities. Each region will then work within these constraints and tailor the knowledge management system for local deployment. A region should choose the interface that is most appropriate to its users, such as a different color scheme, different knowledge organization schema, and different views of the knowledge. The benefit of this approach is that while there is overall consistency to knowledge management, geographic regions have degrees of freedom to work with in order to customize and personalize the approach to meet their unique needs. This strategy is most often used when organizations choose the international strategy discussed above.

Regionally-commissioned and locally executed is the third strategy. Here, organizations do not seek to develop a global knowledge management in a top-down fashion, as discussed in the previous two options. Rather, the organization works from the bottom up. Regional centers become the centers of activity and they decide how knowledge should be managed within their locality. For example, an organization that operates in the Middle East might arrive at a set of established practices to promote knowledge sharing among offices in Dubai, Doha, Bahrain, and Jeddah. These efforts surfaced from the recognition that local offices in a given region needed to exchange expertise on a frequent basis to operate efficiently and effectively. So, rather than create a corporate-wide effort, the regional headquarters will commission a locale-specific knowledge management effort. Each field office in the region is free to execute its strategy in a manner that achieves goals and policies set at the regional office. The regional centers act in a similar fashion to the headquarters mentioned above. They take responsibility for integrating knowledge sharing across the various local centers. They also serve as connectors to other regional centers. In this example, the Middle East regional center might agree on knowledge transfer mechanisms with the European and South East Asian regional centers. This approach allows for the greatest amount of customizing in terms of building a knowledge management system that addresses local needs. However, the primary disadvantage is that this strategy creates the loosest connected and non-unified structure from a global point of view. Knowledge management practices become quite different as one moves from one region to another. Yet, the interconnection among regional centers will determine the extent to which knowledge flows from one region to another.

All of these variations speak to the *intended* architecture of a knowledge management system. However, arriving at the most appropriate architecture requires more than evaluating the most recent strategic plan from corporate headquarters; announcing your company operations as global, multinational, or international; and then selecting a model from these choices. The contents of any corporate strategy must be validated against the real-world conditions experienced by the different locations and offices. A knowledge management system implementation often generates earnest and productive dialogue about how to resolve differences between the corporate vision and the actual practice. Therefore, it is helpful to examine how employees are actually performing work in addition to how they are organized structurally.

MANAGING KNOWLEDGE ACROSS THE EXTENDED ENTERPRISE[2]

Internal participants are not the sole contributors to a company's knowledge base. Organizations today operate in complex business networks. Consider the case of supply chain networks, as organizations depend on a collection of business partners for their raw materials, assembly of products, delivery of products to customer, and even in some cases the handling of after-sale services. Most computer equipment organizations (e.g., Dell, Hewlett Packard) do not do most of their production and delivery of products in-house. Organizations have realized that they must partner with external entities for ideas, know-how, and capabilities, and therefore a knowledge management system needs to be designed to support such partnerships.

Organizations have become highly specialized in niche areas, often focusing their capabilities on specific expertise, services, or products. Most have realized that they must develop their core capabilities and engage with business partners to supplement, expand, and apply knowledge. Often, business partnerships emerge from the need to secure raw materials and administrative resources. Innovating in isolation can be risky and costly. Out of ten research and development projects, five on average fail, three are abandoned, and two go on to become successful (Rizova, 2006). A large number of innovative ideas fail due to lack of market orientation, such as with poorly engineered products that do not address customer needs. Companies usually have strong incentives to be overly innovative in new product development; however, continual launches of new products and line extensions add complexity throughout a company's operations, and as the costs of managing that complexity multiply, margins shrink. If a company creates a sustainable competitive advantage through its relationships with business partners, then its knowledge management systems need to clearly identify which knowledge should and should not be shared freely with partners.

Interorganizational collaboration in the form of strategic alliances is one of the more common strategies for tapping into external sources of innovation. There are many challenges to this process, but by considering the organizations involved, including the type of project and the ways to integrate knowledge between and within organizations, the chances of success can be maximized. One of the main motivations for these innovation-focused alliances is the quest for new knowledge and learning. When two organizations are already competitively strong, one or both parties may want to acquire critical knowledge while maintaining their own capabilities (Doz and Hamel, 1997; Kogut and Zander, 1992). Alliances enable a company to intercept the technology of another company and to close skill gaps faster than internal development would allow (Karim and Mitchell, 2004). Alliances also foster intense interaction, and that collaboration enables the transfer of tacit knowledge between members.

The key issues when managing knowledge within the extended enterprise include developing standards, balancing knowledge sharing with protection of intellectual property, and the establishment of a trust relationship between organizations with separate goals and objectives. The development of standards is critical for getting organizations to collaborate and share knowledge effectively. The simplest form of a standard is a document and naming convention for electronic files. Unless these are adhered to, the knowledge shared between organizations will easily be misplaced, misunderstood, or simply excluded from the appropriate circulation. The development of standards can be top-down, but often, extended enterprise configurations emerge because they recognize similar standards and work processes across organizational boundaries. Both the establishment of standards for knowledge sharing and processes to govern appropriate boundaries around what knowledge is shared is critical for enabling a zone of trust between organizations engaged in knowledge exchange. This trust is an important phenomenon for the progress of corporate culture. Realized efficiencies and significant productivity gains can be realized by an increased cooperation and knowledge sharing between organizations operating in the same vertical market.

Knowledge Integration across the Extended Enterprise: Wipro

When Wipro, a global software development firm based in India, set out to create a knowledge management program, it started by interviewing its top management about the business problems that the company was facing (Chatzkel, 2004). It asked which of these problems might be successfully addressed by better access to knowledge and information. Using existing business problems as the basis for the direction of your knowledge management program provides several lasting advantages. First, it provides a clear scope for the program. Second, it enables business leadership not familiar with knowledge management theory or techniques the chance to understand the value proposition in terms that are familiar to them. Third, if the business problems are well understood, the costs of the problems and benefits of the solutions are well understood providing a solid basis for program metrics. Lastly, the success of addressing known business problems is the fastest way to spreading buy-in to your program. Knowledge management is not a magic bullet, it is not a religion, and it is not a new way of doing business. In fact, knowledge management teaches us to do very little that is not already documented as best practice in business—lessons learned, mentoring, and careful documentation. It does, however, pull many of these techniques together in a way that can provide a legitimate business advantage. The key is to focus on how the acquisition and use of knowledge and information can address business problems and increase business performance. Knowledge management initiatives should always start and end by trying to solve real, defined business problems.

Too often, corporations approach knowledge sharing opportunities like a financial transaction or as a zero sum game. However, knowledge is a currency of a slightly different character in that it can be utilized by two organizations at the same time, as discussed in Chapter 2. Sharing ideas across organizations participating in the same value chain has the potential to drive innovation and increase productivity for all participants from start to finish. Exploring the ground rules for knowledge management system collaboration spaces and content sharing possibilities with partner organizations is an important activity in knowledge management system design.

FROM LOCAL TO GLOBAL: SYSTEMS OF KNOWLEDGE

Regardless of the structure of a global knowledge management system and the composition of the system's management team, there are certain common issues that can create further barriers to a well-designed and well-executed knowledge management program. Management of these issues requires the human component of the system be equipped with a relatively high degree of emotional intelligence. Within organizations, emotional intelligence is considered to be the ability to perceive and manage the impact of varying contexts and emerging technologies on cultural dynamics such as trust.

Understanding local cultures refers to understanding the differences between one locality and another including why differences exist. Once you have acquired knowledge on the local cultures through experience or by learning from others, then it is possible to integrate and build bridges across the localities. Neglecting the need to understand and appreciate different cultures can risk building a greater divide between two cultures. Understanding local cultures, whether it is the culture of a profession or a geographic location, is paramount to understanding the following:

1. The incentive structure that will motivate individuals to engage in knowledge sharing
2. Mechanisms that are already in place to promote knowledge sharing
3. The structure in place that governs how knowledge is created, stored, and applied

It is through appreciation of these three aspects of local knowledge management that one can begin to see what is common, and consequently what might be different, across various cultures. Occasionally it is discovered that few differences exist across the local cultures, and what has prevented knowledge sharing are issues such as a lack of trust. Hence, there is no need for the redesign of a global knowledge management system but an equally challenging proposition exists regarding how to build trust.

Understanding local cultures is done by observing, interviewing individuals, and in some cases even bringing people from the local cultures onto the knowledge management team. Individuals from the knowledge management team can embed themselves into the local cultures and seek to understand how work is performed, the knowledge flows and the informal structure of the organizations, and the accepted values and norms of the culture. Observations have the advantage of discovering knowledge that was not originally intended. Latent and emergent findings can reveal very important information for building an adequate global knowledge management system. However, the more data collected the longer it takes to analyze which can cause a shift from the original goals. Observations are expensive and take time when compared to gathering data from interviews. Interviews have the advantage of being focused and cost-effective. Yet data collected from an interview is only as good as the questions being asked and the information elicitation methods. Interviews can range from being highly structured to being unstructured. The critical challenge when interviewing people in order to understand local cultures is that the individuals will not be able to articulate the nuances of knowledge management. Much knowledge we possess about culture is tacit knowledge and is difficult to share with others.

The most common approach to bring about cultural awareness is to enroll individuals from the local cultures on the knowledge management team. This is done through the creation of cross-regional teams or global task forces. Each of the local cultures will receive representation on the team and have the opportunity to contribute. Hence, choosing the right individual to represent the local culture becomes very important. The individual chosen should not only be respected by the local members, but also have the necessary skills and capabilities to communicate on behalf of the locals. Many times, the right individual might not be one who has a formal position of authority, but rather one who has a central place in the informal network. Understanding local cultures and the methods employed by organizations to gain this cultural knowledge must be done as a first step to building a global knowledge management program.

One of the most difficult challenges to overcome when bringing individuals from different communities together is creating trust between different groups and cultures. Without ensuring that individuals from each group trust individuals in other groups, one cannot expect to see individuals engage in dialogue and collaborative work. Trust is one of the most studied concepts in the social sciences. At the most basic level, two forms of trust exist. The first kind is trust in the whole individual. For example, this is reflected when someone declares that they trust another person, friend, or family member. The trust we place in others allows us to believe in the knowledge they share. The second kind of trust is the trust we place in the abilities of individuals. Here, we do not necessarily know enough to make a holistic judgment on the individual. We instead focus on the skills, expertise, and knowledge that the individual holds. For example, many people implicitly trust teachers, doctors, lawyers, and accountants. Because of our inability to accurately judge and make decisions on the knowledge they provide us, we have to rely on an established base of trust. While these two kinds of trust are not comprehensive, they do accurately illustrate the two kinds of trust organizations need to understand which will exist between people in knowledge sharing activities.

When trying to connect localities into a global world, we most often are trying to transfer knowledge from one locality that is desired by other localities, and possibly by the whole organization. Hence, it becomes important that once localities are connected, knowledge flows are encouraged. This requires individuals to learn to trust the ability of those whom they transfer knowledge to and receive knowledge from. It is important to appreciate that the individuals from other foreign locations are competent in (1) producing knowledge, (2) consuming knowledge that is provided to them, (3) storing knowledge and securing its value, and (4) sharing knowledge. This means trusting their knowledge management abilities and relying on them. Too often, due to proximity and long histories of prior collaboration, individuals default to reliance on those who are close to them, and seldom look to others who may be at a distance, either at a functional distance or geographically. Trust is often formed when organizations are small and newly formed, such as the trust between two entrepreneurs creating a new business. This trust helps them collaborate, rely on each other's skills and expertise, and create a successful organization. As individuals are hired in the organization, and the organization grows, trust in both ability and skills becomes more common and over time it is this kind of trust that permeates the organization. Individuals are hired because they are trustworthy, and individuals are promoted to positions because they are seen as trustworthy.

Trust is important when consuming and contributing knowledge to other individuals. This is especially true when individuals do not have prior experience working with each other. When individuals from two communities have not worked together in the past, trust will be absent; over time, and through positive experiences, trust will emerge and become stronger. Early on, it is important to acknowledge the absence of trust and build explicit processes to create trust. Often building a process for early resolution of issues that arise during knowledge transfer begins the formation of trust between individuals. For example, if there is a delay in one unit providing knowledge to another, this might be because of a misunderstanding in how the other group perceived the urgency of the request and not because they lack expertise or knowledge and should be mistrusted. Creating avenues where dialogue can occur during the initial periods of knowledge transfer is important. Therefore good communication mechanisms need to be in place to resolve issues, especially early on in knowledge management endeavors. In the case where groups have worked together in the past, and an environment of mistrust exists, the challenge becomes more difficult. Managers must find a way for the individuals involved from each community to give the other a fair chance and move on from previous events. It is important to acknowledge a difficult past, and then describe how the new knowledge processes will address any outstanding issues.

Knowledge is context sensitive, which implies it requires context to create meaning for others. Sharing knowledge is not as simple as sharing information (Szulanski, 1996). The integrity of information can be preserved quite adequately when it is shared from one location to another. However, knowledge does not operate under the same principle. As discussed in Chapter 2 and earlier in this chapter, translating content between languages may cause the meaning to be lost. The greater the distance between the two communities, the greater the chance that context might distort knowledge as it moves from one setting to another. In building global knowledge management systems, it is important to take active steps to preserve the context of knowledge as it moves between localities.

Today, most knowledge management programs are enhanced by technology. Therefore, it becomes very important to understand the differences in the technological infrastructures found across different locations that will utilize a knowledge management system. If there are variations in the technology infrastructure across localities, the access to valuable knowledge may be uneven, and variations occur often with systems that span multiple countries. Therefore, it is critical to ensure that the effects of variations upon the technical infrastructure are understood.

Organizations will normally choose one of two modes to address discrepancies in technology infrastructure. The first is to build a system that satisfies the lowest common denominator. Here, the focus is to build a system that everyone can access and use with ease. The locality with the least sophisticated technology infrastructure is used as the standard on which the global knowledge management system is built. The advantage created is that everyone has access to a uniform set of resources, and is assured access without inconvenience. The obvious disadvantage is those with more sophisticated technology capabilities could perceive the system as immediately out-of-date or tedious to use. Another strategy is to build a system that can be used in a range of environments without much loss of functionality in any environment. For example, it is possible to access Google's Gmail using its standard interface, or choose a more basic HTML version. The basic HTML version has less functionality, but still allows for the essential functions of reading and responding to email. Not only does having these options benefit those who have no choice but also to use Gmail on low bandwidth, but it also benefits mobile workers who access Gmail on telecommunication infrastructures of varying sophistication. Most websites provide the option to view content in basic HTML format, which is ideal in locations where limited and under-developed technology infrastructures exist. The benefit of such a strategy is individuals are not disadvantaged by a system that does not fully exploit these resources. A system can provide videos, images, audio files, a social networking tool, chat rooms and discussion forums, and sophisticated graphics, but not limit access to a certain group of users. Those who have advanced technology resources can take full advantage of all of the features of the system. A drawback of this strategy is that it does not build a truly "global" system; there are still divides and differences among the localities. This can serve as a temporary strategy while upgrading the technological resources of the localities.

CONCLUSION

Many of the first generation knowledge management systems failed due to the significant number of factors that must be taken into consideration for the successful deployment of a system that serves both global and local needs of a multinational corporation. The basic questions addressed when creating a knowledge management system include where knowledge originates from, who will possess important knowledge, how knowledge is stored and shared within the organization, and how knowledge will be used. The questions can have multiple answers based on the many cultures and localities served by the organization. Economic, political, and technological changes in the global infrastructure create a multifaceted, dynamic environment that influences how knowledge management systems are designed and implemented.

As global companies develop an appreciation of how knowledge should flow to improve decision making and accelerate key business processes, they recognize that the design of a KMS must account for employees' existing work processes, and their cultural norms and psychological differences, not to mention the geographical distances that separate them.

Global factors cause the requirements for a knowledge management system to be quite diverse. The ability to assemble elements from an organization's strategic plan, its varied IT infrastructure and operations processes, its cultural characteristics, occupational tendencies, and personal preferences is essential for success. The knowledge gained from learning about and participating in a global context should be translated into requirements for a system that facilitates collaboration and knowledge activities across the organization.

Recap: The Major Points for Knowledge Managers to Consider When Building Global Knowledge Management Systems

1. As businesses look globally and adjust their strategies to tackle global issues, knowledge strategies must follow suit to take advantages of the opportunities a global economy presents.
2. A fundamental challenge in communicating knowledge is overcoming language barriers, which may require intermediaries or technological solutions.
3. Many external factors, commonly referred to as flatteners, can impact a global organization. They may be social, economic, political, or technological.
4. Globalization adds a new dimension to the notion of culture: the national culture that may be experienced as an organization begins operations in a country different than its own.
5. Geographical distance can be overcome easily by technology when transferring explicit knowledge. However, the transfer of tacit knowledge requires more specialization, networking, and personal connections that may require a knowledge manager to go beyond technical solutions and attempt to bridge distances through new, creative means.
6. As an organization's strategy becomes more global, so must the knowledge management strategy. Considerations for acquiring global knowledge from local communities and individuals, the transfer of knowledge across many geographical and cultural boundaries, and the use of knowledge by a heterogeneous set of people must all be factored in to the goals and objectives of the strategy.
7. Many times a global knowledge management system can span boundaries and increase knowledge flows across vast distances, but the need to keep this system flexible, adaptable and easily maintained becomes very significant.
8. Creating trust across a globalized firm is a challenge that is often not spoken of, as it can be extremely challenging to have employees working at a distance to create a trusting community that supports knowledge work.
9. Deciding on the balance between the locus of control, whether situating decision-making authority with the head office or distributing it to local offices, will impact the knowledge strategy and utilization within the firm.
10. The one constant in a global environment is change, and any knowledge management strategy, project, and manager must be able to adapt to an unpredictable, dynamic world.

DISCUSSION QUESTIONS

1. The global flatteners that encourage the globalization of markets can create many threats for organizations. However, they present many opportunities as well. What opportunities can these forces create for an organization that is building a knowledge management system to connect offices in different countries around the

globe? How can these flatteners contribute towards an organization's knowledge management practices?

2. Organizations operating in a global environment interact with many different cultures on a daily basis. What challenges does a heterogeneous group of cultures present for an organization's knowledge management activities? What challenges does it present for its design and implementation of a knowledge management system?

3. An organizational culture can have profound effects on how an organization operates or what strategies it can pursue. Can an organizational culture be changed or adapted to new strategies that require different attitudes and beliefs towards knowledge activities and utilization? What is required to change an organizational culture?

4. One of the most significant challenges to a global knowledge management strategy is the geographic separation between offices. What methods and technologies can an organization use to not only bridge the distance between people, but also build the relationships needed to facilitate knowledge sharing among individuals and groups?

5. Why would a multinational organization coordinate knowledge-sharing activities at the head office and disseminate all policies and technology from that central location? Conversely, when would it be appropriate for the head office to relinquish control of knowledge management processes and procedures to local offices?

6. Consider a global knowledge management system that operates in many different countries which have few political similarities. What aspects of designing the system should be considered to ensure the system meets the employees' needs, complies with all local laws and regulations, and suits the local marketplace? Are there areas of design that cannot be standardized due to the uniqueness of many countries?

7. Outline the different strategies that are available to an organization implementing a global knowledge management system. What are the advantages and disadvantages to utilizing each strategy? Provide an example where each strategy would be most appropriate.

NOTES

1. The following section draws heavily on Desouza, K. C., and J. R. Evaristo. 2003. "Global Knowledge Management Strategies." *European Management Journal* 21, no. 1: 62–67.

2. The following section draws from Baloh, P., S. Jha, K. C. Desouza, J. Y. Kim, Y. Awazu, and C. Dombrowski. 2006. "Building Partnerships for Innovation." Technical Report, Institute for Innovation in Information Management, The Information School, University of Washington.

REFERENCES

Baily, M. N., and D. J. Elliott. 2009. "The U.S. Financial and Economic Crisis: Where Does It Stand and Where Do We Go From Here?" Brookings Institution. June 15. http://www .brookings.edu/papers/2009/0615_economic_crisis_baily_elliott.aspx.

Baloh, P., S. Jha, K. C. Desouza, J. Y. Kim, Y. Awazu, and C. Dombrowski. 2006. "Building Partnerships for Innovation." Technical Report, Institute for Innovation in Information Management, The Information School, University of Washington.

Bartlett, C. A., and S. Ghoshal. 1989. *Managing Across Borders: The Transnational Solution.* Boston: Harvard Business School Press.

Barzilai-Nahon, K., and R. M. Mason. 2010. "How Executives Perceive the Net Generation." *Information, Communication & Society* 13, no. 3: 396–418.

Bourdieu, P., and J. C. Passeron. 1973. "Cultural Reproduction and Social Reproduction." In *Knowledge, Education and Cultural Change. Papers in the Sociology of Education,* edited by Richard K Brown. London: Tavistock.

Bourdieu, P., and J. C. Passeron. 1990. *Reproduction in Education, Society and Culture.* London, Newbury Park, CA: Sage Publications.

Bylin, K. 2009. "The Digital Natives: A Generation of Broken Robots (Part One)." HypeBot.com, February. http://www.hypebot.com/hypebot/2009/02/the-digital-natives-a-generation-of-broken-robots-part-one-of-five.html.

Chatzkel, J. 2004. "Establishing a Global KM initiative: The Wipro story." *Journal of Knowledge Management* 8, no. 2: 6-18.

Choo, C. W., C. Furness, S. Paquette, H. van den Berg, B. Detlor, P. Bergeron, et al. 2006. "Working with Information: Information Management and Culture in a Professional Services Organization." *Journal of Information Science* 32, no. 6: 491–510.

Cook, S. D., and D. Yanow. 1993. "Culture and Organizational Learning." *Journal of Management Inquiry* 2, no. 4: 373–390.

Daft, R. L., and R. H. Lengel. 1986. "Organizational Information Requirements, Media Richness and Structural Design." *Management Science* 32, no. 5: 554–571.

Daft, R. L., and J. Wiginton. 1979. "Language and Organization." *Academy of Management Review* 4, no. 2: 179–191.

Desouza, K. C. 2005. "Mind Your Language." *IET Engineering Management* 47(October/November).

Desouza, K. C., and Y. Awazu. 2006. "Integrating Local Knowledge Strategies." *KM Review* 9, no. 4: 20–23.

Desouza, K. C., and J. R. Evaristo. 2003. "Global Knowledge Management Strategies." *European Management Journal* 21, no. 1: 62–67.

Desouza, K. C., and J. R. Evaristo. 2004. "Managing Knowledge in Distributed Projects." *Communications of the ACM* 47, no. 4: 87–91.

Desouza, K. C., and J. R. Evaristo. 2006. "Project Management Offices: A Case of Knowledge-Based Archetypes." *International Journal of Information Management* (October 1): 414.

Desouza, K. C., and T. Hensgen. 2003. "Every Citizen a Missile: The Need for an Emergent Systems Approach for Law Enforcement." *Government Information Quarterly* 20, no. 3: 259–280.

Doz, Y., and G. Hamel. 1997. "The Use of Alliances in Implementing Technology Strategies." In *Managing Strategic Innovation and Change,* edited by M. L. Tushman and P. Anderson, 556–580. New York: Oxford University Press.

Dugger, Celia W. 2009. "South Africa Is Seen to Lag in H.I.V. Fight." *New York Times,* July 19. http://www.nytimes.com/2009/07/20/world/africa/20circumcision.html?scp=3&sq=kwazulu-natal&st=cse.

The Economist. 2008. "Cracks in the Crust." Economist.com, December 11. http://www.economist.com/node/12762027?story_id=12762027.

Evaristo, J. R., and P. Fenema. 1999. "A Typology of Project Management: Emergence and Evolution of New Forms." *International Journal of Project Management* 17, no. 5: 275–281.

Evaristo, J. R., R. Scudder, K. C. Desouza, and O. Sato. 2004. "A Dimensional Analysis of Geographically Distributed Project Teams: A Case Study." *Journal of Engineering and Technology Management* 21, no. 3: 175–189.

Florida, R. L. 2008. *Who's Your City?: How the Creative Economy Is Making Where to Live the Most Important Decision of Your Life*. New York: Basic Books.

France24. 2009. "South Africa Hit by Recession for the First Time in 17 Years." France24.com, May 26. http://www.france24.com/en/20090526-south-africa-hit-recession-first-time-17-years-gdp-economic-crisis.

Friedman, T. 2007. *The World Is Flat: A Brief History of The Twenty-First Century*. 1st Picador ed. (further updated and expanded). New York: Picador/Farrar, Straus and Giroux.

Gallupe, B. 2001. "Knowledge Management Systems: Surveying the Landscape." *International Journal of Management Reviews* 3, no. 1: 61–77.

Geertz, C. 1973. *The Interpretation of Cultures*. New York: Basic Books.

Ghemawat, P. 2007. *Redefining Global Strategy: Crossing Borders in a World Where Differences Still Matter*. Boston: Harvard Business School Press.

Ghoshal, Sumantra, and Christopher A. Bartlett. 1990. "The Multinational Corporation as an Interorganizational Network." *The Academy of Management Review* 15, no. 4: 603–625.

Haugen, B. 2005. "The Impact of Globalization on Law Libraries." *International Journal of Legal Information* 33, no. 3. http://scholarship.law.cornell.edu/ijli/vol33/iss3/8.

HM Treasury, Bank of England and Financial Services Authority. 2007. "News Release: Liquidity Support Facility for Northern Rock Plc." September 14.

Hofstede, G. 2001. *Culture's Consequences: Comparing Values, Behaviors, Institutions, and Organizations Across Nations*. 2nd Edition. Thousand Oaks, CA: Sage Publications.

ipl2 Consortium. 2011. "ipl2: Information You Can Trust." ipl2.org. Accessed March 15. http://www.ipl.org/div/about/mission_and_vision.html.

Jarvenpaa, S., and D. Leidner. 1998. "Communication and Trust in Global Virtual Teams." *Journal of Computer-Mediated Communication and Organizational Science* 14: 29–64.

Karim, S., and W. Mitchell. 2004. "Innovating through Acquisition and Internal Development: A Quarter-Century of Boundary Evolution at Johnson & Johnson." *Long Range Planning* 37, no. 6: 525–547.

Kingsbury, A. 2006. "The World Is Not Flat." *U.S. News & World Report*, September 10. http://www.usnews.com/usnews/news/articles/060910/18qa.htm.

Kogut, B., and U. Zander. 1992. "Knowledge of the Firm, Combinative Capabilities, and the Replication of Technology." *Organization Science: A Journal of the Institute of Management Sciences* 3, no. 3: 383–397.

Msinga Municipality. 2011. "Msinga Municipality: IDP Phase 3." Msinga Municipality. Accessed March 16. http://www.msinga.org/msinga_municipality_IDP_sector_plans.htm.

Paik, Yongsun, and D. Choi. 2005. "The Shortcomings of a Standardized Global Knowledge Management System: The Case Study of Accenture." *The Academy of Management Executive* 19, no. 2: 81–84.

Paquette, S., and L. Moffat. 2005. "Corporate Portals for Supply Chain Collaboration." *Journal of Internet Commerce* 4, no. 3: 69–94.

Parr, B. 2009. "Iran Election Crisis: 10 Incredible YouTube Videos." Mashable.com, June. http://mashable.com/2009/06/20/iran-youtube/.

Pastore, E. 2009. *The Future of Museums and Libraries: A Discussion Guide* (IMLS-2009-RES-02). Institute of Museum and Library Services, Washington, D.C.

Peirce Edition Project. 1982–2010. *Writings of Charles S. Peirce: A Chronological Edition*. Vols. I–VIII. Bloomington, IN: Indiana University Press.

Rizova, P. 2006. "Are You Networked for Successful Innovation?" *MIT Sloan Management Review* 47, no. 3: 49.

Ruppel, C. P., and S. J. Harrington. 2001. "Sharing Knowledge Through Intranets: A Study of Organizational Culture and Intranet Implementation." *IEEE Transactions on Professional Communication* 44, no. 1: 37–52.

Saussure, F. D. 1916. *Course in General Linguistics*. New York: McGraw Hill.

Schein, E. H. 1991. "What Is Culture." In *Reframing Organizational Culture*, edited by P. J. Frost, L. F. Moore, M. Reis Louis, C. C. Lundberg, and J. Martin, 243–253. Newbury Park, CA: Sage Publications.

Schein, E H. 2004. *Organizational Culture and Leadership*. 3rd ed. San Francisco: Jossey-Bass.

Shah, A. 2008. "Global Food Crisis 2008." Global Issues. August 10. http://www.globalissues .org/article/758/global-food-crisis-2008.

Szulanski, G. 1996. "Exploring Internal Stickiness: Impediments to the Transfer of Best-practice within the Firm." *Strategic Management Journal* 17 (Winter Special): 27–43.

Tonta, Y. 2008. "Libraries and Museums in the Flat World: Are They Becoming Virtual Destinations?" *Library Collections, Acquisitions, & Technical Services* 32, no. 1: 1–9.

Turner, J. R. 1993. *The Handbook of Project-Based Management*. Maidenhead, Berkshire, England: McGraw Hill.

Building the Business Case for Knowledge Management

Kevin C. Desouza

OBJECTIVES

- Explore the challenging issue of building a business case for knowledge management.
- Present guidelines for creating a business case.
- Discuss the importance of resource allocation for knowledge management efforts.
- Understand the role of the organization's strategy goals, objectives, and key performance indicators in the business case.

INTRODUCTION[1]

In the preceding chapters, we explored the details and intricacies of the major concepts that create the foundation for knowledge management. However, understanding these concepts is only the initial step to establishing an organizational knowledge management initiative. Why? Simply put, *resources* are needed in order to invest in knowledge management. Whether it is discretionary resources to acquire a new system for knowledge discovery or a budget to buy items, such as a gift cards, to be used as incentives to promote knowledge sharing between employees, it is important to note that access to resources can make or break a knowledge management effort. Not all resources are of a monetary nature. Many times, the most valuable resource required is attention. Employee attention to the knowledge management activities is also important for success. Employee attention begins with capturing the attention of senior executives, who then give their attention to the projects in which they invest significant *resources* under their control. Therefore, securing resources for knowledge management is a critical success factor for any KM project.

Unfortunately, few knowledge managers know how to write business cases that attract the necessary resources for their knowledge management efforts. A **business case** is a cohesive and well-evidenced argument of why someone should invest in a project. Business cases are strategic artifacts aimed to sell internal and/or external stakeholders on the merits of a project. Upon reading a business case, one should have a clear strategic understanding of the project and its value proposition, confidence in the project team, assurance that the budget for the project is reasonable, and awareness that the high-level project plan is sound. Based on our consulting experience, out of every 20 business cases for a knowledge management–related effort, about one is funded at the level requested, up to three are funded at 30 percent below what was requested (or lower), and the rest are not funded at all. Three reasons for this must be acknowledged upfront.

The first and most important reason for the poor success rate is that organizations, just like individuals, have almost unlimited desires, but limited resources that can be used to satisfy these wishes. This problem of resource scarcity means that organizations do not have unlimited resources (such as capital, or even more intangible resources, like managerial attention), so all needs will not be met. Because the scarcity problem is critical, an organization considering a business case for investing in a knowledge management initiative will evaluate such a request against all other cases requesting funding or people. Too often, knowledge management business cases do not acknowledge and account for this reality, and therefore do not not receive executive approval.

The second reason for a poor KM success rate is that proposed knowledge management efforts fail to include cogent analysis and justification of the expected returns and risks. Investment in knowledge management should provide returns that are more than, or the very least, equal to, the returns you would earn from other capital investments in order to appear attractive to investors. Further, investors are often seeking to minimize risks. Therefore, why should an organization invest in a perceived risk-laden effort such as knowledge management? The hope of securing a better rate of return is one common justification. In an organizational context, return on investment is compared across projects that are candidates for investments. Business cases that demonstrate returns that are worthy of the effort and present convincing arguments on why the return will guide the organization toward its future objectives have higher chances of being funded. However, simply claiming a high return is not sufficient for a knowledge management case to be competitive. The business case must provide sufficient evidence to demonstrate that achieving the projected returns is reasonable. Managers of knowledge projects acknowledge that making the case for a knowledge management effort and calculating return on investments is not straightforward as compared to making the business case for a new piece of manufacturing equipment or the management of other tangible assets. Investing in a piece of new machinery can be directly tied to increases in product quality and/or quantity through multiple metrics (e.g., lower defect rates or more finished products per hour). Calculating the payoffs for investments in knowledge management efforts is not as easy, and direct effects are difficult if not impossible to measure. Knowledge management efforts lead to changes in behaviors, approaches, and methods that on their own may not have direct bottom-line impacts. However, when these are mapped and traced to organizational processes, the impacts can be measured and articulated. Significant effort, ability, and creativity are often required to identify these indirect impacts and calculate their effectiveness. The effort to measure and quantify the impacts is further complicated by the lag time between the investments in knowledge management efforts and realizing their outcomes (i.e., in terms of financial or other forms of economic benefits).

The third important characteristic of KM programs that accounts for the low rate of investment is that these efforts often require large, organization-wide resource commitments. Consider the case of investing in initiatives such as the prevention of global warming by lowering greenhouse gas emissions or the promotion of fair trade practices. Most people agree that preventing global warming or increasing the adoption of fair trade practices benefits society. The challenge arises when the question becomes, who will take responsibility for investing and paying for these efforts? If taxes were raised to support these efforts, many citizens would not be pleased. Rational individuals often want others to bear the cost of common efforts and gladly enjoy the benefits, yet hesitate to initiate responsibility. A similar predicament faces knowledge management efforts. Departments within an organization want their peer units to invest in a common effort. Each department might see knowledge management as a task someone else should provide resources for and hence decline to spend its own resources. In some organizations, knowledge management efforts might be viewed as a tax levied on a department's resources. Departments do not want to pay this tax, yet any outcomes from the tax, such as infrastructure (e.g., a new intranet), will benefit all departments. When organizational departments expend their scarce resources on common efforts, they will be displeased if the efforts do not perform to their expectations.

The three challenges outlined here, while significant, are not insurmountable. Knowledge managers can develop strong business cases for knowledge management projects that will lead to success for an organization. In the following sections, we will discuss the components of a general business case and how they are related to a proposal for a knowledge management project or initiative. We discuss not only the quantitative financial components of a KM business case, but other qualitative arguments that can strengthen the probability that a business case for knowledge management will be accepted and supplied with adequate resources.

WHAT IS A BUSINESS CASE?

A business case represents a well-argued and logically structured document that puts forth the business rationale for investing in a course of action. Business cases are best visualized as persuasive arguments. The business case must clearly establish the following:

- The key arguments for the project
- The costs and risks of doing nothing
- A description of the proposed actions;
- How the proposed actions compare to other viable alternatives
- How the proposed actions fit with the current and future strategic goals of the organization
- The cost-benefit, risk, and financial assessments of the proposed actions
- A tentative, high-level, project plan
- A statement on how the proposed action, if implemented, would change the organization
- Expectations for results of the project

Business cases can range from formally prepared documents (20 to 200 pages) to informal persuasive arguments made in a few paragraphs. Normally, the greater the level of investment required in a project, the greater the care and time required to write the business case. Larger investments are subject to greater scrutiny before funding is provided because the impact of failure would be greater for the organization. The burden for evidence, including sound analysis of the costs, benefits, and risks of the project, increases with the level of investment. The greater the level of investment, the greater the need to guarantee not only that the principal invested in the project can be recovered, but that there is the realistic expectation of gaining additional returns in the form of financial or competitive advantage or operating efficiencies. The business case must include a detailed analysis of the financial merits of the project. The financial analysis must show how the proposed alternative compares to both doing nothing (the baseline case) and other reasonable alternatives. The financial analysis is complemented with an analysis of the cost-benefit and risk assessment of the proposed alternative.

Is a Business Case the Same as a Business Plan?

Business cases are written for undertakings within an existing organization, while, business plans are normally written to start up new business ventures. The two documents might share common elements (such as an executive summary, financial analysis, or risk assessments), but they are quite distinct. On one hand, a *business plan* is written to attract investment (normally by a venture capitalist) or loans (from financial institutions) to get a business started, or move a business from its current state to its next level of growth. A business plan contains a formal statement of the business vision, mission, goals and objectives; the market analysis of the business opportunity; a financial analysis and projection of the expected investment and returns; analysis of competitors (both current and future); industry and customer analysis; a description of the management team; and a projected growth plan. Business plans are used to guide the creation and/or renovation of an organizational entity. Business cases are written by employees within an organization to propose the organization invest in a course of action that will support the attainment of strategic goals and objectives.

When an existing organization is preparing to open a new venture, business plans and business cases can appear interchangeable. As an example, consider the case of a university that decides to open a new campus in China. Is the document prepared to propose such an initiative a business plan or a business case? It can be referred to as either, since it must have elements of a business plan including the vision and mission of the new campus, the management team who will lead the effort, and the projected financial impact. This document will be prepared by internal stakeholders of the university and must include material including how the proposed new campus fits the current mission and goals of the university, how the venture compares with other investment alternatives and priorities of the university, and the risks associated with the venture. As a general rule the goal is to start a new business venture, then the document being prepared is a business plan. If the business plan is being written within the context of an existing business, then the document should clearly outline the business case for investing in the new venture in comparison to other investment candidates.

CONSTRUCTING THE BUSINESS CASE

The goal of a business case is to put forth the best arguments possible for the course of action that will address the needs of the organization. It is important that the process used to create a business case is well executed, is methodologically sound and rigorous, and involves the necessary stakeholders. This section reviews the steps in developing a business case, highlighting key activities. The process to develop a general business case is presented first, followed by guidance specific a knowledge management business case.

No two business cases will look the same in structure, content, or size, as they will be written for a different audience. Each business case needs to be tailored to the specific project and to the audience evaluating the effort. Some organizations will provide their employees with pro forma business case templates to assist in writing a case and offer a level of standardization for cross-case comparison. A business case can be written either by one person on behalf of a team, or collaboratively by an entire team. If the team designates one person to take the lead in writing the case, it is important that the rest of the team members provide comments and input throughout the process and assist with the revisions. The advantage of having one person write the document is the consistency in writing style, tone, and language. If different individuals are working on various sections of the document, the team must ensure that there is a logical flow to the document and the writing is consistent. The benefit of collaborative writing is that different individuals have varying skills and expertise, which may make them stronger in writing various sections. For example, an individual who has expertise with accounting and finance may find it easier to present the financial assessment, whereas one who is skilled in marketing and public relations may be the best candidate to write the business opportunity and executive summary.

The Business Case for Public Libraries

In a climate of severe state and local budget cuts, libraries are in a position, more than ever, where they need to provide a clear-cut business case for their value as public institutions. In California, for example, "Gov. Jerry Brown … [is] proposing that lawmakers triage the state's fiscal hemorrhage by cutting off entire state-level programs that help keep public libraries afloat" (Goldberg, 2011). Under the threat of furloughs, downsizing of services, and outright closures, it is not enough to assert that public libraries are valuable and well-liked institutions. Instead, libraries are faced with the challenge of demonstrating their value in terms of the bottom line.

In a recent study, "the University of Pennsylvania's Fels Institute of Government adds bottom-line evidence that the return on investment in library service more than justifies the costs" (Goldberg, 2011). The study looks at how Philadelphia's public libraries help drive the city's economic engine by connecting users with information and programs that support literacy, growth of small businesses, and employment. It concludes that "the library created more than $30 million worth of economic value to the city in FY2010" (Goldberg, 2011). Further, it correlates a premium in homes values with proximity to a public library: "Researchers found that Philadelphia homes located within a quarter-mile of a branch library were worth an average of $9,630 more than homes outside that radius" (Goldberg, 2011).

The findings regarding significant areas of library usage are supported in a large-scale study of the impact of free access to the computers and the Internet in US public libraries published by the Institute of Museum and Library Services. The study illustrates how "libraries have been a silent partner in workforce development, educational achievement, health information delivery, and bringing government services to citizens" (Becker et al., 2010: 8–9).

Such evidence makes explicit the value of public libraries and provides the business case for budgetary support. Further, it provides the justification for policy changes to enhance public libraries' impact in their communities.

The following subsections present the key components of a business case for a knowledge management implementation, in the order in which they normally appear in the finished document. Please note that some elements of the business case, such as the financial analysis and the business opportunity, can be prepared concurrently.

Executive Summary

The **executive summary** is a brief and convincing statement that clearly articulates the need for the project, provides a brief project description, and projects the expected returns on the investment. The executive summary should entice the reader to continue reading the rest of the document. Be mindful that the reader may not read the entire document; therefore, the summary should convey the essence of the proposed effort. The executive summary is normally written last, since by the time the rest of the document is prepared, the project team has a clear understanding of the overall project, the intricacies of various assumptions, organizational constraints, cost-benefit and risk assessments, and key value drivers of the effort. An executive summary is normally 300 to 500 words in length.

In a knowledge management business case, these are the key elements on which to focus the reader:

- What knowledge one is proposing to manage and why
- How the knowledge is going to be managed
- What operational, tactical, or strategic gains the organization will witness due to the knowledge management project

It is important to keep the executive summary clear and concise, emphasizing the strategic objectives of the project. Two key questions to ask when writing an executive summary:

1. Does it clearly articulate how the project contributes to the strategic goals of the organization?
2. Does it clearly describe how *not* investing in the proposed effort will hamper the future growth and survivability of the organization?

Defining the Business Opportunity

What are the drivers for the proposed project? What opportunity requires this knowledge management project? What business problem will the project address? These are the key questions answered in this section; no project will be funded unless it clearly demonstrates that a business opportunity exists. In this section, the document should clearly describe the current situation facing the organization and why undertaking the proposed knowledge project is in the organization's best interest. The important point to convey is why remaining inactive is an unacceptable alternative, and this argument can be supported by the findings from the strategic assessment and the needs analysis outlined in this chapter. In writing the business opportunity, the primary objective is to build a convincing argument for readers and draw them into the case. A well-written business opportunity section helps ensure that readers stay connected with the rest of the document and retains their interest in the case.

In writing the business opportunity description for a knowledge management project, it is common practice to document the current state and the ideal state, and then illustrate why resolving the gap between the two will be beneficial for the organization—for example, one common approach to writing this section is to describe the current state of how customer knowledge is being managed, then describe the ideal state of the improvements and efficiencies will enable the organization to acquire and share customer knowledge. It is important to focus the reader on the strategic deliverables and outcomes. To use the previous example, simply writing about the merits of managing customer knowledge is not sufficient; it is essential to acknowledge the impacts of managing knowledge in terms of the changes to the organization's profitability, market standing, or industry position. The project must realize an overall incentive such as increased revenue, lower cost of operations, or strategic gains for the organization.

Strategic Assessment

A business case requires knowledge managers to conduct a strategic assessment of the business. This phase focuses on understanding the *business needs* and *opportunities*. Unless the authors clearly understands the current state of the business, its desired future state, and the trajectories that are available to reach the future state, a successful business case cannot provide adequate direction for the organization. Any knowledge management projects must clearly lead the organization toward this desired state, and they must fit with the current undertakings and future aspirations of the business. If the business case fails to make a connection to these states, readers will perceive that the effort being proposed is not in the best strategic interest of the organization or simply does not meet the current organizational needs. Conducting a strategic assessment will help determine the key problems and opportunities that are consuming the attention of senior leaders. These become important pieces of information on which to anchor the arguments presented in a business case. The key components of a Strategic Assessment are outlined in Table 9.1.

The strategic assessment needs to consider what strategic projects are currently underway in the organization. At any given time an organization may be undertaking several large and resource intensive projects. The best way to recognize these efforts is

Table 9.1. Key Components of a Strategic Assessment

Component	Description
Determine current state	• Determine current strategic initiatives/projects that are underway (projects where a high level of internal and external attention is focused).
Identify executive sponsor	• Identify executive sponsor and decision maker and understand his or her needs, concerns, and priorities.
Analyze strategic initiatives	• Analyze current and future strategic initiatives/projects from a knowledge management perspective.
Demonstrate support for strategic initiatives	• Show the value that knowledge management brings to the strategic initiatives.

by determining where a high level of internal and external attention is focused. Key executives normally lead these efforts, and they will involve major customers and market segments. These efforts are normally centered on the launch of major new initiatives, products, and services. If the business case being proposed can relate directly to other major strategic projects, the business case will more likely be successful, since the organization has already committed resources to these courses of actions and is likely to support supporting initiatives. However, the business case will have to compete with numerous other initiatives, including current projects that are also vying for similar resources and attention.

It is essential that the executive sponsor for the business case be identified in this assessment. Ultimately, funding for the business case will be at the discretion of this senior-level sponsor. Protocol may dictate to begin by talking with one's supervisor/manager/director, then continuing up the organizational hierarchy until one finds the person who has not only) budgetary control and resources to sponsor the project, but also is responsible for the work being proposed in the business case. Many times, substantial resources are spent developing the business case only to result in a well-developed document that generates no funding interest. Identifying the potential executive sponsors will help to assure that time is not wasted in the development of a case. Seek the counsel of sponsoring executives in order to identify their needs and concerns, determine who they have identified as their key stakeholders, learn what their experiences have been with related projects, and understand how a business case under development would help them. It is important to be mindful that business cases must appeal to a specific executive audience. Chances of developing an innovative product are higher if customers are involved in the development process and their needs and concerns are addressed. When developing a business case, the executive sponsor is the customer who ultimately has to buy what the business case is proposing to build.

In developing a knowledge management business case, it is important to use strategic assessment to identify the critical initiatives that the organization is currently engaged in or planning to begin. These initiatives need to be thoroughly examined from a knowledge management perspective. What will the role of knowledge management be in these efforts? For example, is knowledge being underutilized or misappropriated in the current initiatives? Is the organization unprepared to exploit the current knowledge base for innovation and new product development? If the company is planning to enter foreign markets, are there adequate protocols to facilitate knowledge transfer? These are just a few of the questions that one will need to think through from a strategic perspective.

Knowledge management efforts should *support* and *facilitate* ongoing strategic initiatives. Hence, it is very important that a proposed knowledge management effort be tied to these initiatives in as direct a manner as possible. Normally, any strategic initiative will have a number of tactical and operational objectives. The knowledge management efforts should be tied to these objectives. For example, if the strategic effort is to "build industry leading products," it may be translated into objectives such as "increasing the quality of products," "increasing innovation and new product development," and "improving customer experience." The related knowledge management questions to ask: "How is knowledge about the current products being managed?" "How is knowledge about product defects and solutions being managed?" and "How is customer knowledge being utilized for innovation?" These questions tie directly into the objectives and the overall strategic goals of the organization. Showing the value that the knowledge management perspective brings to the current strategic initiatives and projects will provide an entry point to make the case for a supporting knowledge management initiative. It is vital to communicate the value proposition of the knowledge management effort to the strategic initiative. This is where acting as an internal *consultant* may be beneficial. Effective management consultants are able to sell a concept to executive sponsors by demonstrating the fit of the proposed effort through the lens of their own goals and objectives.

For example, if the executive of a nonprofit is interested in increasing the number and diversity of donors to the organization, a good consultant will frame the knowledge management effort within these concepts. If a consultant determines a new website will help the organization with achieving these goals, he or she will emphasize that donors retrieve product information through the website, note the prominence of blogs and wikis in developing online communities, and explain how these online spaces can be used to attract new donors and increase their commitment to the organization. A presentation that encompasses these strategies will have a higher probability of receiving a positive response from the executive than one that ignores strategic objectives. Leading executives to visualize the overall value of the knowledge management perspective and expertise is the critical outcome of the strategic assessment stage.

Frameworks for Developing a Business Case: Nonprofits

It is likely that nonprofit organizations are familiar with the mechanics of developing a business case based on their experiences in fundraising and advocacy. The process of developing a fundraising proposal for a new program or project follows similar steps. In its grant seeking efforts, the organization defines the problem (unmet need), provides evidence for the problem identified, and develops a solid case for its preferred alternative to address the problem, including the budget, impacts, outcomes, and evaluation methods. As identified in a toolkit developed by the Texas Commission on the Arts and highlighted by the National Council of Nonprofits, the components of a successful funding request include the following:

- Problem statement
- Qualifications
- Funding sources
- Funder benefits
- Evaluation
- Budget (Texas Commission on the Arts, 2011b)

Further, nonprofit organizations may have experience with developing robust arguments as part of their advocacy efforts, which can be applied to developing a successful business case. In carrying out advocacy efforts, nonprofits must develop strong and compelling communications that include a formal statement of their position, consider the audience and decision makers, and anticipate questions and opposition (Texas Commission on the Arts, 2011a). The process to develop an advocacy campaign may be useful as a framework in the early stages of developing a business case.

Needs Analysis

In the needs analysis (also sometimes referred to as the requirements definition) phase, the business opportunity is documented. Any issue can be viewed as a problem or an opportunity. In defining the opportunity, one needs to first be clear in identifying the objectives, the measurable outcomes expected upon the completion of the proposed projects. These objectives should be tied to outcomes from the strategic assessment phase, such as the current or desired states of the business or the current business needs. Objectives are normally classified as first-order (critical), second-order (important), and third-order (nice to have). Classifying objectives ensures a focus on the important issues, and the other objectives that are secondary to the goals of the project. If cuts to the proposed project become necessary due to receiving partial only funding, the least important objectives are removed. In defining the objectives, one must also be clear on the scope of the business initiative. What are the limits or boundaries of the opportunity? The availability of funding or the number of customers that are involved defines the scope of an opportunity. The more clearly the scope is defined, the greater the chance to devise an effective solution. See Table 9.2 for a summary of the key components of a Needs Analysis.

The identification of stakeholders is a critical undertaking in this phase. A business case might affect numerous stakeholders: employees that interact with a particular product or service, managers with responsibility for organizational projects, customers, or business partners. Identifying these stakeholders will help ensure that interactions and expectations are carefully managed. Then a careful analysis is conducted to map their influences on the proposed project. Influences can be either in support of or in opposition to the project. Stakeholders impact a business case in many ways, from raising roadblocks to new ideas and innovations to nonparticipation in critical phases of the project, thereby limiting success or increasing risk. Some stakeholders can even conduct activities or projects that undermine the proposed efforts. Not all stakeholder impacts need to be negative; if stakeholders are engaged appropriately they can make many positive contributions to the business case, such as building coalitions to support the case, helping bear some of the risks in the project, or providing resources to support

| Table 9.2. Key Components of a Needs Analysis ||
Component	Description
Define the project scope and high-level objectives.	• Define the project scope and prioritize the objectives (i.e., the measurable outcomes expected upon the completion of the proposed project).
Identify stakeholders.	• Identify the key stakeholders across the organization who will participate in and be impacted by the project.
Gather feedback from executive sponsors and stakeholders.	• Meet with executive sponsors and stakeholders in order to gather and document their feedback regarding the results of the needs assessment; use their feedback to assist in developing the solution alternatives.
Define specific project objectives.	• Define specific project objectives (requirements) in order to better design and evaluate solution alternatives.
Map objectives to outcomes.	• Map objectives to specific process-level and strategy-level outcomes (intermediate and longer term) for measurement, tracking, and accountability.

the effort. Once stakeholder influences are mapped, a careful analysis is conducted to understand the key drivers behind these influences. Drivers can include political nuances (e.g., the proposed project undermines the stakeholder's position in the organization by reducing his or her staff), to economic considerations (e.g., the cost of the project might detract resources from his or her current efforts).

Upon completion of the needs analysis, it is important that one meets with the executive sponsor and stakeholders to review the work performed to date. The feedback received allows for the revision and clarification of the business opportunity. This knowledge exchange also initiates the process to address stakeholder concerns. These concerns can be clearly documented and used as supporting information in the evaluation of the business case's alternatives.

In the needs analysis stage, the knowledge management effort is defined and conceptualized. Given the strategic assessment, the goal here is to clearly establish what the opportunity might be for a knowledge management project. It is important to stay true to the outcomes of the strategic assessment and to focus on aligning the opportunity definition to strategic priorities of the organization. In this stage, it is vital to make the knowledge management effort as specific and clear as possible. For instance, instead of simply stating "customer knowledge needs to be managed," describe what type of customer knowledge from which kind of customers (e.g., customers who are advanced users of a product, customers in a specific geographic region, or customers who have witnessed problems with the products); how the customer knowledge will be collected (e.g., at what frequency, through what medium); why customer knowledge is important; and what we mean by *manage* customer knowledge (i.e., simply collecting and presenting knowledge, or ensuring real-time access and application of the knowledge by sales personnel, or both). Being specific allows you to begin to define the boundaries of the need. Further, being specific and arriving at a clear definition of the need will help you to better design the alternatives (solutions) to address the need.

A business case should specify the objectives in the needs analysis. Here the focus should not be solely on knowledge management outcomes, but on showing how the knowledge management outcomes contribute to the strategic goals of the organization. Figure 9.1 depicts a common approach.

Knowledge management outcomes should be tied to *process-level outcomes*; that is, tools, techniques, strategies, and procedures should show measurable changes to organizational processes. As an example, if the knowledge transfer protocol as facilitated by a new organization-wide knowledge map increases the efficiency and effectiveness of locating expertise across the organization, one might expect that this would positively

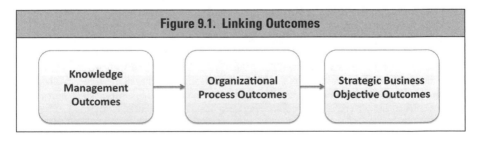

Figure 9.1. Linking Outcomes

Knowledge Management Outcomes → Organizational Process Outcomes → Strategic Business Objective Outcomes

contribute to organizational processes such as higher efficiency and effectiveness of customer query resolution. This may result in less time for customer calls, lower frequency of repeat calls on the same topic by the customer, or the faster discovery of solutions by customer service staff. Next, these outcomes can be tied into the *strategic-level outcomes*. In this example, the outcomes are tied to strategic-level goals such as increasing customer satisfaction, increasing customer retention, or increasing sales of products. Since it is difficult to tie knowledge management efforts directly to the strategic outcomes, mapping the intermediate organizational process outcomes becomes critical. Following this process also demonstrates the overall connection to the knowledge management solution argued by the business case. Moreover, the mapping of impacts to process-level outcomes helps identify stakeholders that need to be addressed.

Stakeholders who have responsibility for the various intermediary organizational outcomes need to be consulted. Their input on how the knowledge management effort might impact the various outcomes guides the refinement of the business case. It is important that their advice be sought on their preferred knowledge management solutions and the challenges they envision in deploying such a solution. For example, do they think that their employees might not use the solution? Should the solution be automated or manual? Should employees be able to access the solution via mobile devices or laptops? It is these stakeholders who will eventually be evaluating whether the knowledge management was a success or failure. If stakeholders are appropriately engaged in this stage, they can contribute to the success of the project by getting others involved, encouraging their employees to view the effort positively, and assigning other staff as contact points. Soliciting their buy-in early is critical to the success of the overall knowledge management project.

Interview with Neal Myrick, Executive Director of Groundwire

The following are excerpts from an e-mail conversation between Kevin Desouza and Neal Myrick, the executive director of Groundwire. Groundwire is a 501(c)(3) organization based in Washington State that aims to "make sure hundreds of environmental groups have the online tools needed to accomplish real social change" (http://www.groundwire.org/about/what-we-do/).

Mr. Myrick responded to questions regarding his experience in the nonprofit space, including his experience in developing business cases and his thoughts on the challenges that nonprofits face in the economic downturn.

Q: What is the mission of Groundwire; what got you excited to take on the role as executive director?
A: Groundwire's mission is to provide technology to engage people, organizations, and communities in building a sustainable society. I am excited to be in this role for two reasons: (1) because we are the perfect organization for making an impact at this moment in the environmental movement's history. Environmental organizations have largely focused on policy level decision makers over the last 25 years at the expense of forming and maintaining deep, reliable relationships with citizens.... The general belief is that they will never be able to compete with the money big corporations invest in fighting climate change legislation so they need to change the game and use the power of people. We help them use online strategies, technology, and data to build, and maintain power through people.... (2) I personally highly value diversity in all of its forms and am excited to be in a position to influence and encourage environmental organizations to consider diversification as a strategy for building great power.

(Continued)

Interview with Neal Myrick, Executive Director of Groundwire *(Continued)*

Q: Can you describe your current role as executive director at Groundwire?

A: I am the CEO and am therefore responsible for the health and success of the organization. I spend a great deal of time building and maintaining relationships: externally with clients, peers, and funders and internally with staff and my board....I basically spend 40 percent of my time fundraising, 40 percent working on program issues, and 20 percent on finance and administration.

Q: What do you see as the major challenges Groundwire faces in enabling non-profits to leverage technologies successfully towards their organizational mission?

A: Money and time. The classic problem....Even with the benefit of open source software and cloud computing, the cost of implementing and supporting technology is expensive because it takes a lot of time–time is money....and most nonprofits cannot get frequent enough or big enough grants to meet IT needs....we can provide technology solutions to nonprofits at a discount and help them compete. We still run into the problem, though of funding the project but finding it difficult to fund the ongoing training, support, and maintenance/upgrades.

Q: What process do you, and your teams, follow when preparing business cases for funding? How do you know that you have a good business case?

A: We don't have a specific process because each business case is different depending on the project and who we are proposing the project to....Internally, we are driven by our mission to ensure our work results in positive environmental impacts...We assess the client, their theory of change, and their readiness to utilize and support technology to engage people as part of their overall strategy for achieving their mission. We reject projects where potential clients simply want website work done without focusing on how the website is going to engage people in support of their mission. If we have strong values and mission alignment with a project it is easier to develop a compelling business case....The approach to the funder and the business case depends on the funder. Each funder has a unique perspective on the world and a unique theory for how they are going to change it. We focus first on finding alignment in values and program focus. If I am working on a project for the North Cascades, for example, I find funders (either individual or foundation) who care deeply about protecting that amazing environment (values) and who believe, like we do, that an important strategy for protecting beautiful ecosystems is getting people to experience and fall in love with them (program focus).

Q: What lessons have you learned over the years in terms of writing successful (and unsuccessful) business cases for technology projects?

A: Proposals help people have the courage to take a risk on an idea. Documenting the logic and data that supports a proposal is culturally required but the actual decisions about whether or not to approve a proposal are typically not based on the data. In my experience decisions to take risks are made based on reputation, emotion, timing, and trust.

- *Reputation*: People have less and less bandwidth every day and so they look for reliable shortcuts to support their decisions. Reputation is a fairly reliable shortcut. If a person/organization has a reputation for proposing and implementing successful technology projects they are halfway to getting a proposal accepted. Even with internal business proposals IT teams should include subtle reminders of past successes in order to help decision makers recognize the reputation short cut.

- *Emotion*: Emotion obviously plays a significant role in decision making. When writing a proposal I have learned to communicate a sense of urgency and to discuss benefits (either opportunities seized, risks averted, etc.) in a way that stirs an emotional response. I typically need to amp up the emotional quotient in nonprofit work because people are often in nonprofit work for emotional reasons. A lack of emotional connection can be detrimental to a proposal in a nonprofit setting. Too much emotion can be detrimental in a business setting.

(Continued)

Interview with Neal Myrick, Executive Director of Groundwire *(Continued)*

- *Timing:* This seems obvious, but proposals must be made in the context of what's going on in the current work environment and with the decision makers involved. A technology project proposal to proactively prevent a problem might fail when presented as a proactive solution and then succeed immediately after the problem happens. I have also learned to time proposals with significant organization events (such as an IPO) and take advantage of the momentum and emotion around that important event to get support for projects that in some way have a connection. Proposal writers must also be keenly aware of who the decision makers are and what is going on with them individually that might impact the proposal because, again, decisions are made based on emotion and other not-so-logical factors. For example, I used to wait for my boss to be sick in order to get certain proposals approved because I knew she would rely on my reputation and her trust in me more than anything else.

- *Trust:* Relationships are the key to everything. No amount of data can convince someone to take a risk with you if they don't have at least some level of trust. If I know I am gearing up for a big proposal in the fall I typically start building and deepening relationships with the appropriate stakeholders in the spring. Even if I have worked somewhere for five years I will increase the frequency of interaction with certain people, plant seeds, and get feedback on ideas long before I start writing the proposal. This is especially true in the nonprofit world where the only way to get a funder to give you money is if they trust you—no matter how good your reputation is. Your reputation will get you in the door (and thereby halfway there) but trust will get you the money.

Q: What are the top five things that you look for when evaluating the merits of a business cases made by your employees or when serving on committees?

A: This is strictly from my nonprofit perspective: (1) Mission and values alignment, (2) Impact (or potential for impact), (3) Thoroughness of authentic thought (not just upsides but also risks, downsides—balance), (4) Impact on funding (cost, potential for fundraising), (5) Passion and investment the person/team has for making it successful (will someone be and stay the champion and who is that person). ROI (and supporting data) would likely replace #4 in a for-profit setting.

Q: Nonprofit agencies of all kinds are facing tough budget crises; what recommendations can you offer them in terms of strategically deploying their resources?

A: Focus on the core—strengths, programs, clients. It is easy to experience mission bloat in the nonprofit world because it is difficult to reject an idea to help people or animals. Nonprofits can find partners to potentially provide non-core services to their constituents if they lose funding for non-core programs.

Keep staff focused on the priority work. Nonprofit workers work very hard but can suffer job bloat because their constituents often need more help than they can provide. Over time, the staff can lose sight of what the priority work is because all the work becomes critical. Staff need permission and tools to focus their work.

Don't be afraid to ask funders for help. I can't tell you how many funders have told me they wished they would have known a nonprofit was in such dire straits before it folded. Boards and EDs alike need to be willing to swallow their pride and call for help when needed.

Collaborate or merge. Nonprofits who are struggling financially can find other nonprofits in similar fields of work and talk about merging or collaborating. I worked with an ED who was trying to get seven other nonprofits to lease a building together and share administrative overhead like copiers, IT, etc. She was pursuing a cost-reduction strategy. I worked with another ED who managed a nonprofit through a merger because the alternative was shutting the doors. She realized that the programs were important and not the nonprofit institution that provided them.

Crafting Alternatives

The design and evaluation of alternatives for addressing the business opportunity is the next phase of developing a business case. At the start, it is best to be open to many possible solutions and then evaluate their feasibility. Once initial ideas are generated through a process of refining and filtering, a manageable set of alternatives is derived. Document the process and the outcomes during the design of alternatives so that they can be communicated in the business case. The readers of the business case should understand the process that was used to develop the alternatives; this knowledge will create transparency and demonstrate the due diligence employed, instilling a level of confidence.

Once the alternatives are determined, each alternative is then evaluated based on defined criteria. The benefits and costs for each alternative are enumerated by comparing the different alternatives with each other and with the default state of maintaining the current state. In addition to financial costs and benefits, it is important to focus on the strategic advantages of each alternative. Does one alternative put the organization in a better strategic position than others? Alternatives are also evaluated as to their impacts on the identified stakeholders. An alternative that has minimal disruption to the stakeholders can be desirable in cases where the proposed work is innovative or risky. See Table 9.3 for a common framework for defining and evaluating alternatives in terms of risks and rewards.

Furthermore, the organizational readiness for each alternative must be considered, addressing a key question: how ready is the organization to implement each alternative? An alternative might appear very good in theory, but not be viable due to the state of readiness of the organization. Consider the case of implementing an electronic knowledge sharing system such as an intranet. This alternative is suitable to consider when an organization already has an established knowledge-sharing culture. Conversely, implementing it in an organization that has not yet developed an environment that encourages knowledge sharing may result in a failed investment.

The stage of devising alternatives for knowledge management offers the opportunity to present the organization's best ideas to address the business case. While each knowledge management project will be different and each framework for defining the alternatives varied, some standard guidelines can be used. Business cases should attempt to keep the plan simple, and begin by securing small successes. Being too aggressive and ambitious is one of the most common reasons knowledge management business cases do not gain support. Starting small, also referred to as prototyping the

Table 9.3. Evaluating Alternatives in Terms of Risks and Rewards		
Project Alternative	**Risks**	**Rewards**
Aggressive	High	High
Conservative	Medium	Medium
No action (status quo)	Low	Low

project into smaller segments, will help the KM project in several ways. Ideas can be tested and any challenges will be identified before the project is implemented on a larger scale. Second, it will also help demonstrate a proof of concept and engage the stakeholders with the initial results. Showing proof of concept is a method used to convert skeptics of the project into enthusiastic supporters. Third, managers are willing to invest a portion of the total budget required, and then wait to evaluate the initial results. If the results are positive, they have the option to increase the investment to continue the success. Fourth, you might have put forth "the most ideal" alternative in the business case, but it is possible that this alternative has not been fully tested or implemented in the organizational context. The other alternatives—those that were evaluated but not selected—might be feasible yet face similar issues. Sometimes starting small provides the opportunity to test alternatives and to ensure that the organization and its employees are prepared to commit to the larger goals and objectives.

Each alternative must be evaluated with the business objectives in mind. Too often, knowledge managers are excited about a particular technology or process, and this obscures the evaluation process. Ultimately, it is not the novelty of the tool that is going to win over stakeholders and make a contribution to the organization. Instead, choosing the best tool to fit the organizational objectives is the most effective course of action. It is vital that a knowledge manager not be solely focused on the technology. Viewing the opportunity from the business perspective and choosing the approach that will attain the overall objectives is much more advisable.

Project Description

This section presents details regarding the proposed project, but the discussion is still at a strategic level, as the goal is not to produce an operational plan. This proposed project is the one selected from the alternatives that best meets the strategic goals and objectives of the organization. In this section, readers will look for how the project fits the current needs of the organization, compares with other alternative being considered, and demonstrates the overall project concept and the value proposition. This section draws heavily on findings from the needs analysis and the alternatives sections to justify the recommendation. Any processes that describe how the decision was made can be explained in this section in order to allow for the process to be transparent to the readers of the business case. The overall goal of this section is to leave readers with the evidence necessary for them to understand the chosen solution and why it was preferable to the other listed alternatives, which should include the alternative of no action.

One of the crucial mistakes managers make when writing project descriptions is to get caught up in jargon-laden writing. Too often, project descriptions are difficult to understand for outsiders who are removed from the effort. It is important to remember that readers of the business case are seldom individuals who know the nitty-gritty of the effort or the language used by experts. Put another way, the project description should be written for a generalist, who with little help can understand the gist of the effort. When in doubt, incorporate guides such as flowcharts, diagrams, tables, or a list of abbreviations to help communicate the major points to your readers.

Financial Analysis

The next step in creating the business case for a knowledge management project is to understand the financial feasibility of the selected alternatives. Is it economically possible to purchase the solution? Are the necessary financial resources available to commit to the design and implementation of the solution? What are the impacts of investing cash in the proposed project instead of investing it in other organizational initiatives? Table 9.4 outlines the key components of a financial analysis.

There are several important things to bear in mind when conducting a financial analysis, with the time horizon of the project being one of the most critical issues. The longer the duration of the proposed project, the greater the difficulty and the inherent risk of financial analysis, as it is difficult to forecast conditions into the distant future. A better chance for accuracy exists when conducting a financial analysis for a project that is completed in the short term, when compared to one that spans many years. The estimates for goods and services, property, expected sales prices, and other costs have a higher chance of changing over longer forecasting periods.

One critical component of an effective financial analysis is the **sensitivity analysis**. Sensitivity analysis is a financial modeling technique that allows for the identification of critical variables affecting the outcomes of the project. If a project requires a particular raw material and the current price of the item is $10, the initial financial analysis may indicate the project is feasible. But if the price of the raw material increases to $15 or even $20, the impacts to the outcomes of the project need to be identified through a sensitively analysis. The project might still be feasible with raw material prices at $15, though it will take additional years to recoup the investment. In a second example,

Table 9.4. Key Components of a Financial Analysis	
Component	**Description**
Determine the time horizon.	• The length of the project contributes to the confidence and accuracy in the financial analysis; it is difficult to forecast accurately over a longer duration due to the increased likelihood of changes over time (such as changes in the costs of goods and services).
Carry out a sensitivity analysis.	• Determine how each of the alternatives will be impacted by changes in the key variables and devise risk mitigation strategies.
Identify the project cost components.	• Identify tangible and intangible costs and document how they contribute to the project outcomes.
Determine the viability of the project based on the time horizon.	• Determine the viability of the project in terms of cash outlays and receipts over the life of the project using calculations such as the Net Present Value (NPV), Internal Rate of Return (IRR), and Payback Period. When considered together, these measures help to demonstrate whether the project alternatives will earn a favorable return on investment within the expected time horizon.

assume that one customer will purchase 50 percent of the product. What will the impact be on the proposed project if the customer becomes insolvent or lowers the demand for the product? Performing a sensitivity analysis will help illustrate how each of the alternatives is impacted by changes to key variables and what risk mitigation strategies should be considered. Risk mitigation strategies are devised to reduce the impact of the variables and to plan for counter measures. If a sensitivity analysis shows that the project is too risky because it is reliant on one major customer, a risk mitigation strategy would be to solicit more customers during the early phases of the project. As with many of the other issues, documenting the sensitivity analysis process is essential, as the risks and risk mitigation strategies must be documented in the eventual business case.

Unlike traditional business projects, completing a financial analysis for a knowledge management business presents additional issues. For example, knowledge management initiatives seldom produce an immediate financial return. Knowledge management initiatives take time and effort in order to create change in the organization. Cultural barriers to knowledge behaviors such as sharing need to be addressed, training needs to be provided, and small incentives may need to be identified and distributed. With knowledge-sharing initiatives, it is important to factor into the financial analysis the time lag that will occur before results are noticeable and measureable.

When estimating costs of a knowledge management effort, it is a good practice to clearly document what costs are allocated to tangible versus intangible items. Tangible items can include new hardware, software, and applications. Intangibles are items such as training and development, community building initiatives, and networking events. Documenting this difference between the two forms of expenses is important because spending on tangible artifacts can be easily visualized and managed, whereas spending on intangibles is less impactful. Yet, the intangibles can be more important to the success of the overall initiative. In additional, the impact of two types of expenses is spread across different time horizons. Buying a piece of software or hardware equipment may be a one-time cost, but training costs can occur for multiple years and vary over time. Intangible expenses are usually the first target for cuts in tough budget times. It is common thinking that these can be done away with or are less important than their tangible counterparts. This is where clearly segmenting these out, and explicitly identifying their criticality, will allow executive sponsors to understand their value and appreciate their impacts on the overall business objectives.

The financial analysis discusses the project's financial intricacies, including the timeframe that the expected costs and benefits will be realized. Most projects call for cash outlays at various periods during the effort. Similarly, the income from the project will occur at varying time intervals. For instance, only after the project is completed may you begin to see income from the effort, and this income could be spread across several years. The financial analysis must capture these intricacies and compare the money spent over the life of the project to the expected income realized either during or after the completion of the project. Three common indicators of the viability of the project are net present value, internal rate of return, and the payback period.

Net present value (NPV) helps normalize future cash flows (both cash outlays and cash receipts) into their present value. Simply put, receiving $1 today is better than receiving $1 tomorrow. Similarly, it is better to hold onto cash today and pay bills at a later date (assuming, they are paid before a creditor charges interest and penalties). To calculate NPV, the following formula is used:

$NPV = FV_{r,n}[1/(1+r)^n]$ where NPV = net present value, FV = future value, r = rate of return, and n = time

Consider the case of receiving \$1,000 three years from now. Currently, the annual savings rate at a bank is 2 Percent. What is the present value of the investment?

$PV = FV_{r,n}[1/(1+r)^n]$
$PV = \$1000[1/(1+.02)^3]$
$PV = \$942.32$

If a person promised to pay \$950 today, versus the proposal just discussed (\$1,000 in three years), the best option is \$950 today, as it is greater than the NPV of the other proposal. This example is simplistic, but demonstrates the concept of the changing value of money over time.

More complex formulae can be used to compute NPV for an annuity (i.e., where payments are received, or made, over time). As a general rule, if the NPV of a project is greater than zero, then it is advised to invest in the project. When the NPV is negative, the company should not invest in the project because the future cash flows do not justify the present investment. Also, the greater the time period to recoup the investment, the greater the chance of securing a positive NPV.

The **internal rate of return (IRR)** is another important financial measure of a project; this process calculates the discount rate, also known as the investment yield rate, for the project. The IRR is the rate at which the NPV for a project is equal to zero. When comparing two projects, the one with the higher IRR is preferred. Another option to the IRR is to present the ROI (Return on Investment). This value represents, as the name implies, the savings (benefit) one will get out of the project for the investment (cost) outlays.

The **payback period** helps one estimate how quickly the investment will be recouped. Put another way, it is the time required for the savings to equal the cost. Naturally, the shorter the payback period, the better. When comparing two nearly similar alternatives, the rational company will choose the project with the shorter payback period.

No one financial metric will be adequate for evaluating a project's feasibility or its value proposition. Metrics are best used in conjunction with each other, as each measure provides a slightly different value perspective. For example, the payback period will tell a company which project will pay back the investment quicker, while the IRR gives the savings received from the project. Both of these measures are valuable and should be taken into account when considering various proposals for uses of capital.

Unlike traditional (e.g., manufacturing) projects, financial analysis for a knowledge management case is more complicated. First, much of the projected benefits from the knowledge management effort are based on soft facts, or nonmeasurable and qualitative data. It is difficult to determine precise figures for many elements and impacts of KM projects. For example, how much will an organization save from better knowledge transfer protocols between customer service representatives? Since the exact amount cannot be projected, an estimate based on experience or a knowledge manager's tacit knowledge must be used. If it currently costs $50 to resolve a customer complaint, and it takes approximately one hour, basic mathematics derive the cost savings from a knowledge management intervention. Assuming that the availability of a better organized product knowledge base will lower the time that it takes to resolve each complaint by 30 percent (so rather than one hour, it will now take 42 minutes), then the cost savings is $15 ($50 − $35) per complaint. If 1,000 calls per day are received with customer complaints, the cost per savings per year is $365,000. This information should be part of the financial analysis, but it is equally important to clearly document how the 30 percent reduction in time to resolve calls was estimated. Was this based on industry data? Was data collected from the staff to determine how long they spent searching for information? Were staff observed performing their daily routines? Where exact figures do not exist, sharing evidence and rationale for numbers is very important. If the reader of the business case lacks confidence in the source of the numbers, the chances of the assessment being convincing are low.

Second, as noted, there will be a time lag between when the knowledge management intervention is deployed and when observable returns might be realized. In the financial analysis section, it is very important to document this clearly. For example, if the

---

IT Project Challenges in the Public Sector

The public sector faces a number of challenges related to IT projects. Common issues in the sector include overpayment for technology solutions. For example, findings from a recent analysis conducted by Compass Management Consultants in the United Kingdom indicate that "the public sector is paying around 40% above the market rate for outsourced services, and there is every indication that this trend is a global one" (Woods, 2010). Another challenge in the public sector is the length of time that is required to carry out a project due to rules and regulations "which means that at the end of the day, the deal taken may not be the best one" (Woods, 2010). Further, the public sector often has the challenge of designing projects to meet the needs of large, diverse stakeholder groups, where private companies may be focusing on the organization itself. These issues contribute to poor outcomes for IT projects such as "cancelled projects and projects that fail to meet objectives or live up to expectations" (Woods, 2010).

These issues can be identified and addressed through developing sound business cases in order to improve outcomes for IT projects. Business cases, following the private sector model, help to ensure that "all IT initiatives [should] also be geared at improving efficiency, in order to allow government organisations to spend less, yet deliver more services" (Woods, 2010).

By using a business case approach, government entities can avoid common issues with IT projects. For example, a "report commissioned by the Texas Comptroller's office" identified a significant cost savings of "between $10 and $20 million" if it provided an online tax application because a number of processing functions would simply go away, and "eventually, the agency could cut the number of employees in half" (Deloitte Research, 2003: 19). But the financial analysis identified a significant risk to the project: "the big savings don't kick in until a significant percentage of taxpayers file their taxes online" due to the need to maintain parallel systems and processes (Deloitte Research, 2003: 19). By building this finding regarding the required uptake rate built into the design and implementation phases, it is possible to achieve the desired efficiencies and cost savings where similar e-government initiatives may have stumbled. For example, in the UK, "only 13% of the population used e-government services in 2002, despite large investments in online government by the Blair administration" (Deloitte Research, 2003: 20).

installation of a social networking tool that helps connect experts within the organization is followed by a projected six- to nine-month lag period before results are experienced, then the financial analysis needs to account for this delay.

In analyzing and making a case for a KM project, the bottom line is that the project needs to make financial sense. The project needs to show that it can recoup the investments made and that, when compared to other projects, it will earn a favorable return on capital invested. In some cases, a project that does not have the best financial outlook may still win approval due to other project features such as the risk assessment or the planning details as described in the remainder of the project proposal.

Planning the Project

Assuming that the project is financially feasible and risks can be sufficiently managed, the project can be designed. In this stage, the business case answers the question of *how the work* will be done. The first task is to clearly document the steps of the project. It is important to be clear on what work will be performed, the scope of the work, and what impact the work will have on the organization. The work description should be as jargon-free and nontechnical as possible. Even if the work being undertaken involves complex procedures and technologies, a business case should remain at the strategic level and be written in a manner that can be understood by people who may not have in-depth knowledge of the specific area.

The second task is to assemble the project team. The skills and expertise needed and the personnel available are two important factors in the selection of employees. In cases where the business case does not represent regular assigned duties for personnel, special accommodations are required to bring them on to the project, and in this example careful consideration is needed to calculate the true cost of these people to project.

The third task involves creating a high-level project plan, also called the implementation plan. The project plan needs to document the key tasks, milestones, and the personnel who will be involved in the specific work effort. Important personnel to document are the project leader, the project sponsor and other key stakeholders, and the team leaders. When constructing a project plan, it is necessary to be both realistic and conservative. Therefore, allowing for slack in the plan can provide much need flexibility. In addition, with large-scale initiatives it is important to clearly map the interdependencies between major tasks, which allows one to see how the various pieces of the project fit together and illustrates where delays and other problems have a cascading impact throughout the entire effort.

The knowledge management project typically supports a business opportunity that is linked to a specific functional unit; therefore it is vital that representation from the business unit is included on the project team. Representation must ensure that individuals from the functional units can provide valuable input on the intricacies of the unit so that the project plan satisfies the business needs. It is important that the representatives take an active role in crafting the project plan and provide input on how the project tasks impact other strategic projects within their department. This is useful when devising the most ideal implementation plan that minimizes disruption within the unit.

Risk Assessment

All knowledge management projects have some element of risk. Risk is a normal aspect of doing business and cannot be avoided. While risk is natural, management of risk is essentially a human undertaking. Effective managers know how to plan for risks and manage strategies to protect against their possible impact to the organization. They understand the probabilities of risk; their triggers, enhancers, suppressors; and the expected outcomes. Ineffective managers are more likely to ignore or underestimate risks, thereby avoiding the critical act of planning for their occurrence. In the context of a knowledge management business case, it is important that risks be clearly documented. Table 9.5 summarizes the key components of a risk assessment.

Risks need to be classified as those that are internal to the project and those that are external. Internal risks are related to the technology being implemented and the complexity of the project. External risks are related to outside factors such as customers or government. Classifying risks helps to focus on those risks that are under one's control and can be managed. It is important to acknowledge the risks that are uncontrollable and explain the precautions taken within the business case. For every risk, probabilities of occurrence are calculated through the use of historic data. For example, historic weather information can help in estimating chances of severe weather. Similarly, industry data can be used to estimate the likelihood of product failure or business failure. In cases, where historic data is not available, a manager's intuition and tacit knowledge is utilized. Best guesses are made, and the rationale for these estimates must be explained in the case.

Table 9.5. Key Components of a Risk Assessment	
Component	**Description**
Identify external and internal project risks.	• Identify project risks that are internal (i.e., within management control) and external risks related to factors that should be monitored and handled through appropriate precautions but over which the project management has no control (e.g., the economic climate, competitors' actions).
Determine the risk probability.	• Use historical data to determine the probability of occurrence; if historical data is not available, use management best guesses to arrive at estimates and provide the rationale.
Identify project cost components.	• Identify tangible and intangible costs and document how they contribute to the project outcomes.
Categorize risks.	• Categorize risks based on probability (e.g., Improbable, Unlikely, Possible, Likely, and Very Likely).
Estimate costs of damages.	• Estimate costs of damages, focusing on likely risks.
Develop contingency plans.	• Develop and document contingency plans for likely risks that are determined to be material (significant cost to the project or organization). The contingency plans should include the actions to be taken in the event that the risk occurs.

Risks are then classified into various categories based on their likelihood of occurrence; for example, (1) Improbable, Unlikely, Possible, Likely, and Very Likely or (2) Definite, Probable Distinct, Possible Given Time, Remote, and Improbable. Categorizing risks enables managers to focus their attention on the risks that are more likely to occur, and then allocate resources toward mitigating these risks. The extent of expected damage should the risk occur needs to be estimated. Once again, historic data is used to identify the cost of damage for a given risk. At this point decisions need to be made regarding the threshold for acceptable risks. What constitutes an acceptable risk will vary from organization to organization. Some organizations might be more risk averse, while others might be risk seekers. Organizations can exhibit different risk preferences depending on the type of project, customer involved, business segment impacted, or other intricacies to the project.

It is important to present contingency plans and countermeasures to the probable risks to a project or organization. Not all risks have a contingency plan, as the concept of *materiality* is used to determine what actions should be taken. Materiality states that an organization should focus on risks that will have a significant impact on the business. The costs of some risks are immaterial to the organization, or will have little or no impact to its operations and success. Materiality helps direct the effort in devising contingency plans for risks where the benefits of such plans outweigh the costs.

In the risk assessment section, the process and outcomes of the steps to identifying, assessing, and costing risks are documented. It is vital that risks be explained clearly as the risk assessment section is one of the most heavily scrutinized sections of the business case.

Budget Pressures in the Public Sector and Privatization

In the current economic climate, there is increasing pressure to cut budgets, especially in local governments. A "national survey conducted by the Public Technology Institute and Input "showed that 50 percent of local government IT budgets will be cut over the next couple of years." (Katims, 2010). The risk is that, especially in the public sector setting where the focus tends to be on the most pressing near-term issues, "because IT infrastructure doesn't show signs of wear…it's very easy to put things off" and "deferred maintenance will backfire" (Katims, 2010). Yet research suggests that budget pressures may present an opportunity to take actions such as consolidation, integration, and outsourcing in order to create efficiencies and "capture savings from IT investments" (Deloitte Research, 2003: 17). These types of projects have been less common in the public sector because public sector entities, especially at the local level, often function as silos and have historically had few incentives to seek out such efficiencies. In order to effectively address budget cuts, public sector managers need to approach IT projects by "developing more rigorous business cases and Return on Investment (ROI) models on the front end" (Deloitte Research, 2003: 17).

There are "many avenues local governments can take to be more cost efficient" (Katims, 2010). And budget pressures and lack of discretionary funds have increasingly caused governments to turn to public–private partnerships as a means to balance their budgets. But some projects have been criticized for giving up longer-term value and public good for short-term gains. For example, the city of Chicago partnered with a private company to manage the Chicago Skyway, and handed over its parking meter system to "a Morgan Stanley-backed group a concession that continues the city's strategy of privatizing its public assets" (Martin, 2008). Privatizing parking meters may result in "pricing [it] at a point, potentially, where many can't afford it" (Martin, 2008). Business cases can help governments evaluate options through cogent analysis of short-term and long-term benefits and risks.

Assumptions and Constraints

Every business case is built upon assumptions. In this section, the various assumptions made during the development of the business case are stated. For instance, in the case of installing new equipment, an assumption would be stated regarding how much downtime of the factory is required. In the case of hiring personnel, if there were assumptions made on the ease of recruiting and hiring good candidates, these need to be documented. Other assumptions might include probabilities of winning client deals, securing funding, or interdependencies between organizational processes.

Assumptions, like risks, are necessary evils. Assumptions help us make sense of the environment and guide our perception of the organization. In this section of the business case, one ensures that one's own assumptions are conveyed to the reader. After all, the reader will bring his or her own assumptions to bear when evaluating the proposal. Constraints are specific kinds of assumptions that limit or restrict the effort of the proposed project. In organizations, it is common to have funding limits for proposals. For example, an organization might request proposals for funding that are below $250,000. This constraint may limit the extent of work proposed in the business case. Documenting what might be possible if this constraint were not in place will be part of this section. Other types of constraints might be the availability of personnel, time, space, or know-how.

Recommendations and Conclusions

This section lists the key overall recommendations of the business case to summarize the actions and benefits that will occur. Strong business cases provide unambiguous, feasible recommendations that are directly related to the core strategies of the business. The recommendation section is written very much like the executive summary. It should be brief, concise, and clear on the proposed knowledge management project, rationale for action, benefits, costs and risks.

Appendix

Most business cases will include a series of appendices. This section is used to present auxiliary information. Common appendices might include detailed comparisons between the various alternatives, in-depth financial analyses, a more detailed project plan, or letters of endorsement from the various stakeholders who support the project effort.

FROM FUNDING TO THE EXECUTION OF THE BUSINESS CASE

Achieving success in receiving funding and approval for a business case is noteworthy. However, now the work begins in order for the project to progress as it was envisioned. It is from this point onward that the project will be judged as a success or failure.

Once the project receives initial approval, the first step is to take the feedback received during the business case presentation and funding deliberations to make any necessary changes to the project goals, objectives, scope, and deliverables. Seldom does a business case get funded "as-is." It is more common to have a business case go through revisions and changes as it is being reviewed and funding considerations are debated. The project may have to be scaled back, as the funding provided may not have been for the total amount requested. This can have a significant impact on the deliverables, and therefore the expectations for the project. Occasionally the project may need to be extended in scope as a condition of funding. For example, the project may need to incorporate more customers or segments of the business than originally accounted for as a condition for approval, which will impact the project timeline, implementation plans, and/or personnel allotted.

As the project work is performed, it is vital to keep stakeholders updated on the progress. Stakeholders should receive routine updates on the critical tasks being undertaken, milestones completed, challenges and issues that arise, and other details. It is always important to alert stakeholders on issues and challenges in a proactive, rather than a reactionary, manner. A common method used is to create a project overview, or dashboard, that marks tasks with a color-coding scheme. Green indicates everything is going well; the tasks are scheduled to be completed on time and on budget. Yellow denotes tasks that are starting to face unexpected challenges and concerns that need attention. This calls for management attention and immediate intervention in order to prevent a situation from becoming worse and impacting the overall project. Red is assigned to a task that is experiencing serious trouble and will run over the estimated time or above the estimated budget. A standard rule is to inform stakeholders about tasks that reach a yellow state, allowing for interventions aimed at preventing the task from progressing to a red state. Keeping stakeholders in the communication loop is essential to maintain support in the event a project begins to slightly deviate from plans. Whenever possible, the project should publicize and communicate small successes that it achieves. This helps keep people energized and committed to the effort. Stakeholders maintain their support when they can inform others that they are supporting a successful project. In the communication of good news, a project manager should not overstate the project's achievements.

Throughout the duration of the project, especially for projects that span over multiple years, it can be expected that the organization will implement strategic changes. For example, the organization may change its strategic focus, prominent executives might leave the organization, or divisions and departments might be outsourced. It is therefore important to routinely evaluate whether the ongoing knowledge management effort continues to be aligned with the strategic goals of the organization. If a knowledge management project's objective was to build a social networking tool to help connect engineers in a new product development group, and the organization decides to outsource product development or acquires another engineering firm that already utilizes a tool that is used for knowledge sharing among engineers, then the KM project will have to be reevaluated or evolve. A common mistake is to fall into a sunk-cost trap—a situation where a company that has already invested in a course of action decides not to change directions or stop a project, even if the evidence points toward such a decision.

One important element of the execution of a project is building the capacity to reflect and learn from the knowledge gained during the course of the project. Learning is a critical method through which a novice project manager (or novice organization that may be at only the early stages of knowledge management) becomes an expert. In cases where a good postmortem analysis is conducted, the lessons can be applied to successive projects, improving their chances for successful results. Learning can occur in a collective setting involving the whole team, or can also be an individual exercise where the project manager reflects on the project and his/her own observations. A project manager should use evidence of learning and collaboration on the part of the project team to do performance evaluations. Employees will seldom be honest in their evaluations of the project if they know that their input will affect their performance evaluation.

Historical Perspective: The Knowledge Workstation at Johns Hopkins Medical Institutions

It is difficult to imagine the technical and operational challenges faced in the early days of large-scale knowledge management initiatives, given how far we have come in terms of institutional and personal knowledge management. In the 1980s, knowledge management initiatives brought together relatively new technologies (such as the Internet) and approaches to user-centered interface design in order to develop comprehensive, novel solutions. One such example is the Integrated Advanced Information Management System (IAIMS) planning model, started and funded under the National Library of Medicine in the 1980s. An early example of the application of the IAIMS approach was carried out at Johns Hopkins beginning in 1984.

The goal of IAIMS at Johns Hopkins Medical Institutions (JHMI) was to bring together its "specialized clinical and operational databases" into a comprehensive knowledge management workstation, which fused two components, called an IAIMS workstation and a clinical workstation (CWS) (Lucier et al., 1988: 248). "The ruling design principle for the CWS is a healthcare worker's desktop...should be able to perform on the CWS virtually all tasks he or she would be able to do at a desk" (Lucier et al., 1988: 248).

At the same time, Johns Hopkins' Welch library carried out a strategic planning initiative. It was a leader in technology, having been one of the first libraries to develop a National Library of Medicine (NLM) public domain integrated library system (ILS) (Lucier et al., 1988). Rather than resell its ILS, the Welch library opted to enter the database creation and management business because it perceived that this would have a bigger benefit to "affirm the role of the library within the JHMI as a content manager, offering maximum opportunities for developing information and knowledge management expertise" (Lucier et al., 1988: 249).

With this objective in mind, JHMI and Welch embarked on a unique project that became "the foundation for the library's work in knowledge management" (Lucier et al., 1988: 249). The four strategic components of the IAIMS initiative included: (1) JHMI initiative to develop a set of network standards, (2) Welch mandate to "manage, develop, and improve access to academic databases," (3) recommendation to create a Division of Medical Informatics, and (4) IAIMS executive committee expansion to include representatives from the schools of Public Health and Nursing (Lucier et al., 1988).

Regarding the organization's goals for the knowledge management workstation, the team based its vision on "Vannevar Bush's Memex....contemporary developments such as the Scholar's Workstation, and Feigenbaum's concept of autoknowledge" and articulated its goal: "Within the next decade, it is planned that the JHMI workers will be able to meet the majority of their biomedical literature and clinical information needs through a hierarchical network of local and remote electronic databases. They will regularly use local desktop workstations existing on a communications network that is part of a larger internet" (Lucier et al., 1988: 249).

(Continued)

**Historical Perspective: The Knowledge Workstation at
Johns Hopkins Medical Institutions** *(Continued)*

In descriptions of the knowledge management workstation, the team emphasized that while "initially text-oriented, the environment will eventually support voice and image processing. The distant goal is a knowledge management environment, a network of databases that an individual would tap as one would one's own memory to satisfy a need for knowledge" (Lucier et al., 1988: 250). As it was envisioned, the KW would be used for information transfer and knowledge management, which was defined as a set of related functions, including accessing information; maintaining information using a set of online user tools; and organizing and personalizing information (Lucier et al., 1988).

The project also employed a unique philosophy in terms of its development and implementation which included system autonomy and "the use and modification of public domain software, sharing of resources with others for collective benefit" (Lucier et al., 1988: 251). This software included as the WELMED common search interface with navigation and IRX (Information Retrieval Experiment), a UNIX based retrieval system with natural language capabilities, indexing, and ranking, and Intermedia to create links, described as "ties between selected information in one document.... and any selected information in another document" (Lucier et al., 1988: 253). Further, its principles would include "the use of prototype software in development" (Lucier et al., 1988: 251).

The JHMI/Welch team articulated that information transfer and knowledge management were two ends of a continuum. And therefore it would use a prototype approach to develop the IAIMS workstation, which included the functions for information transfer and tools for knowledge base creation (which would support a critical mass of users), and a separate prototype for the CWS workstation with the user tools for manipulation and personalization of information (Lucier et al., 1988). At the point when both were robust, the prototypes would converge in the knowledge workstation (KW). As such, the implementation would include three stages of development, with the first stage focusing on establishing common network standards and capabilities, and developing and providing access to bibliographic databases and user interfaces; the second stage focusing on diffusion (i.e., building out the same infrastructure in other units); and the third stage providing access for all units in JHMI to networks, databases (including full-text journals), and interfaces along with integration with CWS (Lucier et al., 1988).

The IAIMS initiative at JHMI illustrates first principles around implementation of knowledge management systems in an institutional setting, along with employing technology and software development principles and practices that are in common use today.

CONCLUSION

In this chapter, we covered the process of preparing and writing a business case for a knowledge management initiative. Without a strong business case, knowledge management will remain a theoretical and impractical concept in organizations. Good business cases give individuals the opportunity to put theory into practice by providing resources for implementing knowledge management programs, processes, and technologies. Writing good business cases requires time, effort, and practice. The goal of this chapter was to provide the foundational knowledge required for writing successful knowledge management business cases. It is important to learn from each business case experience in order to refine a manager's skills and competencies in proposing, implementing, and leading knowledge management projects in organizations.

Recap: The Major Points for Knowledge Managers to Consider When Building a Business Case for Knowledge Management

1. Resources are required to invest in knowledge management, and it is the job of the knowledge manager to acquire the appropriate mix of resources for an organization's KM initiatives.
2. It is normal to have a higher failure rate for knowledge management funding proposals, and therefore it is in the best interest of the knowledge manager to partner with other business units to jointly acquire resources.
3. Knowledge managers can utilize a business case, a well-argued and logically structured document that puts forth the business rationale for investing in a course of action, when communicating their ideas for a KM initiative.
4. In the strategic assessment section of a business case, the knowledge manager puts forth the argument that the proposed KM project is aligned with the corporate strategy and supports the goals and objectives of the firm.
5. A focus of the decision makers in the organization will be the financial analysis section, as they will be interested in the financial return they will receive on their investment. Although this is often hard to calculate, it is an important part of the business case.
6. Whether it is a for-profit, not-for-profit, public, or private firm, a business case of some form is always required to acquire the resources that a successful KM initiative demands.
7. When a business case for KM is accepted and funded, the work of a knowledge manager has only begun. Now managers must employ their project management skills to ensure the project will deliver what was promised to the organization.
8. A challenge for the implementation of a knowledge management plan is the constantly changing internal and external environments, and a good plan will integrate flexibility in order for the end product to be a success.
9. Communication to the stakeholders of the knowledge management program is essential throughout the entire process of building a business case. They can provide valuable knowledge regarding the formation of a case before and after the case has been submitted and accepted.
10. Writing a business case is an art, and takes practice and determination in order to be successful. The tacit knowledge gained by the experience of both business case successes and failures will over time develop the project manager into an organizational leader who can build consensus for large and impactful knowledge management projects.

DISCUSSION QUESTIONS

1. Why are some companies hesitant to invest in knowledge management related projects? What strategies can knowledge managers use to overcome these reservations and demonstrate the value of KM?
2. Every business case will be different based on the project and the business situation. What are the "must have" sections in a business case intended for knowledge management programs, and which ones are optional depending on the project?
3. How does an organization know it needs to create business case for a new knowledge management program? What can occur either internally within the organization or externally in the business environment that triggers the recognition of the need for a business case?

4. What is the link between a business case and the organization's strategy? What needs to be included in a knowledge management project's business case in order to ensure alignment with the business strategy?
5. Not all business cases requesting resources for knowledge management initiatives will be approved. What steps should a knowledge manager take after receiving a rejection? What knowledge can be gained from the processes to benefit future business case submissions?
6. A fundamental challenge in writing a business case for knowledge management is determining how the outcomes will be measured. What are some of the quantitative and qualitative measures that could apply to such a KM business case?
7. How can stakeholders, knowledge workers and users, and different functional areas of an organization be used to assist in the creation of a business case for knowledge management? Identify some of these key individuals and groups and their contribution to the formulation of a business case.
8. Business cases not only generate and support knowledge management within an organization, but knowledge management can support the creation of business cases. Where are the opportunities in the business case development process for using knowledge management activities (such as knowledge creation and acquisition or knowledge from external organizations) to improve the quality of arguments and information presented in the business case?

SUGGESTED READING

Developing a Business Case: Expert Solutions to Everyday Challenges. 2011. Pocket Mentor Series. Boston, MA: Harvard Business Review Press.

NOTE

1. This chapter is based on Desouza, K. C. 2010. "Winning the Business Case for Knowledge Management." *Business Information Review* 27, no. 3: 159–174.

REFERENCES

Becker, S., M. D. Crandall, K. E. Fisher, B. Kinney, C. Landry, and A. Rocha. 2010. "Opportunity for All: How the American Public Benefits from Internet Access at U.S. Libraries." Technology and Social Change U.S. IMPACT Study, March. http://www.tascha.washington.edu/usimpact/documents/OPP4ALL_FinalReport.pdf.

Deloitte Research. 2003. "Cutting Fat, Adding Muscle: The Power of Information Technology in Addressing Budget Shortfalls." Nebraska Information Technology Commission. http://nitc.nebraska.gov/news/0310/CuttingFat.pdf.

Goldberg, B. 2011. "Spread the Word: There's New Evidence of Libraries' ROI." *American Libraries Magazine*, January 19. http://americanlibrariesmagazine.org/news/01192011/spread-word-there-s-new-evidence-libraries-roi.

Katims, L. 2010. "CIOs Project Continued Local Government IT Budget Cuts." Government Technology.com. Last modified October 21. http://www.govtech.com/budget-finance/CIOs-Project-Continued-Local-Government-IT-Budget-Cuts.html.

Lucier, R. E., N. W. Matheson, K. A. Butter, and R. E. Reynolds. 1988. "The Knowledge Workstation: An Electronic Environment for Knowledge Management." *Bull Medical Library Association* 76, no. 3: 248–255.

Martin, T. W. 2008. "Chicago Banks on Private Parking." *Wall Street Journal*, December 13. http://online.wsj.com/article/SB122826399442774223.html.

Texas Commission on the Arts. 2011a. "Advocacy: When Testifying to Decision Makers." Texas Commission on the Arts. Accessed January 9. http://www.arts.state.tx.us/toolkit/advocacy/testify.asp.

Texas Commission on the Arts. 2011b. "Fundraising & Development: When Putting Together a Proposal." Texas Commission on the Arts. Accessed January 9. http://www.arts.state.tx.us/toolkit/fundraising/proposal.asp.

Woods, S. 2010. "Governing IT in the Public Sector." ITNewsAfrica.com. Last modified August 13. http://www.itnewsafrica.com/?p=8625.

10

Managing Knowledge for Organizational Value

Scott Paquette and Kevin C. Desouza

OBJECTIVES

- Summarize the key points of the book.
- Emphasize the importance of leadership and governance in knowledge management.
- Suggest ideas and techniques that can be used to overcome the challenges of knowledge management in organizations.
- Provide actionable guidance for current and future knowledge managers.

INTRODUCTION

Managing knowledge within an organization requires much effort from all employees and stakeholders. It involves acquiring and creating new knowledge for the firm, sharing it amongst employees in different departments, offices, or countries. It also includes organizing the knowledge so it can easily be retrieved and used, managing the various knowledge assets used by an organization including knowledge management systems, and taking a global view of knowledge. All of these activities require support from the senior executive team, middle managers and operational positions. Simply put, knowledge management is an organization-wide endeavor.

Building a business case for knowledge management can be the first step in an organization's path toward leveraging knowledge to create a strategic or competitive advantage. By convincing the executives of an organization of the importance of knowledge, resources can be allocated to knowledge management projects. It is essential that these projects have a leader or a leadership team guiding the knowledge work in order to ensure value is generated from their activities. The importance of leadership that takes ownership for an organization's knowledge management cannot be overstated, as these are the individuals who will promote, maintain, measure, and support an organization's progress towards mature knowledge processes. Communication with other areas of the firm is essential to ensure that goals are accomplished, and having knowledge leadership integrated with other leaders within the firm is essential to KM success.

In this chapter we conclude our discussion of knowledge management by first examining the importance of leadership for the knowledge management function. The roles of knowledge leaders are discussed, including how they integrate their work with other areas of the organization. Next, we will look specifically at the idea of a project management office, which can be an important vehicle for managing the knowledge activities of a firm. We also discuss the idea that knowledge professionals are very similar to consultants, as they require the same perspective of the organization and require skills to impart their knowledge to others. The overall challenges that a knowledge manager must be aware of are identified, but also the valuable resources available, whether online or offline, educate and inform knowledge managers about new technologies and developments in KM. The management of knowledge can appear to be a daunting task for any manager, but with the support of an organization's leadership, the appropriate organizational and governance structure to support knowledge activities, the awareness of challenges that may be experienced and the paths towards finding solutions to these challenges, it is very possible for a manager to create and sustain a successful knowledge management strategy.

ESTABLISHING KNOWLEDGE MANAGEMENT LEADERSHIP

Knowledge management efforts need to contribute to the organization at the strategic level, in addition to being able to achieve operational and tactical objectives. Knowledge has its broadest impact when it can be shared and used by the entire organization. In order to do so, it is pivotal for the leaders of knowledge management efforts to be involved in strategic goal setting and deliberations. Without the senior leadership of an organizing taking responsibility for the management of an organization's knowledge, any KM efforts are bound to fail.

In leading organizations, roles such as chief knowledge officers (CKOs) or chief learning officers (CLOs) represent the knowledge management function at the strategic level. General Electric has appointed a CLO with the intent of creating an environment where employees can do their best work by providing them with opportunities to learn and develop their skills. The company believes that by developing employees it is easier to retain them and their knowledge. It takes a global view of knowledge management and often brings managers and executives from around the world together with the purpose of creating a learning experience through the sharing of tacit knowledge (Hartley, 2010). When Intel wanted to augment its operations in China, it relied on its CLO to manage the expansion and the development of the growing workforce. The CLO worked in conjunction with the HR managers to identify the right talent for the expanding areas and the managers that would lead them (Summerfield, 2008).

In other organizations, the knowledge management leader reports to the chief information officer (CIO) or the chief talent officer (also known as the head of human resources), which may be as effective in some cases, but if the management of knowledge is a critical success factor for the organization, a dedicated executive to oversee all knowledge activities may be required (Awazu and Desouza, 2004; Bontis, 2000). Some organizations have grouped the role of knowledge leaders with other IT management functions and placed this responsibility under the chief financial officer (CFO) or other accounting and finance professionals, but this is not the optimal solution. By demonstrating an organizational commitment to knowledge management by appointing a senior leader to oversee all knowledge activities and KM projects, an organization demonstrates to all of its members the importance of knowledge for their success.

The main role of KM leaders is to take a strategic view of how knowledge is being leveraged within and across an organization for advancing strategic causes. They become the champion for knowledge management initiatives and take responsibility for ensuring the success of KM projects. The first responsibility is to define the knowledge management strategy of the firm. This is normally performed through consultation with other leaders of the business units or departments in order to ensure that the knowledge management strategy is aligned with the overall corporate strategy. The normal process for knowledge strategy formulation begins with ensuring the organizational strategy and goals are well defined and known to all those responsible for managing organizational knowledge. Next, after an inventory of the knowledge assets has been performed, these assets can be mapped to the organizational strategy to ensure the organization is aware of what knowledge is supporting critical organizational activities (Wong, 2005).

A gap analysis is then performed to identify missing knowledge. The organization must ask itself what knowledge it needs not only to perform its daily routines and activities, but to support future business endeavors that will lead to its success. Is there new knowledge that must be acquired or created, or does knowledge exist that should be transferred through the organization? Are there opportunities to experience greater returns from automated knowledge applications and other important knowledge management systems? Once the gap analysis is completed, the organization now has a list of knowledge assets that are needed in order to support the business. An overall knowledge strategy can be devised that accomplishes two goals. First, it ensures that the existing knowledge assets are managed appropriately and are allotted sufficient resources to be make them useful for employees. Secondly, it lays out an overall plan to improving the stock of knowledge within the organization by identifying knowledge that needs to be acquired by the firm. From this knowledge strategy, a tangible action plan can be devised to perform these KM activities, including the measures that will be applied to judge the success of the KM projects and activities. These plans can be the driver for acquiring resources (whether financial or human) that will make up the project teams responsible for making the knowledge strategy a reality.

As mentioned, an important aspect of a knowledge leader's job is to ensure that any knowledge management activities are closely aligned with the business strategy. Knowledge management is the most effective when it directly supports the strategic direction of an organization. If the organization and its knowledge management strategy are working to achieve the same goals and objectives, it is more likely that the organization will be successful in executing its strategy. However, alignment works both ways, so knowledge management leaders need to be knowledge advocates and inform the rest of the organization how they can leverage knowledge to improve their work. Furthermore, they have the ability to provide a knowledge management perspective on any organizational strategic decisions. For example, in a merger and acquisition

---

The Value of a Knowledge Audit

In order for an organization to know what knowledge assets it possesses, it can conduct a knowledge audit. These audits identify specific categories of knowledge assets to be identified and then survey the organization to determine what resources are available to knowledge workers. These resources can be technical, structural, financial, or human resources.

Northrop Grumman, the American defense contractor and manufacturer, is an example of an organization that created value to its knowledge strategy formulation by conducting a knowledge audit. Company executives realized that they needed to encourage the maturation of their knowledge programs, but did not know the barriers to knowledge creation and transfer that existed in the organization. They hired an outside consulting firm to work with the employees of the many divisions and locations to understand the knowledge-sharing habits of the employees and how knowledge was incorporated in their work. The results were used not only to create a solid understanding of knowledge management within the company, but to identify the gap between the existing and desired state of knowledge management. This gap served as a guideline for the formulation of a new knowledge strategy, and was instrumental in generating a proposal for a major KM project to use technology and people to make sharing knowledge easier (Santosus, 2001).

---

context, a knowledge project can evaluate how this strategic change will impact the knowledge structure of both firms through considering such ideas as redundancies, knowledge gaps, new innovation capabilities, and knowledge system integration.

Leadership must carefully manage the knowledge management budget and decide which resources should be allocated toward the projects that will produce the most gains. Do they go for quick wins that might be possible through smaller projects, or do they group their resources to support a major project that will have an organization-wide impact? They are involved in hiring personnel to create a knowledgeable workforce, and investing in the appropriate technological solutions that will further improve their knowledge capabilities. If the desired resources are not available, it is up to the knowledge management leadership to lobby other senior management for additional resources, or make the important decisions on what aspects of the knowledge management strategy will be fully resourced.

Any decisions made by the leadership team must be communicated to the organization. All levels of the firm must be informed of not only the ongoing knowledge projects, but also the value of these projects to the business and how they will impact the employees in their daily routines and tasks. Everyone within the organization must understand their roles and responsibilities in the management of the organization's knowledge. Knowledge managers should develop an internal communication plan with the help of the human resources department or the area responsible for internal communications. They should determine the best channels and forms of communication to reach the organization's employees. During large projects with large implications for the entire firm, managers should have additional means to reach people and keep them constantly informed. The control of the messages should also be part of the larger KM strategy. Connecting with internal employees is a great opportunity to share the success stories of how KM is contributing to the organization and its strategy. Communication can also play an important role in ensuring that all employees can see how they can use knowledge management practices and technologies in their roles to the benefit of the individual (more efficient and effective work routines) and the entire organization (coordinating many different efforts). Sometimes communication can be as simple as sending a regular e-mail, posting updates on the corporate intranet, or routinely hosting seminar and brown-bag lunches so that employees can share ideas on how they are managing knowledge and learn from one another. These are just a few examples of tools used to promote KM activities, and creative knowledge managers will use unique methods that are suited towards the organizational culture in which they work.

The Librarian as a Knowledge Leader

An example of knowledge management leadership can be found at Harvard Business School's Baker Library, where Mary Lee Kennedy holds the position of executive director. She describes her role as a knowledge manager because she sees an important aspect of her job as ensuring that the school can exchange ideas, information, and expertise. More importantly, she has discovered the importance of aligning the library's priorities with those of the business school, which entails gaining an understanding of how courses are taught, what research is being conducted, the principles of lifelong learning, and how people within the school collaborate. Kennedy has become an important driver for collaboration, information exchange, and knowledge use within the school; she is focused on connecting people and their knowledge. She acts as a liaison between knowledge sources and contributes to the work of the school's professors by being involved early in their knowledge search processes and guiding people to knowledge resources that include internal and external people, books, or online sources.

Recently, the library has seen a shift from traditional tools for information organization (such as the OPAC), to more web based resources and offline strategies such as communities of practice. However, Kennedy's strategy for KM includes developing knowledge leaders who can work with the changing nature of knowledge and create better decision-making methods for the school's leadership. This innovative leader has expanded the traditional role of the librarian to demonstrate her in-depth understanding of information and knowledge management in order to provide new and valuable services to the business school and its members (Kennedy, 2006, 2011).

Finally, any activities that support the knowledge strategy must be evaluated and measured to demonstrate to other executives the value that is being created through managing knowledge. The knowledge management leader's decision on what metrics are most appropriate for the specific knowledge activities is an important one. It is not an easy decision, as much knowledge and the associated activities are difficult to measure. However, to ensure the sustainability of any KM programs, the return of the investment in a KM strategy should be demonstrated to those who allocate organizational resources.

THE PROJECT MANAGEMENT OFFICE[1]

In recent years, many organizations have implemented a project management office (PMO) to help lower the typical risks facing projects, including those risks centered on knowledge. Whether implementing a one-time project with a defined start and end, or managing an ongoing program with several projects, experienced project managers are essential for successful, on-time, within-budget delivery. CIO Magazine and the

Project Management Institute (PMI) surveyed 450 managers and found that 67 percent of their organizations had a PMO in place (Santosus, 2003). The same survey concluded that the longer a PMO was operative, the higher was its impact on improving project success. The findings indicate that PMOs can instill project management discipline and align project management processes with an organization's overall strategic objectives. The same is true for the success of the implementation and use of a knowledge management system. A management group should be established to combine the deliverable and focused discipline of knowledge management with the conceptual and analytical strengths of business consultancy.

Since many organizations have been transitioning to a project-based structure where they tackle problems by dividing them up into projects, the notion of a central office to assist in the management projects is significant. Knowledge management has taken a similar approach in recent years, as more and more knowledge initiatives are structured as projects with formal management, administration, and reporting requirements. Any implementation of a knowledge management system will be structured under an organization's project management methodology, and knowledge managers should leverage this methodology in their planning and design of any knowledge-based system. Most knowledge managers are expected to have skills in project management, as this is a key success factor in implementing a successful knowledge project. The following outlines this emerging trend in the management of knowledge projects, and links the foundational concepts of project management to knowledge management.

Definition of a PMO

Providing a singular, generalizable blueprint for a PMO is not possible. Just as the technology structure of a knowledge management system should be designed around a specific company's cultural characteristics and business processes, so too should the project management structure. Most PMOs in IT organizations have certain common characteristics. First, they are chartered with a responsibility to contribute to the success of project management in the organization. The precise nature and scope of their contribution will vary depending on the PMO class and archetype. Second, most PMOs are responsible for ensuring that projects being undertaken (or projects being considered) are in alignment with the strategic goals of the organization. This is very important for knowledge projects that require alignment with organizational strategy. Third, most PMOs are designed as independent units in the organization, with their own budgets and resources. Fourth, the composition of a PMO normally involves a fluid mix of experienced business and technology professionals, including individuals who have extensive knowledge on all aspects of software management. Fifth, PMOs are responsible for the development of standards and methodologies for project management and improving the capability of the organization in the practice of these methodologies.

With these objectives, the PMO may integrate any combination of the following:

- *Project knowledge management*: Leveraging knowledge in the form of best practices in how projects are managed, and also lessons learned from conducting projects. This knowledge flows through the other areas of the organization, such as engineering, research and development, and product development, so as to improve the products and services of the organization.

- *Project processes and procedures*: Defining the knowledge management methodology of the organization, and the metrics used to evaluate projects in terms of successes (or failures). An outcome of such an effort is a defined and reusable project management framework that governs how work is conducted in the organization.
- *Training for project teams*: Managing the educational requirements of project managers to ensure that they are best equipped to deal with project complexities, managing the working knowledge of the project, and engaging the project team with the proper collaboration tools.
- *Knowledge portfolio management*: Managing and coordinating the multiple sources and repositories of organizational knowledge and looking at current projects in terms of their knowledge needs, knowledge assets produced and comparing them to artifacts from past projects to improve organizational learning.

Depending on the role of a PMO, they can be categorized into offices that operate at three levels: strategic, tactical, and operational. At the strategic level, the role of the PMO is to ensure that the knowledge management system and the knowledge management practices employed on projects are aligned with the strategic objectives of the organization so that knowledge is captured, organized, and shared effectively. Efficient and effective organizational learning is also encouraged in order to improve the policies, practices, and methodologies employed within the company. At the tactical level, the role of the PMO is to ensure appropriate collaboration between project initiatives, ensuring that adequate coordination among the various projects is being undertaken at the organization, and that lessons learned in one project have the best chance of being applied in another. When documenting knowledge derived from the execution of projects, monitoring the projects for defined standards and methodologies will support consistent quality of knowledge. Knowledge sharing among the members of the projects via collaboration tools and methodologies is designed to overcome organizational, geographic and cultural barriers. Finally, at the operational level, the PMO is responsible for conducting project evaluations by creating the process for codifying the lessons learned, and documenting any innovative practices.

Overall, a PMO is a vehicle that can be used by any organization to place structure, standards and consistency around their projects. This will only serve to benefit the knowledge managers who may undertake multiple KM projects where a successful implementation and launch are essential. Furthermore, a knowledge manager can work with individuals within the PMO to help them manage project knowledge, and assist the organization's project managers in gathering knowledge about the project, and knowledge contained within the project. Knowledge managers and project managers can create a symbiotic relationship that benefits each of their own projects and goals.

KM PROFESSIONALS AS ORGANIZATIONAL CONSULTANTS

A good knowledge management professional needs to act as an organizational consultant who can work with different areas of the organization to improve their knowledge management capabilities. Five specific skills required to be a consultant can apply to those managing knowledge. First, they need to have a big picture view of the organization. They must understand the strategy that an organization pursues, and what that means for all levels of the firm. This high level approach gives them the ability to ensure knowledge management practices are aligned with the organization's strategy and goals. Second, even though they require the ability to think at a strategic level, they need to translate this knowledge to an operational level. Making the connection between a knowledge strategy and what it means for the daily job routines of employees is important to ensure any knowledge strategy can be operationalized and communicated to the lower levels of the firm. Therefore, the third important skill of a knowledge manager is to have a strong understanding of all the departments and business units within a firm. Although it is assumed they will have experience with knowledge activities such as facilitating knowledge creation or sharing, they need to apply this experience to all aspects of the organization to ensure any knowledge management initiative is truly an organization-wide initiative. KM should transcend boundaries and be compatible with all parts of an organization.

Fourth, not only is a strong understanding of the internal workings of the firm essential, but having strong ties to the external or business environment assists in their ability to transfer knowledge to internal employees. They need to be adept in environmental scanning to ensure they are current with new and emerging technologies and business practices. They can also act as gatekeepers and liaisons to encourage knowledge from outside the organization. This external knowledge augments their internal knowledge to improve their KM experience. Finally, any knowledge manager

---

Interview with a KM Leader

Name: Stan Garfield

Current Title and Organization: Community Evangelist, Global Consulting Knowledge Management, Deloitte Touche Tohmatsu Limited

Biography: Mr. Garfield began as a computer programmer, research assistant, and manager at Washington University School of Medicine and St. Louis University from 1975 to 1983. He then moved to Digital Equipment Corporation (later, Compaq and HP) and held a wide variety of field and headquarters management roles in presales, consulting and system integration. Among his many achievements, he launched DEC's first knowledge management program in 1996, helped develop the corporate KM strategy for Compaq in 2000, and led the Worldwide Consulting & Integration Knowledge Management Program for Hewlett-Packard, 2004–2008. After leaving HP, he briefly served as Retail and Consumer Knowledge Domain Manager at PricewaterhouseCoopers before joining Deloitte Touche Tohmatsu Limited. Through the years, he has kept abreast of his work in the knowledge management field. We hope that this interview will give you an appreciation of what it takes to be a KM leader.

Q: Can you tell us a bit about your first job as a knowledge manager and how did you get this role (i.e., how did you make the transition to a knowledge manager, if it was not your first job)?
A: In 1996 I was asked by the senior vice president of systems integration at Digital Equipment Corporation to start a knowledge management program after we visited Ernst & Young's Center for Business Knowledge in Cleveland, Ohio. When he heard that Ernst & Young had a Chief Knowledge Officer, he turned to me and said, "I want you to be our CKO." I had been doing knowledge

(Continued)

Interview with a KM Leader *(Continued)*

A *(continued)*

management for many years in addition to my official duties in professional services management, but we didn't call it that. It has been referred to as something like "resource management" or "capability development" or "information."

My job was to launch the first KM program at DEC. I had to define the strategy and approach we would use, and start the process of implementing changes incorporating people, process, and technology elements.

Along the way, I had to endure many ups and downs, enlist allies in the cause to join my virtual team, get executive sponsorship from a succession of leaders, increase investment and commitment to the program, deal with constant organizational change, adjust to changing technology, migrate from and integrate with legacy software, exercise diplomacy with many other groups, and cope with two large-scale corporate mergers.

Q: What did you learn from this experience? What were three of the major challenges you faced? How did you overcome these challenges?

A: I learned:

1. Put a strong KM leader in place, and ensure that the KM team has only strong members.
2. Balance people, process, and technology components, with a project leader for each category.
3. Establish a governance and collaboration process to engage all groups within the organization (e.g., business units, regions, functions), and to formally manage and communicate on all projects—appoint KM leaders in each major group.
4. Hold annual worldwide face-to-face meetings to get all KM leaders informed, energized, and collaborating.
5. Communicate regularly through newsletters, training, websites, and local events.
6. Get the senior executive to actively support the program.
7. Engage with other KM programs, both internal and external, to learn, share ideas, and practice what you preach.
8. Focus on delivering tangible business benefits that match the overall objectives of the organization.
9. Deliver regular improvements to make the KM environment effective and easy to use.
10. Set three basic goals for employees and stick to them for at least a year.

Three keys to the success of a KM program:

1. Set three simple goals and stick with them for the long term. Communicate them regularly. Incorporate the goals and metrics into as many parts of the organization as possible (e.g., employee goals, incentive and rewards programs, and newsletters).
2. Keep the people, process, and technology components of the KM program in balance. Don't allow one element (e.g., technology) to dominate the other two.
3. Lead by example. Model the collaboration and knowledge sharing behaviors you want the organization to adopt in how you run the KM program.

Five pitfalls to avoid:

1. Trying to take on too much
2. Focusing on technology
3. Not engaging the constituents
4. Doing too much studying and planning and not enough prototyping and piloting
5. Not reusing what others have already learned and implemented

Q: Over the years, can you describe what has changed in your approach to leading knowledge management programs in organizations?

(Continued)

Interview with a KM Leader *(Continued)*

A: My approach has evolved as opposed to changed. I emphasize understanding the needs of the organization and responding to those needs, rather than trying to roll out a system and try to get it adopted. Here are 13 insights I have drawn from my 14 years in KM:

1. Collect content; connect people.
2. Try things out; improve and iterate.
3. Lead by example; model behaviors.
4. Set goals; recognize and reward.
5. Tell your stories; get others to tell theirs.
6. Use the right tool for the job; build good examples.
7. Enable innovation; support integration.
8. Include openly; span boundaries.
9. Prime the pump; ask and answer questions.
10. Network; pay it forward.
11. Let go of control; encourage and monitor.
12. Just say yes; be responsive.
13. Meet less; deliver more.

Q: Can you share with us some successful vignettes of knowledge management and their outcomes?

A: When I took over the worldwide KM program for HP Consulting & Integration, one of the three goals we set was to ensure that a collaborative team space was established for each customer project. Previously, there was no standard way of doing this, and project deliverables were often lost, misplaced, or otherwise unavailable. After establishing this goal and monitoring progress against it, we were able to declare success and replace that goal with another one. Establishing a goal, measuring performance against the goal, and regularly reporting on it allowed it to be achieved.

Another goal was to collect a project profile for all customer projects. The problem was that the quality of the information submitted was often poor, with missing or inaccurate data. We assigned the people who supported our knowledge help desk an additional task: review all project profile submissions, and approve only those that met a minimum quality test. Those submissions which failed this test were followed up to ensure good data. We measured and reported on the quality, and after a year, the quality was nearly 100% and the process was working perfectly.

Threaded discussion boards at HP did not allow posting and replying entirely by e-mail. As a result, adoption and usage was low. We made the commitment to add this functionality by having one of my team members write custom code. Upon release, this led to a significant increase in adoption and usage, and as a result, we could make the promise that for most topics, if a user posted a question to the relevant discussion board, at least one useful answer would be posted within 48 hours. This was a major success factor for communities of practice.

Q: What is your approach for designing robust processes to promote knowledge transfer in global organizations?

A: Tie KM processes to existing business processes as much as possible. Modify existing processes to add KM steps, with appropriate monitoring and enforcement. Add or modify policies as needed. When adding new processes, make them as easy as possible to use. Include incentives, recognition, and rewards to get people to do what you want.

Answer these three questions:

1. What existing processes need to be modified to incorporate KM activities? Identify all processes which already exist and need to be part of the KM program.

   For example, there may be existing methodologies. Some collaboration methods may already be in use. Workflow may be performed using some technology. Compile a list of all processes currently in use which you can include in the KM initiative, either as is or by adapting them.

2. What new processes need to be created? In answering the previous question, which processes don't currently exist, but are needed? Identify all additional processes which are needed but are not currently available.

   For example, there may not be any process for capturing and reusing knowledge. Lessons learned and proven practices may not be collected currently. The organization may not be aware of appreciative inquiry as a technique. Choose the most critical missing processes for

(Continued)

Interview with a KM Leader *(Continued)*

A 2. *(continued)*

inclusion in the program. Consider the potential difficulty in implementation and the anticipated benefits of each in making your selections.

3. What policies will need to be changed or created to ensure desired behaviors? Adopting, enhancing, and creating processes will be of limited value unless there are associated policies which require their use. For the most important processes, plan to create policies to enforce adoption.

For example, a content management policy may be required to specify how content is created, stored, and reused. A classification standard which defines the organization's taxonomy and how it is to be deployed may be needed. A standard procedure for how intellectual property is to be valued may need to be enforced.

Q: Can you provide us any advice on how to make a strong business case for knowledge management in organizations?

A: Start by identifying the top three KM objectives that match key business goals of the organization. The business case must be tied directly to what the business views as its top priorities.

You need to get the top leader of your organization to sponsor the program you intend to launch. The best way to do this is to create a springboard story to motivate the leadership team, using narrative to ignite action and implement your new ideas.

Look for a successful case of sharing, innovating, reusing, collaborating, or learning that can serve as a good example of what should become institutionalized. Start by looking within your organization, then to other organizations within your enterprise, and finally to other enterprises. What you need is a simple example of how a KM principle was applied to one of the challenges or opportunities in your top three objectives list with the desired results.

Tell this springboard story to the senior executive and the leadership team. Tie it to major opportunities and challenges facing them.

Q: What advice would you give budding knowledge managers as they enter their roles?

A: Before starting a knowledge management initiative, you should learn more about the field. To start, read books, periodicals, websites, blogs, and Twitter feeds; attend training and conferences; and participate in professional communities and Twitter chats to deepen your understanding of the field of knowledge management. This is practicing what you preach, and will allow you to learn from the experience of others, reuse the best ideas, and avoid the usual pitfalls.

It's a good idea to attend a KM conference before starting a KM program. After that, try to attend one every year, choosing a different one as much as possible.

Many conferences feature training before, during, or after the event. Take advantage of this whenever possible.

When attending conferences and training courses, make every effort to get to know the other attendees. Seek them out during meals, breaks, and social events. Ask them questions, share your thoughts, and exchange contact information. Try to schedule visits with the most energetic colleagues to learn more about their KM programs.

If you have the funds to engage an outside consultant, you can benefit from their knowledge and experience. If not, you can still learn from visiting their websites and reading their literature and publications.

For KM communities, discussion lists, and chat groups, start by reading any discussions, and then post questions. If events are held, try to attend, especially face-to-face events.

Learning about the field of KM is an ongoing responsibility. There is a great amount of content to digest, and new material is published every day. Start with a simple goal such as reading one book or attending one conference, accomplish it, and then set your next goal. As you learn more, it will become easier to tackle each successive step.

must be a good teacher. They must be able to impart both their explicit and tacit knowledge to others in order for the organization to learn new processes. They should be able to work with people of different backgrounds and cultures in order to communicate the importance of KM throughout the organization. The role of a knowledge manager is to take their knowledge and work with business partners to, not only create knowledge management capabilities, but leverage value from organizational knowledge.

KEY CHALLENGES FOR KNOWLEDGE MANAGERS

Whether attempting to create, transfer, organize, or use knowledge, knowledge workers will face many challenges. The role of the leadership with responsibility for knowledge management is to devise strategies to overcome these challenges and make their KM activities successful. A large challenge faced by KM project teams is time. Much of the foundation of a knowledge management strategy relies on the organization's ability to create behavioral changes in how employees perform their work. Other tasks require realignment of the organizational structure and the corresponding incentive systems. Once again, these are not small changes and will take a great deal of time to plan and implement correctly. Therefore, creating changes in how an organization manages its knowledge is a long-term commitment, and results will not be realized quickly. As many organizations manage their business with a short-term view, it is challenging to demonstrate the true value of knowledge management over the short term. Organizations must be patient and be willing to commit resources for a long-term duration in order to make their KM programs successful. If not, KM projects with great potential may be abandoned in their infancy before they benefit the organization.

Whenever resources are involved in decisions, these decisions can become very political. Power struggles can emerge as managers attempt to gain resources for their own departments and uses. The knowledge manager must be aware that they are

---

When Resources Are Scarce

Knowledge managers are not always able to procure the resources they desire to implement large KM projects. However, many new technologies offer low-cost solutions that can substitute for more expensive applications. Take the case of iCrossing, a digital marketing firm that wanted to create an internal knowledge system but could not acquire the resources necessary to implement and maintain a large intranet software application suite. Instead of letting this lack of resources halt its knowledge management progress, the firm turned to wikis. These very inexpensive solutions allowed for the creation of a corporate intranet that was developed by the people within the organization.

iCrossing was able to identify a wiki product that would be easy to use for all levels of users, and would encourage the creation of content by a diverse group of people. The initial wiki grew as employees found value in its use, and new features such as job posting from human resources and specific pages dedicated to projects and industry news was added. Instead of the implementation of a top-down intranet, it became a bottom-up knowledge resource for the firm. It was eventually opened up to all the company's 600 employees. The wiki met the company's needs by providing a cost effective solution that allows for the management of its knowledge (Lynch, 2008).

competing for limited resources along with the other areas of the firm, and therefore can find themselves in a political battle that is adding little to no value to their work. Many KM managers align themselves with more powerful departments within the organization and jointly compete for resources in order to complete their projects. Newer initiatives such as KM will find themselves in an uphill battle with older, more established areas and may have to be creative in their approach to securing the financial and human resources necessary to make knowledge management a success in the organization.

For knowledge management to be truly successful, it must become ingrained in the organizational culture to allow for the evolution of a knowledge culture. As most KM activities are based with the individual, it is crucial that managing knowledge

---

Making the Case for KM and Engaging Stakeholders: The British Council

The British Council, the "UK's international cultural relations body" (British Council, 2011), undertook a knowledge management initiative starting in 2002, hiring a KM director with the goal of moving from a traditional focus on sharing documents to a focus on who should be linked up within the organization (i.e., shifting its view of knowledge management as a two-way communication process) (Cheuk, 2006). The components of the KM initiative included (1) performing a knowledge audit, (2) developing KM strategies for business units, (3) enhancement of intranet collaboration tools, (4) applying Social Network Analysis (SNA) to understand and support collaboration, and (5) applying narrative approaches to doing project debriefs (Cheuk, 2006).

An important component of the KM initiative included efforts to engage the British Council's leadership in order to promote the value of knowledge management and stimulate knowledge sharing efforts. At the time that the Council undertook its KM initiative, it underwent a reorganization effort that included forming a global leadership team. The Council engaged the team in "a series of activities [that were] developed to promote knowledge sharing among global leadership team" (Cheuk, 2006). Social network analysis (SNA) was introduced through facilitated exercises in part to help improve strategic decision making in global leadership team.

The SNA component of the British Council's KM initiative included three steps (Cheuk, 2006):

1. *Data collection*: The global leadership team members responded to a questionnaire asking them (1) to whom/from whom do you do send and receive information? and (2) with whom do you have informal discussions regarding your work and new ideas?

2. *Facilitated visualization*: The team was presented with an SNA map showing the formal and informal connections between members of the organization and asked them to identify patterns, determine where they sit on the map, and identify strengths and weaknesses of the network.

3. *Reflection*: The team members were then asked: What needs to be changed in next three months in order to achieve global leadership team objectives? As an individual, what would you like to change?

A significant impact of the SNA exercise is that it helped to reinforce the case for KM by showing the value of knowledge flow beyond sharing documents, and the need to balance document sharing with people-to-people networking (Cheuk, 2006). Specific weaknesses identified by the team included that there were a preponderance of nodes that were tied to headquarters and that there were few ties (representing little knowledge sharing) between global leaders. As a result of its learning, the leadership team identified interventions such as forming a subgroup to work on knowledge sharing, agreeing to nurture informal subgroups, and engaging in monthly web meetings to work on KM as a team. Outcomes of the initiative included increased knowledge sharing between team members regarding important projects.

become "simply what people do," and part of normal routines and tasks. Firms that can encourage the development of a knowledge culture place the motivation and responsibility for the creation, transfer, and use of knowledge with the individuals. Less control and direct supervision of knowledge work is required as employees understand and promote the value of good knowledge management practices. But like any cultural change, converting an existing organizational culture into a strong knowledge culture is extremely challenging and will take a great deal of time and effort. The leadership (and especially the knowledge management leadership) must be committed to knowledge management as an organizational strategy, and convince all members of the organization of its importance. Many firms have been quite successful in embracing and creating knowledge cultures, and this is often demonstrated in their ability to innovate and generate new knowledge.

The impact of technology on knowledge management cannot be discounted, especially in a dynamic and constantly shifting business environment. New technologies can bring new opportunities for managing knowledge, and improve the effectiveness of an existing knowledge management program. Innovation can cause established KM practices to become obsolete or inefficient, so the knowledge manager must constantly survey the technological landscape to understand how new technologies can impact organizational KM programs. If technology is established as the foundation for a KM program, it should be recognized that the need for flexibility, adaptability and resilience is paramount for the KM program, as the technology used today will not necessarily be the best solution for tomorrow.

Many forces impact an organization's ability to create and maintain an effective knowledge management program. Both internal and external factors influence the effectiveness of a knowledge management strategy. A strong knowledge manager will be knowledgeable about these influences, and understand what they mean for current and proposed KM projects. By creating strategies that recognize and mitigate project and operational risks surrounding knowledge management, an organization can develop very successful knowledge projects, activities and knowledge workers that impact their success in the business environment.

REMAINING RELEVANT IN THE KNOWLEDGE MANAGEMENT FIELD

Many resources are available to those responsible for leading knowledge management initiatives. Staying current with innovations in knowledge management is easy given the resources that the Internet and social media can provide. Of course, many offline resources and conferences exist as well.

One of the best resources for KM practitioners is local communities of practice that form to discuss issues and ideas surrounding KM. Many knowledge managers meet regularly to build their professional network and learn from the experiences of others. There is no substitute for experience, and learning from others can be very valuable. Connecting through online means can also be a rewarding experience. Search for online discussion groups, forums and professional groups in LinkedIn. Even Twitter has an active knowledge management group that informs their followers of KM ideas and resources via the #KM hashtag.

Many other online resources have regular articles and columns on knowledge management geared towards the practitioner. Of course, a diligent knowledge manager will also keep an eye on advances in academic research that can impact how knowledge management and associated technologies can be used effectively. Table 10.1 provides an introductory list of knowledge management recourses.

Knowledge management professionals should practice what they preach. So making connections, networking, sharing knowledge and assisting others with their knowledge management challenges should come naturally!

Table 10.1. An Introductory List of Knowledge Management Resources	
Resource	**Description**
KM World (http://www.kmworld.com/)	An online magazine dedicated to KM
KM World Conference (http://www.kmworld.com/conference/)	An annual conference targeted toward practitioners with a diverse group of speakers
CIO.com (http://www.cio.com/)	CIO Magazine's website with many articles on KM
International Conference on Information Systems (http://home.aisnet.org/displaycommon.cfm?an=1&subarticlenbr=79)	An annual academic conference that includes research on KM
The Journal of Knowledge Management	An academic journal with research on KM
The International Journal of Knowledge Management	An academic journal with research on KM
Knowledge Management Research & Practice	An academic journal with research on KM
Business Information Review	A journal for both academics and practitioners with many articles on KM
Hawaiian International Conference on System Sciences (http://www.hicss.hawaii.edu/)	An academic conference with a specific track dedicated to KM
Ross Dawson's Blog (http://www.rossdawsonblog.com/)	A blog dedicated to discussing issues surrounding leveraging knowledge in networks
Gurteen Knowledge Website (http://www.gurteen.com/gurteen/gurteen.nsf/)	A repository of relevant articles, commentary, and events on KM
Stan Garfield's KM Site (http://stangarfield.googlepages.com)	A repository or interesting presentations on KM
NHS Knowledge Management Specialist Library (http://www.library.nhs.uk/knowledge management/)	A repository of KM material from a health library perspective
KM.gov (http://wiki.nasa.gov/cm/wiki/?id=1926)	A repository of KM material from the Federal Knowledge Management Working Group

---

**Recap: The Major Points for Knowledge Managers to Consider
When Creating Value with Knowledge**

1. Having dedicated leadership for an organization's knowledge management strategy is essential.
2. The knowledge leader should take responsibility for the knowledge strategy and its alignment with the corporate strategy.
3. Communicating aspects of the knowledge strategy to internal people is often neglected, yet one of the most important factors in getting employees to embrace KM.
4. Any organizational activity that requires resources is susceptible to political decisions, and KM is no exception. Managers should be aware of the internal politics that govern the allocation of resources.
5. Measuring the outcomes of knowledge management projects is key to demonstrating the value of organizational knowledge to senior executives.
6. Project management offices are one structure that can help enable an organization's KM strategy and facilitate the sharing and storage of organizational knowledge.
7. Knowledge managers have many similarities to organizational consultants in the way that they view the organization, their need for a broad set of knowledge regarding the different departments of the organization, and their ability to share experiential knowledge and teach it to other people in the organization.
8. Implementing and executing a knowledge management strategy does not occur without facing many challenges. Managers should be aware of the possible barriers they may face and devise a plan for overcoming these challenges that could hamper a knowledge management strategy.
9. Any knowledge management project or strategy should be flexible, adaptable, and resilient to changes from both internal and external forces.
10. Although keeping up with changes in the environment and innovations within the practice of knowledge management may appear to be a daunting task, there are many resources available to help knowledge managers connect with other professionals, learn about their profession, and share their ideas and knowledge.

CONCLUSION

We intended for this book to take you on a journey that explored knowledge management and how it impacts individuals, groups, organizations, and society. We began with the foundations of knowledge and management, and then discussed the many aspects of knowledge management, including creation, sharing and transfer, organization and use. We discussed the idea of a knowledge management strategy, including the impact of knowledge management systems on organizations. Guidance for managers was given, including how to create a business case of knowledge management within an organization. Keeping the focus on individuals and relating their impact to groups, teams, projects, and organizations provided a deeper understanding of knowledge practiced and routines found within organizations.

Throughout this book it was our intention to highlight the impact of social media on knowledge management. We view this as an emerging technology that is causing businesses to rethink how they can create new knowledge or share knowledge both internally and externally. We also took a global view of knowledge management, as we can no longer assume any organization operates and competes locally.

As current or future managers of knowledge, it is essential that you constantly refresh your knowledge and skills in order to keep up with a fast-paced and demanding environment. By ensuring that any plans and strategies encompassing the knowledge of an organization are flexible and adaptable, you can ensure that the knowledge within your organization will continue to provide value to employees, guide managers and strategic decision makers, and allow your organization to remain competitive in the future.

DISCUSSION QUESTIONS

1. Why is it important for knowledge managers to take an organization-wide view of knowledge activities?
2. What are the major functions performed by the knowledge leadership in the organization?
3. How can the establishment of a project management office support knowledge management activities?
4. Scarcity of organizational resources can be a challenge for any knowledge manager. What can they do to overcome resource shortages in order to implement their knowledge management projects? How can they deal with organizational politics to ensure they are well positioned to complete their projects?

NOTE

1. The following section draws on K.C. Desouza and J. R. Evaristo. 2006. "Project Management Offices: A Case of Knowledge-Based Archetypes." *International Journal of Information Management* 26, no. 5: 414–423.

REFERENCES

Awazu, Y., and K. Desouza. 2004. "The Knowledge Chiefs: CKOs, CLOs, and CPOs." *European Management Journal* 22, no. 3: 339–344.

Bontis, N. 2000. "CKO Wanted—Evangelical Skills Necessary: A Review of the Chief Knowledge Officer Position." *Knowledge and Process Management* 8, no. 1: 29–38.

British Council. 2011. "About Us." British Council. http://www.britishcouncil.org/new/.

Cheuk, B. 2006. "Case Study: The British Council." *Inside Knowledge* 10, no. 2. http://www.ikmagazine.com.

Hartley, D. 2010. "Learning Gets Switched On." Chief Learning Officer. Last modified September 26. http://clomedia.com/index.php?url=articles/view/3842.

Hislop, D. 2010. "Knowledge Management as an Ephemeral Management Fashion?" *Journal of Knowledge Management* 14, no. 6: 779–790.

Kennedy, M. L. 2006. "Interview." Harvard University Library Notes. http://hul.harvard.edu/publications/hul_notes_1330/mlk.html.

Kennedy, M. L. 2011. "Preparing for Conversations with Mary Lee Kennedy: Sensemaking." Association of Knowledgework. Accessed March 13. http://kwork.org/Stars/kennedy.html.

Lynch, G. G. 2008. "Building a Better (and Useful) Corporate Intranet Starts with a Wiki." CIO. Last modified October 1. http://www.cio.com/article/452183/Building_a_Better_and_Useful_Corporate_Intranet_Starts_With_a_Wiki?taxonomyId=3011.

Santosus, M. 2001. "Knowledge Management at Northrop Grumman." CIO. Last modified September 1. http://www.cio.com/article/30481/Knowledge_Management_at_Northrop_Grumman?page=2&taxonomyId=3011.

Santosus, M. 2003. "Why You Need a Project Management Office." CIO. July 1. http://www.cio.com/article/29887/Why_You_Need_a_Project_Management_Office_PMO_.

Summerfield, B. 2008. "Intel in China." Chief Learning Officer. Last modified June 2. http://clomedia.com/articles/view/intel_in_china.

Wong, K. Y. 2005. "Critical Success Factors for Implementing Knowledge Management in Small and Medium Enterprises." *Industrial Management & Data Systems* 105, no. 3: 261–279.

Glossary

adaptation: The process in which organizations learn new knowledge about their internal and external environments, and change in order to survive the dynamic business conditions.

appropriability: The ability of the owner or creator of knowledge to receive a return equal to the value of the knowledge created.

A-Space (Analytic Space): A Facebook-type platform that allows individuals from the CIA, FBI, and the NSA to connect and share intelligence information on similar subjects that might not normally leave one agency's boundaries. New ideas, theories, and information can be shared in a collaborative workspace where analysts come together to create new meaning and knowledge out of many smaller pieces of knowledge.

ba: A shared space for individual relationships to converge in order to create knowledge. It can be a physical, virtual, or mental space that forms a platform for creating knowledge. It allows for an area where the exchange and formation of new ideas is encouraged, and allows individuals to interact with other individuals and the environment.

blog: A website typically maintained by an individual or group with regular posts of commentary, descriptions of events, or other multimedia materials such as graphics or videos. A comment section is available for readers to begin a conversation on the materials presented in the post.

boundary objects: Items used to span boundaries and allow knowledge to flow. These objects are not necessarily physical objects, but devices used to enable both the course and the recipient of the knowledge to connect and share knowledge.

business case: A well-argued and logically structured document that puts forth the business rationale for investing in a course of action. Business cases are best visualized as persuasive arguments.

business intelligence (BI): A category of applications, technologies, and concepts for gathering, storing, analyzing, and providing access to data to help business users make better decisions.

business plan: A document intended to attract investment or loans to get a business started, or move a business from its current state to its next level of growth. It contains a formal statement of the business vision, mission, goals, and objectives; the market analysis of the business opportunity; a financial analysis and projection of the expected investment and returns; analysis of competitors; industry and customer analysis; a description of the management team; and a projected growth plan.

classification: A spatial, temporal, or spatio-temporal segmentation of the world, and therefore a set of boxes (metaphorical or literal) into which things can be put to then do some kind of work.

combination: The process by which two objects of explicit knowledge are merged to create a new piece of explicit knowledge, then can be shared within or beyond the organization.

common knowledge: The knowledge that is learned through performing an organization's daily business routines, processes, and procedures. Each individual company will have its own common knowledge, and this will distinguish it from other firms in the industry. Common knowledge creates a foundational base of knowledge which members can build upon to create and share new knowledge.

competitive intelligence (CI): Collecting, analyzing, synthesizing, and communicating information on targets of interest, most notably the competitors of the organization. It involves scouring through the available public information on the target and arriving at actionable knowledge on competitive moves and positions, areas of investment, and even senior personnel hires and transfers.

creativity: The generation or production of knowledge and ideas that are both novel and useful. It is the first step in innovation, as innovation is simply the successful implementation of creative ideas.

crowdsourcing: Polling vast numbers of people in order to gain a small piece of their knowledge, then analyzing the knowledge as a whole to determine what the "crowd knows."

culture: A shared set of assumptions invented, discovered, or developed by a group as it learns to cope with its problems of external adaptation and internal integration. It has worked well enough to be considered valid, and is to be taught to new members of the group as the correct way to perceive, think, and feel in relation to those problems.

customer knowledge: The knowledge residing within a firm's customers, as opposed to the information about these customers. Customer knowledge allows an organization to convert its customers from passive recipients of products and services into partners who generate and cocreate knowledge.

data: Raw facts and numbers that are not useful or meaningful on their own, and require interpretation or processing in order to add value to the organization. Data is easy to collect, yet has a low level of value to the organization.

data warehouse/warehousing: A collection of decision support technologies, aimed at enabling the knowledge worker to receive knowledge to improve decision making. It is a subject-oriented, integrated, time varying, nonvolatile collection of data that is used primarily in organizational decision making.

databases: Structures that are used for the storage or operational and transactional data. It is usually data that will not be kept long term, but is used either by the business applications to process transactions, or the accounting information systems to prepare daily, weekly, and monthly financial reports. Any data that needs to be kept on a long-term basis is archived in separate databases for retrieval.

data-driven approach to knowledge creation: The process of creating knowledge through beginning with data collection, and progressing toward new knowledge through the analysis and understanding of the data.

decision support system (DSS): A system designed to alleviate the burden of human decision makers by performing very complex computations. They are often used to summarize, reduce, and compress a large quantity of original data into chunks manageable for human minds.

design thinking: When balance and harmony are used to connect analytical thinking that uses logic (deductive and inductive reasoning) to find answers through analysis, and intuitive thinking, which relies on insight and creative thinking.

Dewey Decimal System: A categorization system used to sort books into ten general categories. Mainly used by libraries, it is based on the metric system and allows for easy retrieval of books and other information courses.

digital natives: A term similar to Millennials or Generation Y that refers to the new generation of corporate workers who share a heightened sense of obligation to make a positive contribution to society and to the health of the planet, seek flexible working arrangements, value social connections, and prize other rewards of employment over monetary compensation. Unlike previous generations who have expressed loyalty to companies, digital natives have chosen to demand change or leave rather than be patient and wait for change.

doxie: A significant facet of what defines cultural behavior, or behavior based on values or priorities that are not explicitly thought through or even conscious.

dynamic capabilities: The ability to integrate, build, and reconfigure internal and external competencies to address rapidly changing environments.

enumerative classification: Top-down, deductive procedures that divide a large group into smaller groups, and those small groups into even smaller groups. This is a hierarchical approach that does not allow for complex relationship structures, or can encourage the extreme subdivision of lasses where these subjects created become too narrow.

environmental scanning: The process of searching the external environment for information and knowledge that is relevant and useful to the organization. It attempts to acquire such information and knowledge in order to transfer it to the individuals who require the knowledge to do their job or make decisions.

executive information system (EIS): A system capable of aggregating relevant data throughout an organization, and presenting a highly condensed summary to senior executives. They allow reliable and accurate insights of the state of the entire company to be available in a timely fashion.

executive summary: A brief and convincing statement that clearly articulates the need for the project, a brief project description, and the expected returns on the investment. It should entice the reader to continue reading the rest of the document.

expert transfers: The transfer of unusual or non-routine problems, and occur when one part of the organization is seeking help from another. This transfer deals with non-documented or non-codified knowledge that requires connections in order to be transferred. The key is the ability of the organization to bring different people together in order to share knowledge.

explicit knowledge: Knowledge that has been codified, is formal and systematic, and is easily written down in documents or systems. It is readily captured, can be articulated, is expressed in words or numbers, and shared formally amongst members of an organization as it can be located and processed with ease. Usually it is transmitted in the form of items such as documents, manuals, technical specifications, blueprints, scientific formulas, or organizational designs. As it can be processed, transmitted, and stored relatively easily, it is not difficult for organizations to capture this knowledge in repositories, systems, or operating technologies and share it throughout organization.

externalization: The process of taking tacit knowledge and converting it to explicit knowledge that can be shared amongst others. It allows tacit knowledge to be transferred to others in order for those other employees to create their own knowledge, but it is a challenging procedure because most forms of tacit knowledge are difficult to convert and codify.

faceted classification: An approach that requires the construction of schedules from an inductive or bottom-up procedure. This requires extensive experience and familiarity with the knowledge being organized in order to create accurate and meaningful subjects; however, it is a more flexible system that can be maintained with some ease.

far transfer: Moving knowledge that is related to a nonroutine task, or a situation that does not normally occur during the course of business. It usually is tacit knowledge that has been learned from an action, and the company wishes to ensure that other teams who might encounter a similar situation will receive this knowledge.

flow: A mental state where a person becomes completely immersed in a task and does not pay attention to external stimulus. Because it involves extreme focus and concentration, flow causes a distorted sense of time, a feeling of complete control over the activity, and, in many cases, a sense of intrinsic reward.

gatekeepers: People who convey external knowledge to internal organizational networks, allowing for the external knowledge to cross the organizational boundary and be shared amongst different people within the organization. These individuals are normally the communication stars of an organization and have many connections to outside sources. This role is very specialized, as usually gatekeepers have a few areas or fields of information in which they are most knowledgeable and it is from these fields that they are able to acquire and share knowledge. Gatekeepers act as filters and provide the services of identifying knowledge external to their organization, determining how to acquire that knowledge, and bringing that knowledge into their organization. At this point, they act as a filter and can not only facilitate knowledge into the organization, but also block other knowledge from being acquired.

global: Relating to or involving the entire world, going beyond local contexts and boundaries to involve multiple nations, cultures, and people.

global flatteners: Forces that act upon organizations, countries, and people encouraging shifts toward the globalization of markets. They change the dynamics, rules, and context of economies and require organizations to shift in how they react to their external environments.

groupthink: A phenomenon that occurs during group or team sessions where knowledge is being introduced in the decision-making process. Individuals begin to act in homogeneous and non-individualistic patterns, leading to the suspension of critical thinking and moral judgment. Groups attempt to remain cohesive and in total agreement, rather than explore all options fully by introducing external, conflicting, and challenging information into their decision making.

incremental innovation: The creation of new knowledge by directly building upon previous knowledge in order to incrementally improve or alter a product or service. It is usually referred to as competence enhancing and does not alter the business, industry, or related strategies.

information: Data that has been converted to have meaning in a particular context. It has value to the organization, yet requires effort to acquire and use.

informational knowledge: The equivalent to knowing "what" one needs to know about a topic. It is the base or foundation for tasks that require specific goals to be achieved, and focuses on beliefs about information and relationships that exist amongst variables.

innovation: The use of new knowledge to offer a product or service that is in demand by an organization's customers or patrons. It is an idea, thing, procedure or system that is perceived to be new by whomever is adopting it.

intangible assets: Those possessed by an individual or organization that are not physical in nature, such as knowledge, brand recognition, customer loyalty, or goodwill. They are difficult to identify, locate and measure from a financial perspective.

intelligence: The act and state of knowing something, and the ability to comprehend a piece of information for a particular purpose, or the ability to analyze and synthesize relevant information.

intermediaries: People or technologies that reside between the source and the recipient of a message or knowledge. They assist in bridging boundaries such as geography, language, or differences in practice.

internal rate of return (IRR): A financial measure of a project that calculates the discount rate, also known as the investment yield rate, for the project. It is the rate at which the net present value for a project is equal to zero.

internalization: When an explicit knowledge transfer leads to the development of new tacit knowledge. This usually occurs when an individual acquires the explicit knowledge and over time develops a deeper understanding of the knowledge, which results in new tacit knowledge.

interpretivism: Views knowledge as inseparable from the people who possess it. It is a complex, foundationless, constructed idea that cannot exist on its own, but is constructed in social interaction between people.

intertextuality: A concept that states that relationships between knowledge and knowledge sources should be established in order to make connections between different yet connected knowledge sources.

knowledge: The beliefs of an individual based on the meaningful accumulation of information. It can be derived from experiences, or through the identification and use of other information and knowledge resources.

knowledge assets: The physical and logical manifestations of knowledge, where knowledge management helps an organization utilize its knowledge assets in the attainment of objectives and goals.

knowledge creation: The organizational processes that develop new knowledge or replace existing knowledge within an organization's knowledge repository and encompasses activities such as new product development, business process design, skill development, and other innovative activities. The knowledge materializes as product and services designs, business processes, working skills, and other organizational capabilities.

knowledge dictionaries: A list of key concepts and terms that are used within a classification system or taxonomy to allow for its use by members of the organization.

knowledge discovery from databases (KDD): The development of processes and techniques that can be leveraged to make sense of the data. It addresses the basic problem of mapping low-level data into other forms that might be more compact, more abstract, or more useful. It strives to understand the data collected by the firm, and use this understanding to create new and valuable organizational knowledge.

knowledge management: The systematic, explicit, and deliberate building, renewal, and application of knowledge to maximize an enterprise's knowledge related effectiveness and returns from its knowledge assets. It involves getting the right knowledge to the right people at the right time so they can make the best decision.

knowledge management system: A system applied to managing organizational knowledge. They are usually (but not limited to) IT-based systems developed to support and enhance the organizational processes of knowledge creation, storage/retrieval, transfer, and application.

knowledge markets: The logical space where buyers and sellers can engage in exchange knowledge products and services.

knowledge taxonomies: Groups of concepts arranged in a hierarchy; can be represented in a graphical depiction to reflect the concepts and relationships amongst those concepts in either a particular field or one organization.

knowledge workers: Those individuals whose job is primarily focused on the identification, acquisition, creation, and use of knowledge. They use knowledge as both the input and output of their work, and may not create a tangible product.

knowledge-based view of the firm: A theory that attempts to explain how an organization creates a competitive advantage over its competitors by describing its internally possessed knowledge as a valuable, rare, difficult to imitate, and non-substitutable asset. It is a derivative of the resource-based view of the firm.

liaisons: Individuals whose principal role is to identify and create the connections to outside knowledge sources that are necessary for their organization to find and transfer knowledge. Through the development of both their professional and social networks, they learn where valuable knowledge exists and how to acquire that knowledge.

management: The motivation of resources, both human (employees) and artificial (technologies) to work in a coordinated fashion toward the achievement of organizational goals and strategies. It is concerned with planning, organizing, controlling, and leading.

metadata: Data about data, or the description created about the knowledge. It is structured in order to aid individuals or technology in the identification, retrieval, and manipulation of the knowledge. It is a form of knowledge representation, but is not intended to replace or substitute for the original knowledge.

microblogging: The sharing of brief text updates, usually less than 200 characters in length, via text messaging, instant messaging, e-mail or the web in order to broadcast within a social network or to the general public.

near transfer: The transfer of explicit knowledge that has been learned through the repeated process of performing certain actions. Involves knowledge that can be easily replicated, as it refers to a task that is routinely and sometimes continually performed by employees. Quite often this knowledge becomes the basis for best practices that can be shared through a knowledge management system or another electronic communications system.

net present value (NPV): Normalizes future cash flows (both cash outlays and cash receipts) into their present value, and assumes receiving $1 today is better than receiving $1 tomorrow.

noise: Other information or knowledge that gets added to a message, introducing errors into the knowledge system that increase the uncertainty of the information, or creates difficulties for the receiver to receive the knowledge accurately.

object: Something that can be stored and manipulated, and exists separately from the human mind.

operational planning: planning concerned with the details surrounding the processes and procedures necessary to achieve each goal and objective. Multiple projects are typically determined during the tactical planning process, and the managers assigned to each project are responsible for developing a specific project plan.

organizational charts: The most common visual tools used to depict how employees are organized within the organization structure. These charts also provide insight as to what areas the organization considers important.

organizational culture: The set of accepted values, ideals, expectations, norms, behaviors, and patterns of interaction within an entity.

organizational knowledge: The sum total of knowledge residing in individuals or the social collective.

organizational learning: Organizational activities that result in any of its units or people acquiring knowledge that is deems potentially useful and valuable. This knowledge should be accessible to other parts of the organization via knowledge sharing and transfer mechanisms, and can be stored for future use.

organizational memory: Consists of all the tangible and intangible rules, processes, procedures, and cultural instructions that dictate the ways in which the organization operates.

outsourcing: The contracting out of specific business operations (partially or entirely) to a third-party contactor. The outsourced work can take place either in the same country as the outsourcer, or in a different one (called offshoring). The objective is to allow organizations to realize economic gains and to focus on the core competencies of their business.

payback period: Estimates how quickly the investment will be recouped, or the time required for the financial savings to equal the project cost. When comparing two nearly similar alternatives, the rational company will choose the project with the shorter payback period.

positivism: Views knowledge as an object that exists separately and independently of people. Knowledge is a stock, or organizational asset that can be codified, stored, transferred and measured.

pragmatic boundaries: As knowledge can be "practice-based" and rooted in activity or action, much knowledge, especially tacit knowledge, is created in practice or during the act of performing a job. This context becomes very hard to communicate without a foundation of knowledge that is rooted in that particular act.

procedural knowledge: The equivalent of knowing how to go about accomplishing a task. It is the foundation for tasks that focus on how a specific goal or objective will be achieved. This form of knowledge outlines the processes or means that should be used to perform the desired tasks, and is the knowledge that process-oriented tasks rely upon and is associated mainly with tacit knowledge.

project: An endeavor in which human, material, and financial resources are organized in a novel way, to undertake a unique scope of work, for a given specification, within constraints of cost and time, so as to achieve beneficial changes defined by quantitative and qualitative objectives.

radical innovations: Products or services that are built on new knowledge that is substantially different from any existing knowledge and in fact renders that existing knowledge obsolete. These innovations can remove the existing competencies of a firm and demand that new strategies be created in order to manage the resulting change.

satisficing: The process in which decision makers search for a solution that is "good enough" or satisfies the problem, as opposed to searching for the optimal solution (ch3, ch4).

self-service technologies (SSTs): Technology that allows individuals to complete service transactions, such as checking out at a grocery store or printing a boarding pass at the airport, through interactions with software-based interfaces. They are especially suitable for handling highly repetitive transactions following simple and explicit procedures.

semantic boundaries: Prevent two employees from having the means to learn about differences and dependencies in their work. This recognizes that although the knowledge source and recipient are syntactically compatible and are speaking the same language, interpretations or understandings of the knowledge may vary making collaboration difficult.

sensitivity analysis: A financial modeling technique that allows for the identification of critical variables affecting the outcomes of the project. It helps illustrate how each of the alternatives are impacted by changes to key variables and what risk mitigation strategies should be considered.

serial transfer: When knowledge has been gained by part of the organization in one setting, and it is transferred to another part of the organization in a different setting. Usually this process takes the knowledge gained by a team and moves it into the public space, making it available to other teams.

social network analysis: A technique to understanding the connections and relationships between people. It involves both the mapping and measuring of relationships between people, groups, organizations, or other knowledge sources. A map is created with nodes representing the people or groups, with links illustrating the relationships or knowledge flows between the nodes.

socialization: The process of tacit knowledge being converted into new tacit knowledge. This occurs mainly in social settings where experience is shared with individuals, and through these experiences, new tacit knowledge is created.

strategic planning: Planning at the highest level of the organization; conducted by senior management to define a direction or the future state they wish to achieve. The vision and mission statement are important parts of a strategic plan, as they provide guidance for determining what business strategies are most suitable for an organization.

strategic transfer: When knowledge is received by a team during a task that is not routine or occurs infrequently yet deals with work at a strategic level. The knowledge usually impacts large parts of the organization, such as lessons learned during disaster scenario planning. Most often, this form of transfer is used when tacit or experiential knowledge is involved, and involves many face-to-face meetings or the formation of knowledge network connections.

syntactic boundary: When the knowledge source and recipient do not share a common syntax for communicating or representing the knowledge. Simply, if they do not speak the same language and cannot understand each other, knowledge cannot be transferred.

tacit knowledge: Knowledge that has both cognitive and technical elements. The cognitive element consists of mental models such as paradigms, schemata, beliefs, perspectives, and intuitions. The technical elements are personal know-how, crafts, and skills that apply to a specific context, developed over the years. It is highly personal and is difficult to articulate and transfer to others. Tacit knowledge is deeply rooted in action, procedures, commitment, ideals, values, and it can be only indirectly accessed.

tactical planning: Establishing key initiatives that will help achieve the overall strategy. Goal and objective formulation are examples of important pieces of tactical planning, and this can involve both senior and middle-level management.

text mining: The process of deriving high-quality information from text. It involves the process of structuring the input text, deriving patterns within the structured data, and finally evaluating and interpreting the output.

theory-driven approach to knowledge creation: The process of creating knowledge by beginning with an idea, or theory, and designing a research project to collect data that will ultimately support or disprove the theory.

Web 2.0: The new features of the Internet that allow for interaction and the creation of new knowledge and content by a diverse and large group of people. It replaces many of the concepts of Web 1.0 where information was presented for users only to absorb, whereas now the creation and distribution information and knowledge are easily facilitated. The evolution of websites to become much more interactive provided a richer user-experience, and involved the users more in order to harness their collective intelligence. This increase in interaction and collaboration are common results of these new online resources, tools, and services.

web mining: The application of data mining techniques to discover patterns from websites and other information sources on the Internet.

wiki: A website that can be edited by many people, possibly at the same time, to combine the knowledge in order to create new, explicit knowledge accessible by others.

wisdom: An individual's accumulated knowledge and experience applied to a particular context. Wisdom assists in choosing the best course of action when a decision situation arises, and points to the most rational means to reach the alternatives.

Index

Page numbers followed by the letter "f" indicate figures; those followed by the letter "t" indicate tables.

About the Authors
and Contributors

Dr. Kevin C. Desouza is an associate professor at the University of Washington Information School. He holds adjunct appointments in the UW's College of Engineering and at the Daniel J. Evans School of Public Affairs. He currently serves as the director of the Institute for Innovation in Information Management (I3M) and is an affiliate faculty member of the Center for American Politics and Public Policy, both housed at the University of Washington. He founded the Institute for National Security Education and Research, an interdisciplinary, university-wide initiative, in August 2006 and served as its director until February 2008. He holds a visiting professorship at the Faculty of Economics, University of Ljubljana, Slovenia. He has held visiting positions at the Center for International Studies at the London School of Economics and Political Science, the University of the Witwatersrand in South Africa, Groupe Sup de Co Montpellier (GSCM) Business School in France, and the Accenture Institute for High Business Performance in Cambridge, Massachusetts (USA). In the private sector, he founded the Engaged Enterprise and its think tank, the Institute for Engaged Business Research. The Engaged Enterprise was a global strategy consulting firm with expertise in the areas of knowledge management, crisis management, strategic deployment of information systems, and government and competitive intelligence assignments.

Dr. Desouza has seven books to his name. In addition, he has published articles in prestigious practitioner and academic journals. His work has also been featured by a number of publications such as *Sloan Management Review, Washington Internet Daily, Computerworld, KM Review, Government Health IT, Information Outlook*, and *Human Resource Management International Digest*. He has been interviewed by the press on outlets including Voice of America and Manager (Slovenia). He has been invited to edit special issues of several prominent journals such as *Technology Forecasting and Social Change, Information Systems Journal*, and the *Journal of Strategic Information Systems*, among others. In addition, he serves on a number of editorial boards such as the *Journal of Strategic Information Systems*, and has reviewed research for government agencies such as the Research Council of Norway, Finnish Funding Agency for Technology and Innovation, and the Qatar National Research Fund-Qatar Foundation, among others.

Dr. Desouza has advised, briefed, and/or consulted for major international corporations and government organizations on strategic management issues ranging from management of information systems, to knowledge management, competitive intelligence, government intelligence operations, and crisis management. He is frequently an invited speaker on a number of cutting-edge business and technology topics for national and international, industry, and academic audiences. Dr. Desouza has received over $1.4 million in research funding from both private and government organizations. Dr. Desouza is a fellow of the Royal Society of Arts.

Scott Paquette is a visiting professor in the College of Information Studies at the University of Maryland. He is affiliated with the Center for the Advanced Study of Communities and Information (CASCI), and the Center for Information Policy and e-Government (CPEG). He completed his PhD at the Faculty of Information Studies of the University of Toronto, where his research focused on the management of customer knowledge and knowledge management systems.

Dr. Paquette's professional experience includes working as a manager of domestic banking systems for a Canadian bank, extensive project management and consulting experience with a telecommunications company, and working in a large professional accounting firm as a senior consultant in technology risk management and IT security. Scott has also consulted with many organizations on knowledge management and social media strategy.

Dr. Paquette's current research focuses on knowledge creation and the transfer of knowledge across boundaries in organizations, including the use of social media. Scott's publications have appeared in the *International Journal of Information Management*, *Journal of Information Science*, the *Journal of Internet Commerce*, the *Journal of Information Technology and Politics*, *Business Information Review*, and *Government Information Quarterly*, and have been presented at conferences worldwide.

✳ ✳ ✳

Peter Baloh is a member of the executive board at BISOL—an innovative and rapidly growing photovoltaic module producer and solar power plant solution provider. His responsibilities include strategy, innovation management, and business process change—bringing order, learning habits and agility into chaos which is caused by quick growth. He holds a position as associate professor of technology and Innovation at IEDC Bled School of Management, an award-winning boutique business school. Additionally, he has founded and managed a niche consultancy firm, Catch the Knowledge.

Jongmin T. Moon is a doctoral student in Information Science at the University of Washington. His research focuses broadly on innovation and entrepreneurship, and his current focus is on corporate entrepreneurship (i.e., intrapreneurship). Prior to entering the PhD program, Mr. Moon obtained a MS in information management (MSIM) and a BA in Japanese linguistics from the University of Washington. He has published in *Business Information Review*.

Chris Rivinus studied cultural anthropology at Vassar College before turning his attention to international business. He holds an MBA from Colorado State University and an additional master's in international commerce from Denver University's Graduate

School for International Studies. He has led and consulted on the design and implementation of several global knowledge systems, bringing an approach that accounts for both the cultural and social elements of human behavior in the pursuit of tangible business results. He is currently the head of IS Services at Tullow Oil plc, and is based in London.

Chen Ye is an assistant professor of management information systems at the Reginald F. Lewis School of Business, Virginia State University. He received his PhD from University of Illinois at Chicago. His main research area is information technology use at the individual level.